MIND HUNTER

MIND HUNTER

INSIDE THE FBI'S ELITE SERIAL CRIME UNIT

JOHN DOUGLAS
AND MARK OLSHAKER

G

GALLERY BOOKS
New York   London   Toronto   Sydney   New Delhi

G

Gallery Books
An Imprint of Simon & Schuster, Inc.
1230 Avenue of the Americas
New York, NY 10020

First Gallery Books trade paperback edition October 2017

GALLERY BOOKS and colophon are registered trademarks
of Simon & Schuster, Inc.

For information about special discounts for bulk purchases,
please contact Simon & Schuster Special Sales at 1-866-506-1949
or business@simonandschuster.com.

The Simon & Schuster Speakers Bureau can bring authors
to your live event. For more information or to book an event,
contact the Simon & Schuster Speakers Bureau at 1-866-248-3049
or visit our website at www.simonspeakers.com.

Manufactured in Italy

20

ISBN 978-1-5011-9196-1
ISBN 978-0-6848-6447-1 (ebook)

To the men and women of the FBI Behavioral Science
and Investigative Support Units, Quantico, Virginia,
past and present—fellow explorers,
partners on the journey.

Foul deeds will rise,
Though all the earth o'erwhelm them,
to men's eyes.

—WILLIAM SHAKESPEARE,
  Hamlet

Authors' Note

This book has been very much a team effort, and it could not have been accomplished without the tremendous talents and dedication of each member of that team. Chief among them are our editor, Lisa Drew, and our project coordinator and "executive producer" (and Mark's wife), Carolyn Olshaker. Right from the beginning, they both shared our vision and provided the strength, confidence, love, and good counsel that nurtured us through the effort to realize it. Our profound gratitude and admiration go equally to Ann Hennigan, our talented researcher; Marysue Rucci, Lisa's able, indefatigable, and endlessly cheerful assistant; and our agent, Jay Acton, who was the first to recognize the potential of what we wanted to do and then made it happen.

Our special thanks go to John's father, Jack Douglas, for all of his recollections and for so carefully documenting his son's career, making organization a breeze; and to Mark's father, Bennett Olshaker, M.D., for all of his advice and guidance on issues of forensic medicine and psychiatry and the law. We are both extremely fortunate to have the families we do, and their love and generosity are always with us.

Finally, we want to express our appreciation, admiration, and heartfelt thanks to all of John's colleagues at the FBI Academy in Quantico. Their character and contribution is what made the career chronicled in this work possible, which is why the book is dedicated to them.

—JOHN DOUGLAS AND MARK OLSHAKER,
July 1995

Contents

Twenty Years Later

John Douglas and Mark Olshaker

Much has changed in the more than two decades since we wrote *Mindhunter: Inside the FBI's Elite Serial Crime Unit*, the first of our books together. But much has also remained the same.

We've lost close friends and associates mentioned in these pages: Robert Ressler, John's original partner in the serial killer study and fellow profiler; Roy Hazelwood, the Bureau's sex crimes expert and one of the brightest lights at Quantico; and Ken Baker, the Secret Service veteran who worked with John's Investigative Support Unit—ISU—and contributed so much to the understanding of the assassin personality. Our parents have also since passed away, so we are now "the older generation."

Speaking of which, a new generation of FBI profilers has emerged—no longer "buried" in offices sixty feet below ground level (ten times deeper than dead people, we used to say) but stationed across US Route 1 from Marine Corps Base Quantico in a government office building. The profilers' group is now known as the Behavioral Analysis Unit—BAU.

Just like practicing medicine, profiling remains somewhere in that nether region between science and art. And, like physicians, some profilers are better and more experienced than others. In the years since *Mindhunter*'s initial publication, television and the Internet have been full of men and women calling themselves profilers, most of whom have no discernible credentials or actual experience. Often they do more harm than good, and we've seen a number of cases where academic-oriented profilers have misinterpreted evidence and sent either the investigation or the defense's strategy off in a completely wrong direction. It's imperative to remember that a talented and experienced profiler working in cooperation with a highly professional local law enforcement agency can produce results often leading to a quicker arrest and a more successful prosecution.

Several suspects involved in the crimes we covered have been caught, and we will discuss the apprehension of the Unabomber, the Green River Killer, and the BTK Killer a little later. Larry Gene Bell was executed for the vicious murder of seventeen-year-old Shari Faye Smith and nine-year-old Debra May Helmick. Lust killers Jerome Brudos, Joseph Christopher, and Arthur Shawcross, along with Martin Luther King Jr.'s assassin James Earl Ray, all died in prison. Would-be murderers John Hinckley Jr. and Arthur Bremer have been released from confinement. California's "Trailside Killer" David Carpenter and the ultimate boogeyman Charles Manson are in their eighties and still behind bars as of this writing. And Joe Del Campo, John's FBI partner in crime(solving) from their Milwaukee street agent days, recently starred in a season of the TV reality show *Survivor*. You never know what a former G-man is capable of.

Any author would be gratified to have a book remain in print and selling for more than twenty years, and we're certainly no exception. The reaction from readers has been truly amazing and a great source of pride and satisfaction to both of us and our families. We like to think that *Mindhunter*'s continued success, the subsequent books it has spawned, the television shows and movies whose producers have admitted their indebtedness to our work, and now the original Netflix dramatic series based on *Mindhunter* have something to do with the compelling mysteries and life-and-death stories we told. Although science, technology, and certain investigative techniques have made significant leaps forward in the past two decades, the basics of the human mind and motivation remain the same and likely always will.

We are frequently asked why true crime is so compelling to readers and viewers, given its often grisly subject matter and tragic endings. The answer, we believe, is that, by its very nature, true crime deals with the essentials and fundamentals of what we loftily call "the human condition." By this we mean the instincts and emotions we all feel: love, hate, jealousy, revenge, ambition, lust, joy and sadness, terror, disappointment and despair, and feelings of grandiosity and personal entitlement . . . often coupled with equal measures of deep-seated inadequacy and self-loathing. True-crime narratives represent the human condition writ large: ordinary people operating at the terrifying extremes of those instincts and emotions. In this vein, every mystery we relate, every case we report, every outcome we track, becomes its own morality play, complete with heroes, villains, and victims.

After retirement, whenever John has accepted a consulting case, whether he's working for the prosecution or defense, and whether he's a paid consultant or working pro bono, his standard line is "You can hire me, but the one I'm working for is the victim." That is our first responsibility—always.

Now, let's take a brief look at some of the cases that have been closed since *Mindhunter*'s initial publication.

The one that remains the most visceral for us, since it nearly ended John's life, is that of Washington State's Green River Killer. All told, Gary Leon Ridgway confessed to the murders of forty-eight women and later admitted to killing at least seventy-one—many of them runaways, prostitutes, or otherwise vulnerable victims—along the so-called Sea-Tac Strip of the Pacific Highway.

The initial profile of the UNSUB (UNknown SUBject of

an investigation) was fairly straightforward: a blue-collar loner, probably a long-distance truck driver who could easily pick up hitchhikers and had a private cab where he could strangle his victims and subsequently dispose of their bodies in the Green River Gorge or other places along his routes. But what John and his FBI associates warned the law enforcement task force was that the profile wasn't the key element; the post-offense behavior was. This was a guy who would somehow inject himself into the investigation and return to the crime scenes and/or body disposal sites to relive his fantasies with these women.

Because the probe was so comprehensive, John felt there would be a good chance that the actual UNSUB would be picked up and interviewed at some point, especially if he happened to fit our profile. He would probably have a love-hate relationship with prostitutes and runaways and therefore feel justified in "punishing" them. For that reason John advised against relying on polygraph tests as a way to eliminate suspects. Plus lie detectors aren't all that reliable, which is why their results are seldom admitted as evidence in court. While they may work pretty well with ordinary people, lying to a metal box with wires sticking out of it is no big deal for a sociopath.

Gary Ridgway was arrested on November 30, 2001, as he was leaving the Kenworth truck factory in Renton, Washington, where he worked as a spray painter. Taken in on charges of soliciting prostitution, he was then linked to four of his victims through DNA, demonstrating the value of that newly emerging science. The former truck driver had been arrested back in 1982 on charges relating to prostitution, and in 1983 he became a suspect in the Green River case. He was given a polygraph examination, which he passed, eliminating him from further police consideration. Subsequent analysis of that test suggested it might not have been interpreted properly. (What do you know!)

The authorities looked at him again in 1987, which is

not unusual in a long-unsolved case, and at that point they took hair and saliva samples. Twenty-four years later it was the subsequent DNA analysis of these on-file samples that finally cracked the case. In 2003, Ridgway pled guilty to forty-nine charges of aggravated first-degree murder; an additional charge was added as part of his plea bargain. In exchange he received consecutive life sentences with no possibility of parole rather than execution.

In hindsight, the main point that the profile got wrong was its prediction that the UNSUB would be single. In fact, Ridgway had been married three times and had a string of girlfriends, all of whom spoke of his voracious sexual appetite. He had been in the Navy during the Vietnam War, and had frequent relations with prostitutes there. Given that Ridgway caught gonorrhea from one of these encounters, this may have accounted for his feeling of entitlement to punish prostitutes—a kind of triggering event not unusual in this type of serial killer.

Over the years and as more research was compiled, profilers wouldn't be as quick to conclude that a prolific serial killer—even one who spent a lot of time on the road— would necessarily be single or not be in a relationship. In Chapter 13 ("The Most Dangerous Game"), you'll meet Alaskan baker Robert Hansen, who was able to keep his married life completely separate from his passion for picking up prostitutes, flying them in his private plane out into the wild, and then hunting them like animals.

The self-proclaimed BTK Killer of Wichita, Kansas, Dennis Rader was also a hunter of sorts but stalked his prey in their own homes, proud of his artistic ability to "Bind, Torture, and Kill" entire families and draw detailed pictures of his murder scenes. John and FBI colleagues Roy Hazelwood and Ron Walker realized those pictures and the language Rader used to describe the crimes suggested a renegade or former cop or, perhaps even likelier, a law enforcement wannabe. Serial killers get off on their power over their victims and therefore tend to envy the power they perceive police officers to possess.

From an investigative standpoint, the strange thing about the BTK case was that there would be a spate of killings and then they would cease. Normally when this happens, we think there is a good chance the UNSUB has either moved to another area, been incarcerated for a crime not tied to his serial murders, or died.

With BTK, however, the crimes would resume after years of dormancy. He murdered five people in 1974, then two in 1977, then went quiet until claiming one victim each in 1985 and 1986, and finally waited more than five years until killing his last victim in 1991. Very few if any of these killers ever see the evil of their ways and decide to go straight, so there had to be another explanation. Was Rader able to control himself and live off the fantasies of his past crimes for longer and longer periods?

The world started hearing from him again in 2004. He was bragging about his work and claiming a previous crime that had never been definitively linked to him. We were not surprised that Rader couldn't help reaching out to the media. For almost all of these serial sexual predators, their crimes are the most important, gratifying, and "successful" aspects of their lives. And if communicating with the authorities or the media is one of their signature elements— the part that gives them the emotional satisfaction—it is unlikely they're going to stop.

In late 2004, as if to prove BTK's bona fides, the UNSUB mailed to Wichita police a victim's driver's license and a female doll with bound hands and feet and a plastic bag over its head—another example of his "art." In one of his ever-growing series of letters to the authorities, he asked if he could be traced from material on a floppy disk that he planned to send to a local television station. Through a pre-arranged communication system involving a classified ad in the *Wichita Eagle*, the police conceded they would not be able to trace him.

On February 16, 2005, a package purportedly from BTK was received by local Fox television affiliate KSAS that contained a gold chain, the photocopied cover of a paperback novel about a killer who bound and gagged his victims, several index cards, one of which gave instructions for further communication through the *Wichita Eagle* . . . and a Memorex floppy disk. The disk's contents were disappointingly prosaic: nothing about the murders, only a file that read "This is a test" and directing police to consult the index cards.

Contrary to what they had told BTK, Wichita PD was able to analyze the disc's metadata—a term we'd never even heard when we first wrote *Mindhunter*—and discovered that it had been used on a computer belonging to Christ Lutheran Church and was last modified by "Dennis." An Internet search listed a Dennis Rader as president of the church council. Rader's car, a black Jeep Cherokee, matched the description of a vehicle noted leaving the scene where one of BTK's packages had been left.

In order to determine whether there was a DNA connection to Rader, the district attorney's office obtained a warrant to test a pap smear taken of Rader's daughter at the Kansas State University Medical Clinic when she was a student. The Kansas Bureau of Investigation analyzed the sample and found it bore a familial DNA connection to a sample taken from one of BTK's victims. After his arrest, Dennis Rader eventually confessed and, like Gary Ridgway, pled guilty to avoid the death penalty.

The original profile for the BTK Killer from previous FBI Behavioral Science Unit research predicted that the perpetrator of such sadistic crimes was likely to be single, but it also stated "if UNSUB has a girlfriend or is married, we would expect the woman to be of a very passive, compliant and/or dependent position." This turned out to be a pretty accurate assessment.

Dennis Rader was not a policeman but a municipal compliance officer for Park City, Kansas—someone who makes sure your grass doesn't get too long, your dog is on its leash, and your sidewalk is shoveled after a snowfall. He was extremely strict about giving out citations, and one family went so far as to complain that he euthanized their dog for no reason. Before that job, he had been in the Air Force, obtained a bachelor's degree from Wichita State in the administration of justice, and worked for a home security firm. Starting to see a pattern here?

Not only that, but successive prison interviews revealed that Rader had tortured small animals as a child and stolen underwear from his female victims.

Once the trial and sentencing were over, John had the opportunity to interview Rader at the El Dorado Correctional Facility in El Dorado, Kansas. The question that haunted John was why Rader had repeatedly stopped and restarted his brutal killings.

As Rader related, it was simple and, in its own way, pretty "human." One afternoon his wife, Paula, had returned home unexpectedly and found him dressed in women's clothing and the underwear of his victims, although Paula had no way of knowing where the bra and panties had come from. She was shocked and disgusted. He tried to explain away his "harmless" fetish and that he had been wrestling with his own psyche to try and get past it. She threatened to leave him if it ever happened again.

Whether this was enough to get him back on the wagon is hard to say, but Rader certainly realized that if he ever gave Paula a reason to call in the police or anyone else, it might not take very long to connect him and his souvenirs with the BTK murders.

For a while he was able to content himself with his memories, drawings, and souvenirs, but eventually the urges became too strong, and Rader went back to breaking into homes and staging his scenes of bondage and torture. And again he was caught by his wife wearing his victims' clothing. Fortunately for him, Paula still didn't put two and two together. While she did fit our profile of a passive and dependent significant other, Paula got up enough courage to seek a divorce as soon as the truth about her husband came out.

John also knew from Dennis Rader's insistence on a public title that, as BTK, he followed and admired other serial killers. It turned out Rader idolized Harvey Glatman, the "Lonely Hearts Killer" of 1950s Los Angeles, who would entice women to his apartment or some other place with bogus offers of jobs as photographic models for pulp fiction magazines, then tie them up, sexually assault them, strangle them, and dump their bodies in the desert. He was finally arrested in 1958 after a woman he attempted to abduct managed to escape and ran to the police. He was tried, convicted, and executed in the San Quentin State Prison gas chamber on September 18, 1959.

Dennis Rader quoted Harvey Glatman as saying, "It was all about the rope." What exactly does that mean? The rope symbolized total control. The ultimate fantasy would be to keep these victims alive and dominated indefinitely, although both men knew that wasn't possible.

The difference in the length of Glatman's and Rader's killing careers was as much a matter of luck as anything else. Neither Rader nor, for example, Gary Ridgway turned out to be of any great intellect. They were just obsessed with their crimes and were fortunate to avoid having the dots connected sooner. Ironically, however, Rader's undoing was similar to that of another serial killer whose identity remained unknown at the time we published *Mindhunter*. He was probably a good deal smarter than all three of these murderers put together.

In Chapter 17 ("Anyone Can Be a Victim") we reported on the then-unidentified Unabomber, who had sent a series of sophisticated mail bombs to academics and people in the technology sector. Three of his victims died and twenty-three others were injured. He even got one of his devices into the cargo hold of an American Airlines passenger jet flying out of Chicago, but the package began smoking before it exploded and the alert pilot made a well-timed emergency landing.

Unlike Dennis Rader, the Unabomber didn't give himself his public identity. The name came from the FBI's major case code name: UNABOM, for UNiversity and Airline BOMber. In profiling this particular UNSUB, there was disagreement within the FBI and the ever-growing task force as to whether he was more likely to be someone associated with the airline—perhaps a mechanic who would have the technical skills necessary to build bombs—or the profile that John had constructed, theorizing that he was more likely associated with a university, since he seemed highly intelligent in his strategy and bomb-making skills. The UNSUB would also include false clues and extraneous objects like pieces of wood and tree bark.

Once the Unabomber began sending letters to the *New York Times* complaining of big-business tactics and the despoliation of the environment from incidents like the *Exxon Valdez* oil spill, John became even more convinced of his academic credentials due to the tone and style of his writing. The specific complaints and use of wood in the bombs led to the conclusion that he was a neo-Luddite, self-styled, anti-technology champion.

Finally, after years of intermittent bombings, the Unabomber sent the *New York Times* an ultimatum. He would stop his activities if the *Times* and the *Washington Post* would publish his "manifesto" about technology. Otherwise he would continue.

There was much debate and soul-searching over this demand—both in the journalistic and law enforcement communities, and in conferences between them. The *Times* and *Post* managements worried over the precedent this would set. Could newspapers now be held hostage by any dangerous lunatic who wanted his opinions heard? The law enforcement community was equally concerned, as it always is, over encouraging copycats and giving in to a killer's demands.

At the Investigative Support Unit in Quantico, the opinion was more clear-cut: The public is often our greatest partner. Once all logical and reasonable leads have been exhausted, give ordinary citizens a chance to help solve the case. Attorney General Janet Reno went along with ISU's recommendation.

This mind-set had worked well in the past. As you'll see in more detail later on, *Mindhunter* chronicles special agent and profiler Jana Monroe, who, in trying to solve a Tampa Bay triple murder, had the idea to reproduce on donated billboards a set of directions believed to be in the UNSUB's handwriting. This led to the arrest, prosecution, and conviction of Oba Chandler, who has since been executed for his crimes.

The Unabomber case has a now-famous outcome. After the newspapers agreed to publish his 35,000-word essay, "Industrial Society and Its Future," in special sections, a woman named Linda Patrik convinced her youth counselor/ social worker husband, David Kaczynski, that the writing sounded alarmingly similar to ideas expressed by his older brother, Ted, of whom she was already suspicious. Theodore "Ted" Kaczynski was a Harvard University and University of Michigan–trained Ph.D. mathematician who, for decades, had been living in the remote woods of Montana as a hermit in a tiny cabin without electricity or running water.

Mark spoke to David Kaczynski about the moral agony he and Linda went through in deciding they had to turn in his brother. Before identifying his brother, David delicately made a deal with authorities to assure that Ted would not be executed for his crimes. Although we both favor the death penalty for certain serial and predatory murders, we can't fault David and Linda for their decisions and actions, which were truly heroic. Ted is now serving multiple life sentences at the federal "supermax" prison in Florence, Colorado.

Would an Oba Chandler or Unabomber manifesto–type strategy have worked in identifying and stopping BTK earlier? We'll never know, but we think there is a very good chance it would have. Even though their crimes were completely different, the one thing the maladjusted genius Ted Kaczynski and the sadistic but banal underachiever Dennis Rader shared was a monumental sense of ego. Neither one of them could bear to let his brilliance go unrecognized by the public, and that was their downfall in both cases.

It's easy to second-guess, and one thing you learn in this business is that every case looks obvious once it's solved. Police investigators are understandably reluctant to give out case details known only to the offender. But had the Wichita police released some of the BTK sketches, crime scene descriptions, and other communications, it is quite possible someone within Dennis Rader's workplace, at his church, in his social circle, or even at home might have recognized his handiwork or at least had enough of a suspicion to contact authorities.

Since we wrote *Mindhunter*, the prevalence of certain crimes has changed. Violent crime in general has been on a downward trend, but the number of predatory sexually oriented killers has remained relatively the same. The reason, we believe, is because this type of criminal pathology is not as responsive to societal conditions or improved policing as other criminal enterprises. In the past sixteen years we have become concerned with domestic and international terrorism, a phenomenon that was just beginning when we cited the 1995 Oklahoma City federal building bombing. Mass shootings have become alarmingly commonplace, unlike Charles Whitman's 1966 killing spree from the top of the University of Texas tower. (Though Whitman's autopsy revealed a small brain tumor, our consultation with a distinguished neurologist confirmed that its location would not have affected the areas controlling this type of behavior.)

As we suggested earlier, even though the types of crimes have changed, we have found that the basic motivators remain the same.

Whether we're talking about a mail bomber like Ted Kaczynski, Charles Whitman or any number of school shooters, or the raft of religious terrorists who have come to plague much of the world, we're exploring similar psyches. These are people who take up mass violence as a personal assertion or political statement to compensate for their own hopelessness, pathos, failure, and/or lack of purpose. Again, that inner despair may be in constant conflict with a sense of personal grandiosity and unfulfilled entitlement, but these individuals are all, without exception, inadequate nobodies who want to be somebodies and find meaning in their lives. They may have personal courage—choosing to die for a cause, however misguided, is not a casual decision—but they have also found that violence is their only proof of power.

In the years since John retired from the Bureau and began taking cases from the outside, his perspective has broadened—as has Mark's, which is reflected in our subsequent books. In the Investigative Support Unit, agents could work only cases brought to them by police departments and sheriffs' offices, not defendants. But when John branched out, we came to see things from the other side and we recognized that not all official investigations are complete or accurate.

Such cases as the 1993 murder of three eight-year-old boys in Arkansas, attributed to the so-called West Memphis Three; the still-unsolved 1996 Christmas Day slaying of six-year-old JonBenét Ramsey in Boulder, Colorado; and the 2007 killing of twenty-one-year-old British exchange student Meredith Kercher in Perugia, Italy, for which American student Amanda Knox and her Italian boyfriend Raffaele Sollecito were charged and convicted graphically demonstrated the horrifying consequences when a police investigation starts off on the wrong foot, driven by preconceived notions and prejudices rather than where the evidence points. Inadequate preservation of crime scenes and physical evidence; improper interview techniques that can lead to false confessions; junk science and convenient reliance on jailhouse snitches who have their own goals independent of the truth—all of these factors can and do contribute to wrongful convictions.

When we recently began reflecting on the eye-opening cases that John had investigated and that we analyzed and wrote about in *Mindhunter*, we had to confront some of our own long-held ideas and impressions. In Chapter 7 ("The Heart of Darkness"), you'll read about the interview John and Bob Ressler conducted with William Heirens at State-ville Prison in Crest Hill, Illinois, when they were pursuing their initial serial killer study. Heirens was the notorious "Lipstick Killer" of post–World War II Chicago, who confessed to and was convicted of the horrific murder and dismemberment of six-year-old Suzanne Degnan.

After the interview, John was so overwhelmed by Hei-rens's insistence on his innocence that, as we wrote, "when we got back to Quantico, I dug out all the case files. In addition to the confession and other compelling evidence, I found that his latent fingerprints had been lifted from the Degnan crime scene. Yet Heirens had spent so much time sitting in his cell and thinking and giving himself all the answers that if they polygraphed him at that point, he probably would have passed with no trouble."

The reason he would have done so, we finally concluded after a detailed analysis many years after writing those words, was because there was a better-than-even chance that William Heirens was innocent. Yes, he had been a proven breaking-and-entering guy during college but, despite possessing a firearm, he gave no previous impression of being a violent man or lust killer. He definitely did not represent the profile John would have come up with had he worked the original case. But the police seemed to lose interest in the best suspect they had developed once they'd arrested Heirens and the public was satisfied that a depraved killer had been caught.

Considering the accumulated experience of more than two decades of John's full-time profiling and criminal investigative analysis; the Chicago PD's reputation in the 1930s and 1940s—they frequently beat confessions out of suspects, including William Heirens and an African American they'd previously arrested in their investigation who was completely innocent—knowing how easy it can be to plant and stage evidence; and understanding that profiling can be only as good as the information and evidence supplied by the requesting local law enforcement agency, the prospect of Heirens's actual innocence becomes increasingly believable.

But, as is all too common, there was ultimately no resolution. When the eighty-three-year-old wheelchair-bound William Heirens passed away on March 5, 2012, at the Dixon Correctional Center in Dixon, Illinois, he was the longest-serving prisoner in the United States.

While there may have been a momentary inclination to change or update specific aspects of the narrative for this new edition of *Mindhunter*, we stand proudly by what we wrote back in the mid-1990s and feel it best serves the book to update the reader with this introduction rather than changing any of the text. Just as the basics of the human mind and motivation remain the same, so do the essentials of good criminal investigation. Despite the advantages offered by advances in technology, computers, DNA, serology, and arson science—and the reevaluation of such standard tools as fingerprints and ballistic analysis—there remains no substitution for good gumshoe detective work and investigative analysis. This involves examining the crime scene and all the evidence, studying the victimology, knocking on doors, and following up every reasonable lead. The bottom line is that we're never going to take the human element out of crime solving.

What was true more than twenty years ago is true today, and will be as far into the future as we can imagine:

Behavior reflects personality. The best indicator of future violence is past violence. To understand the "artist," you must study his "art." The crime must be evaluated in its totality. There is no substitute for experience, and if you want to understand the criminal mind, you must go directly to the source and learn to decipher what he tells you. And, above all: *Why + How = Who.*

And now we invite you once again to embark upon the hunt with us.

I Must Be in Hell

I must be in hell.

It was the only logical explanation. I was tied down and naked. The pain was unbearable. My arms and legs were being lacerated by some kind of blade. Every orifice of my body had been penetrated. I was choking and gagging from something shoved down my throat. Sharp objects had been stuck in my penis and rectum and felt like they were tearing me apart. I was bathed in sweat. Then I realized what was happening: I was being tortured to death by all the killers and rapists and child molesters I'd put away in my career. Now I was the victim and I couldn't fight back.

I knew the way these guys operated; I'd seen it over and over again. They had a need to manipulate and dominate their prey. They wanted to be able to decide whether or not their victim should live or die, or how the victim should die. They'd keep me alive as long as my body would hold out, reviving me when I passed out or was close to death, always inflicting as much pain and suffering as possible. Some of them could go on for days like that.

They wanted to show me they were in total control, that I was completely at their mercy. The more I cried out, the more I begged for relief, the more I would fuel and energize their dark fantasies. If I would plead for my life or regress or call out for my mommy or daddy, that would really get them off.

This was my payback for six years of hunting the worst men on earth.

My heart was racing, I was burning up. I felt a horrible

jab as they inched the sharp stick even farther up my penis. My entire body convulsed in agony.

Please, God, if I'm still alive, let me die quickly. And if I'm dead, deliver me quickly from the tortures of hell.

Then I saw an intense, bright white light, just like I'd heard about people seeing at the moment of death. I expected to see Christ or angels or the devil—I'd heard about that, too. But all I saw was that bright white light.

But I did hear a voice—a comforting, reassuring voice, the most calming sound I'd ever heard.

"John, don't worry. We're trying to make it all better."

That was the last thing I remembered.

"John, do you hear me? Don't worry. Take it easy. You're in the hospital. You're very sick, but we're trying to make you better," was what the nurse actually said to me. She had no idea whether or not I could hear her, but she kept repeating it, soothingly, over and over again.

Though I had no idea at the time, I was in the intensive care unit of Swedish Hospital in Seattle, in a coma, on life support. My arms and legs were strapped down. Tubes, hoses, and intravenous lines penetrated my body. I was not expected to live. It was early December of 1983, and I was thirty-eight years of age.

The story begins three weeks earlier, on the other side of the country. I was up in New York, speaking on criminal-personality profiling before an audience of about 350 members of the NYPD, the Transit Police, and the Nassau and Suffolk County, Long Island, Police Departments. I'd given this speech hundreds of times and could just about do the whole thing on autopilot.

All of a sudden, my mind started to wander. I was aware I was still talking, but I'd broken out in a cold sweat and I was saying to myself, *How in hell am I going to handle all these cases?* I was just finishing up with the Wayne Williams child-killing case in Atlanta and Buffalo's ".22-Caliber" race murders. I had been called in to the "Trailside Killer" case in San Francisco. I was consulting with Scotland Yard on the "Yorkshire Ripper" investigation in England. I was going back and forth to Alaska, working on the Robert Hansen case, in which an Anchorage baker was picking up prostitutes, flying them out into the wilderness, and hunting them down. I had a serial arsonist targeting synagogues in Hartford, Connecticut. And I had to fly out to Seattle the week after next to advise the Green River Task Force in what was shaping up as one of the largest serial murders in American history, the killer preying mainly on prostitutes and transients in the Seattle-Tacoma corridor.

For the past six years, I had been developing a new approach to crime analysis, and I was the only one in the Behavioral Science Unit working cases full-time. Everyone else in the unit was primarily an instructor. I was handling about 150 active cases at a time with no backup, and I was on the road from my office at the FBI Academy in Quantico, Virginia, about 125 days a year. The pressure was tremendous from local cops, who themselves were under tremendous pressure to solve cases, from the community, and from the families of victims, for whom I always had enormous empathy. I kept trying to prioritize my workload, but new requests kept pouring in daily. My associates at Quantico often said I was like a male whore: I couldn't say no to my clients.

During the New York speech, I continued talking about criminal-personality types, but my mind kept wandering back to Seattle. I knew that not everyone on the task force wanted me there, that was par for the course. As in every major case for which I was called in to provide a new service that most cops and many Bureau officials still considered one step removed from witchcraft, I knew I'd have to "sell" them. I had to be persuasive without being overconfident or cocky. I had to let them know I thought they'd done a thorough, professional job while still trying to convince the skeptics the FBI might be able to help. And perhaps most daunting, unlike the traditional FBI agent who dealt with "Just the facts, ma'am," my job required me to deal in *opinions*. I lived with the constant knowledge that if I was wrong, I could throw a serial investigation far off the mark and get additional people killed. Just as bad, it would hammer the lid on the new program of criminal-personality profiling and crime analysis I was struggling to get off the ground.

Then there was the traveling itself. I had already been to Alaska on several occasions, crossing four time zones, connecting to a white-knuckle flight close to the water and landing in darkness, and practically as soon as I got there and met with the local police, I would get back on the plane and fly down to Seattle.

The free-floating anxiety attack lasted maybe a minute. I kept saying to myself, *Hey, Douglas, regroup. Get a grip on yourself.* And I was able to do it. I don't think anyone in that room knew anything was wrong. But I couldn't shake the feeling that something tragic was going to happen to me.

I couldn't shake this premonition, and when I got back to Quantico, I went to the personnel office and took out additional life insurance and income-protection insurance in case I became disabled. I can't say exactly why I did this, except for that vague but powerful feeling of dread. I was physically run-down; I was exercising too much and probably drinking more than I should have been to cope with the stress. I was having difficulty sleeping, and when I did fall asleep, often I'd be awakened by a call from someone needing my instant help. When I would go back to sleep, I'd try to force myself to dream about the case in hopes that that would lead me to some insight about it. It's easy enough in retrospect to see where I was headed, but at the time there didn't seem to be anything I could do about it.

Just before I left for the airport, something made me stop off at the elementary school where my wife, Pam, taught reading to learning disabled students, to tell her about the extra insurance.

"Why are you telling me this?" she asked, very concerned. I had a wicked headache on the right side and she said my eyes were bloodshot and strange-looking.

"I just wanted you to know about everything before I left," I replied. At that time, we had two young daughters. Erika was eight and Lauren was three.

For the trip to Seattle, I brought along two new special agents, Blaine McIlwain and Ron Walker, to break them in on the case. We arrived in Seattle that night and checked into the Hilton Hotel downtown. As I was unpacking, I noticed I had only one black shoe. Either I hadn't packed the other one or somehow I'd lost it along the way. I would be making a presentation to the King County Police Department the next morning, and I decided I couldn't go on without my black shoes. I have always been something of a flashy dresser, and in my fatigue and stress, I became obsessed with having black shoes to wear with my suit. So I tore out into the downtown streets, rushed around until I found an open shoe store, and came back to the hotel, even more exhausted, with a suitable pair of black shoes.

The next morning, a Wednesday, I made my presentation to the police and a team that included Port of Seattle representatives and two local psychologists who had been brought in to help with the investigation. Everyone was interested in my profile of the killer, whether there could be more than one offender, and what type of individual he, or they, might be. I tried to get across the point that in this type of case, the profile wouldn't be all that important. I was pretty sure of what kind of guy the killer would turn out to be, but just as sure there'd be a lot of guys who would easily fit the description.

More important in this ongoing cycle of murders, I told them, was to begin going *proactive*, using police efforts and the media to try to lure the guy into a trap. For example, I suggested the police might set up a series of community meetings to "discuss" the crimes. I was reasonably certain the killer would show up at one or more of these. I also thought it would help answer the question of whether we were dealing with more than one offender. Another ploy I wanted the police to try was to announce to the press that there had been witnesses to one of the abductions. I felt that might draw out the killer to take his own "proactive strategy" and come forward to explain why he might have been innocently seen in the vicinity. The one thing of which I felt most certain was that whoever was behind these kills wasn't going to burn out.

I then gave the team advice on how to interrogate potential subjects—both those they generated on their own and the many sad crazies who inevitably come forward in a high-profile case. McIlwain, Walker, and I spent the rest of the day touring body dump sites, and by the time we got back to the hotel that evening, I was wiped out.

Over drinks at the hotel bar, where we were trying to unwind from the day, I told Blaine and Ron I wasn't feeling well. I still had the headache, thought I might be coming down with the flu, and asked them to cover for me with the police the next day. I thought I might feel better if I spent the next day in bed, so when we said good night, I put the Do Not Disturb sign on my door and told my two associates I'd rejoin them Friday morning.

All I remember is feeling terrible, sitting on the side of the bed and beginning to undress. My two fellow agents went back to the King County Courthouse on Thursday to follow up on the strategies I had outlined the day before. As I'd requested, they left me alone all day to try to sleep off my flu.

But when I didn't show up for breakfast on Friday morning, they began to get concerned. They called my room. There was no answer. They went to the room and knocked on the door. Nothing.

Alarmed, they went back to the front desk and demanded a key from the manager. They came back upstairs and unlocked the door, only to find the security chain on. But they also heard faint moaning from inside the room.

They kicked in the door and rushed inside. They found me on the floor in what they described as a "froglike" position, partially dressed, apparently trying to reach the telephone. The left side of my body was convulsing, and Blaine said I was "burning up."

The hotel called Swedish Hospital, which immediately dispatched an ambulance. In the meantime, Blaine and Ron stayed on the phone with the emergency room, giving them my vitals. My temperature was 107 degrees, my pulse, 220. My left side was paralyzed, and in the ambulance I continued having seizures. The medical report described me with "doll's eyes"—open, fixed, and unfocused.

As soon as we arrived at the hospital, they packed me in ice and began massive intravenous doses of phenobarbital in an attempt to control the seizures. The doctor told Blaine and Ron he could practically have put the entire city of Seattle to sleep with what they were giving me.

He also told the two agents that despite everyone's best efforts, I was probably going to die. A CAT scan showed the right side of my brain had ruptured and hemorrhaged from the high fever.

"In layman's terms," the doctor told them, "his brain has been fried to a crisp."

It was December 2, 1983. My new insurance had become active the day before.

My unit chief, Roger Depue, went to Pam's school to give her the news in person. Then she and my father, Jack, flew out to Seattle to be with me, leaving the girls with my mother, Dolores. Two agents from the FBI's Seattle Field Office, Rick Mathers and John Biner, picked them up at the airport and brought them straight to the hospital. That's when they knew how serious it was. The doctors tried to prepare Pam for my death and told her that even if I lived, I'd probably be blind and vegetative. Being a Catholic, she called in a priest to give me last rites, but when he found out I was Presbyterian, he refused. So Blaine and Ron gave him the hook and found another priest who didn't seem to have these hang-ups. They asked him to come pray for me.

I hovered in the coma between life and death all week. The rules of the intensive care unit allowed only family members to visit, so my Quantico colleagues and Rick Mathers and others from the Seattle Field Office suddenly became close relatives. "You've certainly got a big family," one of the nurses commented wryly to Pam.

The idea of the "big family" wasn't a complete joke in one sense. Back at Quantico, a number of my colleagues, led by Bill Hagmaier of the Behavioral Science Unit and Tom Columbell of the National Academy, took up a collection so that Pam and my dad could stay out in Seattle with me. Before long, they'd taken in contributions from police officers from all over the country. At the same time, arrangements were being made to fly my body back to Virginia for burial in the military cemetery at Quantico.

Toward the end of the first week, Pam, my father, the agents, and the priest formed a circle around my bed, joined hands, and took my hands in theirs and prayed over me. Late that night, I came out of the coma.

I remember being surprised to see Pam and my father and being confused about where I was. Initially, I couldn't talk; the left half of my face drooped and I still had extensive paralysis on my left side. As my speech came back, it was slurred at first. After a while I found I could move my leg, then gradually, more movement returned. My throat was painfully sore from the life-support tube. I was switched from phenobarbital to Dilantin to control the seizures. And after all the tests and scans and spinal taps, they finally offered a clinical diagnosis: viral encephalitis brought on or complicated by stress and my generally weakened and vulnerable condition. I was lucky to be alive.

But the recovery was painful and discouraging. I had to learn to walk again. I was having memory problems. To help me remember the name of my primary physician, Siegal, Pam brought in for me a figurine of a seagull made of shells and sitting on a cork base. The next time the doctor came to give me a mental status exam and asked if I remembered his name, I slurred, "Sure, Dr. Seagull."

Despite the wonderful support I was getting, I was tremendously frustrated with the rehabilitation. I'd never been able to sit around or take things slow. FBI director William Webster called to encourage me. I told him I didn't think I could shoot anymore.

"Don't worry about that, John," the director replied. "We want you for your mind." I didn't tell him I was afraid there wasn't much of that left, either.

I finally left Swedish Hospital and came home two days before Christmas. Before leaving, I presented the emergency room and ICU staffs with plaques expressing my profound gratitude for all they had done to save my life.

Roger Depue picked us up at Dulles Airport and drove us to our house in Fredericksburg, where an American flag and a huge "Welcome Home, John" sign were waiting. I had dropped from my normal 195 to 160 pounds. My kids, Erika and Lauren, were so upset by my appearance and the fact that I was in a wheelchair that for a long time afterward, they were afraid every time I went away on a trip.

Christmas was pretty melancholy. I didn't see many friends; only Ron Walker, Blaine McIlwain, Bill Hagmaier, and another agent from Quantico, Jim Horn. I was out of the wheelchair, but moving around was still difficult. I had trouble carrying on a conversation. I found I cried easily and couldn't count on my memory. When Pam or my dad would drive me around Fredericksburg, I'd notice a particular building and not know if it was new. I felt like a stroke victim and wondered if I'd ever be able to work again.

I was also bitter at the Bureau for what they'd put me through. The previous February, I'd spoken with an assistant director, Jim McKenzie. I told him I didn't think I could keep up the pace and asked him if he could get me some people to help out.

McKenzie was sympathetic but realistic. "You know this organization," he'd said to me. "You have to do something until you drop before anyone will recognize it."

Not only did I feel I wasn't getting support, I felt I wasn't getting any appreciation, either. Quite the contrary, in fact. The previous year, after working my butt off in the Atlanta "Child Murders" case, I was officially censured by the Bureau for a story that appeared in a newspaper in Newport News, Virginia, just after Wayne Williams was apprehended. The reporter asked me what I thought of Williams as a suspect, and I replied that he looked "good," and that if he panned out, he'd probably be good for at least several of the cases.

Even though the FBI had asked me to do the interview, they said I was speaking inappropriately about a pending case. They claimed I'd been warned before doing a *People* magazine interview a couple of months before. It was typical of government bureaucracy. I was hauled up before the Office of Professional Responsibility at headquarters in Washington, and after six months of bureaucratic tap dancing, I got a letter of censure. Later, I would get a letter of commendation for the case. But at the time, this was the recognition from the Bureau for helping crack what the press was then calling the "crime of the century."

So much of what a law enforcement officer does is difficult to share with anyone, even a spouse. When you spend your days looking at dead and mutilated bodies, particularly when they're children, it's not the kind of thing you want to bring home with you. You can't say over the dinner table, "I had a fascinating lust murder today. Let me tell you about it." That's why you so often see cops drawn to nurses and vice versa—people who can relate in some way to each other's work.

And yet often when I was out in the park or the woods, say, with my own little girls, I'd see something and think to myself, *That's just like the such-and-such scene, where we found the eight-year-old.* As fearful as I was for their safety, seeing the things I saw, I also found it difficult to get emotionally involved in the minor, but important, scrapes and hurts of childhood. When I would come home and Pam would tell me that one of the girls had fallen off her bike and needed stitches, I'd flash to the autopsy of some child her age and think of all the stitches it had taken the medical examiner to close her wounds for burial.

Pam had her own circle of friends who were involved with local politics, which didn't interest me at all. And with my travel schedule, she ended up with the lion's share of responsibility for raising the children, paying the bills, and running the house. This was one of the many problems with the marriage at the time, and I know that at least our oldest, Erika, was aware of the tension.

I couldn't shake my resentment at the Bureau organization for letting this happen to me. About a month after I returned home, I was out burning leaves in the backyard. On an impulse, I went in, collected all the copies of profiles I had in the house, all the articles I'd written, carried them outside, and threw them all onto the fire. It felt like a catharsis, just getting rid of all of this stuff.

Some weeks after that, when I could drive again, I went to Quantico National Cemetery to see where I would have been buried. Graves are positioned by date of death, and if I had died on December 1 or 2, I would have gotten a lousy site. I noticed it happened to be near that of a young girl who had been stabbed to death on her driveway not far from where I lived. I'd worked on her case and the murder was still unsolved. As I stood there ruminating, I recalled how many times I'd advised police to surveil grave sites when I thought the killer might visit, and how ironic it would be if they were watching here and picked me up as a suspect.

Four months after my collapse in Seattle, I was still out on sick leave. I'd developed blood clots in my legs and lungs as a complication of the illness and so much time in bed, and I still felt as if I was struggling to get through every day. I still didn't know if I'd physically be able to work again and didn't know if I'd have the confidence even if I could. In the meantime, Roy Hazelwood, from the instructional side of the Behavioral Science Unit, was doubling up and had taken on the burden of handling my ongoing cases.

I made my first visit back to Quantico in April of 1984 to address an in-service group of about fifty profilers from FBI field offices. I stepped into the classroom, wearing slippers because my feet were still swollen from blood clots, and got a standing ovation from these agents from all over the country. The reaction was spontaneous and genuine from the people who, better than anyone, understood what I did and what I was trying to institute within the Bureau. And for the first time in many months, I felt cherished and appreciated. I also felt as if I had come home.

I went back to work full-time a month later.

1

Inside the Mind of a Killer

Put yourself in the position of the hunter.

That's what I have to do. Think of one of those nature films: a lion on the Serengeti plain in Africa. He sees this huge herd of antelope at a watering hole. But somehow—we can see it in his eyes—the lion locks on a single one out of those thousands of animals. He's trained himself to sense weakness, vulnerability, something different in one antelope out of the herd that makes it the most likely victim.

It's the same with certain people. If I'm one of them, then I'm on the hunt daily, looking for my victim, looking for my victim of opportunity. Let's say I'm at a shopping mall where there are thousands of people. So I go into the video arcade, and as I look over the fifty or so children playing there, I've got to be a hunter, I've got to be a profiler, I've got to be able to profile that potential prey. I've got to figure out which of those fifty children is the vulnerable one, which one is the likely victim. I have to look at the way the child is dressed. I have to train myself to pick up the nonverbal clues the child is putting out. And I have to do this all in a split second, so I have to be very, very good at it. Then, once I decide, once I make my move, I've got to know how I am going to get this child out of the mall quietly and without creating any fuss or suspicion when his or her parents are probably two stores down. I can't afford to make any mistakes.

It's the thrill of the hunt that gets these guys going. If you could get a galvanic skin response reading on one of them as he focuses in on his potential victim, I think you'd get the same reaction as from that lion in the wilderness. And it doesn't matter whether we're talking about the ones who hunt children, who hunt young women or the elderly or prostitutes or any other definable group—or the ones who don't seem to have any particular preferred victim. In some ways, they're all the same.

But it is the ways they are different, and the clues that they leave to their individual personalities, that have led us to a new weapon in the interpretation of certain types of violent crimes, and the hunting, apprehension, and prosecution of their perpetrators. I've spent most of my professional career as an FBI special agent trying to develop that weapon, and that's what this book is about. In the case of every horrible crime since the beginning of civilization, there is always that searing, fundamental question: what kind of person could have done such a thing? The type of profiling and crime-scene analysis we do at the FBI's Investigative Support Unit attempts to answer that question.

Behavior reflects personality.

It isn't always easy, and it's never pleasant, putting yourself in these guys' shoes—or inside their minds. But that's what my people and I have to do. We have to try to feel what it was like for each one.

Everything we see at a crime scene tells us something about the unknown subject—or UNSUB, in police jargon—who committed the crime. By studying as many crimes as we could, and through talking to the experts—the perpetrators themselves—we have learned to interpret those clues in much the same way a doctor evaluates various symptoms to diagnose a particular disease or condition. And just as a doctor can begin forming a diagnosis after recognizing several aspects of a disease presentation he or she has seen before, we can make various conclusions when we see patterns start to emerge.

One time in the early 1980s when I was actively interviewing incarcerated killers for our in-depth study, I was sitting in a circle of violent offenders in the ancient, stone, gothic Maryland State Penitentiary in Baltimore. Each man was an interesting case in his own right—a cop killer, a child killer, drug dealers, and enforcers—but I was most concerned with interviewing a rapist-murderer about his modus operandi, so I asked the other prisoners if they knew of one at the prison I might be able to talk to.

"Yeah, there's Charlie Davis," one of the inmates says, but the rest agree it's unlikely he'll talk to a fed. Someone goes to find him in the prison yard. To everyone's surprise, Davis does come over and join the circle, probably as much out of curiosity or boredom as any other reason. One thing we had going for us in the study is that prisoners have a lot of time on their hands and not much to do with it.

Normally, when we conduct prison interviews—and this has been true right from the beginning—we try to know as much as we can about the subject in advance. We go over the police files and crime-scene photos, autopsy protocols, trial transcripts; anything that might shed light on motives or personality. It's also the surest way to make certain the subject isn't playing self-serving or self-amusing games with you and is giving it to you straight. But in this case, obviously, I hadn't done any preparation, so I admit it and try to use it to my advantage.

Davis was a huge, hulking guy, about six foot five, in his early thirties, clean-shaven, and well groomed. I start out by saying, "You have me at a disadvantage, Charlie. I don't know what you did."

"I killed five people," he replies.

I ask him to describe the crime scenes and what he did with his victims. Now, it turns out, Davis had been a part-time ambulance driver. So what he'd do was strangle the woman, place her body by the side of a highway in his driving territory, make an anonymous call, then respond to the call and pick up the body. No one knew, when he was putting the victim on the stretcher, that the killer was right there among them. This degree of control and orchestration was what really turned him on and gave him his biggest thrill. Anything like this that I could learn about technique would always prove extremely valuable.

The strangling told me he was a spur-of-the-moment killer, that the primary thing on his mind had been rape.

I say to him, "You're a real police buff. You'd love to be a cop yourself, to be in a position of power instead of some menial job far below your abilities." He laughs, says his father had been a police lieutenant.

I ask him to describe his MO: he would follow a good-looking young woman, see her pull into the parking lot of a restaurant, let's say. Through his father's police contacts, he'd be able to run a license-plate check on the car. Then, when he had the owner's name, he'd call the restaurant and have her paged and told she'd left her lights on. When she came outside, he'd abduct her—push her into his car or hers, handcuff her, then drive off.

He describes each of the five kills in order, almost as if he's reminiscing. When he gets to the last one, he mentions that he covered her over in the front seat of the car, a detail he remembers for the first time.

At that point in the conversation, I turn things further around. I say, "Charlie, let me tell you something about yourself: You had relationship problems with women. You were having financial problems when you did your first kill. You were in your late twenties and you knew your abilities were way above your job, so everything in your life was frustrating and out of control."

He just sort of nods. So far, so good. I haven't said anything terribly hard to predict or guess at.

"You were drinking heavily," I continue. "You owed money. You were having fights with the woman you lived with. [He hadn't told me he lived with anyone, but I felt pretty certain he did.] And on the nights when things were the worst, you'd go out on the hunt. You wouldn't go after your old lady, so you had to dish it out to someone else."

I can see Davis's body language gradually changing, opening up. So, going with the scant information I have, I go on, "But this last victim was a much more gentle kill. She was different from the others. You let her get dressed again after you raped her. You covered up her head. You didn't do that with the previous four. Unlike the others, you didn't feel good about this one."

When they start listening closely, you know you're onto something. I learned this from the prison interviews and was able to use it over and over in interrogation situations. I see I have his complete attention here. "She told you something that made you feel bad about killing her, but you killed her anyway."

Suddenly, he becomes red as a beet. He seems in a trancelike state, and I can see that in his mind, he's back at the scene. Hesitantly, he tells me the woman had said her husband was having serious health problems and that she was worried about him; he was sick and maybe dying. This may have been a ruse on her part, it may not have been—I don't have any way of knowing. But clearly, it had affected Davis.

"But I hadn't disguised myself. She knew who I was, so I had to kill her."

I pause a few moments, then say, "You took something from her, didn't you?"

He nods again, then admits he went into her wallet. He took out a photograph of her with her husband and child at Christmas and kept it.

I'd never met this guy before, but I'm starting to get a firm image of him, so I say, "You went to the grave site, Charlie, didn't you?" He becomes flushed, which also confirms for me he followed the press on the case so he'd know where his victim was buried. "You went because you didn't feel good about this particular murder. And you brought something with you to the cemetery and you put it right there on that grave."

The other prisoners are completely silent, listening with rapt attention. They've never seen Davis like this. I repeat, "You brought something to that grave. What did you bring, Charlie? You brought that picture, didn't you?" He just nods again and hangs his head.

This wasn't quite the witchcraft or pulling the rabbit out of the hat it might have seemed to the other prisoners. Obviously, I was guessing, but the guesses were based on a lot of background and research and experience my associates and I had logged by that time and continue to gather. For example, we'd learned that the old cliché about killers visiting the graves of their victims was often true, but not necessarily for the reasons we'd originally thought.

Behavior reflects personality.

One of the reasons our work is even necessary has to do with the changing nature of violent crime itself. We all know about the drug-related murders that plague most of our cities and the gun crimes that have become an everyday occurrence as well as a national disgrace. Yet it used to be that most crime, particularly most violent crime, happened between people who in some way knew each other.

We're not seeing that as much any longer. As recently as the 1960s, the solution rate to homicide in this country was well over 90 percent. We're not seeing that any longer, either. Now, despite impressive advances in science and technology, despite the advent of the computer age, despite many more police officers with far better and more sophisticated training and resources, the murder rate has been going up and the solution rate has been going down. More and more crimes are being committed by and against "strangers," and in many cases we have no motive to work with, at least no obvious or "logical" motive.

Traditionally, most murders and violent crimes were

relatively easy for law enforcement officials to comprehend. They resulted from critically exaggerated manifestations of feelings we all experience: anger, greed, jealousy, profit, revenge. Once this emotional problem was taken care of, the crime or crime spree would end. Someone would be dead, but that was that and the police generally knew who and what they were looking for.

But a new type of violent criminal has surfaced in recent years—the serial offender, who often doesn't stop until he is caught or killed, who learns by experience and who tends to get better and better at what he does, constantly perfecting his scenario from one crime to the next. I say "surfaced" because, to some degree, he was probably with us all along, going back long before 1880s London and Jack the Ripper, generally considered the first modern serial killer. And I say "he" because, for reasons we'll get into a little later, virtually all real serial killers are male.

Serial murder may, in fact, be a much older phenomenon than we realize. The stories and legends that have filtered down about witches and werewolves and vampires may have been a way of explaining outrages so hideous that no one in the small and close-knit towns of Europe and early America could comprehend the perversities we now take for granted. Monsters had to be supernatural creatures. They couldn't be just like us.

Serial killers and rapists also tend to be the most bewildering, personally disturbing, and most difficult to catch of all violent criminals. This is, in part, because they tend to be motivated by far more complex factors than the basic ones I've just enumerated. This, in turn, makes their patterns more confusing and distances them from such other normal feelings as compassion, guilt, or remorse.

Sometimes, the only way to catch them is to learn how to think like they do.

Lest anyone think I will be giving away any closely guarded investigative secrets that could provide a "how-to" to would-be offenders, let me reassure you on that point right now. What I will be relating is how we developed the behavioral approach to criminal-personality profiling, crime analysis, and prosecutorial strategy, but I couldn't make this a how-to course even if I wanted to. For one thing, it takes as much as two years for us to train the already experienced, highly accomplished agents selected to come into my unit. For another, no matter how much the criminal thinks he knows, the more he does to try to evade detection or throw us off the track, the more behavioral clues he's going to give us to work with.

As Sir Arthur Conan Doyle had Sherlock Holmes say many decades ago, "Singularity is almost invariably a clue. The more featureless and commonplace a crime is, the more difficult it is to bring it home." In other words, the more behavior we have, the more complete the profile and analysis we can give to the local police. The better the profile the local police have to work with, the more they can slice down the potential suspect population and concentrate on finding the real guy.

Which brings me to the other disclaimer about our work. In the Investigative Support Unit, which is part of the FBI's National Center for the Analysis of Violent Crime at Quantico, we don't catch criminals. Let me repeat that: *we do not catch criminals*. Local police catch criminals, and considering the incredible pressures they're under, most of them do a pretty damn good job of it. What we try to do is *assist* local police in focusing their investigations, then suggest some proactive techniques that might help draw a criminal out. Once they catch him—and again, I emphasize *they*, not *we*—we will try to formulate a strategy to help the prosecutor bring out the defendant's true personality during the trial.

We're able to do this because of our research and our specialized experience. While a local midwestern police department faced with a serial-murder investigation might be seeing these horrors for the first time, my unit has probably handled hundreds, if not thousands, of similar crimes. I always tell my agents, "If you want to understand the artist, you have to look at the painting." We've looked at many "paintings" over the years and talked extensively to the most "accomplished" "artists."

We began methodically developing the work of the FBI's Behavioral Science Unit, and what later came to be the Investigative Support Unit, in the late 1970s and early 1980s. And though most of the books that dramatize and glorify what we do, such as Tom Harris's memorable *The Silence of the Lambs*, are somewhat fanciful and prone to dramatic license, our antecedents actually do go back to crime fiction more than crime fact. C. Auguste Dupin, the amateur detective hero of Edgar Allan Poe's 1841 classic "The Murders in the Rue Morgue," may have been history's first behavioral profiler. This story may also represent the first use of a proactive technique by the profiler to flush out an unknown subject and vindicate an innocent man imprisoned for the killings.

Like the men and women in my unit a hundred and fifty years later, Poe understood the value of profiling when forensic evidence alone isn't enough to solve a particularly brutal and seemingly motiveless crime. "Deprived of ordinary resources," he wrote, "the analyst throws himself into the spirit of his opponent, identifies himself therewith, and not infrequently sees thus, at a glance, the sole methods by which he may seduce into error or hurry into miscalculation."

There's also another small similarity worth mentioning. Monsieur Dupin preferred to work alone in his room with the windows closed and the curtains drawn tight against the sunlight and the intrusion of the outside world. My colleagues and I have had no such choice in the matter. Our offices at the FBI Academy in Quantico are several stories underground, in a windowless space originally designed to serve as the secure headquarters for federal law enforcement authorities in the event of national emergency. We sometimes call ourselves the National *Cellar* for the Analysis of Violent Crime. At sixty feet belowground, we say we're ten times deeper than dead people.

The English novelist Wilkie Collins took up the profiling mantle in such pioneering works as *The Woman in White* (based on an actual case) and *The Moonstone*. But it was Sir Arthur Conan Doyle's immortal creation, Sherlock Holmes, who brought out this form of criminal investigative analysis for all the world to see in the shadowy gaslit world of Victorian London. The highest compliment any of us can be paid, it seems, is to be compared to this fictional character. I took it as a real honor some years back when, while I was working a murder case in Missouri, a headline in the *St. Louis Globe-Democrat* referred to me as the "FBI's Modern Sherlock Holmes."

It's interesting to note that at the same time Holmes was working his intricate and baffling cases, the real-life Jack the Ripper was killing prostitutes in London's East End. So completely have these two men on opposite sides of the law, and opposite sides of the boundary between reality and imagination, taken hold of the public consciousness that several "modern" Sherlock Holmes stories, written by Conan Doyle admirers, have thrown the detective into the unsolved Whitechapel murders.

Back in 1988, I was asked to analyze the Ripper murders for a nationally broadcast television program. I'll relate my conclusions about this most famous UNSUB in history later in this book.

It wasn't until more than a century after Poe's "Rue Morgue" and a half century after Sherlock Holmes that behavioral profiling moved off the pages of literature and into real life. By the mid-1950s, New York City was being rocked by the explosions of the "Mad Bomber," known to be responsible for more than thirty bombings over a fifteen-year period. He hit such public landmarks as Grand Central and

Pennsylvania Stations and Radio City Music Hall. As a child in Brooklyn at the time, I remember this case very well.

At wit's end, the police in 1957 called in a Greenwich Village psychiatrist named Dr. James A. Brussel, who studied photographs of the bomb scenes and carefully analyzed the bomber's taunting letters to newspapers. He came to a number of detailed conclusions from the overall behavioral patterns he perceived, including the facts that the perpetrator was a paranoiac who hated his father, obsessively loved his mother, and lived in a city in Connecticut. At the end of his written profile, Brussel instructed the police:

> Look for a heavy man. Middle-aged. Foreign born. Roman Catholic. Single. Lives with a brother or sister. When you find him, chances are he'll be wearing a double-breasted suit. Buttoned.

From references in some of the letters, it seemed a good bet that the bomber was a disgruntled current or former employee of Consolidated Edison, the city's power company. Matching up the profile to this target population, police came up with the name of George Metesky, who had worked for Con Ed in the 1940s before the bombings began. When they went up to Waterbury, Connecticut, one evening to arrest the heavy, single, middle-aged, foreign-born Roman Catholic, the only variation in the profile was that he lived not with one brother or sister but with two maiden sisters. After a police officer directed him to get dressed for the trip to the station, he emerged from his bedroom several minutes later wearing a double-breasted suit—buttoned.

Illuminating how he reached his uncannily accurate conclusions, Dr. Brussel explained that a psychiatrist normally examines an individual and then tries to make some reasonable predictions about how that person might react to some specific situation. In constructing his profile, Brussel stated, he reversed the process, trying to predict an individual from the evidence of his deeds.

Looking back on the Mad Bomber case from our perspective of nearly forty years, it actually seems a rather simple one to crack. But at the time, it was a real landmark in the development of what came to be called behavioral science in criminal investigation, and Dr. Brussel, who later worked with the Boston Police Department on the Boston Strangler case, was a true trailblazer in the field.

Though it is often referred to as *deduction*, what the fictional Dupin and Holmes, and real-life Brussel and those of us who followed, were doing was actually more *inductive*—that is, observing particular elements of a crime and drawing larger conclusions from them. When I came to Quantico in 1977, instructors in the Behavioral Science Unit, such as the pioneering Howard Teten, were starting to apply Dr. Brussel's ideas to cases brought to them in their National Academy classes by police professionals. But at the time, this was all anecdotal and had never been backed up by hard research. That was the state of things when I came into the story.

I've talked about how important it is for us to be able to step into the shoes and mind of the unknown killer. Through our research and experience, we've found it is equally important—as painful and harrowing as it might be—to be able to put ourselves in the place of the victim. Only when we have a firm idea of how the particular victim would have reacted to the horrible things that were happening to her or him can we truly understand the behavior and reactions of the perpetrator.

To know the offender, you have to look at the crime.

In the early 1980s, a disturbing case came to me from the police department of a small town in rural Georgia. A pretty fourteen-year-old girl, a majorette at the local junior high school, had been abducted from the school bus stop about a hundred yards from her house. Her partially clothed body was discovered some days later in a wooded lovers'-lane area about ten miles away. She had been sexually molested, and the cause of death was blunt-force trauma to the head. A large, blood-encrusted rock was lying nearby.

Before I could deliver my analysis, I had to know as much about this young girl as I could. I found out that though very cute and pretty, she was a fourteen-year-old who looked fourteen, not twenty-one as some teens do. Everyone who knew her assured me she was not promiscuous or a flirt, was not in any way involved with drugs or alcohol, and that she was warm and friendly to anyone who approached her. Autopsy analysis indicated she had been a virgin when raped.

This was all vital information to me, because it led me to understand how she would have reacted during and after the abduction and, therefore, how the offender would have reacted to her in the particular situation in which they found themselves. From this, I concluded that the murder had not been a *planned* outcome, but was a panicked reaction due to the surprise (based on the attacker's warped and delusional fantasy system) that the young girl did not welcome him with open arms. This, in turn, led me closer to the personality of the killer, and my profile led the police to focus on a suspect in a rape case from the year before in a nearby larger town. Understanding the victim also helped me construct a strategy for the police to use in interrogating this challenging suspect, who, as I predicted he would, had already passed a lie-detector test. I will discuss this fascinating and heartbreaking case in detail later on. But for now, suffice it to say that the individual ended up confessing both to the murder and the earlier rape. He was convicted and sentenced and, as of this writing, is on Georgia's death row.

When we teach the elements of criminal-personality profiling and crime-scene analysis to FBI agents or law enforcement professionals attending the National Academy, we try to get them to think of the entire story of the crime.

My colleague Roy Hazelwood, who taught the basic profiling course for several years before retiring from the Bureau in 1993, used to divide the analysis into three distinct questions and phases—what, why, and who:

What took place? This includes everything that might be behaviorally significant about the crime.

Why did it happen the way it did? Why, for example, was there mutilation after death? Why was nothing of value taken? Why was there no forced entry? What are the reasons for every behaviorally significant factor in the crime?

And this, then, leads to:

Who would have committed this crime for these reasons?

That is the task we set for ourselves.

2

My Mother's Name Was Holmes

My mother's maiden name was Holmes, and my parents almost chose that as my middle name instead of the more prosaic Edward.

Other than that, as I look back, not much about my early years indicated any particular future as a mindhunter or criminal profiler.

I was born in Brooklyn, New York, near the border with Queens. My father, Jack, was a printer with the *Brooklyn Eagle*. When I was eight, concerned about the rising crime rate, he moved us to Hempstead, Long Island, where he became president of the Long Island Typographical Union. I have one sister, Arlene, four years older, and from early on she was the star of the family, both academically and athletically.

I was no academic standout—generally a B-/C+ student— but I was polite and easygoing and always popular with the teachers at Ludlum Elementary despite my mediocre performance. I was mostly interested in animals and at various times kept dogs, cats, rabbits, hamsters, and snakes—all of which my mother tolerated because I said I wanted to be a veterinarian. Since this endeavor showed promise of a legitimate career, she encouraged me down this path.

The one pursuit in school for which I did show a flair was telling stories, and this might, in some way, have contributed to my becoming a crime investigator. Detectives and crime-scene analysts have to take a bunch of disparate and seemingly unrelated clues and make them into a coherent narrative, so storytelling ability is an important talent, particularly in homicide investigations, where the victim can't relate his or her own story.

At any rate, I often used my talent to get out of doing real work. I remember once in ninth grade, I was too lazy to read a novel for an oral book report before the class. So when my turn came (I still can't believe I had the balls to do this), I made up the title of a phony book, made up a phony author, and began telling this story about a group of campers around a campfire at night.

I'm making it up as I go along, and I'm thinking to myself, *How long can I keep pulling this off?* I've got this bear stealthily stalking up on the campers, just about to pounce, and at that point I lose it. I start cracking up and have no choice but to confess to the teacher that I'd made up the whole thing. It must have been the guilty conscience, proving I wasn't a complete criminal personality. I'm up there, exposed as a fake, knowing I'm going to flunk, about to be embarrassed in front of all my peers, and I can already anticipate what my mother's going to say when she finds out.

But to my surprise and amazement, the teacher and the other kids are totally into the story! And when I tell them I've been making it up, they all say, "Finish it. Tell us what happens next." So I did, and walked away with an A. I didn't tell this to my own children for a long time because I didn't want them to think that crime does pay, but I learned from it that if you can sell people your ideas and keep them interested, you can often get them to go along with you. This has helped me innumerable times as a law officer when I had to sell my own superiors or a local police department on the value of our services. But I have to admit that to a certain extent, it's the same talent that con men and criminal predators use to get by.

By the way, my fictitious campers did end up escaping with their lives, which was far from a foregone conclusion since my real love was animals. So, in preparation for becoming a vet, I spent three summers on dairy farms in upstate New York in the Cornell Farm Cadet Program sponsored by the university's veterinary school. This was a great opportunity for city kids to get out and live with nature, and in exchange for this privilege, I worked seventy to eighty hours a week at $15 per, while my school friends back home were sunning themselves at Jones Beach. If I never milk another cow, I won't feel a huge void in my life.

All of this physical labor did get me in good shape for sports, which was the other consuming passion of my life. At Hempstead High School, I pitched for the baseball team and played defensive tackle in football. And as I look back on it, this was probably the first real surfacing of my interest in personality profiling.

On the mound, it rather quickly dawned on me that throwing hard and accurate pitches was only half the battle. I had a solid fastball and a pretty decent slider, but a lot of high school pitchers had that, or equivalent stuff. The key was to be able to psych out the batter, and I realized that that had mainly to do with establishing an air of confidence for yourself and making the guy standing at the plate as insecure as possible. This came into play in a remarkably analogous way years later when I began developing my interrogation techniques.

In high school, I was already six foot two, which I used to my advantage. Talent-wise, we were a so-so team in a good league, and I knew it was up to the pitcher to try to be a field leader and set a winning tone. I had pretty good control for a high schooler, but I decided not to let the opposing batters know this. I wanted to appear reckless, not quite predictable, so the batters wouldn't dig in at the plate. I wanted them to think that if they did, they risked being brushed back or even worse by this wild man sixty feet away.

Hempstead did have a good football team, for which I was a 188-pound defensive lineman. Again, I realized the psychological aspect of the game was what could give us an edge. I figured I could take on the bigger guys if I grunted and groaned and generally acted like a nut. It didn't take long before I got the rest of the linemen to behave the same way. Later, when I regularly worked on murder trials in which insanity was used as a defense, I already knew from my own experience that the mere fact that someone acts like a maniac does not necessarily mean he doesn't know exactly what he's doing.

In 1962, we were playing Wantagh High for the Thorpe Award, the trophy for the best high school football team on Long Island. They outweighed us by about forty pounds a man, and we knew chances were good we were going to get the crap knocked out of us before a full house. So before the game, we worked out a set of warm-up drills whose sole objective was to psych out and intimidate our opponents. We formed up in two lines with the first man in one line tackling—practically decking—the first man in the other line. This was accompanied by all the appropriate grunts and groans and shrieks of pain. We could see from the faces of the Wantagh players that we were having the intended effect. They must have been figuring, "If these jokers are stupid enough to do that to each other, God knows what they'll do to us."

In fact, the entire episode was carefully choreographed. We practiced wrestling throws so we could appear to hit the ground hard, but without getting hurt. And when we got into the actual game, we kept up the general level of craziness to make it appear we'd only been let out of the asylum for this one afternoon and were going straight back as soon as the game was over. The contest was close all the way, but when the dust finally settled, we had won, 14–13, and captured the Thorpe Award for 1962.

My first brush with "law enforcement," in fact, my first "real" experience with profiling, came at age eighteen, when I got a job as a bouncer in a bar and club in Hempstead called the Gaslight East. I was so good at it that later I was given the same position at the Surf Club in Long Beach. At both places, my two main responsibilities were to keep out those below legal drinking age—in other words, anyone younger than me—and to short-circuit or break up the inevitable fights that crop up in places where alcohol is consumed.

Standing at the door, I would request an ID from anyone whose age was questionable, then ask the person for his or her date of birth to see if it matched up. This is pretty standard procedure and it's what everyone expects, so they're all prepared for it. Seldom will a kid who's gone to the trouble of coming up with a fake ID be so careless as to fail to memorize the birth date on it. Looking straight into their eyes as I questioned them was an effective technique with some people, particularly girls, who generally have a more developed social conscience at that age. But those who want to get in can still get past most scrutiny if they just concentrate on their acting for a few moments.

What I was actually doing while I quizzed each group of kids as they got to the front of the line was discreetly scrutinizing the people about three or four rows back—watching them as they prepared to be questioned, observing their body language, noticing if they looked at all nervous or tentative.

Breaking up fights was more of a challenge, and for that I fell back on my athletic experience. If they see a look in your eyes that tells them you're not quite predictable and you act just a little overtly screwy, then sometimes even the big guys will think twice about tangling with you. If they think you're just off enough not to be worried about your own safety, then you become a far more dangerous opponent. Almost twenty years later, for example, when we were conducting the prison interviews for the major serial-killer study, we learned that the typical assassin personality is far more dangerous in certain crucial ways than the typical serial-killer personality. Because unlike the serial killer, who will only choose a victim he thinks he can handle and then will go to elaborate lengths to avoid capture, the assassin is obsessively concerned with his "mission" and is generally willing to die to achieve it.

The other consideration in making people have a particular opinion of you—such as that you're irrational and crazy enough to do something unpredictable—is that you have to maintain that persona all the time on the job, not just when you think people are looking at you. When I interviewed Gary Trapnell, a notorious armed robber and airplane hijacker, at the federal prison in Marion, Illinois, he claimed that he could fool any prison psychiatrist into believing he had any mental illness I cared to specify. The key to pulling it off, he informed me, was to behave that way all the time, even alone in your cell, so that when they interviewed you, you wouldn't have to "think" your way through it, which was what gave you away. So, long before I had the benefit of this type of "expert" advice, I seemed to have some instinct for thinking like a criminal.

When I couldn't manage to scare people out of a fight at the bar, I tried to use my amateur profiling techniques to do the next best thing and head it off before it got serious. I found that with a little experience, by closely observing behavior and body language, I was able to correlate this with the sort of action that ended up breaking out into fights so I could anticipate if an individual was about to start something. In that case, or when in doubt, I always pounced first, using the element of surprise and attempting to get the potential offender out of the building and back out into the street before he knew exactly what was happening to him. I always say that most sexual killers and serial rapists become skilled in domination, manipulation, and control—the same skills I was trying to master in a different context. But at least I was learning.

When I graduated from high school, I still wanted to be a

vet, but my grades weren't nearly good enough for Cornell. The best I could do to get a similar type of program was Montana State. So in September of 1963, the Brooklyn and Long Island boy headed out to the heart of Big Sky country.

The culture shock upon arriving in Bozeman couldn't have been greater.

"Greetings from Montana," I wrote in one of my early letters home, "where men are men and sheep are nervous." Just as Montana seemed to embody all the stereotypes and clichés of western and frontier life to me, that is how I came across to the people I met there as an easterner. I joined the local chapter of Sigma Phi Epsilon, which was composed almost exclusively of local boys, so I stood out like a sore thumb. I took to wearing a black hat, black clothing, and black boots and sported long sideburns like a character out of *West Side Story*, which was very much how New Yorkers like me were perceived in those days.

So I made the most of it. At all the social gatherings, the locals would be wearing western garb and dancing the two-step, while I had spent the last several years religiously watching Chubby Checker on TV and knew every conceivable variation of the twist. Because my sister, Arlene, was four years older than I was, she'd long before enlisted me as her practice dance partner, so I quickly became the dance instructor for the entire college community. I felt like a missionary going into some remote area that had never before heard English spoken.

I had never had much of a reputation as a scholar, but now my grades hit an all-time low as I concentrated on everything but. I'd already worked as a bouncer in a bar in New York, but here in Montana, the drinking age was twenty-one, which was a real comedown to me. Unfortunately, I didn't let that stop me.

My first run-in with the law happened when one of my fraternity brothers and I had taken out these two swell girls who had met in a home for unwed mothers. They were mature for their age. We stopped at a bar and I went in to buy a six-pack.

The bartender says, "Show me your ID." So I show him this phony Selective Service card, carefully done. From my bouncer experience, I'd learned some of the pitfalls and mistakes of false identification.

The guy looks at the card and says, "Brooklyn, huh? You guys back East are big bastards, aren't you?" I kind of laugh self-consciously, but everyone in the bar has turned around, so I know there are witnesses now. I get back out to the parking lot and we drive away drinking this beer, and unbeknownst to me, one of the girls put the beer cans on the trunk of the car.

All of a sudden, I hear a police siren. A cop stops us. "Get out of the car."

So we get out of the car. He starts searching us, and even at the time I know this is an illegal search, but I'm certainly not going to mouth off to him. As he gets down, he's expos-ing his gun and billy club to me, and I get this crazy flash that in a split second, I could take the club, crunch him on the head, grab the gun, and take off. Fortunately for my future, I didn't. But knowing he's getting to me, I take my ID out of my wallet and stuff it down into my undershorts.

He takes all four of us back to the station, separates us, and I'm really sweating because I know what they're doing and I'm afraid the other guy is going to cop out on me.

One of the officers says to me, "Now, son, you tell us. If that guy back at the bar didn't ask for your ID, we'll go back there. We've had trouble with him before."

I respond, "Back where I come from, we don't rat on people. We don't do that kind of stuff." I'm playing George Raft, but I'm really thinking to myself, *Of course he asked for my ID, and I gave him a phony one!* All the while, it's slipped so low in my shorts, it's pinching my vitals. I don't know if they're going to strip-search us or what. I mean, this is the frontier out here as far as I'm concerned, and God knows what they do. So I quickly size up the situation and feign illness. I tell them I'm sick and have to use the rest room.

They let me go in unaccompanied, but I've seen too many movies, so when I get in there and look in the mirror, I'm afraid they're looking at me from the other side. I go way to the side of the room, stick my hands down my pants, and pull out the ID, then I go over to the sink and make out as if I'm throwing up in case they're watching. I go over to the stalls and flush the Selective Service card down the john, then come back with a lot more confidence. I ended up with a $40 fine and probation.

My second encounter with the Bozeman police came my sophomore year, and it was worse.

I go to a rodeo along with two other guys from back East and one guy from Montana. We're leaving at the end, driving a '62 Studebaker, and we have beer in the car, so here we go again. It's snowing like crazy. The kid at the wheel is from Boston, I'm in the front passenger seat, and the local is between us. Anyway, the guy driving goes through a stop sign, and—wouldn't you know it?—there's a cop right there. That seems to be the hallmark of my Montana life. Whatever they say about cops not being around when you need them—not true in Bozeman in 1965.

So this idiot fraternity brother of mine—I can't believe it—he doesn't stop! He takes off with this cop in the back in hot pursuit.

Every time we make a turn and get out of the cop's view for a second, I'm throwing beer cans out of the car. We keep driving and reach this residential neighborhood, hitting speed bumps: *boom, boom, boom*. We come to a roadblock; the cop must have radioed ahead. We drive right around the roadblock, up across someone's lawn. All the time, I'm yelling, "Stop the goddamned car! Get me out of here!" But this idiot keeps going. The car's spinning, it's still snowing like crazy, then right behind us we hear the sirens.

We reach an intersection. He slams on the brakes, the car goes into a 360-spin, the door flies open, and I'm thrown out of the car. I'm hanging by the door and my ass is dragging in the snow on the ground, and all of a sudden someone yells, "Run!"

So we run. All in different directions. I end up in an alley, where I find an empty pickup truck and get in. I'd ditched my black hat while I was running, and I'm wearing a reversible black and gold jacket, so I take it off and turn the gold side outward for some disguise. But I'm sweating and fogging up the windows. I'm thinking, *Oh, shit, they're going to be able to see me.* And I'm afraid the owners are going to come back any minute, and out here, they probably have guns. So I wipe off a small area on the glass so I can see out, and there's all kinds of activity around the car we've abandoned: cop cars, tracking dogs, you name it. And now they're coming up the alley, their flashlights are shining on the pickup, and I'm about ready to shit my pants. But I can't believe that they drive right by and leave me there!

I steal back to school and everyone's already heard about this thing, and I find out that the other two eastern guys and I got away, but they caught the one from Montana and he spilled his guts. He names names and they come after each of us. When they get to me, I cop a plea that I wasn't in control of the car, that I was scared and pleading with the guy to stop. Meanwhile, the driver from Boston gets thrown in a jail cell with springs and no mattress, bread and water and the whole bit, while my incredible luck holds out and I just get slapped with another $40 fine for possession of alcohol, and probation.

But they notify the school, they notify our parents, who are all royally pissed off, and things aren't going any better academically. I have a straight-D average, I've failed a speech class because I never went to class—which is my all-time low since I'd always felt that being able to talk was about my best asset—and I'm not figuring out any way to pull myself out of this morass. By the end of the second year, it's clear that my adventure in the western wilderness is at an end.

If it appears that all of my memories from this period are of mishaps and personal screwups, that's the way it seemed to me at the time. I came home from college, living under the eyes of my disappointed parents. My mother was especially upset, knowing now I'd never become a veterinarian. As usual when I didn't know what to do with myself, I fell back on my athletics and took a job lifeguarding for the summer of 1965. When the summer ended and I wasn't going back to school, I found a job running the health club at the Holiday Inn in Patchogue.

Not long after I started working there, I met Sandy, who worked at the hotel as a cocktail waitress. She was a beautiful young woman with a young son and I was instantly crazy about her. She looked spectacular in her little cocktail outfit. I was still in great shape physically from all of my exercise and working out, and she seemed to like me, too. I was living at home and she would call me all the time. My father would say to me, "Who the hell is calling you all hours of the day and night? There's always this child crying and screaming in the background."

Living at home didn't provide the opportunity for much action, but Sandy told me that if you worked at the hotel, you could get an unbooked room really cheap. So one day we got a room together.

The next morning, early, the phone rings. She answers it and I hear, "No! No! I don't want to talk to him!"

As I wake up, I say, "Who is that?"

She says, "The front desk. They said my husband's here and he's on his way up."

Now I'm wide awake. I say, "Your husband? What do you mean, your husband! You never told me you were still married!"

She pointed out that she'd never told me she wasn't, either, then went on to explain that they were separated.

Big deal, I'm thinking as I begin to hear this maniac running down the hall.

He starts pounding on the door. "Sandy! I know you're in there, Sandy!"

The room had a window onto the hallway made of glass louvers, and he's tearing at them, trying to rip them off the frame. Meanwhile, I'm looking for a place to jump from—we were on the second floor—but there's no window for me to jump out of.

I ask, "Does this guy carry guns or anything?"

"Sometimes he carries a knife," she says.

"Oh, shit! That's great! I've got to get out of here. Open the door."

I get into this pugilistic stance. She opens the door. The husband comes running in. He comes straight at me. But then he sees me in silhouette in the shadows, and I must look big and tough, so he changes his mind and stops.

But he's still yelling: "You son of a bitch! You get the hell out of here!"

Figuring I've been macho enough for one day—and it's still early—I say, very politely, "Yes, sir. I was just going as it was." I'd lucked out again, getting out of another scrape with my hide intact. But I couldn't avoid the truth that everything in my life was going to hell. Incidentally, I'd also cracked the front axle of my father's Saab racing my friend Bill Turner's red MGA.

It was early one Saturday morning that my mother came into my room with a letter from Selective Service saying they wanted to see me. I went down to Whitehall Place in Manhattan for a military physical with three hundred other guys. They had me do deep knee bends and you could hear the cracking as I went down. I'd had cartilage taken out of my knee from football, just like Joe Namath, but he must have had a better lawyer. They held up the decision on me for a while, but eventually I was informed that Uncle Sam did, indeed, want me. Rather than take my chances in the Army, I quickly signed up for the Air Force, even though it meant a four-year hitch, figuring there were better educational opportunities there. Maybe that was just what I needed. I sure as hell hadn't made much of educational opportunities in New York or Montana.

There was another reason for going for the Air Force at that point. This was 1966 and Vietnam was escalating. I wasn't terribly political, generally considering myself a Kennedy Democrat because of my father, who was an official of the Long Island printers' union. But the notion of having my ass shot off in support of a cause I understood only vaguely wasn't all that appealing. I'd remembered an Air Force mechanic once telling me that they were the only service in which the officers—the pilots—went into combat while the enlisted men stayed back to support them. Having no intention of becoming a pilot, that sounded okay to me.

I was sent to Amarillo, Texas, for basic training. Our flight (what an Air Force training class is called) of fifty was about evenly divided between New Yorkers like myself and southern boys from Louisiana. The drill instructor was always on the northerners' asses, and most of the time I thought it was justified. I tended to hang around with the southerners, whom I found more likable and far less obnoxious than my fellow New Yorkers.

For a lot of young men, basic training is a stressful experience. With all the discipline I'd experienced from coaches in team contact sports, and as much of a jerk-off as I'd acknowledged to myself I'd been the last several years, I found the DI's rap almost a joke. I could see through all his head trips and psych jobs, and I was already in good physical condition, so basic training was kind of a snap for me. I qualified quickly as an expert marksman on the M16, which was probably a carryover from the aim I'd developed as a high school pitcher. Up until the Air Force, the only riflery experience I'd had was shooting out streetlamps with a BB gun as a young teen.

During basic training I was developing another sort of badass reputation. Pumped up from lifting weights and with my head shaved close, I became known as "the Russian Bear." A guy in another flight had a similar reputation, and someone got the bright idea that it would be good for base morale if we boxed each other.

The bout was a big event on base. We were very evenly matched, and each of us refused to give an inch. We ended up beating the holy hell out of each other, and I got my nose broken for the third time (the first two having come during high school football).

For whatever it was worth, I ended up third out of the fifty in my flight. After basic training, I was given a battery of tests and told I was well qualified for radio-intercept school. But radio-intercept school was filled and I didn't feel like waiting around until the next class began, so they made me a clerk typist—even though I couldn't type. There was an opening in Personnel at Cannon Air Force Base, about a hundred miles away outside of Clovis, New Mexico.

So that's where I ended up, spending all day long pecking out DD214s—military discharge papers—with two fingers, working for this idiot sergeant and saying to myself, *I have to get out of here.*

Again, here's where my luck comes in. Right next door to Personnel was Special Services. When I say this, most people think of Special Forces, like the Green Berets. But this was Special Services, specifically, Special Services—Athletics. With my background, that seemed an excellent way to defend my country in its time of need.

I start snooping around, listening at the door, and I hear one of the guys in there saying, "This program's going to hell. We just don't have the right guy."

I'm thinking to myself, this is it! So I walk around, knock on the door, and say, "Hello, I'm John Douglas, let me tell you a little about my background."

As I talk, I'm looking at them for reactions and "profiling" the kind of guy they want. And I know I'm clicking, because they keep looking at each other like, "This is a miracle! He's exactly what we want!" So they get me transferred out of Personnel, and from that day forward, I never had to wear a uniform, they paid me extra money as an enlisted man for running all the athletic programs, I became eligible for Operation Bootstrap, where the government paid 75 percent of my education costs to go to school at nights and on weekends—which I did, at Eastern New Mexico University in Portales, twenty-five miles away. Since I had to overcome my D average from college, I had to get all A's to stay in the program. But for the first time, I felt as if I had some focus.

I did such a good job of representing the Air Force in such rigorous sports as tennis, soccer, and badminton that eventually they put me in charge of the base golf course and pro shop, even though I'd never played a hole in my life. But I did look great running all the tournaments in my Arnold Palmer sweaters.

One day the base commander comes in and he wants to know what compression ball he should use for this particular tournament. I had no idea what he was talking about, and like my ninth-grade book report almost ten years before, I got found out.

"How in hell did you end up running this thing?" he wanted to know. I was immediately taken off golf and moved into women's lapidary, which sounded exciting until I found out it meant stonework. I was also put in charge of women's ceramics and the officers' club pool. I'm thinking, these officers are flying over Vietnam getting their asses shot and I'm here getting chairs and towels for their flirtatious wives and teaching their kids how to swim and they're paying me extra for this while I get my college degree?

My other responsibility seemed to hearken back to my bouncer days. The pool was next to the officers' bar, which was often full of young pilots training with the Tactical Air

Command. More than once I had to pull wild, drunken pilots off of each other or off of me.

About two years into my Air Force hitch, while I was pursuing my undergraduate degree, I found out about a local association that helped handicapped children. They needed help with their recreational programs, so I volunteered. Once a week, accompanied by a couple of civilian staffers, I took about fifteen children roller-skating or to play miniature golf or bowling or to some type of sports situation where the kids could develop their individual skills and abilities.

Most of the youngsters faced serious challenges such as blindness or Down's syndrome or severe motor-control problems. It was tiring work, for example, skating around and around a rink with a child in each arm, trying to make sure they didn't hurt themselves, but I absolutely loved it. In fact, I've had few other experiences in life I've enjoyed as much.

When I pulled up in my car at their school each week, the kids would all run out to greet me, crowd around the car, and then I'd get out and we'd all hug. At the end of each weekly session, they were all as sad to see me leave as I was to have to go. I felt I was getting so much out of it, so much love and companionship at a time in my life when I wasn't really getting it from any other sources, that I started coming in in the evenings to read stories to them.

These children were such a contrast to the healthy, so-called normal kids I worked with on the base who were used to being the centers of attention and getting everything they wanted from their parents. My "special" children were so much more appreciative of anything that was done for them and, in spite of their handicaps, were always so friendly and eager for adventure.

Unbeknownst to me, I was being observed much of the time I spent with the children. It must say something about my powers of observation that I never found out! At any rate, my "performance" was being evaluated by members of the Eastern New Mexico University psychology department, who then offered me a four-year scholarship in special education.

Though I had been thinking about industrial psychology, I loved the kids and thought this might be a good choice. In fact, I could stay in the Air Force and become an officer with this as a career. I submitted the university's offer to the base's civilian-run personnel board, but after consideration, they decided the Air Force didn't need anyone with a degree in special education. I thought this was rather strange because of all the dependents on base, but that was their decision. So I gave up my thoughts of going into special ed as a career, but continued the volunteer work I loved so much.

Christmas of 1969, I was going home to see my family. I had to drive the hundred miles back to Amarillo to catch the plane to New York, and my Volkswagen Beetle wasn't in such great shape for the trip. So my best friend in the Air Force, Robert LaFond, swaps me his Karmann Ghia for the trip. I didn't want to miss the Special Services Christmas party, but that was the only way I could get to Amarillo in time for the flight.

When I got off the plane at La Guardia, my parents met me. They looked grim, almost shell-shocked, and I couldn't figure out why. After all, I was turning my life around and finally giving them reason not to be disappointed in me.

What had happened was, they'd received a report of an unidentified driver killed near the base in a VW that matched the description of mine. Until they saw me get off the plane, they didn't know if I was alive or dead.

It turned out that Robert LaFond, like a lot of other guys, had gotten drunk and passed out at the Christmas party. People who were there told me that some of the officers and noncoms had carried him out to my car, put him in with the key in the ignition, and when he came to, he tried to drive off the base. It was snowing and freezing out; he hit a station wagon head-on with a military mother and her children inside. Thank God, they weren't hurt, but in my flimsy car, Robert went into the steering wheel, through the windshield, and was killed.

This haunted me. We were very close and I was plagued by the thought that this might not have happened if he hadn't lent me the good car. When I got back to base, I had to claim his personal effects, box up all his possessions, and ship them off to his family. I kept going back to look at my wrecked car, I kept having dreams about Robert and the crash. I was with him the day he'd bought a Christmas present for his parents in Pensacola, Florida, a gift that arrived in the mail the same day Air Force officers came to the house to tell them their son had died.

But I wasn't only grief-stricken, I was also angry as hell. Like the investigator I later became, I kept asking around until I'd narrowed it down to the two men I thought were responsible. I found them in their office, grabbed them, and put them up against the wall. I started hammering on them, one by one. I had to be pulled off them. I was so mad, I didn't care if I got court-martialed. As far as I was concerned, they had killed my best friend.

A court-martial would have been a messy affair, since they would have had to deal with my formal accusation against the two men. Also, by this time, American involvement in Vietnam was beginning to wind down, and they were offering early outs to enlisted men with only a few months to go. So to smooth things out as best they could, the personnel people discharged me several months early.

While I was still in the service, I'd finished my undergraduate degree and begun a master's in industrial psychology. Now I was living on the GI Bill in a $7-a-week, windowless, basement apartment in Clovis, fighting the legions of three-inch waterbugs that went into attack formation every time I came in and switched on the lights. Not having access to the base facilities anymore, I joined a cheap, run-down health club whose atmosphere and decor roughly matched that of my apartment.

During the fall of 1970, I met a guy at the club named Frank Haines, who turned out to be an FBI agent. He ran a one-man resident agency in Clovis. We got friendly while working out together. It turned out he had heard about me through the retired base commander and started trying to interest me in applying to the Bureau. Frankly, I'd never given a single serious thought to law enforcement. I was planning a career in industrial psychology once I finished my degree. Working for a large company, dealing with such issues as personnel matters, employee assistance, and stress management, seemed to offer a solid, predictable future. The only direct contact I'd had with the FBI up until then was one time back in Montana when a trunk I'd shipped home had been stolen. One of the local field agents interviewed me, thinking I might have set up the crime to collect on the insurance. But nothing came of it, and if that was the kind of cases the FBI handled, there didn't seem to me to be much to the job.

But Frank was persistent in thinking I would make a good special agent and kept encouraging me. He invited me to his house for dinner several times, introduced me to his wife and son, showed me both his gun and his paycheck stub, neither of which I could match. I had to admit, next to my shabby lifestyle, Frank was living like a king. So I decided to take a crack at it.

Frank stayed in New Mexico, and years later, our paths would cross when I came out to testify in the trial for a homicide he'd worked in which a woman was brutally killed and her body burned to avoid detection. But in the fall of 1970, this kind of action was far from my mind.

Frank sent my application to the field office in Albuquerque. They gave me the standard law test for nonlawyers. Despite my physical conditioning and muscular build, my 220 pounds was 25 over the FBI limit for my six-foot-two-inch height. The *only* one in the Bureau who could exceed the weight standards was the legendary director, J. Edgar Hoover, himself. I spent two weeks on nothing but Knox gelatin and hard-boiled eggs to get down to the weight. It also took three haircuts before I was deemed presentable for an ID photo.

But finally, in November, I was offered a probationary appointment, at an initial salary of $10,869. Finally, I was getting out of my depressing, windowless basement room. I wonder what I would have thought at the time had I known I'd be spending a major part of my Bureau career in another windowless basement room, pursuing far more depressing stories.

3

Betting on Raindrops

Many apply, few are chosen.

That was the message continually drummed into us as new recruits. Nearly everyone interested in a career in law enforcement aspired to become a special agent of the United States Federal Bureau of Investigation, but only the very best could hope to have that opportunity. A long, proud heritage went all the way back to 1924 when an obscure government lawyer named John Edgar Hoover took over a corrupt, underfunded, and badly managed agency. And the same Mr. Hoover—by the time I joined, seventy-five years of age—still presided over the revered organization it had become, ruling as always with a square jaw and an iron fist. So we'd better not let the Bureau down.

A telegram from the director instructed me to report to Room 625 in the Old Post Office Building on Pennsylvania Avenue in Washington at 9 a.m. on December 14, 1970, to begin the fourteen weeks of training that would transform me from an ordinary citizen into a special agent of the FBI. Before this I went home to Long Island, where my dad was so proud, he flew the American flag in front of the house. With what I'd been doing the last several years, I didn't have any dress-up civilian clothes, so my dad bought me three "regulation" dark suits—a blue, a black, and a brown—white shirts, and two pairs of wing tips, one black and one brown. Then he drove me down to Washington to make sure I'd be on time for my first day of work.

It didn't take long to become inculcated with FBI ritual and lore. The special agent leading our induction ceremony told us to take out our gold badges and stare at them as we recited the oath of office. We all spoke in unison, staring at the blindfolded woman holding the scales of justice while solemnly swearing to support and defend the Constitution of the United States against all enemies, foreign and domestic. "Bring it closer! Closer!" the special agent ordered, until we were all staring at these badges cross-eyed.

My new-agent class was made up solely of white men. In 1970, there were few black FBI agents and no women. That wouldn't really open up until after Hoover's long tenure, and even from beyond the grave he continued to exert a ghostly and powerful influence. Most of the men were between twenty-nine and thirty-five, so at twenty-five, I was one of the youngest.

We were indoctrinated to be on the lookout for Soviet agents, who would try to compromise us and get our secrets. These agents could be anywhere. We were told particularly to beware of women! The brainwashing was so effective I turned down a date with an extremely good-looking woman who worked in the building who had actually asked me out to dinner. I was afraid it was a setup and I was being tested.

The FBI Academy on the Marine base in Quantico, Virginia, wasn't fully built and operational yet, so we took our firearms and physical training there and the classroom work in the Old Post Office Building in Washington.

One of the first things every trainee is taught is that an FBI agent only shoots to kill. The thinking that went into this policy is both rigorous and logical: if you draw your weapon, you have already made the decision to shoot. And if you have made the decision that the situation is serious enough to warrant shooting, you have decided it is serious enough to take a life. In the heat of the moment, you seldom have the latitude to plan your shot or time to indulge in a lot of mental gymnastics, and attempting merely to stop a subject or bring him down is too risky. You do not take any unnecessary chances for yourself or a potential victim.

We were given equally rigorous training in criminal law, fingerprint analysis, violent and white-collar crime, arrest techniques, weapons, hand-to-hand combat, and the history of the Bureau's role in national law enforcement. One of the units I remember best, though, came fairly early in the course of study. We all referred to it as "dirty-words training."

"Doors closed?" the instructor asked. He then handed each of us a list. "I want you to study these words." The list, as I recall, contained such gems of Anglo-Saxon usage as *shit, fuck, cunnilingus, fellatio, cunt,* and *dickhead.* What we were supposed to do was commit these words to memory so that if they ever came up in field usage—such as during the interrogation of a suspect—we'd know what to do. And what we were supposed to do was to make sure any case report containing any of these words was given to the office's "obscene steno"—I'm not kidding!—rather than the regular secretary. The obscene steno would traditionally be an older, more mature and seasoned woman, better able to handle the shock of seeing these words and phrases. Remember, this was all men in those days, and in 1970 the national sensibility was somewhat different from what it is today, at least within Hoover's FBI. We were actually given a spelling test on these words, after which the papers were collected and—I presume—graded before being burned in the metal trash can.

Despite this kind of silliness, we were all idealistic about fighting crime, and we all thought we could make a difference. About halfway through new-agent training, I was called in to the office of the assistant director for training, Joe Casper, one of Hoover's trusted lieutenants. People in the Bureau called him the Friendly Ghost, but the nickname was definitely used ironically rather than affectionately. Casper told me I was doing well in most areas, but that I was way below average in "Bureau communications," the methodology and nomenclature through which the diverse elements of the organization communicate with each other.

"Well, sir, I want to be the best," I responded. Guys this eager were described as having blue flames coming out of their asses. This could help you get ahead, but also made you a marked man. If a blue-flamer succeeded, he was headed for the top of the world. But if he screwed up, the crash and burn would be very long and very public.

Casper may have been tough but he was nobody's fool, and he'd seen many a blue-flamer in his time. "You want to be the best? Here!" whereupon he threw the entire manual of terms at me and told me to have them all memorized by the time I got back from the Christmas break.

Chuck Lundsford, one of our class's two Academy counselors, got the word on what had happened and came over to me. "What did you say when you went in there?" he asked me. I told him. Chuck just rolled his eyes. We both knew I had my work cut out for me.

I went home to my parents' house for the holidays. While the rest of the family was making merry, I had my nose buried deep in the manual of communications. It wasn't much of a vacation.

When I got back to Washington in early January, still sweating out the consequences of my blue-flame performance, I had to take a written test of what I'd learned. I can't express how relieved I was when our other counselor, Charlie Price, told me I'd scored a 99 percent. "You actually scored a hundred," Charlie confided to me, "but Mr. Hoover says no one's perfect."

About halfway through the fourteen-week program we were each asked our preference for a first field-office assignment. Most of the FBI was dispersed among fifty-nine field offices around the country. I sensed there must be some gamesmanship in the choosing—a giant chess match between the new recruits and headquarters—and as always, I tried to think like the other side. I was from New York and had no particular interest in going back there. I figured L.A., San Francisco, Miami, possibly Seattle and San Diego, would be the most sought-after postings. So if I selected a second-tier city, I'd be much more likely to get my first choice.

I chose Atlanta. I got Detroit.

Upon graduation, we were all given permanent credentials, a Smith & Wesson Model 10 six-shot .38 revolver, six bullets, and instructions to get out of town as fast as possible. Headquarters was always terrified that the raw new agents would get in trouble in Washington, right under Mr. Hoover's nose, which would reflect badly on everyone.

The other item I was given was a booklet entitled "Survival Guide to Detroit." The city was among the most racially polarized in the country, still reeling from the repercussions of the 1967 riots, and could claim the title of the nation's crime capital, with more than eight hundred murders a year. In fact, we had a gruesome pool in the office, betting on exactly how many homicides would be chalked up by year's end. Like most new agents, I started out idealistic and energetic, but soon realized what we were up against. I had spent four years in the Air Force, but the closest to combat I'd been was in a bed in the base hospital next to wounded Vietnam vets when I had my nose operated on for football and boxing injuries. So until I got to Detroit, I'd never been in the position of being the enemy. The FBI was hated in many quarters; they'd infiltrated college campuses and had set up networks of urban informers. With our somber black cars, we were marked men. In many neighborhoods, people threw rocks at us. Their German shepherds and Dobermans didn't like us much, either. We were told not to find ourselves in some sections of the city without extremely heavy backup and firepower.

Local police were angry at us, too. They accused the Bureau of "scooping" cases, putting out press releases before a case was complete, then adding police-solved crimes to the FBI's own clearance-rate stats. Ironically, around the time of my rookie year, 1971, about a thousand new agents were hired, and the bulk of our practical street training came not from the Bureau but from local cops who took us under their protective wings. Much of the success of my generation of special agents unquestionably is attributable to the professionalism and generosity of police officers all over the United States.

Bank robberies were particularly prevalent. On Fridays, when the banks stocked up with cash to handle paydays, we averaged two or three armed robberies, sometimes as many as five. Until bullet-resistant glass became commonplace in Detroit banks, the murder and wounding of tellers was appalling. We had a case captured on a bank surveillance camera in which a manager was shot and killed at his desk, execution style, while a terrified couple sitting across from him, applying for a loan, looked on helplessly. The robber was unhappy that the manager couldn't open the timed vault. And it wasn't just bank officials with access to tens of thousands of dollars in cash. In certain neighborhoods, workers at places like McDonald's were equally at risk.

I was assigned to the Reactive Crimes Unit, which meant, in effect, reacting to crimes that had already happened, bank robbery or extortion, for example. Within that unit, I worked with the UFAP Squad: Unlawful Flight to Avoid Prosecution. This turned out to be excellent experience because this squad always saw a lot of action. In addition to the office-wide yearly homicide pool, we ran a contest in the unit to see who could make the most arrests in a single day. It was just like the competitions car dealers run for who can make the most sales in a given time.

One of our busiest lines of work in those days was what was referred to as the 42 Classification: military deserters. Vietnam had ripped the country in two, and once most of these guys went absent from the service, they did not want in the worst way to go back. We had more assaults against law officers registered with 42 Classifications than with any other type of fugitive.

My first encounter with a UFAP came when I'd tracked

an Army deserter to the service garage where he worked. I identify myself and think he's going to come along quietly. Then suddenly, he pulls this filed-down, makeshift knife with a black-tape handle on me. I pull back, just narrowly avoiding getting stabbed. I lunge at him, throw him up against the glass garage door, then force him down on the ground with a knee on his back and my gun up to his head. Meanwhile, the manager is raising hell with me for taking away a good worker. *What the hell have I gotten myself into?* Was this really the career I'd envisioned? Was it worth continually risking my hide to bring in this kind of lowlife? Industrial psychology was looking awfully good.

Going after deserters often brought with it emotional turmoil as well as creating resentment between the military and the FBI. Sometimes we'd follow up on an arrest warrant, locate the guy, and grab him right on the street. Infuriated, he would stop us, rap with his knuckles on an artificial leg, and tell us he'd gotten a Purple Heart and a Silver Star for that in Nam. What was happening over and over was that deserters who either returned voluntarily or were picked up by the Army itself were routinely sent over to Vietnam as punishment. Many of these guys subsequently distinguished themselves in combat, but the military hadn't told us anything. So as far as we knew, they were still AWOL. This aggravated the hell out of us.

Worse yet was when we'd go to a deserter's listed residence and be told by tearful and rightfully enraged wives or parents that the subject had died a hero's death. We'd be chasing down dead men, killed in action, and the military never got around to letting us know.

Regardless of the profession you're in, when you get out into the field, you start realizing all the big and little things they never taught you in school or training. For one, what do you do with your gun in various situations, such as while using a public men's room stall? Do you leave it on your belt down on the floor? Do you try to hang it up on the stall door? For a while I tried holding it in my lap, but that made me very nervous. It's the kind of thing each of us faces, but not the kind of thing you feel comfortable discussing with your more experienced colleagues. By the time I'd been on the job a month, it became a problem.

When I moved to Detroit, I'd bought another Volkswagen Beetle, the same kind of car, ironically, that was becoming the serial killer vehicle of choice. Ted Bundy had one and it was one of the ways he was ultimately identified. Anyway, I'd stopped in a local shopping center to go into a men's store to buy a suit. Knowing I'm going to be trying on clothes, I figure I'd better leave my gun someplace safe. So I stick it in the glove compartment and head into the store.

Now, the VW Beetle had a couple of interesting characteristics. Since it was a rear-engine car, the spare tire was stored in the trunk in front. Since it was practically ubiquitous in those days—not to mention easy to break into—spare tires were an extremely common theft item. After all, just about everyone needed one. And last but not least, the trunk was opened through a switch in the glove compartment.

I'm sure you can guess the rest. I come out to the car and find the window broken. As I reconstruct this highly sophisticated crime, the tire thief breaks into the car, goes in the glove compartment to open the trunk for the tire, but sees there a much greater prize. I deduce this because my gun is gone but the tire's still there.

"Oh, shit!" I'm saying to myself. "I've been on the job less than thirty days and I'm already supplying weapons to the enemy!" And I know that losing your gun or your credentials means an instant letter of censure. So I go to my squad supervisor, Bob Fitzpatrick. Fitzpatrick's a big guy, a real father figure. He dresses dapper and is something of a living legend in the Bureau. He knows my ass is on the line and how bad I feel. The gun loss has to be reported to the Director's Office, which is just great since that'll be the first field entry in my personnel file. He says we've got to come up with something really creative, revolving around how I'm so concerned with maintaining the public peace that I didn't want to take the chance of alarming anyone in the store if they suddenly saw a gun and thought they were being robbed. Fitzpatrick reassures me that since I'm not up for promotion for a couple of years, the letter of censure shouldn't hurt me as long as I keep my nose clean from now on.

So that's what I tried to do, though that gun continued to haunt me for a long time. The Smith & Wesson Model 10 I turned in to the Quantico armory almost twenty-five years later when I retired from the Bureau was actually the replacement of my original weapon. Thank God, that first gun never turned up in a crime. In fact, it essentially disappeared.

I lived with two other single agents, Bob McGonigel and Jack Kunst, in a furnished town house in Taylor, Michigan, a southern suburb of Detroit. We were great friends and Bob would later be best man at my wedding. He was also a maniac. He would wear crushed-velvet suits and lavender shirts, even during inspections. He seemed to be the only one in the entire FBI who wasn't afraid of Hoover. Later, Bob went into undercover work where he wouldn't have to wear a suit at all.

He had started out in the Bureau as a clerk, taking the "inside route" to become a special agent. Some of the best people in the FBI began as clerks, including several I selected for the Investigative Support Unit. But in certain circles, former clerks were resented, as if they'd had special preference to become agents.

Bob was the greatest I have ever known at "pretext calls." This was a proactive technique we developed to catch offenders, particularly useful when the element of surprise was paramount.

Bob was an artist with accents. If the suspect was in the mob, he'd do an Italian accent. For the Black Panthers, he could pass as a street dude. He also had a Nation of Islam persona, an Irish brogue, immigrant Jew, Grosse Point WASP. Not only did he have the voices down cold, he would alter the vocabulary and diction to suit the character. Bob was so good at this that he once called Joe Del Campo— another agent you'll read about in the next chapter—and convinced Joe he was a black militant who wanted to turn FBI informant. In those days, there was a lot of pressure to develop inner-city sources. Bob sets up a meeting with Joe, who thinks he's onto something big. No one shows up for Joe's meeting, and the next day in the office he's really pissed off when Bob greets him with the pretext voice!

Arresting the bad guys was one thing, but soon I found myself becoming interested in the thought processes that went into the crime. Whenever I would arrest someone, I'd ask him questions, such as why he chose one bank over another or what made him select this particular victim. We all knew that robbers preferred to hit banks on Friday afternoons because that was when the most money would be on the premises. But beyond that, I wanted to know what decisions went into the planning and execution of the hit?

I must not have seemed very intimidating. Just as they had in school, people felt comfortable opening up to me. The more I questioned these guys, the more I came to understand that the successful criminals were good profilers. They each had a carefully thought through and well-researched profile of the type of bank they preferred. Some liked banks near major thoroughfares or interstates so that getaways would be easier and they could be many miles away before a pursuit could be organized. Some liked small, isolated branches, such as the temporary ones set up in trailers. Many would case a bank ahead of time to get the layout down, to find out how many people worked there and how many customers could be expected in the lobby at any given time. Sometimes they would keep visiting bank branches until they found one where no males worked, and that would become the target. Buildings with no windows out to the street were best, since no one on the outside could witness the robbery in progress and witnesses on the inside would be unable to identify the getaway car. The best practitioners had come to the conclusion that a holdup note was better than a public announcement, waving a gun, and they'd always remember to take the note back before they left so as not to leave evidence. The best getaway car was a stolen one, and the best scenario of all was to have the car parked ahead of time so that it isn't noticed pulling up. You walk up to the bank, then drive away after the job. A robber who'd been particularly successful at a particular bank might watch it for a while, and if conditions remained the same, he'd hit the same one again within a couple of months.

Of all public facilities, banks are about the best set up to deal with robbery. Yet I was continually amazed when I did follow-up investigations at how many would have neglected to load film in the surveillance cameras, how many had set off a silent alarm accidentally and then forgotten to reset it, or tripped it so often that the police would respond slowly because they figured it was just another accident. This was like hanging out a Rob Me! sign to a sophisticated criminal.

But if you started profiling the cases—I hadn't attached this term to the process yet—you could begin seeing patterns. And once you began seeing patterns, you could start taking proactive measures to catch the bad guys. For example, if you started to see that a rash of bank robberies all seemed to fit together, and if you'd talked to enough perpetrators to understand what it was in each of these jobs that appealed to them, you could obviously and heavily fortify all the bank offices that met the criteria except for one. This one, of course, would be under constant police and/or FBI surveillance with plainclothes details inside. In effect, you could force the robber to select the bank of your choosing and be ready for him when he did. When this kind of proactive tactic was employed, bank-robbery clearance rates went way up.

Whatever we did in those days, we did under the looming presence of J. Edgar Hoover, just as our predecessors had since 1924. In this age of musical-chairs appointments and trial by public opinion, it's difficult to convey the degree of power and control Hoover exercised, not only over the FBI, but government leaders, the media, and the public at large. If you wanted to write a book or a script about the Bureau, such as Don Whitehead's huge 1950s best-seller *The FBI Story*, or the popular James Stewart movie based on it, or produce a TV series, such as Efrem Zimbalist Jr.'s *The FBI* of the 1960s, you had to have Mr. Hoover's personal approval and blessing. Likewise, if you were a high government official, you would always have that nagging fear that the director "had something" on you, particularly if he called in friendly tones to let you know the FBI had "uncovered" a nasty rumor that he would do everything he could to make sure never became damagingly public.

Nowhere was Mr. Hoover's personal mystique stronger than in the FBI branch offices and among the Bureau's management. It was an accepted fact that the FBI held the prestige and admiration it did because of him. He had almost single-handedly built the agency into what it was, and he was tireless in his fights for budget increases and pay raises. He was both revered and feared, and if you didn't think much of him, you kept it to yourself. Discipline was fierce, and branch inspections were bloodbaths. If the inspectors didn't find enough things that needed improvement, Hoover might suspect they weren't doing their jobs exhaustively enough, which meant they would require a certain number of letters of censure from each inspection, whether the conditions warranted them or not. It was like a quota for issuing traffic tickets. It got so bad that special agents in charge, known as SACs, would find sacrificial lambs who weren't immediately up for promotion so that letters of censure wouldn't hurt their careers.

One time, in a story that no longer has a very humorous

ring after the horrific 1995 bombing of the federal building in Oklahoma City, a bomb threat to the FBI office was
called in after an inspection. The call was traced to a phone
booth just outside the federal building downtown where
the field office was located. Authorities from headquarters
came in and removed the entire phone booth and wanted to
compare the fingerprints on the coins in the phone box with
those of all 350 individuals in the office. Fortunately for
all of us, reason prevailed and the examination never took
place. But that was an example of the tension Mr. Hoover's
policies could cause.

There were standard operating procedures for everything. Though I never had the opportunity to meet Mr.
Hoover in a one-on-one setting, I did (and still do) have a
personally autographed photo of him in my office. There
was even a standard procedure for getting such a photo as a
young agent. The SAC would tell you to have his secretary
write a kiss-ass letter for you, elaborating on how proud you
were to be an FBI special agent and how much you admired
Mr. Hoover. If you'd written your letter properly, you'd receive a photo with best wishes to you as a sign for all to see
of your personal connection to the leader.

Certain other procedures, we never knew for sure where
they came from, whether they were Hoover's personal
directives or merely an overzealous interpretation of the
director's wishes. Everyone in the office was expected to
put in overtime, and everyone was supposed to be above
the office average. I'm sure you see the dilemma. Month by
month, like some crazy pyramid scheme, the hours would
keep growing. Agents who came into the Bureau with the
highest morals and character would be forced to learn to
inflate their time sheets. There was to be no smoking or coffee drinking in the office. And like a force of door-to-door
salesmen, agents were discouraged from hanging around
the office at all, even to use the telephone. Therefore, each
man developed his own work habits to get around this. I

spent a lot of time going over my cases at a carrel at the public library.

One of the greatest adherents to the Gospel According to Saint Edgar was our SAC, Neil Welch, nicknamed the Grape. Welch was a big guy, about six four, with heavy horn-rim glasses. He was stern and stoic, not at all warm and fuzzy. He enjoyed a distinguished career in the Bureau, going on to head field offices in Philadelphia and New York, among others. There was some talk he would take Hoover's place when (or should I say, if) the inevitable day finally arrived. In New York, Welch formed a group that was the first to effectively use the federal RICO conspiracy statutes (Racketeer Influenced and Corrupt Organizations) against organized crime. But back in Detroit, he went by the book.

Naturally and inevitably, Welch and Bob McGonigel would clash, and it happened one Saturday when we were at home. Bob got a call that the Grape wanted to see him immediately, along with our squad supervisor, Bob Fitzpatrick. So McGonigel goes in, and Welch tells him someone's been using the phone to call New Jersey. It's against the rules to use the phone for personal business. Actually, what he'd been doing could have been interpreted either way, but in the FBI, you erred on the side of caution.

Welch, who could be really fierce, starts out generally, using good interrogation techniques that put the subject on the spot. "Okay, McGonigel, what about those telephone calls?"

So Bob starts confessing to any call he can think of because he's afraid Welch might have something more serious on him and maybe he can satisfy the SAC's wrath by giving him the petty stuff.

Welch rises to his full imposing height, leans over his desk, and points his finger menacingly. "McGonigel, let me tell you something: you've got two strikes against you. First, you're a former clerk. I hate fucking clerks! The second thing is, if I ever see you wearing a lavender-colored shirt, particularly during inspection, I'm gonna kick your ass up and down East Jefferson Street. And if I ever see you near a telephone, I'm gonna throw your ass down the elevator shaft. Now get out of my office!"

Bob comes home a beaten man, convinced he's going to be fired. Jack Kunst and I really feel sorry for him. But what Fitzpatrick tells me the next day is that after McGonigel left, he and Welch sat there laughing their asses off.

Years later, when I headed up the Investigative Support Unit, I would get asked if—with all that we knew about criminal behavior and crime-scene analysis—any of us could commit the perfect murder. I always told them no, that even with all we knew, our postoffense behavior would still give us away. I think the incident between McGonigel and Welch proves that even a first-rate FBI agent isn't immune to the pressures of the right interrogator.

By the way, from the moment he left the SAC's office that Saturday afternoon, Bob wore the whitest shirts in town . . . until Neil Welch was transferred to Philadelphia.

Much of Hoover's leverage in getting his funding requests through Congress had to do with the statistics he could throw around. But for the director to be able to use these numbers, everyone in the field had to deliver.

Early in 1972, so the story goes, Welch promised the boss 150 gambling arrests. That, apparently, was the category needing a boost in numbers at the time. So we set up an elaborate sting with informants, wiretaps, and military-like planning, all to culminate on Super Bowl Sunday, the biggest illegal-gambling day of the year. The Dallas Cowboys, who'd lost a close contest to the Baltimore Colts the year before, were playing the Miami Dolphins in New Orleans.

Arrests of bookies have to be lightning-fast, precision procedures because they use flash paper (which burns instantly) or potato paper (which is water soluble). The operation promised to be something of a mess because there had been intermittent showers all day.

Our sting netted more than two hundred gamblers on that rainy afternoon. At one point, I had a subject handcuffed in the back of the car, bringing him back to the armory where we were booking them all. He was a charming guy, friendly. He was handsome, too; looked like Paul Newman. He said to me, "Sometime when this is all over, we ought to get together for some racquetball."

He was approachable enough, so I started asking him questions, just the way I'd been asking bank robbers. "Why do you do this stuff?"

"I love it," he replied. "You can arrest all of us today, John. It won't make a bit of difference."

"But for a smart guy like you, making money legitimately should be easy."

He shook his head, like I still didn't get it. It was raining harder now. He glanced to the side, directing my attention to the car's window. "You see those two raindrops?" He pointed. "I'll bet you the one on the left will get to the bottom of the glass before the one on the right does. We don't need the Super Bowl. All we need is two little raindrops. You can't stop us, John, no matter what you do. It's what we are."

For me, this brief encounter was like a bolt out of the blue, like an instant cessation of ignorance. It may seem naive in retrospect, but suddenly, everything I'd been asking, all of my research with bank robbers and other criminals, came crystal clear.

It's what we are.

There was something inherent, deep within the criminal's mind and psyche, that compelled him to do things in a certain way. Later, when I started research into the minds and motivations of serial murderers, then, when I began analyzing crime scenes for behavioral clues, I would look for the one element or set of elements that made the crime and the criminal stand out, *that represented what he was.*

Eventually, I would come up with the term *signature*

to describe this unique element and personal compulsion, which remained static. And I would use it as distinguishable from the traditional concept of modus operandi, which is fluid and can change. This became the core of what we do in the Investigative Support Unit.

As it turned out, all the hundreds of arrests we made that Super Bowl Sunday were thrown out of court on technical procedure. In everyone's haste to get the operation up and running, an assistant to the attorney general, rather than the attorney general himself, had signed the search warrants. But the SAC Welch had fulfilled his promise and delivered his numbers to Hoover, at least long enough for them to have the desired impact on Capitol Hill. And I had come up with an insight that was to become critical in my law enforcement career, simply by betting on raindrops.

4

Between Two Worlds

It was a hijacking case involving the interstate theft of a truckload of J&B Scotch worth about $100,000. It was spring of 1971 and I had been on the job in Detroit going on six months. The warehouse foreman had tipped us off where they were going to make the exchange of money for the stolen booze.

We were working it as a joint FBI–Detroit police operation, but both organizations had met separately for planning. Only the higher-ups had talked to each other, and whatever they'd decided hadn't filtered down to the street. So when the time came to make the arrest, no one was quite sure what anyone else was doing.

It's nighttime, the outskirts of the city, by a set of railroad tracks. I'm driving one of the FBI cars with my squad supervisor, Bob Fitzpatrick, in the seat next to me. The informant was Fitzpatrick's, and Bob McGonigel was the case agent.

Word comes over the radio, "Bust 'em! Bust 'em!" We all come screeching to a halt, surrounding this semi. The driver opens the door, bolts out, and starts running. Along with an agent in another car, I open the door and get out, pull out my gun, and start running after him.

It's dark, we're all dressed down—no suits or ties or anything—and I will never ever forget the whites of his eyes as I see a uniformed cop holding a shotgun aimed directly at me and he's yelling, "Halt! Police! Drop the gun!" We're less than eight feet from each other, and I realize, this guy's about to shoot me. I freeze, at the same time coming to grips with the fact that if I make one wrong move, I'm history.

I'm about to drop my gun and put up my hands when I hear Bob Fitzpatrick's voice frantically shouting, "He's FBI! He's an FBI agent!"

The cop lowers his shotgun, and instinctively I take off again after the driver, adrenaline pumping, trying to make up the distance I've lost. The other agent and I reach him together. We tackle him to the ground and cuff him, more roughly than necessary, I'm so keyed up. But that frozen couple of seconds when I thought I was going to be blown away was one of the most terrifying experiences I've ever had. Many times since then, as I've tried to put myself in the shoes and heads of rape and murder victims, as I've forced myself to imagine what they must have been thinking and going through at the moment of attack, I've recalled my own fear, and it's helped me to really understand cases from the victim's point of view.

At the same time that a lot of us younger guys were busting our humps trying to make as many arrests as we could, many of the burnt-out old-timers seemed to have the attitude that rocking the boat was senseless, that you got paid the same whether you put yourself out on the limb or not, and that initiative was something for salesmen. Since we were encouraged to spend most of our time out of the office, window-shopping, sitting in the park, and reading the *Wall Street Journal* became favorite pastimes for a certain segment of the agent force.

Being the blue-flamer that I was, I took it upon myself to write a memo suggesting a merit pay system to encourage the people who were being most productive. I gave my memo to our ASAC, pronounced "a-sack," or assistant special agent in charge, Tom Naly.

Tom calls me into his office, closes the door, picks up the memo from his desk, and smiles benevolently at me. "What are you worried about, John? You'll get your GS-11," he says as he rips the memo in half.

"You'll get your GS-12," he says as he tears it in half

again. "You'll get your GS-13." Another rip, and by now, he's really laughing. "Don't rock the boat, Douglas," is his final advice as he lets the pieces of the memo flutter into the trash can.

Fifteen years later, long after J. Edgar Hoover was dead and at least somewhat gone, the FBI did implement a merit pay system. Though, when they finally got around to it, they obviously managed it with no help from me.

One evening in May—actually, I remember it was the Friday after May 17, for reasons that will become clear in a moment—I was with Bob McGonigel and Jack Kunst in a bar where we used to hang out, across the street from the office, called Jim's Garage. There's a rock-and-roll band playing, we've all had a few too many beers, when suddenly this attractive young woman comes in with a girlfriend. She reminds me of a young Sophia Loren, dressed in the trendy outfit of the times—this short blue dress and go-go boots practically up to her groin.

I call out, "Hey, blue! Come on over here!" So, to my surprise, she and the friend do. Her name is Pam Modica and we start joking around, hitting it off. Turns out it was her twenty-first birthday and she and the friend are out celebrating her legal right to drink. She seems to be into my sense of humor. Later, I find out her first impression of me was good-looking but kind of nerdy with my short, government-issue haircut. We leave Jim's and spend the rest of the night bar-hopping.

In the next couple of weeks, we got to know each other better. She lived within the city of Detroit and had gone to Pershing High, a practically all-black school where basketball great Elvin Hayes went. When I met her, she was attending Eastern Michigan University in Ypsilanti.

Things developed pretty quickly between us, although not without its social costs to Pam. This was 1971, the Vietnam War was still on, and distrust of the FBI was rampant on college campuses. Many of her friends didn't want to associate with us, convinced I was an establishment plant who was reporting back on their activities to some higher authority. The entire notion that these kids were important enough to be spied on was ludicrous, except that the FBI was doing that sort of thing back then.

I remember going with Pam to a sociology class. I sat in the back of the room, listening to the lecturer, a young, radical assistant professor; very cool, very "with it." But I kept looking at the professor and her gaze kept coming back to me, and it was obvious she was really bothered by my being there. Anyone from the FBI was the enemy, even if he was the boyfriend of one of her students. Looking back on the incident, I realized how unsettling an effect you can sometimes have just by being yourself, and my unit and I used this to our advantage. In a vicious murder case up in Alaska, my colleague Jud Ray, who is black, got a racist defendant to come unglued on the witness stand by sitting next to and being friendly to the man's girlfriend.

During Pam's early college years at Eastern Michigan, a serial killer was working, though we didn't yet use that terminology. He'd struck first in July of 1967, when a young woman named Mary Fleszar disappeared from the campus. Her decomposed body was found a month later. She had been stabbed to death and her hands and feet hacked off. A year later, the body of Joan Schell, a student at the University of Michigan in nearby Ann Arbor, was discovered. She'd been raped and stabbed almost fifty times. Then another body was found in Ypsilanti.

The killings, which became known as the "Michigan Murders," escalated, and women at both universities lived in terror. Each body that turned up bore evidence of horrible abuse. By the time a University of Michigan student named John Norman Collins was arrested in 1969—almost by chance by his uncle, state police corporal David Leik—six coeds and one thirteen-year-old girl had met grisly deaths.

Collins was convicted and sentenced to life imprison-

ment about three months before I entered the Bureau. But I
often wondered if the Bureau had known then what we do
now, if the monster could have been trapped before he had
been responsible for so much misery. Even after his capture, his specter continued to haunt both campuses, as Ted
Bundy's would haunt other colleges only a few years later.
With the memory of the hideous crimes so much a part of
Pam's recent life, they became a part of mine as well. And I
think it's more than likely, at least on a subconscious level,
that when I began studying, then hunting, serial killers, John
Norman Collins and his beautiful, innocent victims were
very much with me.

I was five years older than Pam, but since she was in
college and I was out in the working world of law enforcement, it often seemed like a generation gap. In public, she
was often quiet and seemingly passive around me and my
friends, and I'm afraid we sometimes took advantage of
this.

One time, Bob McGonigel and I met Pam for lunch at a
hotel restaurant that overlooked the downtown area. We're
both in dark suits and wing tips, and Pam is in perky coed
casual. Afterward, we're taking the elevator back down to
the lobby, and it seems like it's stopping on every floor.
Each time, it gets a little more packed.

About halfway down, Bob turns to Pam and says, "We
really enjoyed ourselves today. Next time we're in town,
we'll definitely give you a call."

Pam is looking down at the floor, trying not to react at
all when I jump in, "And next time, *I'll* bring the whipped
cream and *you* bring the cherries." The other passengers are
all looking at each other, squirming uncomfortably, until
Pam bursts out laughing. Then they look at the three of us
like we're some kind of perverts.

Pam was scheduled to be an exchange student in Coven-
try, England, for the fall semester. By late August, when she

flew over, I was pretty sure she was the girl I wanted to marry. It never occurred to me at the time to ask Pam if she had similar feelings about me. I just assumed that she must.

While she was away, we wrote to each other constantly. I spent a lot of time at her family's house at 622 Alameda Street, near the Michigan State Fairgrounds. Pam's father had died when she was a little girl, but I took advantage of the hospitality of her mom, Rosalie, eating there several nights a week and profiling her, as well as Pam's brothers and sisters, to try to figure out what Pam was like.

During this time, I met another woman whom Pam thereafter referred to (though she had never met her) as the "golf babe." Again, we met at a bar, and when I look back on it, I must have been spending more than my share of time in bars. She was in her early twenties, quite attractive, and recently out of college. We'd practically just met when she insists I come home with her to dinner.

It turns out she lives in Dearborn, which is Ford World Headquarters, and her father is a major auto executive. They live in this big stone house with a swimming pool, original art, fancy furniture. Her father is in his late forties, the image of corporate success. Her mother is gracious and elegant. We're sitting at the dinner table, flanked by my new friend's younger brother and sister. I'm profiling this family, trying to figure out their net worth. At the same time, they're trying to assess me.

Everything is going too well. They seem impressed that I'm an FBI agent, a welcome change from what I'm used to from Pam's circle. But, of course, these people are as establishment as they come. I'm really getting nervous, and I realize the reason is that they've practically got me married off.

The father is asking me about my family, my background, my military service. I tell him about my job running Air Force base athletic facilities. Then he tells me that he and an associate own a golf course near Detroit. He goes on about this fairway and that dogleg and I'm upping my estimate of his assets by the second.

"John, do you play golf?" he asks.

"No, Dad," I respond without missing a beat, "but I'd sure like to learn."

That was it. We all break up. I spent the night there, on the couch in the den. In the middle of the night I was visited by the girl, who had somehow managed to "sleep-walk" down to see me. Maybe it was the idea of being in this fancy house, maybe it was my instinctive fear since I'd joined the Bureau of being set up, but I was scared off by her aggressiveness, which matched that of the rest of her family. I left the next morning, having enjoyed their hospitality and a terrific dinner. But I knew I'd lost my shot at the good life.

Pam came home from England a couple of days before Christmas, 1971. I had decided to pop the question and had bought a diamond engagement ring. In those days, the Bureau had contacts for just about anything you wanted to buy. The company from whom I bought the ring was grateful to us for cracking a jewelry heist and gave excellent deals to agents.

With this preferred price, the biggest diamond ring I could afford was 1.25 carats. But I decided if she first saw it at the bottom of a champagne glass, not only would she think I was exceedingly clever, it would also make the diamond look as if it were three carats. I took her to an Italian restaurant on Eight Mile Road near her house. My intention was that whenever she got up to go to the ladies' room, I'd drop the ring into her glass.

But she never went. So the next night, I took her to the same restaurant again, but with the same results. Having sat on numerous stakeouts by that time, where sitting in a car for hours on end and having to hold it in was a genuine occupational drawback, I really had to admire her. But maybe this was supposed to be some sort of divine message that I wasn't ready to jump into marriage.

The next night was Christmas Eve and we were at her mother's house, with the entire family crowded around. This was my now-or-never moment. We'd been drinking Asti Spumante, which she loved. Finally, she left the room for a minute to go into the kitchen. When she came back, she was sitting in my lap, we drank a toast, and if I hadn't stopped her, she would have swallowed the ring. So much for looking like three carats; she never even saw it until I pointed it out. I wondered if there was a message here.

The important thing, though, was that I had set up my "interrogation scene" to obtain the intended result. Having staged the scene so carefully, surrounding us with her siblings and her mother, who adored me, I hadn't left Pam many options. She said yes. We would be married the following June.

For their second-year assignments, most of the single agents were being sent to New York or Chicago, under the logic that it would be less of a hardship for them than the married guys. I didn't have any particular preference and ended up assigned to Milwaukee, which sounded like an okay city even though I'd never been there and had no real idea where it was. I would move there in January and get settled in, then Pam would join me after the wedding.

I found a place in the Juneau Village Apartments, on Juneau Avenue, not too far from the Milwaukee Field Office in the federal building on North Jackson Street. This turned out to be a tactical mistake, because whatever happened, the response was always, "Go get Douglas. He's only three blocks away."

Even before I arrived in Milwaukee, the women in the office knew who I was: specifically, one of only two single agents. In my first few weeks they fought to take my dictation, even though I had little to do. Everyone wanted to be around me. But after a few weeks, when word gradually got around that I was engaged, I quickly became like the sixth day of a five-day deodorant.

The atmosphere in the Milwaukee Field Office turned out to be a replay of Detroit, only more so. My first SAC there was a man named Ed Hays, whom everyone called Fast Eddie. He was always red as a beet (and dropped dead from high blood pressure shortly after his retirement), and was always walking around snapping his fingers and shouting, "Get out of the office! Get out of the office!"

I said, "Where am I supposed to go? I just got here. I don't have a car. I don't have any cases."

He shot back, "I don't care where you go. Get out of the office."

So I left. In those days, it wasn't uncommon to go into a library or walk down Wisconsin Avenue near the office and find several agents window-shopping because they had nowhere else to be. It was during this time that I bought my next car, a Ford Torino, through a car dealer with whom the Bureau had contacts.

Our next SAC, Herb Hoxie, was brought in from the Little Rock, Arkansas, Field Office. Recruiting was always a big issue for SACs, and as soon as Hoxie arrived, he was already under the gun. Each field office had a monthly quota for both agents and nonclerical personnel.

Hoxie called me into his office and told me I was to be in charge of recruiting. This assignment generally went to a single guy because it involved a lot of traveling around the state.

"Why me?" I asked.

"Because we had to take the last guy off and he's lucky not to be fired." He'd been going into the local high schools and interviewing the girls for clerical positions. Hoover was still alive and there were no female special agents in those days. He would ask them questions, as if from a prepared list. One of them was, "Are you a virgin?" If she answered no, he'd ask her out on a date. Parents started complaining and the SAC had to slam-dunk him.

I started recruiting all over the state. Soon, I was bringing in almost four times the quota. I was the most productive recruiter in the country. The problem was, I was too good. They wouldn't take me off. When I told Herb I really didn't want to do it anymore, that I hadn't joined the FBI to do personnel, he threatened to put me on the civil rights detail, which meant investigating police departments and officers accused of brutalizing suspects and prisoners or of discrimination against minorities. This was not exactly the most popular job in the Bureau, either. I thought this was a hell of a way to reward me for my good work.

So I cut myself a deal. Cockily, I agreed to continue producing the big recruiting numbers if Hoxie would assign me as his primary relief, or substitute, and if I got the use of a Bureau car and a recommendation for Law Enforcement Assistance Administration (LEAA) money for graduate school. I knew that if I didn't want to spend my entire career out in the field, I needed a master's degree.

I was already somewhat suspect in the office. Anyone who wanted this much education must be a flaming liberal. At the University of Wisconsin at Milwaukee, where I began pursuing a master's in educational psychology nights and weekends, I was perceived as just the opposite. Most of the professors were suspicious of having an FBI agent in their classes, and I never had much patience with all the touchy-feely stuff that was so much a part of psychology ("John, I want you to introduce yourself to your neighbor here and tell him what John Douglas is really like").

One class, we were all sitting around in a circle. Circles were big in those days. It gradually dawns on me that no one is talking to me. I try to become part of the conversation, but no one will say anything. Finally, I just said, "What is the problem here, folks?" It turns out I have a metal-handled comb sticking out of my jacket pocket and they all think it's an antenna—that I'm recording the class and transmitting it back to "headquarters." The paranoid self-importance of these people never ceased to amaze me.

At the beginning of May 1972, J. Edgar Hoover died quietly in his sleep, at home in Washington. Early in the morning, Teletype messages flew from headquarters to every field office. In Milwaukee, we were all called in by the SAC to hear the news. Even though Hoover was in his late seventies and had been around forever, no one really thought he'd ever die. With the king now dead, we all wondered where a new king was going to come from to take his place. L. Patrick Gray, a deputy attorney general and Nixon loyalist, was appointed acting director. He was popular at first for such innovations as finally allowing female agents. It wasn't until his administration loyalties began to conflict with the needs of the Bureau that he began to slip.

I was recruiting in Green Bay a few weeks after Hoover's death when I get a call from Pam. She tells me the priest wants to meet with us a few days before the wedding. I'm convinced he thinks he can convert me to Catholicism and score some points with the Church brass. But Pam is a good Catholic who's been brought up to respect and obey what the priests tell her. And I know she'll badger the hell out of me if I don't surrender peacefully.

We come to St. Rita's Church together, only she goes in to see the priest by herself first. It reminds me of the police station back when I was in college in Montana, when they separated all of us to check our stories. I'm sure they're planning the conversion strategy. When they finally call me in, the first thing I say is, "What do you two have in store for the Protestant kid?"

The priest is young and friendly, probably in his early thirties. He asks me these general questions, such as "What is love?" I'm trying to profile him, trying to figure out if there's a particular right answer. These interviews are like the SATs; you're never sure if you've prepared properly.

We get into birth control, how the kids are going to be raised, that sort of thing. I start asking him how he feels about being a priest—being celibate, not having his own family. The priest seems like a nice guy, but Pam has told me St. Rita's is a strict, traditional church and he's uncomfortable around me, maybe because I'm not Catholic; I'm not sure. I think he's trying to break the ice when he asks me, "Where did you two meet?"

Whenever there has been stress in my life, I've always started joking around, trying to relieve the tension. Here's my opportunity, I think, and I can't resist it. I slip my chair closer to him. "Well, Father," I begin, "you know I'm an FBI agent. I don't know if Pam told you her background."

All the while I'm talking I'm getting closer to him, locking in the eye contact I'd already learned to use in interrogations. I just don't want him to look at Pam because I don't know how she's reacting. "We met at a place called Jim's Garage, which is a topless go-go bar. Pam worked there as a dancer and was quite good. What really got my attention, though, was she was dancing with these tassels on each of her breasts, and she got them spinning in opposite directions. Take my word for it, it was really something to see."

Pam is deathly quiet, not knowing whether to say anything or not. The priest is listening in rapt attention.

"Anyway, Father, she got these tassels spinning in opposite directions with greater and greater velocity, when all of a sudden, one of them flew off into the audience. Everyone grabbed for it. I leaped up and caught it and brought it back to her, and here we are today."

His mouth is gaping open. I've got this guy totally believing me when I just break up and start laughing, just as I did for my phony junior high school book report. "You mean this isn't true?" he asks. By this point Pam has broken up, too. We both just shake our heads. I don't know whether the priest is relieved or disappointed.

Bob McGonigel was my best man. The morning of the

wedding was rainy and dreary and I was itching to get on with it. I had Bob call Pam at her mother's house and ask if she'd seen or heard from me. She, of course, said no, and Bob offered as how I hadn't come home the night before and he was afraid I was getting cold feet and backing out. Looking back on it, I can't believe how perverse my sense of humor was. Eventually, Bob started laughing and gave us away, but I was a little disappointed not to have gotten more of a reaction out of her. Afterward, she told me she was so shell-shocked about all the arrangements and so concerned about having her curly hair frizz up in the humidity that the mere disappearance of the groom was a minor concern.

When we exchanged our vows in church that afternoon and the priest pronounced us husband and wife, I was surprised that he had some kind words to say about me.

"I met John Douglas for the first time the other day, and he got me thinking long and hard about how I feel about my own religious beliefs."

God knows what I said to make him think so deeply, but sometimes He works in mysterious ways. The next time I told the tassel story to a priest, it was the one Pam had called in to pray over me in Seattle. And I got him believing it, too.

We had a brief honeymoon in the Poconos—heart-shaped bathtub, mirrors on the ceiling, all the classy stuff—then drove to Long Island where my parents had a party for us since few people in my family had been able to come to the wedding.

After we were married, Pam moved to Milwaukee. She had graduated and become a teacher. New teachers all had to do their time serving as substitutes in the roughest inner-city schools. One junior high was particularly bad. Teachers there routinely were shoved and kicked, and a number of rape attempts had been made against the younger female teachers. I'd finally gotten off the recruiting detail and was putting in long hours on the reactive squad, mostly handling bank robberies. In spite of the inherent danger of my work, I was more concerned about Pam's situation. At least I had a gun to defend myself. One time, four students forced her into an empty classroom, pawing at her and assaulting her. She managed to scream and break away, but I was furious. I wanted to take some other agents down to the school and kick ass.

My best buddy at the time was an agent named Joe Del Campo, who worked with me on bank robbery cases. We would hang around this bagel place on Oakland Avenue, near the University of Wisconsin's Milwaukee campus. A couple named David and Sarah Goldberg managed it, and before too long, Joe and I became friendly with them. In fact, they started treating us like sons.

Some mornings, we'd be in there bright and early, wearing our guns and helping the Goldbergs put bagels and bialys in the oven. We'd eat breakfast, go out and catch a fugitive, follow up on a couple of leads in other cases, then go back for lunch. Joe and I both worked out at the Jewish Community Center, and around Christmas and Hanukkah time, we bought the Goldbergs a membership. Eventually, other agents started hanging around what we simply called "Goldberg's place," and we had a party there, attended by both the SAC and ASAC.

Joe Del Campo was a bright guy, multilingual, and excellent with firearms. His prowess played the central role in perhaps the strangest and most confusing situation I've ever been involved with.

One day during the winter, Joe and I are in the office interrogating a fugitive we'd brought in that morning when we get a call that Milwaukee police have a hostage situation. Joe's been up all night on night duty, but we leave our own subject to cool his heels and head out to the scene.

When we get there, an old Tudor-style house, we learn that the suspect, Jacob Cohen, is a fugitive accused of killing a police officer in Chicago. He's just shot an FBI agent,

Richard Carr, who tried to approach him in his apartment complex, which had been surrounded by a newly trained FBI SWAT team. The crazy guy then ran through the SWAT team perimeter, taking two rounds in the buttocks. He grabs a young boy shoveling snow and runs into a house. Now he's got three hostages—two children and an adult. Ultimately, he lets the adult and one of the kids go. He holds on to the young boy, whose age we estimate at about ten to twelve.

At this point, everyone is pissed off. It's freezing cold. Cohen is mad as hell, not exactly helped by the fact he's now got an ass full of lead. The FBI and Milwaukee police are angry at each other for letting the situation degenerate. The SWAT team is pissed off because this was their first big case and they missed him and let him slip through their perimeter. The FBI in general is now out for blood because he's taken down one of their own. And Chicago police have already gotten out the word that they want to come get him, and that if anyone's going to shoot the suspect, they should have that right.

SAC Herb Hoxie arrives on the scene and makes what I consider a couple of mistakes to compound the ones already made by everyone else. First, he uses a bullhorn, which makes him come across as dictatorial. A private telephone linkup is more sensitive, plus it gives you the flexibility of negotiating in private. Then he makes what I consider his second error: he offers himself as hostage in exchange for the boy.

So Hoxie gets behind the wheel of an FBI car. The police form a circle around the car as it backs into the driveway. Meanwhile, Del Campo tells me to give him a boost onto the roof of the house. Remember, it's a Tudor with steep-sloping roofs that are slick with ice, and Joe's been up all night. The only weapon he's got is his two-and-a-half-inch-barrel .357 magnum.

Cohen comes out of the house with his arm wrapped

around the boy's head, holding him close to his body. Detective Beasley of the Milwaukee Police Department steps out from the circle of cops and says, "Jack, we've got what you want. Leave the boy alone!" Del Campo is still creeping up the pitch of the roof. The police see him up there and realize what he's up to.

The subject and the hostage are getting closer to the car. There's ice and snow everywhere. Then suddenly, the kid slips on the ice, causing Cohen to lose his grip on him. Del Campo comes up over the peak of the roof. Figuring that with the short barrel, the bullet may rise, he aims for the neck and gets off one shot.

It's a direct hit, an amazing shot, right in the middle of the subject's neck. Cohen goes down, but no one can tell whether he's been hit or if it's the boy.

Exactly three seconds later, the car is riddled with bullets. In the crossfire, Detective Beasley is hit in the Achilles tendon. The boy scrambles on his hands and knees in front of the car, which rolls forward on him because Hoxie's been hit by flying glass and has lost control. Fortunately, the boy's not badly hurt.

True to FBI form, the local TV news that night shows the special agent in charge, Herbert Hoxie, on a gurney being moved out of the emergency room with blood trickling from his ear, and while they're wheeling him away, he's giving his statement to the press: "All of a sudden I heard gunfire, bullets were flying everywhere. I guess I was hit, but I think I'm okay . . ." FBI, God, motherhood, apple pie, et cetera, et cetera.

But that wasn't the end of it. Fistfights nearly break out and the police almost beat up Del Campo for taking their shot. The SWAT team isn't any too pleased either because he's made them look bad. They go to ASAC Ed Best to complain, but he stands up for Del Campo and says that Joe salvaged the situation that they let develop.

Cohen had between thirty and forty entrance and exit

wounds but was still alive when they took him away in the ambulance. Fortunately for all concerned, he was DOA at the hospital.

Special Agent Carr, miraculously, survived. Cohen's bullet passed through the trench coat Carr was wearing, into his shoulder, ricocheted off his trachea, and lodged in his lung. Carr kept that trench coat with the bullet hole in it and wore it proudly from that day on.

Del Campo and I were a terrific team for a while, except when we'd get on these laughing jags we couldn't get off of. We were at a gay bar once, trying to develop some informants on a homosexual murder fugitive. It's dark and it takes our eyes some time to adjust. Suddenly, we become aware of all these eyes on us, and we start arguing about which one of us they want. Then we see this sign above the bar, "A Hard Man Is Good to Find," and we just lose it, cracking up like two goofballs.

It never took much. We broke up once talking to an old guy in a wheelchair at a nursing home, and again, interviewing a dapper business owner in his mid-forties whose toupee had slipped halfway down his forehead. It didn't matter. If there was any humor anywhere in a situation, Joe and I would find it. As insensitive as it may sound, this was probably a useful talent to have. When you spend your time looking at murder scenes and dump sites, especially those involving children, when you've talked to hundreds, then thousands, of victims and their families, when you've seen the absolutely incredible things some human beings are capable of doing to other human beings, you'd better be able to laugh at silly things. Otherwise, you're going to go crazy.

Unlike a lot of guys who went into law enforcement, I'd never been a gun nut, but ever since the Air Force I'd always been a good shot. I thought it might be interesting to be on the SWAT team for a while. Every field office had one. It was a part-time job; the five team members were called out as needed. I made the team and was assigned as the sniper—the one who stays farthest back and goes for the long shot. All the others on the team had heavy military backgrounds— Green Berets, Rangers—and here I had taught swimming to pilots' wives and kids. The team leader, David Kohl, eventually became a deputy assistant director at Quantico, and he was the one who asked me to head up the Investigative Support Unit.

In one case, somewhat more straightforward than the Jacob Cohen extravaganza, a guy robbed a bank, then led police on a high-speed chase, ending up barricaded in a warehouse. That was when we were called in. Inside this warehouse, he takes off all his clothes, then puts them back on again. He seems like a real nut case. Then he asks to have his wife brought to the scene, which they do.

In later years, when we'd done more research into this type of personality, we'd understand that you don't do that—you don't agree to this type of demand because the person they ask to see is usually the one whom they perceive as having precipitated the problem in the first place. Therefore, you're putting that individual in great danger and setting them up for a murder-suicide.

Fortunately, in this instance, they don't bring her inside the warehouse, but have her talk to him on the phone. And sure enough, as soon as he hangs up, he blows his brains out with a shotgun.

We'd all been waiting in position for several hours, and suddenly it was over. But you can't always diffuse stress that quickly, which often leads to warped humor. "Jeez, why'd he have to do that?" one of the guys remarked. "Douglas is a crackerjack shot. He could have done that for him."

I was in Milwaukee for a little more than five years. Eventually, Pam and I moved from the apartment on Juneau Avenue to a town house on Brown Deer Road, away from the office, near the northern city limit. I spent most of my time on bank robberies and built up a string of commendations clearing cases. I found I was most successful when I could come up with a "signature" linking several crimes together, a factor that later became the cornerstone of our serial-murder analysis.

My only notable screwup during this time was after Jerry Hogan replaced Herb Hoxie as SAC. Not many perks went along with the job, but one was a Bureau automobile, and Hogan was proud of his new, emerald green Ford Ltd. I needed a car for an investigation one day and none was available. Hogan was out at a meeting, so I asked the ASAC, Arthur Fulton, if I could use the SAC's. Reluctantly, he agreed.

The next thing I know, Jerry's called me into his office and he's yelling at me for using his car, getting it dirty, and—worst of all—bringing it back with a flat. I hadn't even noticed that. Now Jerry and I got along well, so the whole time he's yelling, I can't keep from laughing. Apparently, this was a mistake.

Later that day, my squad supervisor, Ray Byrne, says to me, "You know, John, Jerry Hogan really likes you, but he has to teach you a lesson. He's assigning you to the Indian reservation."

These were the days of the Wounded Knee incident and the groundswell of consciousness over Native American rights. We were hated on the reservations, as much as in the ghettos of Detroit. The Indians had been treated terribly by the government. When I first arrived at the Menominee Reservation up on Green Bay, I couldn't believe the poverty and filth and squalor these people had to live in. So much of their culture had been stripped away from them, they often seemed almost numb to me. Largely as a result of the deplorable conditions and the history of government hostility and indifference, on many of the reservations you saw high incidences of alcoholism, child and spouse abuse, assault, and murder. But because of the utter mistrust of the government, it was nearly impossible for an FBI agent to get any type of cooperation or assistance from witnesses.

The local Bureau of Indian Affairs representatives were of no help. Even family members of victims wouldn't get involved, for fear of being seen as collaborating with the enemy. Sometimes, by the time you would find out about a murder and get to the scene, the body would have been there for several days already, infested with insect larvae.

I spent more than a month on the reservation, during which time I investigated at least six murders. I felt so bad for these people, I was depressed all the time, and I had the luxury of leaving and going home at night. I had just never seen people who, as a group, had so much to overcome. While it was dicey, my time on the Menominee Reservation was the first concentrated dose of murder-scene investigation I'd had, which turned out to be grim but excellent experience.

Without question, the best thing that happened during my time in Milwaukee was the birth of our first child, Erika, in November of 1975. We were to have Thanksgiving dinner at a local country club with some friends, Sam and Esther Ruskin, when Pam went into labor. Erika was born the next day.

I was working long hours on bank robbery cases and finishing up my graduate degree, and the new baby meant even less sleep. But needless to say, Pam bore the brunt of this. I felt much more family-oriented responsibility as a result of fatherhood, and I loved watching Erika grow. Fortunately for all of us, I think, I had not yet begun working child abduction and murder. If I had been, if I'd really stopped and thought about what was out there, I don't know that I could have adjusted to fatherhood as comfortably. By the time our next child, Lauren, was born in 1980, I was well into it.

Becoming a father, I think, also motivated me to try to make more out of myself. I knew that what I was doing wasn't what I wanted to be doing my entire career. Jerry Hogan advised me to put in ten years in the field before I thought about applying for anything else; that way, I'd have the experience for an ASAC and eventually a SAC posting, then maybe eventually make it to headquarters. But with one child and, I hoped, more to come, the life of a field agent, moving from office to office, didn't seem terribly appealing.

As time went on, other perspectives about the job began to evolve. The sniper training and SWAT team exercises had lost their appeal. With my background and interest in psychology—I had my master's by this time—the challenging part of the work, it seemed to me, was trying to manage the situation before it got to the shooting stage. The SAC recommended me for a two-week hostage-negotiation course at the FBI Academy in Quantico, which had only been in operation for a couple of years.

There, under the tutelage of such legendary agents as Howard Teten and Pat Mullany, I got my first real exposure to what was already known then as behavioral science. And that changed my career.

5

Behavioral Science or BS?

I hadn't been back to Quantico since new-agent training almost five years before, and in many ways the place had changed. For one thing, by spring of 1975, the FBI Academy had become a complete and self-contained facility, carved out of a chunk of the U.S. Marine base in the beautiful, gently rolling Virginia woodlands about an hour south of Washington.

But some things hadn't changed. The tactical units still commanded all the prestige and status, and of these, the Firearms Unit was the star. It was headed by George Zeiss, the special agent who had been sent to bring James Earl Ray back from England to face American justice after the 1968 assassination of Dr. Martin Luther King Jr. Zeiss was a huge, powerful bear of a man who broke handcuffs with his bare hands as a parlor trick. One time, some of the guys on the range took a pair and soldered the chain, then gave them to Zeiss to do his thing. He twisted so hard, he snapped his wrist and had to be in a cast for weeks.

Hostage negotiation was taught by the Behavioral Science Unit, a group of between seven and nine special agent instructors. Psychology and the "soft sciences" were never held in much esteem by Hoover and his cohorts, so until he died, this was something of a "back room" endeavor.

In fact, much of the FBI at that time, as well as the law enforcement world in general, considered psychology and behavioral science as they applied to criminology to be so much worthless bullshit. While clearly I never felt this way, I had to acknowledge that a lot of what was known and taught in this field had no real relevance to the business of understanding and catching criminals, a circumstance several of us would try to begin to rectify a couple of years later. When I took over as chief of the operational side of the Behavioral Science Unit, I changed the name to the Investigative Support Unit. And when people asked me why, I told them, quite frankly, I wanted to take the BS out of what we were doing.

The BSU, under Unit Chief Jack Pfaff at the time I took my hostage-negotiation training, was dominated by two strong and insightful personalities—Howard Teten and Patrick Mullany. Teten is about six foot four with penetrating eyes behind wire-rim glasses. Though an ex-Marine, he's a contemplative type—always totally dignified; the model of an intellectual professor. He joined the Bureau in 1962 after serving with the San Leandro, California, Police Department, near San Francisco. In 1969, he began teaching a landmark course called Applied Criminology, which eventually (after Hoover's death, I suspect) became known as Applied Criminal Psychology. By 1972, Teten had gone up to New York to consult with Dr. James Brussel, the psychiatrist who had cracked the Mad Bomber case, who agreed to personally teach Teten his profiling technique.

Armed with this knowledge, the big breakthrough of Teten's approach was how much you could learn about criminal behavior and motives by focusing on the evidence of the crime scene. In some ways, everything we've done in behavioral science and criminal investigative analysis since then has been based on this.

Pat Mullany always reminded me of a leprechaun. At about five ten, he's a roly-poly type with a quick wit and high energy level. He came to Quantico in 1972 from the New York Field Office with a degree in psychology. Near the end of his tenure at Quantico, he would distinguish himself by successfully managing very public hostage situations: in Washington, D.C., when the Hanafi Muslim sect took over the B'nai B'rith headquarters, and in Warrensville Heights, Ohio, when Cory Moore, a black Vietnam vet, grabbed a police captain and his secretary right in the station house. Together, Teten and Mullany represented the first wave of modern behavioral science and made a distinct and unforgettable pair.

The other instructors in the BSU also participated in the hostage-negotiation course. These included Dick Ault and Robert Ressler, who'd arrived at Quantico a short time before. If Teten and Mullany constituted the first wave, Ault and Ressler constituted the second, moving the discipline further along as something that could be of real value to police departments throughout the United States and the world. Though at that time we only knew each other as teacher and student, Bob Ressler and I would soon join forces on the serial-killer study that led ultimately to the modern version of what we do.

About fifty guys were in the hostage-negotiation class. In some ways it was more entertaining than informative, but an enjoyable two-week respite from field work. In class, we examined the three basic types of hostage takers: professional criminal, mentally ill, and fanatic. We studied some of the significant phenomena that had arisen out of hostage situations, such as the Stockholm syndrome. Two years before, in 1973, a botched bank robbery in Stockholm, Sweden, had turned into an agonizing hostage drama for customers and bank employees. Ultimately, the hostages came to identify with their captors and actually assisted them against the police.

We also watched the Sidney Lumet film *Dog Day Afternoon*, which had recently come out, starring Al Pacino as a man who robs a bank to get money for his male lover to undergo a sex-change operation. The film is based on an actual hostage incident in New York City. It was this case, and the protracted negotiations that ensued, that led the FBI to invite Capt. Frank Bolz and Det. Harvey Schlossberg of the NYPD to bring the Academy up to speed on hostage negotiation, an area in which the New York people were the acknowledged national leaders.

We studied the principles of negotiation. Some of the guidelines, such as trying to keep loss of life to a minimum, were obvious stuff. We did have the benefit of audiotapes of actual hostage situations, but it would be years later, when the next generation of instructors came in, before students would be involved in role-playing exercises—the closest you can get in the classroom to hands-on negotiating. It was also somewhat confusing, because a lot of the material had been recycled from the criminal psychology classes and didn't really fit. For example, they would give us photos and dossiers of child molesters or lust killers and discuss how such a personality would react in a hostage situation. Then there was more firearms training, which was still the big thing at Quantico.

Much of what we eventually came to teach about hostage negotiation was learned not in the classroom from other agents but in the cold crucible of the field. As I mentioned, one of the cases that earned Pat Mullany his reputation was that of Cory Moore. Moore, who had been diagnosed a paranoid schizophrenic, made a number of public demands after taking the Warrensville Heights, Ohio, police captain and his secretary hostage in the captain's own office. Among them was that all white people leave the earth immediately.

Now, in negotiating strategy, you don't want to give in to demands if you can possibly help it. Some demands, however, aren't terribly feasible under any circumstances. This certainly qualified as one of those. The case got so much national attention that the president of the United States, Jimmy Carter, offered to speak with Moore and help resolve the situation. While this was certainly well-intentioned on Mr. Carter's part, and indicative of the willingness he subsequently demonstrated for attempting to settle seemingly intractable conflicts around the world, this is not good negotiating strategy and I would never want it to happen in a situation I was managing. Neither did Pat Mullany. The problem with offering up the top guy, in addition to encouraging other desperate little people to try the same thing, is that you lose your maneuvering room. You always want to negotiate through intermediaries, which allows you to stall for time and avoid making promises you don't want to keep. Once you put the hostage taker in direct contact with someone he perceives as a decision maker, everyone is backed against the wall, and if you don't give in to his demands, you risk having things head south in a hurry. The longer you keep them talking, the better.

By the time I was teaching hostage negotiation at Quantico in the early 1980s, we used a disturbing videotape that had been made in St. Louis a couple of years before. Ultimately, we stopped showing it because the St. Louis Police Department was so upset by it. In the tape, a young black man holds up a bar. The robbery's a bust, he gets trapped inside, the police surround the place, and he's got a bunch of hostages.

The police organize a team of black and white officers to talk to him. But as the tape shows, rather than trying to deal with him on an objective level, they start jive-talking him and trying to get down on his level. They're all talking at once, constantly interrupting him, not listening to what he's saying, not trying to figure out what he wants to get out of this situation.

The camera swings away just as the chief of police arrives on the scene—again, I'd never let this happen. Once the chief is there, he "officially" ignores the demands, whereupon the guy points the gun at his own head and blows his brains out for all to see.

Contrast that with Pat Mullany's handling of the Cory Moore case. Obviously, Moore was crazy, and obviously, all the white people weren't going to leave planet Earth. But by listening to the subject, Mullany was able to discern what

Moore really wanted and what would satisfy him. Mullany offered Moore a press conference in which to air his views, and Moore released the hostages bloodlessly.

During the course at Quantico, my name got around the Behavioral Science Unit, and Pat Mullany, Dick Ault, and Bob Ressler recommended me to Jack Pfaff. Before I left, the unit chief called me down to his basement office for an interview. Pfaff was a personable, friendly guy. A swarthy chain-smoker, he looked a lot like Victor Mature. He told me the instructors had been impressed with me and told me to consider coming back to Quantico as a counselor for the FBI National Academy program. I was flattered by the offer and said I'd very much like to do that.

Back in Milwaukee, I was still on the reactive squad and the SWAT team, but was spending much of my time going around the state training business executives on how to deal with kidnapping and extortion threats and bank officers on how to deal with the single-bandit and gang armed robberies that were plaguing rural banks particularly.

It was amazing how naive some of these sophisticated businessmen were about personal security, allowing their schedules, even their vacation plans, to be published in local newspapers and company newsletters. In many cases, they were sitting ducks for would-be kidnappers and extortionists. I tried to teach them and their secretaries and subordinates how to evaluate calls and requests for information, and how to determine whether an extortion call that came in was genuine or not. For example, it wasn't unusual for an executive to get a call that his wife or child had been kidnapped and that he was to take a certain amount of money to such and such a drop. In point of fact, that wife or child was perfectly safe and in no danger the entire time, but the would-be profiteer had known that the family member would be unreachable for whatever reason, and if the criminal had one or two legitimate-sounding facts, he could convince the panicked executive to accede to his demands.

By the same token, we were able to cut down on the success of bank robberies by getting officials to institute some simple procedures. One of the common robbery techniques was to wait outside early in the morning when the branch manager would arrive to open for the day. The subject would grab the guy, then as other unsuspecting employees would arrive for work, they would be taken, too. The next thing you know, you have a whole bank branch full of hostages and a major mess on your hands.

I got some of the branches to institute a basic code system. When the first person arrived in the morning and found that the coast was clear, he or she would do one thing— adjust a curtain, move a plant, turn on a particular light, whatever—to signal to everyone else that all was okay. If that signal was absent when the second person arrived, he or she would not go in, but would call the police immediately.

Likewise, we trained tellers, who are the real key to any bank's security, what to look for and what to do in panic situations without becoming dead heroes. We explained the proper handling of exploding money packs, which were just then going into wide usage. And based on the interviews I'd done with a number of successful bank robbers, I instructed tellers to take the holdup note as it was presented to them, then "nervously" drop it on the floor on their side of the cage rather than hand it back to the robber, thereby preserving a valuable piece of evidence.

I knew from my interviews that robbers don't like to hit banks cold, so it could be extremely valuable to make a note of individuals coming into the branch whom you've never seen before, particularly with a simple or routine request, such as the exchange of paper money for a roll of dimes. If the teller had been able to jot down a license number or noted any kind of ID, a subsequent robbery could often be solved quickly.

I'd begun hanging out with city homicide detectives and around the medical examiner's office. Any forensic pathologist, as well as most good detectives, will tell you that the single most important piece of evidence in any murder investigation is the victim's body, and I wanted to learn as much as I could. I'm sure part of the fascination also went back to my youthful days of wanting to be a veterinarian and to understand how the structures and functions of the body related to living. But though I enjoyed working both with the homicide squad and the ME's staff, what really interested me was the psychological side: what makes a killer tick? What makes him commit a murder under the particular circumstances he does?

During my weeks at Quantico, I'd been exposed to some of the more bizarre murder cases, and one of the most bizarre of all turned out to be practically in my backyard—actually about 140 miles away. But that was close enough.

Back in the 1950s, Edward Gein had been a recluse living in the farming community of Plainfield, Wisconsin—population 642. He had begun his criminal career quietly, as a grave robber. His particular interest was the corpse's skin, which he removed, tanned, and draped across his own body, in addition to adorning a tailor's dummy and various home furnishings. At one point he had considered a sex-change operation—still revolutionary in the midwest of the 1950s—and when that seemed impractical, decided on the next best thing, which was making himself a woman suit out of real women. Some speculate he was trying to become his dead, domineering mother. If this case is starting to sound familiar, aspects of it were used by both Robert Bloch in his novel *Psycho* (made into the Hitchcock film classic) and Thomas Harris in *The Silence of the Lambs*. Harris picked up the story while sitting in on our classes at Quantico.

Gein could probably have continued living in ghoulish obscurity had his fantasy needs not expanded into "creating" more corpses to harvest. When we began our serial-killer study, this escalation is something we came to recognize in virtually all cases. Gein was charged with the murder of two middle-aged women, though likely there were more. In January of 1958, he was found legally insane and then spent the rest of his life in the Central State Hospital at Waupun and the Mendota Mental Health Institute, where he was always a model prisoner. In 1984, Gein died peacefully at age seventy-seven in the Mendota geriatric ward.

Needless to say, as a local detective or a special agent in the field, you don't get to see this sort of thing too often. When I got back to Milwaukee, I wanted to learn as much about the case as I could. But when I checked with the state attorney general's office, I found that the records had been sealed because of the insanity angle.

Saying I was an FBI agent with an educational interest in the crimes, I got the office to open the files to me. I'll never forget going with the clerk and taking the boxes off the endless shelves and actually having to break a wax seal to get in. But inside, I saw photographs that instantly became seared in my mind: headless, naked female bodies, hung upside down by ropes and pulleys, slit open in front all the way from sternum to vaginal area with all genitalia cut out. Other photos showed severed heads lying on the table, their blank, open eyes staring into nothingness. As horrible as these images were to contemplate, I began speculating as to what they said about the person who had created them, and how that knowledge could have aided in his capture. And in a real sense, I've been contemplating that ever since.

At the end of September 1976, I left Milwaukee for my temporary duty assignment, or TDY, as a counselor for the 107th National Academy session at Quantico. Pam had to stay on her own in Milwaukee, running the house and taking care of one-year-old Erika, while still teaching. This was the first of my many professional absences over the years, and I'm afraid too many of us in the Bureau, in the military, and in the foreign service give too little thought to the incredible burdens on the spouse left behind.

The FBI National Academy program is a tough, eleven-week course for senior and accomplished law enforcement officials from around the nation and the world. In many cases, Academy students are trained right alongside FBI agents. The way to tell the difference between trainees is by shirt color. FBI agents wear blue while NA students wear red. Another thing: NA students tend to be older and more experienced. To qualify, you have to be recommended by your local commanding officer and accepted by the Quantico staff. Not only does the National Academy provide expert training in the latest in law enforcement knowledge and techniques, it also serves as an extended and informal environment for the FBI to build personal relationships with local police officers, which has proved an invaluable resource over and over again. The head of the National Academy program was Jim Cotter, a real law enforcement institution whom the police loved.

As a counselor, I was responsible for one section of students—Section B—consisting of fifty men. Even though Director Patrick Gray's, and then Clarence Kelley's, policies were opening the Bureau from the narrow strictures of the Hoover years, no women were yet invited to the National Academy. In addition to the Americans, I had people from England, Canada, and Egypt. You live in the same dormitories and you're expected to be everything from instructor to social director to therapist to den mother. It was a way for the Behavioral Science staff to see how you interacted with police, if you liked the atmosphere at Quantico, and how you handled stress.

And there was plenty of that. Away from their families and living in dorm rooms for the first time in their adult lives, unable to drink in their rooms, sharing the bathroom with people they'd never met before, pushed to physical challenges most of them hadn't had to endure since new-recruit training, the students got an excellent education, but at a price. By about the sixth week, many of the cops were going nuts, bouncing off the white cinder-block walls.

And this, of course, took its toll on the counselors as well. Each one handled the assignment differently. As with everything else in my life, I decided that if we were all going to get through this in one piece, I'd better have a sense of humor. Some counselors took other approaches. One was so strict and intense, he'd be chewing his guys' butts out during intramural games. By the third week, his section was so pissed off, they gave him a set of luggage—the symbolic message being, "Get the hell out of here."

Another counselor was a special agent I'll call Fred. He'd never had a drinking problem until he came to Quantico, but he sure got one there.

The counselors were all supposed to watch for signs of students becoming depressed. In fact, Fred had taken to locking himself in his room, smoking and drinking himself into oblivion. When you're dealing with street-hardened cops, it's survival of the fittest. Any weakness and you're dead meat. A really nice guy, Fred was so sensitive and understanding and gullible, he didn't stand a chance with this crew.

There was a standing rule: no women on the floor. One night, one of the cops comes to Fred saying he "can't take it anymore." That's not something you want to hear as a counselor. His roommate has a different woman in bed every night and he can't sleep. So Fred goes with the guy to the room and sees half a dozen other men standing outside the door, waiting their turn, holding money in their sweaty hands. Fred freaks, he barges in on the guy who's on top of this long-haired blonde, grabs him, and pulls him off the woman, who turns out to be an inflatable doll.

One week later, another cop comes to Fred's room in the middle of the night saying his depressed roommate, Harry, has just opened the window and jumped. First of all, the windows in the dorm building aren't supposed to open. So Fred races down the hall, into the room, peers out the open window, and sees Harry covered with blood lying on the grass. Fred races down the stairs and out to the suicide scene, whereupon Harry jumps up and scares the shit out of him. It happens a bottle of ketchup had been appropriated from the cafeteria that very night! By graduation, Fred's hair was falling out, he wasn't shaving, his leg was numb, and he was walking with a limp. A neurologist could find nothing clinically wrong with him. A year later, back in his field office, he was out on a medical disability discharge. I felt sorry for the guy, but in one respect at least cops are a lot like criminals: you've got to prove how tough you are with each.

Despite my easygoing and humorous approach, I was not immune either, though fortunately, most of it was camp stuff. On one occasion, my group removed all the furniture from my room; on another, they short-sheeted my bed; and on several more, they stretched cellophane across my toilet seat. You have to be able to relieve stress somehow.

There came a point when they were driving me nuts, I was desperate to get away for a little while, and like the good cops they were, they sensed that moment precisely. They prop my green MGB up with cinder blocks, lifting it just enough off the ground so that the wheels missed by a small fraction of an inch. I get in, turn on the engine, I pop the clutch, put the car in gear, and futilely gun the engine, unable to figure out why I'm going nowhere fast. I get out, cursing at the damn British engineering; I open the hood, I kick the tires, I bend down and look under the car. And all of a sudden, the entire parking lot is lit up. They're all in their cars shining their headlights at me. Since they claimed to like me, they actually put the car back on terra firma for me after they'd had their fun.

The foreign students were in for their share, too. A lot of these guys would come over with empty suitcases, go to the PX, and buy like crazy. I particularly remember one high-ranking Egyptian colonel. He'd asked a cop from Detroit what *fuck* meant. (Big mistake.) The cop had told him, somewhat accurately, that this was an all-purpose word that had many, many different usages depending on the situation, but it was almost always appropriate. One of its meanings is "beautiful" or "classy."

So he's in the PX, goes over to the photography counter, points, and booms out, "I wish to buy that fucking camera."

The horrified young woman clerk says, "Excuse me?"

"I want to buy that fucking camera!"

Some of the other guys quickly get to him and explain that while the term does have many usages, it is not used around women and children.

Then there was the Japanese police officer who had dutifully asked one of the other cops the protocol for greeting instructors one holds in high regard. So every time I saw him in the hallway, he would smile, bow respectfully, and greet me with, "Fuck you, Mr. Douglas."

Rather than getting all complicated, I'd bow back, smile, and say, "Fuck you, too."

Generally, when the Japanese sent over someone to the National Academy, they would insist on sending two students. After a while it became clear that one would be the superior officer and the other a subordinate who would be responsible for shining the senior man's shoes, making his bed, cleaning his room, and generally acting as his servant. One time, several of the other students went to Jim Cotter and complained that the top guy was regularly practicing his karate and martial arts by beating the hell out of his companion. Cotter took the top guy aside, explained that every student was equal at the Academy, and stated in no uncertain terms that this kind of behavior would not be tolerated. But it just goes to prove the kind of cultural barriers that have to be overcome.

I sat in on NA classes and got a sense of how they were taught. By the end of the session in December, both the Behavioral Science and Education Units offered me jobs. The Education Unit chief offered to pay for more graduate school, but I thought I'd be more interested in Behavioral Science.

I came back to Milwaukee a week before Christmas, so confident I'd be getting the posting to Quantico that Pam and I bought a five-acre lot in an area south of the FBI Academy in Quantico. In January 1977, the Bureau announced a man-power study, during which time personnel transfers would be frozen. So there went my new job; I was stuck with this lot in Virginia and had to borrow money from my dad for the down payment, and I still had no idea what my future in the Bureau was going to be.

But then, several weeks later, I'm out on a case with an agent named Henry McCaslin when I get a call from head-quarters that I'm going to be transferred to Quantico in June and assigned to Behavioral Science.

At thirty-two years of age, I would be taking the place of Pat Mullany, who was going on to the inspection staff at headquarters. Those were big shoes to fill and I looked for-ward to the challenge. My only real concern was the people I'd be teaching. I knew how they could take apart counselors, even ones they liked. I could only imagine how tough they'd be on instructors who were trying to teach them their own business. I had the right dance down, but I wasn't sure if I knew the song well enough. If I was going to be teaching them behavioral science, I'd better figure out some way to eliminate as much of the BS as I could. And if I was going to be able to say anything of value to a police chief fifteen or twenty years older than me, I knew I'd better have the goods to back it up.

And it was that fear that led me to the next stage of the journey.

6

Taking the Show on the Road

Nine special agents were assigned to Behavioral Science when I joined the unit in June of 1977, all primarily involved in teaching. The main course offered to both FBI personnel and National Academy students was Applied Criminal Psychology. Howard Teten had originated it back in 1972, focusing on the issue with which detectives and other crime solvers are most concerned: motive. The idea was to try to give students an understanding of why violent criminals think and act as they do. Yet as popular and useful as this course was, it was based mainly on research and teaching from the academic discipline of psychology. Some of the material came from Teten's own experience, and later that of the other instructors. But at that time, the only ones who could speak from the authority of organized, methodical, broadly conducted studies were the academics. And there was a dawning realization among many of us that these studies, and this professional perspective, had only limited applicability to the field of law enforcement and crime detection.

Other courses offered at the Academy included: Contemporary Police Problems, which dealt with labor-management issues, police unions, community relations, and associated topics; Sociology and Psychology, which mirrored the typical introductory college curriculum; and Sex Crimes, which often, unfortunately, was more entertaining than useful or informative. Depending on who was teaching Sex Crimes, it was taken with greater or lesser seriousness. One of the instructors set the tone with a dirty-old-man doll dressed in a raincoat. When you pushed down on the head, the raincoat flashed open and the penis popped up. They would also show hundreds of photographs of people with various types of what are now called paraphilias but were then generally known simply as perversions: transvestism, various fetishes, exhibitionism, and so on. These would often elicit an inappropriate laugh from the room. When you're dealing with voyeurism or showing a man dressed in women's clothing, you might be able to squeeze a few chuckles out of a particular photo. When you get into the extremes of sadomasochism or pedophilia, if you're still laughing, then there's something wrong with you or the instructor or both. It took several long years and a lot of sensitization before Roy Hazelwood and Ken Lanning came in and put the study of such topics as rape and the sexual exploitation of children on a serious and professional level. Hazelwood is retired now but still an active consultant, and Lanning will retire soon. These two guys remain among the leading law enforcement experts in the world in their respective fields.

But back in the "just the facts, ma'am" Hoover days, no one in any position of authority considered what became known as profiling to be a valid crime-solving tool. In fact, the very phrase *behavioral science* would have been considered an oxymoron and its proponents might as well have been advocating witchcraft or psychic visions. So anyone "dabbling" in it would have had to do so very informally with no records kept. When Teten and Mullany began offering personality profiles, it was all done verbally, nothing on paper. The first rule was always, "Don't embarrass the Bureau," and you never wanted to document something that could blow up in your—or your SAC's—face.

Through Teten's initiative and based on what he had learned from Dr. Brussel in New York, some informal consulting was provided to individual police officials who requested it, but there was no organized program nor any thought that this was a function the Behavioral Science Unit

should perform. What normally happened was that a graduate of the NA course would call Teten or Mullany to talk
about a case he was having trouble with.

One of the early ones came from a police officer in
California desperate to solve the case of a woman who'd
been murdered by multiple stab wounds. Other than the
viciousness of the killing, nothing in particular stood out,
and there wasn't much to go on forensically. When the
officer described the few facts he had, Teten advised him
to start looking in the victim's own neighborhood—for a
slightly built, unattractive loner in his late teens who had
killed the woman impulsively and was now wrestling with
tremendous guilt and fear of being found out. When you go
to his house and he comes to the door, Teten suggested, just
stand there, stare right at him, and say, "You know why I'm
here." It shouldn't be difficult to get a confession out of him.

Two days later, the officer called back and reported that
they'd begun systematically knocking on doors in the neighborhood. When a kid fitting Teten's "profile" answered at
one house, before the cop could get out his rehearsed line,
the young man blurted out, "Okay, you got me!"

While it probably seemed at the time that Teten was pulling rabbits out of a hat, there was a logic to the type of individual and situation he described. And over the years, we
would make that logic more and more rigorous and make
what he and Pat Mullany were dabbling with in their spare
time an important weapon in the fight against violent crime.

As is often true with advances in a particular field, this
one came about largely by serendipity. The serendipity in
this case was that as a Behavioral Science Unit instructor, I
really didn't think I knew what I was doing and felt I needed
a way to get more firsthand information.

By the time I got to Quantico, Mullany was just about to
leave and Teten was the overall guru. So responsibility for
breaking me in fell to the two guys closest to me in age and
seniority—Dick Ault and Bob Ressler. Dick was about six

years older than I was, and Bob, about eight. Both had done police work in the Army before joining the Bureau. Applied Criminal Psychology represented about forty hours of classroom instruction over the eleven weeks of the National Academy course. So the most efficient way of breaking in a new guy was with the "road schools," where instructors from Quantico taught the same types of courses in highly compressed form to local police departments and academies throughout the United States. These were popular and there was usually a waiting list of requests for our services, mainly from chiefs and senior people who'd been through the full NA course. Going out with a seasoned instructor and watching him perform for two weeks was a quick way of picking up what it was you were supposed to be doing. So I started traveling with Bob.

There was a standard drill to the road schools. You'd leave home on Sunday, teach at one department or academy from Monday morning to Friday noon, then move on to the next school and do it all again. After a while, you started to feel like Shane or the Lone Ranger—riding into town, doing your bit to help the locals, then silently riding out again when your work was done. Sometimes I wanted to leave a silver bullet for them to remember us by.

Right from the beginning, I felt uncomfortable about what amounted to teaching from "hearsay." Most of the instructors—myself prime among them—had no direct experience with the vast majority of the cases they taught. In that way, it was very much like a college course in criminology where, in most cases, the professor has never been out in the streets experiencing the kind of things he's talking about. Much of the course had evolved into "war stories," told originally by whoever the officers on the cases had been, then embellished over time until they had little relationship to the actual events. By the time I came on the scene, it had gotten to the point where an instructor would make a pronouncement about a particular case only to be contradicted in class by a student who had actually worked the case! The worst part of it was, the instructor wouldn't always back down but would often insist he was right, even in the face of someone who'd been there. This kind of technique and attitude can go a long way toward making your class lose faith in everything else you say, whether they have any personal knowledge or not.

My other problem was that I had just turned thirty-two years of age and looked even younger. I was supposed to be teaching experienced cops, many of them ten and fifteen years older. How was I going to sound authoritative or teach them anything? Most of the firsthand experience I had in murder investigation had been under the wings of seasoned homicide cops in Detroit and Milwaukee, and here I was going to be telling people like them how to do their jobs. So I figured I'd better know my shit before I faced these guys, and whatever I didn't know, I'd better learn in a hurry.

I wasn't stupid about it. Before I would start a session I would ask if anyone in the class had any direct experience with any of the cases or criminals I planned on discussing that day. For example, if I was going to be discussing Charles Manson, the first thing I'd ask was, "Anyone here from LAPD? Anyone here work this case?" And if there happened to be someone, I'd ask him to give us all the details of the case. That way, I'd make sure I didn't contradict anything that an actual participant would know to be true.

But still, even though you might be a thirty-two-year-old kid fresh out of a field office, when you taught at Quantico or came to teach from Quantico, you were presumed to speak with the authority of the FBI Academy and all of its impressive resources. Cops would constantly come up to me during breaks, or, during road schools, call my hotel room in the evenings, asking for pointers on active cases. "Hey, John, I've got this case that's kind of similar to what you were talking about today. What do you think about this?" There was no letup. And I needed some authority for what

I was doing; not authority from the Bureau, but personal authority.

Now there comes a point on the road—at least there did for me—when you realize there are only so many songs you can listen to, so many margaritas you can drink, so much time you can hang around the room staring at the television. That point came for me in a hotel cocktail lounge in California early in 1978. Bob Ressler and I were doing a school in Sacramento. The next day, driving away, I commented that most of these guys we're teaching about are still around, and most of them are going to be on ice for the rest of their lives. Let's see if we can talk to them; ask them why they did it, find out what it was like through *their* eyes. All we can do is try. If it doesn't work out, it doesn't work out.

I'd long had a reputation as a blue flamer, and this didn't do much to diminish it in Bob's eyes. But he did agree to go along with my crazy idea. Bob's motto has always been, "It's better to ask for forgiveness than permission," and that certainly seemed to apply here. We knew if we asked for sanction from headquarters, we wouldn't get it. Not only that, anything we tried to do from then on would be scrutinized. In any bureaucracy, you have to watch blue flamers carefully.

California has always had more than its share of weird and spectacular crimes, so that seemed like a good place to start. John Conway was a special agent assigned to the FBI resident agency in San Rafael, just north of San Francisco. He'd had Bob for a class at Quantico, had excellent relations with the California state penal system, and agreed to act as liaison and make the arrangements for us. We knew we needed to have someone we trusted, and who trusted us, because if this little project blew up in everyone's face, there would be plenty of blame to go around.

The first felon we decided to go for was Ed Kemper, who at the time was serving out his multiple life sentences at the California State Medical Facility at Vacaville, about midway between San Francisco and Sacramento. We had been teaching his case at the National Academy without ever having had any personal contact, so he seemed like a good one to start with. Whether he would agree to see us or talk with us was an open question.

The facts of the case were well documented. Edmund Emil Kemper III was born on December 18, 1948, in Burbank, California. He grew up with two younger sisters in a dysfunctional family in which his mother, Clarnell, and father, Ed junior, fought constantly and eventually separated. After Ed displayed a range of "weird" behavior, including the dismemberment of two family cats and playing death-ritual games with his older sister, Susan, his mother packed him off to her estranged husband. When he ran away and went back to his mother, he was sent to live with his paternal grandparents on a remote California farm at the foothills of the Sierras. There, he was miserably bored and lonely, cut off from his family and the little comfort that the familiar surroundings of his own school afforded him. And there, one afternoon in August of 1963, the tall, hulking fourteen-year-old shot his grandmother, Maude, with a .22-caliber rifle, then stabbed her body repeatedly with a kitchen knife. She had insisted he stay and help her with the household chores rather than accompany his grandfather, whom he liked better, into the fields. Knowing Grandpa Ed would not find what he had just done acceptable behavior, when the old man returned home, Ed shot him, too, and left the body lying in the yard. When questioned by the police afterward, he shrugged and said, "I just wondered how it would feel to shoot Grandma."

The seeming motivelessness of the double murder got Ed a diagnosis of "personality trait disturbance, passive-aggressive type," and a commitment to the Atascadero State Hospital for the criminally insane. He was let out in 1969 at age twenty-one, over the objection of state psychiatrists, and placed in the custody of his mother, who had left her third husband and was now working as a secretary at the newly opened University of California at Santa Cruz. By now, Ed Kemper was six foot nine and weighed in at around three hundred pounds.

For two years he held odd jobs, cruised the streets and highways in his car, and made a practice of picking up young female hitchhikers. Santa Cruz and its environs seemed to be a magnet for beautiful California coeds, and Kemper had missed out on a lot in his teens. Though turned down for the Highway Patrol, he got a job with the State Highway Department.

On May 7, 1972, he picked up two roommates from Fresno State College, Mary Ann Pesce and Anita Luchessa. He drove them to a secluded area, stabbed both young women to death, then took their bodies home to his mother's house where he took Polaroid photos, dissected them, and played with various organs. Then he packed up what was left in plastic bags, buried the bodies in the Santa Cruz mountains, and tossed the heads into the deep ravine beside the road.

On September 14, Kemper gave a ride to a fifteen-year-old high school girl, Aiko Koo, suffocated her, sexually assaulted her corpse, then brought it home for dissection. The next morning, when he had one of his periodic visits with state psychiatrists to monitor and evaluate his mental health, Koo's head was lying in his car trunk. The interview went well, though, and the psychiatrists declared him no longer a threat to himself or others and recommended that his juvenile record be sealed. Kemper reveled in this brilliantly symbolic act. It demonstrated his contempt for the system and his superiority to it at the same time. He drove back to the mountains and buried the pieces of Koo's body near Boulder Creek.

(At the time Kemper was active, Santa Cruz could boast the unenviable title of serial-murder capital of the world. Herbert Mullin, a bright, handsome, diagnosed paranoid schizophrenic, was killing both men and women, he claimed, at the urging of voices directing him to help save the environment. On a similar theme, a twenty-four-year-old recluse car mechanic who lived in the woods outside of town—John Linley Frazier—had burned down a house and killed a family of six as a warning to those who would destroy nature. "Materialism must die or mankind must stop," was the note left under the windshield wiper of the family's Rolls-Royce. It seemed as if every week another outrage was taking place.)

On January 9 of 1973, Kemper picked up Santa Cruz student Cindy Schall, forced her into his trunk at gunpoint, then shot her. As had become his custom, he carried her body back to his mother's house, had sex with it in his bed, dissected it in the bathtub, then bagged the remains and flung them over the cliff into the ocean at Carmel. His innovation this time was to bury Schall's head face-up in the backyard, looking toward his mother's bedroom window, since she'd always wanted people "to look up to her."

By now, Santa Cruz was gripped with terror of the "Coed Killer." Young women were warned not to accept rides from strangers, particularly from people outside the supposedly safe confines of the university community. But Kemper's mother worked for the college, and so he had a university sticker on his car.

Less than a month later, Kemper picked up Rosalind Thorpe and Alice Liu, both of whom he shot, then piled in the trunk. They received the same treatment as his previous victims when he got them home. He dumped their mutilated bodies in Eden Canyon, near San Francisco, where they were found a week later.

His compulsion to kill was escalating at an alarming rate, even to him. He considered shooting everyone on the block, but finally decided against it. He had a better idea—what he realized he'd been wanting to do all along. On Easter weekend, as his mother slept in her bed, Kemper went into her room and attacked her repeatedly with a claw hammer until she died. He then decapitated her and raped her headless corpse. As his final inspirational touch, he cut out her larynx and fed it down the garbage disposal. "It seemed appropriate," he later told police, "as much as she'd bitched and screamed and yelled at me over so many years."

But when he turned on the switch, the disposal jammed and threw the bloody voice box back out at him. "Even when she was dead, she was still bitching at me. I couldn't get her to shut up!"

He then called Sally Hallett, a friend of his mother's, inviting her over for a "surprise" dinner. When she arrived, he clubbed and strangled her, cut off her head, and left the body in his own bed while he went to sleep in his mother's bed. On Easter Sunday morning, he took off in his car, driving aimlessly eastward. He kept listening to the radio, expecting to have become a huge national celebrity. Yet there was nothing.

Outside of Pueblo, Colorado, dazed and exhausted from lack of sleep, disappointed that his grand gesture had not had more of an impact, he pulled over at a phone booth beside the road, called the Santa Cruz Police Department, and after repeated attempts to convince them he was telling the truth, confessed to the murders and his identity as the Coed Killer. He then waited patiently as local police were dispatched to pick him up.

Kemper was convicted on eight counts of first-degree murder. When asked what he considered to be the appropriate punishment, he replied, "Death by torture."

Though John Conway had made advance arrangements with the prison officials, I decided it was best to request interviews with the prisoners "cold" when we got there. Even though that meant making the trip without the certainty of cooperation, it seemed the best idea. Nothing stays secret in a prison, and if word got out that a certain inmate had a relationship with, and was talking to, the FBI, he could

be considered a snitch or worse. If we showed up unannounced, it would be clear to the prison population that we
were investigating something or other and didn't have any
prior arrangement or deal. So I was somewhat surprised
when Ed Kemper readily agreed to talk to us. Apparently,
no one had asked him anything about his crimes for quite
some time, and he was curious about what we were doing.

Going into a high-security penitentiary is a chilling experience, even for a federal law enforcement agent. The first
thing you have to do is surrender your gun. Obviously, they
don't want any weapons available in the lockup areas. The
second requirement is that you sign a waiver stating that you
absolve the prison system of responsibility if you are taken
hostage and understand that in such an eventuality, you
will not be bargained for. Having an FBI agent as a hostage
could be an enormous bargaining chip. Those formalities
having been taken care of, Bob Ressler, John Conway, and
I were ushered into a room with a table and chairs to await
Ed Kemper's arrival.

The first thing that struck me when they brought him
in was how huge this guy was. I'd known that he was tall
and had been considered a social outcast in school and in
the neighborhood because of his size, but up close, he was
enormous. He could easily have broken any of us in two. He
had longish dark hair and a full mustache, and wore an open
work shirt and white T-shirt that prominently displayed a
massive gut.

It was also apparent before long that Kemper was a bright
guy. Prison records listed his IQ as 145, and at times during
the many hours we spent with him, Bob and I worried he
was a lot brighter than we were. He'd had a long time to sit
and think about his life and crimes, and once he understood
that we had carefully researched his files and would know if
he was bullshitting us, he opened up and talked about himself for hours.

His attitude was neither cocky and arrogant nor remorseful and contrite. Rather, he was cool and soft-spoken, analytical and somewhat removed. In fact, as the interview went on, it was often difficult to break in and ask a question. The only times he got weepy was in recalling his treatment at the hands of his mother.

Having taught Applied Criminal Psychology without necessarily knowing that everything I was saying was true, I was interested in the age-old question of whether criminals are born or made. Though there is still no definitive answer and may never be, listening to Kemper raised some fascinating questions.

There was no dispute that Ed's parents had had a terrible marriage. He told us that, from early on, he had looked so much like his father that his mother had hated him. Then his size became an issue. By the time he was ten, he was already a giant for his age, and Clarnell worried that he would molest his sister, Susan. So she made him sleep in a windowless basement room near the furnace. Every night at bedtime, Clarnell would close the basement door on him, while she and Susan went to their rooms upstairs. This terrified him and made him totally resentful of the two women. It also coincided with his mother's final breakup from Ed's father. Because of his size, shy personality, and lack of a role model in the house to identify with, Ed had always been withdrawn and "different." Once he was shut up like a prisoner in the basement and made to feel dirty and dangerous without having done anything wrong, his hostile and murderous thoughts began to blossom. It was then that he killed and mutilated the two family cats, one with his pocketknife and the other with a machete. We would later realize that this childhood trait of cruelty to small animals was the keystone of what came to be known as the "homicidal triad," also including enuresis, or bed-wetting, beyond the normally appropriate age and fire-starting.

What was also sad and ironic was that at Santa Cruz, Ed's mother was popular with both administrators and students. She was considered a sensitive, caring person you could go to if you had a problem or just needed to talk something out. Yet at home, she treated her timid son as if he were some kind of monster.

There's no way you can ever date or marry any of these college coeds, was her apparent message. They're all much better than you. Continually exposed to that attitude, Ed eventually decided to fulfill her expectations.

In her own way, it must be said, she did try to take care of him. When he expressed an interest in joining the California Highway Patrol, she endeavored to have his juvenile record expunged so the "stigma" of having murdered his grandparents wouldn't hold him back in adult life.

This desire to work with the police was another interesting revelation, which was to come up over and over again in our serial killer studies. The three most common motives of serial rapists and murderers turn out to be domination, manipulation, and control. When you consider that most of these guys are angry, ineffectual losers who feel they've been given the shaft by life, and that most of them have experienced some sort of physical or emotional abuse, as Ed Kemper had, it isn't surprising that one of their main fantasy occupations is police officer.

A policeman represents power and public respect. When called upon to do so, he is authorized to hurt bad people for the common good. In our research, we discovered that, while few police officers go bad and commit violent crimes, frequently serial offenders had failed in their efforts to join police departments and had taken jobs in related fields, such as security guard or night watchman. One of the things we began saying in some of our profiles was that the UNSUB would drive a policelike vehicle, say a Ford Crown Victoria or Chevrolet Caprice. Sometimes, as in the case of the Atlanta child murders, the subject had purchased a used and stripped police car.

Even more common is the "police buff." One of the things

Ed Kemper told us was that he would frequent bars and restaurants known to be police hangouts and strike up conversations. This made him feel like an insider, gave him the vicarious thrill of a policeman's power. But also, once the Coed Killer was on the rampage, he had a direct line into the progress of the investigation, allowing him to anticipate their next move. In fact, when Kemper called from Colorado at the end of his long, bloody mission, he had a difficult time convincing the Santa Cruz cops that this wasn't all some drunken joke, that the Coed Killer was really their friend Ed. Now, because of what we've learned, we routinely consider the likelihood that a subject will attempt to insinuate himself into the investigation. Years later, working the Arthur Shawcross prostitute murders in Rochester, New York, my colleague Gregg McCrary correctly predicted that the killer would turn out to be someone that many of the police knew well, who hung around their hangouts, and who enthusiastically pumped them for information.

I was extremely interested in Kemper's methodology. That he was getting away with these crimes repeatedly in the same general geographical area meant that he was doing something "right"; that he was analyzing what he was doing and learning to perfect his technique. Keep in mind that for most of these guys, the hunting and killing is the most important thing in their lives, their main "job," so they're thinking about it all the time. Ed Kemper got so good at what he did that when he was stopped one time for a broken taillight while he had two bodies in his trunk, the officer reported how polite he was and let him off with a warning. Rather than being terrified of discovery and arrest, this was part of the thrill to Kemper. He dispassionately told us that had the officer looked in his trunk, he was prepared to kill him. Another time, he talked his way past a university security guard with two women dying of gunshot wounds in the car. Both were wrapped in blankets up to their necks, one next to him in the front seat, the other in the back. Kemper calmly and somewhat embarrassedly explained that the girls were drunk and he was taking them home. The last part of the statement was true. And on one occasion, he picked up a woman hitchhiking with her young teenaged son, planning to kill them both. But as he drove away, he saw out of his rearview mirror that the woman's companion had written down his license-plate number. So he rationally drove the mother and son to where they were going and dropped them off.

As bright as he was, Kemper had actually administered psychological tests in prison, so he knew all the buzzwords and could give you an analysis of his behavior in analytical psychiatric detail. Everything about the crimes was part of the challenge, part of the game, even figuring out how to get the victims into the car without being suspicious. He told us that when he stopped his car for a pretty girl, he'd ask her where she was going, then glance at his watch as if trying to decide if he had enough time. Thinking that she was dealing with a busy man who had other more important priorities than stopping for hitchhikers would immediately put her at ease and erase any hesitations. Aside from giving us a look into a killer's modus operandi, this type of information would start suggesting something important: the normal common-sense assumptions, verbal cues, body language, and so on that we use to size up other people and make instant judgments about them often don't apply to sociopaths. With Ed Kemper, for instance, stopping for a pretty hitchhiker *was* his most important priority, and he had thought long, hard, and analytically about how best to accomplish his objective; much longer, harder, and more analytically than a young woman encountering him casually would have done from her perspective.

Manipulation. Domination. Control. These are the three watchwords of violent serial offenders. Everything they do and think about is directed toward assisting them in filling their otherwise inadequate lives.

Probably the most crucial single factor in the development of a serial rapist or killer is the role of fantasy. And I mean this in its broadest sense. Ed Kemper's fantasies developed early, and they all involved the relationship between sex and death. The game he made his sister play with him involved binding him to a chair as if he were in the gas chamber. His sexual fantasies involving others ended with the partner's death and dismemberment. Because of his feelings of inadequacy, Kemper didn't feel comfortable with normal boy-girl relationships. He didn't think any girl would have him. So in his own mind, he compensated. He had to completely possess his imagined partner, and that meant ultimately possessing her life.

"Alive, they were distant, not sharing with me," he explained in a confession introduced in court. "I was trying to establish a relationship. When they were being killed, there wasn't anything going on in my mind except that they were going to be mine."

With most sexually based killers, it is a several-step escalation from the fantasy to the reality, often fueled by pornography, morbid experimentation on animals, and cruelty to peers. This last trait can be seen by the subject as "getting back" at them for bad treatment. In Kemper's case, he felt shunned and tormented by the other children because of his size and personality. And he told us that before he dismembered the two family cats, he had stolen one of his sister's dolls and cut off its head and hands, practicing what he was planning for living beings.

On another level, Kemper's overriding fantasy was to rid himself of his domineering, abusive mother, and everything he did as a killer can be analyzed in that context. Please don't get me wrong; this in no way excuses what he did. Everything in my background and experience tells me that people are responsible for what they do. But in my opinion, Ed Kemper is an example of someone not born a serial killer but manufactured as one. Would he have had the same murderous fantasies had he had a more stable and nurturing home life? Who knows? But would he have acted on them in the same fashion had he not had this incredible rage against the dominant female personality in his life? I don't think so—because the entire progress of Kemper's career as a killer can be seen as an attempt to get back at dear old Mom. When he finally worked himself up to that final act, the drama was played out.

This was another characteristic we were to see over and over again. Seldom would the subject direct his anger at the focus of his resentment. Though Kemper told us he used to tiptoe into his mother's room at night with a hammer and fantasize bringing it down through her skull, it took him at least six killings before he could actually get up the nerve to face what he really wanted to do. And we've seen many other variations on this displacement theme. For example, a common trait is to take some "trophy" item from the victim after the murder, such as a ring or necklace. The killer would then give that item to his wife or girlfriend, even if that woman was the "source" of his anger or hostility. Typically, he would say he had purchased the jewelry or else found it. Then, seeing her wear it, he both relives the excitement and stimulation of the kill and mentally reasserts domination and control, knowing he could have done to his own partner what he did to his unfortunate victim.

Eventually, in our analysis, we would begin to break down the components of a crime into such elements as pre- and post-offense behavior. Kemper had mutilated each of his victims, which at first suggested to us a sexual sadist. But the mutilation was all postmortem, or after the victim's death, rather than while she was alive, thus not inflicting punishment and causing suffering. After listening to Kemper for several hours, it became clear that the dismemberment was more fetishistic than sadistic and had more to do with the possession part of the fantasy.

Equally significant, I thought, was his handling and disposal of the corpses. The early victims had been carefully buried far from his mother's home. The later ones, including his mother and her friend, had virtually been left out in the open. That, combined with his extensive driving around town with bodies and body parts in the car, seemed to me to be taunting the community he felt had taunted and rejected him.

We ended up doing several lengthy interviews with Kemper over the years, each one informative, each one harrowing in its detail. Here was a man who had coldly butchered intelligent young women in the prime of their lives. Yet I would be less than honest if I didn't admit that I liked Ed. He was friendly, open, sensitive, and had a good sense of humor. As much as you can say such a thing in this setting, I enjoyed being around him. I don't want him out walking the streets, and in his most lucid moments, neither does he. But my personal feelings about him then, which I still hold, do point up an important consideration for anyone dealing with repeat violent offenders. Many of these guys are quite charming, highly articulate, and glib.

How could this man do such a terrible thing? There must be some mistake or some extenuating circumstances. That's what you're going to say to yourself if you talk to some of them; you cannot get the full sense of the enormity of their crimes. And that's why psychiatrists and judges and parole officers are fooled so often, a subject we'll get into in more detail later on.

But for now: *if you want to understand the artist, look at his work.* That's what I always tell my people. You can't claim to understand or appreciate Picasso without studying his paintings. The successful serial killers plan their work as carefully as a painter plans a canvas. They consider what they do their "art," and they keep refining it as they go along. So part of my evaluation of someone like Ed Kemper comes from meeting him and interacting with him on a personal basis. The rest comes from studying and understanding his work.

• • •

The prison visits became a regular practice whenever Bob Ressler or I were on a road school and could get the time and cooperation. Wherever I found myself, I'd find out what prison or penitentiary was nearby and who of interest was "in residence."

Once we'd been doing this for a while, we refined our techniques. Generally, we were tied up four and a half days a week, so I tried to do some of the interviews on evenings and weekends. Evenings could be difficult because most prisons take a head count after dinner and no one is allowed into the cellblock after that. But after a while, you start to understand the prison regimens and adapt to them. I found that an FBI badge could get you into most penitentiaries and a meeting with the warden, so I began showing up unannounced, which often worked out best. The more of these interviews I did, the more confident I began to feel about what I was teaching and telling these veteran cops. I finally felt that my instruction was achieving some reality base, that it wasn't just recycled war stories from those who had actually been there.

It wasn't necessarily that the interviewees were providing profound insight into their crimes and psyches. Very few had that, even someone as bright as Kemper. Much of what they told us parroted their trial testimony or self-serving statements they'd made many times before. Everything had to be interpreted through hard work and extensive review on our part. What the interviews were doing, though, was letting us see the way the offender's mind worked, getting a feel for them, allowing us to start walking in their shoes.

In the early weeks and months of our informal research program, we managed to interview more than half a dozen killers and would-be killers. These included George Wallace's would-be assassin, Arthur Bremer (Baltimore Penitentiary), Sara Jane Moore and Lynette "Squeaky" Fromme, both of whom had tried to kill President Ford (Alderson,

West Virginia), and Fromme's guru, Charles Manson, at San Quentin, just up the bay from San Francisco and the rotting hulk of Alcatraz.

Everybody in law enforcement was interested in Manson. It had been ten years since the grisly Tate and LaBianca murders in Los Angeles, and Manson remained the most famous and feared convict in the world. The case was regularly taught at Quantico, and while the facts were clear, I didn't feel we had any real insight into what made this guy tick. I had no idea what we could expect to get from him, but I thought that anyone who had so successfully manipulated others to do his will would be an important subject. Bob Ressler and I met with him in a small conference area off the main cellblock at San Quentin. It had wire-reinforced glass windows on three sides, the kind of room set aside for inmates and their lawyers.

My first impression of Manson was just about diametrically opposite from what I had of Ed Kemper. He had wild, alert eyes and an unsettling, kinetic quality to the way he moved. He was much smaller and slighter than I'd imagined; no more than five two or five three. How did this weak-looking little guy exert such influence over his notorious "family"?

One answer came right away when he climbed onto the back of a chair positioned at the head of the table so he could look down on us as he talked. In the extensive background preparation I'd done for the interview, I'd read that he used to sit on top of a large boulder in the desert sand when he'd addressed his disciples, enhancing his physical stature for his sermons on the mount. He made it clear to us from the outset that despite the celebrated trial and voluminous news coverage, he didn't understand why he was in jail. After all, he hadn't killed anyone. Rather, he considered himself a societal scapegoat—the innocent symbol of America's dark side. The swastika he had carved into his forehead during the trial was faded but still visible. He was still in contact with his women followers in other prisons through cooperative third parties.

In one sense at least, he was very much like Ed Kemper and so many of the other men we talked to in that he had had a terrible childhood and upbringing; if those two terms can be used at all to describe Manson's background.

Charles Milles Manson was born in Cincinnati in 1934, the illegitimate son of a sixteen-year-old prostitute named Kathleen Maddox. His surname was merely a guess on Kathleen's part as to which of her lovers was the father. She was in and out of prison, pawning Charlie off on a religious aunt and sadistic uncle who called him a sissy, dressed him in girl's clothing for his first day of school, and challenged him to "act like a man." By the time he was ten, he was living on the streets, except for his terms in various group homes and reform schools. He lasted four days at Father Flanagan's Boys Town.

His young adult life was marked by a series of robberies, forgeries, pimpings, assaults, and incarcerations at increasingly tougher institutions. The FBI had investigated him under the Dyer Act for the interstate transport of stolen cars. He was paroled from his latest imprisonment in 1967, just in time for the "Summer of Love." He made his way to San Francisco's Haight-Ashbury district, the West Coast magnet for flower power and sex, drugs, and rock and roll. Looking primarily for a free ride, Manson quickly became a charismatic guru to the turned-on dropout generation still in their teens and twenties. He played the guitar and spoke in elliptical verities to disillusioned kids. Soon he was living for free, with all the sex and illicit stimulants he wanted. A nomadic "Family" of followers of both sexes gathered around him, sometimes numbering as many as fifty. As one of his services to the community, Charlie would preach his vision of the coming apocalypse and race war, which would leave the Family triumphant and him in control. His text was "Helter Skelter" from the Beatles' *White Album*.

On the night of August 9, 1969, four Manson Family members, led by Charles "Tex" Watson, broke into the secluded home of director Roman Polanski and his movie star wife, Sharon Tate, at 10050 Cielo Drive in Beverly Hills. Polanski was away on business, but Tate and four guests—Abigail Folger, Jay Sebring, Voytek Frykowski, and Steven Parent—were viciously slaughtered in a depraved orgy that included slogans scrawled on the walls and victims' bodies with their own blood. Sharon Tate was nearly nine months pregnant.

Two days later, at Manson's apparent instigation, six Family members killed and mutilated businessman Leno La-Bianca and his wife, Rosemary, in their home in the Silver Lake district of Los Angeles. Manson himself didn't participate, but came in the house afterward for the mayhem that followed. The subsequent arrest for prostitution of Susan Atkins, who had participated in both murders, and an arson involving a piece of highway equipment, ultimately led back to the Family and perhaps the most celebrated trials in California history, at least until the O. J. Simpson extravaganza. In two separate proceedings, Manson and several of his followers were sentenced to death for the Tate and LaBianca murders and a number of others traced to them, including the killing and mutilation of Donald "Shorty" Shea, a movie stuntman and Family hanger-on who was suspected of squealing to the police. When the state's capital-punishment laws were overturned, the sentences were reduced to life imprisonment.

Charlie Manson was not your routine serial killer. In fact, it was in dispute whether he'd actually murdered anyone with his own hands. Yet his bad background was beyond question, and so were the horrors his followers had committed at his instigation and in his name. I wanted to know how someone sets out to become this satanic messiah. We had to sit through hours of cheap philosophizing and ramblings, but as we pressed him for specifics and tried to cut through the bullshit, an image began to emerge.

Charlie hadn't set out to be the dark guru. His goal was fame and fortune. He wanted to be a drummer and play for a famous rock band like the Beach Boys. He had been forced to live by his wits his entire life and so had become extremely adept at sizing up the people he met and quickly determining what they could do for him. He would have been excellent in my unit assessing an individual's psychological strengths and weaknesses and strategizing how to get to a killer we were hunting.

When he arrived in San Francisco after his parole, he saw vast hordes of confused, naive, idealistic kids who looked up to him for his life experience and the seeming wisdom he spouted. Many of them, particularly the young girls, had had problems with their fathers and could relate to Charlie's past, and he was astute enough to be able to pick them out. He became a paternal figure, one who could fill their empty lives with sex and the enlightenment of drugs. You can't be in the same room with Charlie Manson and not be affected by his eyes—deep and penetrating, wild and hypnotic. He knew what his eyes could do and what effect they could have. He told us he had spent his early life getting the shit beaten out of him, and with his small stature, there was no way he could win a physical confrontation. So he compensated by invoking the force of his personality.

What he preached made perfect sense: pollution is destroying the environment, racial prejudice is ugly and destructive, love is right and hate is wrong. But once he had these lost souls in his sway, he instituted a highly structured delusional system that left him in complete control of their minds and bodies. He used sleep deprivation, sex, food control, and drugs to gain complete dominance, like a prisoner-of-war situation. Everything was black-and-white and only Charlie knew the truth. He'd strum his guitar and repeat his simple mantra over and over again: only Charlie could redeem the sick and rotting society.

The basic dynamics of leadership and group authority that Manson described for us we were to see repeated over the years in subsequent tragedies of similar dimension. The power over and understanding of inadequate people that Manson possessed would be revisited by the Reverend Jim Jones and the mass murder–suicide of his flock in Guyana, then again by David Koresh at the Branch Davidian compound in Waco, Texas, to name but two. And despite the glaring differences among these three men, what links them together is striking. Insight we got from talking to Manson and his followers contributed to our understanding of Koresh and his actions and other cults.

At the heart of it, the issue with Manson wasn't this messianic vision but simple control. The "helter-skelter" preaching was a way to maintain the mind control. But as Manson came to realize, unless you can exert this control over your flock twenty-four hours a day, you risk losing it. David Koresh realized this and holed up his devotees in a rural fortress where they couldn't leave or be away from his influence.

After listening to Manson, I believe that he did not plan or intend the murders of Sharon Tate and her friends; that, in fact, *he lost control* of the situation and his followers. The choice of the site and victims was apparently arbitrary. One of the Manson girls had been there and thought there was money around. Tex Watson, the good-looking, all-American honor student from Texas, sought to rise in the hierarchy and rival Charlie for influence and authority. Zoned out like the others on LSD and having bought into the leader's new tomorrow, Watson was the primary killer and led the mission to the Tate-Polanski house and encouraged the others to the ultimate depravities.

Then, when these inadequate nobodies came back and told Charlie what they had done, that helter-skelter had begun, he couldn't very well back down and tell them they had taken him too seriously. That would have destroyed his power and authority. So he had to do them one better, as if he had intended the crime and its aftermath, leading them to the LaBianca home to do it again. But significantly, when I asked Manson why he hadn't gone in and participated in the killings, he explained, as if we were dense, that he was on parole at the time and couldn't risk his freedom by violating that.

So I believe from the background information and the interviews we did with Manson that while he made his followers into what he needed, they, in turn, made him into what they needed and forced him to fulfill it.

Every couple of years, Manson comes up for parole and has been turned down every time. His crimes were too publicized and too brutal for the parole board to take a chance on him. I don't want him let out, either. But if he were released at some point, knowing what I do about him, I wouldn't expect him to be a serious violent threat like a lot of these guys are. I think he'd go off into the desert and live out there, or else try to cash in on his celebrity for money. But I wouldn't expect him to kill. The biggest threat would be from the misguided losers who would gravitate to him and proclaim him their god and leader.

By the time Ressler and I had done ten or twelve prison interviews, it was clear to any reasonably intelligent observer that we were onto something. For the first time, we were able to correlate what was going on in an offender's mind with the evidence he left at a crime scene.

In 1979, we'd received about fifty requests for profiles, which the instructors tried to handle between their teaching responsibilities. By the next year, the caseload had doubled and would double again the next. By then, I had pretty much been relieved of teaching and was the only one in the unit devoting full time to operational work. I would still give presentations to National Academy and agent classes as my schedule allowed, but unlike the others, for me teaching had now become a sideline. I did virtually all the homicide cases that came into the unit and whichever rape cases Roy Hazelwood was too busy to handle.

What had been an informal service without official sanction was developing into a small institution. I took on the newly created title of "criminal-personality profiling program manager" and started working with the field offices to coordinate the submission of cases by local police departments.

At one point, I was in the hospital for a week or so. My old football and boxing injuries had messed up my nose, which had made breathing progressively more difficult, and I was in getting my twisted septum straightened out. I remember lying there hardly able to see and having one of the other agents come in and drop twenty case files on my bed.

We were learning more and more with each new prison encounter, but there had to be a way to organize the informal research into a systematized, usable framework. And that step forward came through Roy Hazelwood, with whom I was collaborating on an article about lust murder for the *FBI Law Enforcement Bulletin*. Roy had done some research with Dr. Ann Burgess, a professor of psychiatric mental-health nursing at the University of Pennsylvania School of Nursing and associate director of nursing research for the Boston Department of Health and Hospitals. Burgess was a prolific author and already widely known as one of the nation's leading authorities on rape and its psychological consequences.

Roy brought her to the Behavioral Science Unit, introduced her to Bob and me, and described what we were doing. She was impressed and told us she thought we had an opportunity to do research of a kind that had never been done before in this field. She thought we could contribute toward understanding criminal behavior in the same way *DSM*—the *Diagnostic and Statistical Manual of Mental Disorders*—

had toward the understanding and organization of types of mental illness.

We agreed to work together, with Ann pursuing and eventually obtaining a $400,000 grant from the government-sponsored National Institute of Justice. The goal was to exhaustively interview thirty-six to forty incarcerated felons and see what kinds of conclusions we could draw. With our input, Ann developed a fifty-seven-page instrument to be filled out for each interview. Bob would administer the grant and be the liaison with NIJ, and he and I, with help from agents in the field, would go back into the prisons and face the subjects. We would describe the methodology of each crime and crime scene, and study and document the pre- and postoffense behavior, Ann would crunch the numbers, and we'd write up our results. We expected the project to take about three or four years.

And in that time, criminal-investigative analysis came into the modern age.

7

The Heart of Darkness

The question logically arises, why would convicted felons cooperate with federal law enforcement agents? We wondered about that ourselves when we began the project. However, the overwhelming majority of those we've approached over the years do agree to talk to us, and they do so for a number of reasons.

Some of them are genuinely bothered by their crimes and feel that cooperating on a psychological study is a way to make some partial amends and also come to a better understanding of themselves. I think Ed Kemper fits into this category. Others, as I've indicated, are police and law enforcement buffs and just enjoy being near cops and FBI agents. Some think there might be some benefit in cooperating with the "authorities," though we've never promised anything in return. Some feel ignored and forgotten and just want the attention and the relief from boredom that a visit from us represents. And some simply welcome the opportunity to relive their murderous fantasies in graphic detail.

We wanted to hear whatever these men had to tell us, but we were primarily interested in several basic questions, which we outlined in an article explaining the goals of the study in the September 1980 issue of the *FBI Law Enforcement Bulletin.*

1. What leads a person to become a sexual offender and what are the early warning signals?
2. What serves to encourage or to inhibit the commission of his offense?

3. What types of response or coping strategies by an intended victim are successful with what type of sexual offender in avoiding victimization?
4. What are the implications for his dangerousness, prognosis, disposition, and mode of treatment?

For this program to be valuable, we understood, we would have to be fully prepared and be instantly able to filter what each man told us. Because if you're reasonably intelligent, as many of these guys are, you're going to find a weakness in the system that you can use to your advantage. By their very nature, most serial offenders are good manipulators. If it'll help your case to be mentally unstable, you can be mentally unstable. If it'll help your case to be remorseful and contrite, you can be remorseful and contrite. But whatever seemed to them to be the best course of action to follow, I found that the people who agreed to talk to us were all similar. They had nothing else to think about, so they spent a lot of time thinking about themselves and what they'd done and could give it back to me in minute detail. Our task was to know enough about them and their crimes in advance to make sure they were telling us the truth, because they'd also had enough time to construct alternate scenarios that made them much more sympathetic or guiltless than the record would indicate.

In many of the early interviews, after hearing our convict's story, I'd want to turn to Bob Ressler or whoever was with me and say, "Could he have been railroaded? He had a sensible answer to everything. I wonder if they really got the right guy." So the first thing we'd do when we got back to Quantico was check the record and contact the local police jurisdiction for the case file to make sure there hadn't been some horrible miscarriage of justice.

Growing up as a boy in Chicago, Bob Ressler had been terrified and intrigued by the murder of six-year-old Suzanne Degnan, who had been snatched from her house and killed. Her body was discovered cut up in pieces in the sewers of Evanston. A young man named William Heirens was eventually caught and confessed to the killing and the murders of two other women in an apartment building as part of some burglaries that escalated out of control. In one of them, the murder of Frances Brown, he had scrawled on the wall with her lipstick:

> For heAVens
> SAke cAtch Me
> BeFore I Kill More
> I cannot control myselF

Heirens attributed the murders to a George Murman (probably short for "murder man"), who he claimed lived inside him. Bob has said that the Heirens case was probably one of his early motivations for pursuing a career in law enforcement.

Once the Criminal Personality Research Project was funded and under way, Bob and I went to interview Heirens at Statesville Prison in Joliet, Illinois. He had been incarcerated since his conviction in 1946 and had been a model prisoner for all that time, the first one in the state to complete his college degree. He then went on to graduate work.

By the time we interviewed him, Heirens was denying any connection to the crimes, saying he was railroaded. No matter what we asked him, he had an answer, insisted he had an alibi and wasn't even close to any of the murder scenes. He was so convincing and I was so concerned there might have been a massive miscarriage of justice that when we got back to Quantico, I dug out all the case files. In addition to the confession and other compelling evidence, I found that his latent fingerprints had been lifted from the Degnan crime scene. Yet Heirens had spent so much time sitting in his cell and thinking and giving himself all the answers that if they polygraphed him at that point, he would probably have passed with no trouble.

• • •

Richard Speck, who was serving consecutive life sentences for the murder of eight student nurses in a South Chicago town house in 1966, made it clear he didn't want to be lumped with the other killers we were studying. "I don't want to be on that list with them," he told me. "They're crazy, these people. I'm not a serial killer." He didn't deny what he'd done, he just wanted us to know he wasn't like them.

On one key level, Speck was correct. He wasn't a serial killer, who kills repeatedly with some emotional cycling or cooling-off period between his crimes. He was what I characterized as a mass murderer, who kills more than twice as part of the same act. In Speck's case, he went to the house with burglary as his motive, trying to get money to get out of town. When twenty-three-year-old Corazon Amurao answered the door, he forced his way in with a pistol and knife, saying he was only going to tie her and her five roommates up and rob them. He herded them all into a bedroom. Over the next hour, three more women came home from dates or studying at the library. Once he had them all in his power, Speck apparently changed his mind, engaging in a frenzy of rape, strangling, stabbing, and slashing. Only Amurao survived, huddling terrified in the corner. Speck had lost count.

After he left, she went out on the balcony and called down for help. She told police about the "Born to Raise Hell" tattoo on the attacker's left forearm. When Richard Franklin Speck showed up in a local hospital a week later after a bungled suicide attempt, he was identified by the tattoo.

Because of the brazen brutality of his crime, Speck had been the subject of all kinds of speculation from the medical and psychological communities. Initially, it had been announced that Speck had a genetic imbalance, an additional male (Y) chromosome, which was thought to increase aggressive and antisocial behavior. These vogues come and go with some regularity. More than a hundred years ago, the behaviorists of the times used phrenology—the study of skull shape—to predict character and mental ability. More recently, it was thought that an electroencephalograph reading showing a repeating fourteen-and-six-spike pattern was evidence of severe personality disorder. The jury is still out on the XYY issue, but the indisputable fact is that many, many men have this genetic makeup and display no extraordinary aggressiveness or antisocial behavior. And to cap things off, when a detailed study was performed on Richard Speck, it was found that his genetic makeup was perfectly normal—he didn't even have the extra Y.

Speck, who has since died in prison of a heart attack, didn't want to talk to us. His was one of the unusual cases where we had contacted the warden, who'd agreed to allow us in, but he didn't think it was a good idea to let Speck know in advance of our visit. When we arrived, we concurred. We could hear him screaming and cursing from a holding pen where he'd been taken so we could look at his cell. The other prisoners were going nuts in sympathy with him. The warden wanted to show us the kind of pornography Speck kept, but Speck was protesting furiously over this violation of his space. Prisoners hate anything resembling a shakedown. Their cells are the only semblance of privacy they've got left. As we walked down the three-tiered cellblock at Joliet, windows broken and birds flying up near the ceiling, the warden warned us to stay close to the center so that prisoners couldn't reach us with urine or feces.

Realizing this wasn't getting us anywhere, I whispered to the warden that we'd just keep walking down the corridor without stopping at Speck's cell. With the subject-interview guidelines in effect today, we might not have been able to spring ourselves on him unannounced. In fact, the entire criminal-personality study would be much more difficult to put together now.

Unlike Kemper or Heirens, Speck wasn't exactly a model

prisoner. He had once built and hidden a crude miniature still in the back of a false drawer in the cellblock guard's wooden desk. It produced hardly any alcohol, just enough to create a smell and make the guards go crazy when they couldn't find it. Another time, he found an injured sparrow that had flown in through one of the broken windows and nursed it back to health. When it was healthy enough to stand, he tied a string around its leg and had it perch on his shoulder. At one point, a guard told him pets weren't allowed.

"I can't have it?" Speck challenged, then walked over to a spinning fan and threw the small bird in.

Horrified, the guard said, "I thought you liked that bird."

"I did," Speck replied. "But if I can't have it, no one can."

Bob Ressler and I met him in an interview room at Joliet, accompanied by his prison counselor, something akin to a guidance counselor in high school. Like Manson, Speck chose the head of the table, sitting on a credenza so he could be above us. I started out by telling Speck what we wanted to do, but he wouldn't talk to us, only ranting about the "motherfucking FBI" who wanted to look in his cell.

When I look at these guys, when I sit across a table from them in a prison conference room, the first thing I try to do is visualize what they must have looked like and sounded like when they were doing the crimes. I've prepared myself with all of the case files so I know what each has done and what he's capable of, and what I have to do is project this onto the individual sitting across from me.

Any police-type interrogation is a seduction; each party is trying to seduce the other into giving him what he wants. And you have to size up the individual interviewee before you can figure out how to approach him. Outrage or moral judgment won't accomplish anything. ("What, you sadistic beast! You ate an arm?") You have to decide what's going to ring his bell. With some, like Kemper, you can be straightforward and matter-of-fact, so long as you make clear you know the facts and they can't snow you. With the ones like Richard Speck, I learned to take a more offensive approach.

We're sitting there in the conference room and Speck's making a show of ignoring us, so I turn to the counselor. He was an open, gregarious man, experienced at diffusing hostility—some of the qualities we look for in hostage negotiators. I talk about Speck as if he weren't even in the room.

"You know what he did, your guy? He killed eight pussies. And some of those pussies looked pretty good. He took eight good pieces of ass away from the rest of us. You think that's fair?"

Bob is clearly uncomfortable with this. He doesn't want to get down to the killer's level, and he's squeamish about mocking the dead. Of course, I agree, but in situations like this, I think you do what you have to.

The counselor answers me in kind and we go back and forth like that. We would have sounded like high school boys in the locker room if we weren't actually talking about murder victims, which shifts the tone from immature to grotesque.

Speck listens for a while, shakes his head, chuckles, and says, "You fucking guys are crazy. It must be a fine line, separates you from me."

With that opening I turn to him. "How in the hell did you fuck eight women at the same time? What do you eat for breakfast?"

He looks at us as if we're a couple of gullible rubes. "I didn't fuck all of them. That story got all out of proportion. I just fucked one of them."

"The one on the couch?" I ask.

"Yeah."

As crude and disgusting as this all sounds, it's starting to tell me something. First of all, as hostile and aggressive as he is, he doesn't have much of a macho self-image. He knows he can't control all the women at once. He's an opportunist—he'll rape one for the hell of it. And from the crime-scene photos, we know that the one he chose was facedown on the couch. She was already a depersonalized body to him. He didn't have to have any human contact with her. We can also tell he's not a sophisticated or organized thinker. It doesn't take much for what would have been a relatively simple and successful robbery to degenerate into this mass murder. He admits that he killed the women not in a sexual frenzy, but so that they couldn't identify him. As the young nurses come home, he's putting one in a bedroom, one in a closet, as if he's corralling horses. He has no idea how to handle the situation.

Interestingly, he also claims that the wound that sent him to the hospital and ultimately to capture did not represent a suicide attempt but rather was the result of a bar fight. Without necessarily understanding the significance of what he's saying, he's telling us he wants us to think of him as the "born to raise hell" macho man rather than a pathetic loser whose only way out is to kill himself.

Now, as I'm listening, I'm starting to turn all of this information around in my mind. Not only is it telling me something about Speck, it's telling me something about this type of crime. In other words, when I see similar scenarios in the future, I'm going to have more insight into the type of individual responsible. And that, of course, was the main purpose of the program.

As we processed the study's data, I tried to get away from the academic, psychological jargon and buzzwords and more into clear-cut concepts that would be of use to law enforcement personnel. To tell a local detective that he's looking for a paranoid schizophrenic may be intellectually interesting, but it doesn't tell him much that's useful in catching his UNSUB. One of the key distinctions we came up with was whether an offender was *organized* or *disorganized* or showed a mixed pattern. People like Speck were beginning to give us the pattern of the disorganized offender.

Speck told me he had a troubled early life. The only time I could tell we'd touched a nerve was when I asked him about his family. By the time he was twenty, he had chalked up nearly forty arrests and had married a fifteen-year-old girl, with whom he fathered a child. He left her five years later, angry and bitter, and told us he just never got around to killing her. He did kill several other women, though, including a waitress in a sleazy bar who'd spurned his advances. He also robbed and attacked a sixty-five-year-old woman a couple of months before he murdered the nurses. All things being equal, the brutal rape of an older woman suggests to us a young man, possibly even a teenager, without much experience or confidence or sophistication. Speck was twenty-six when the rape occurred. As the age of the offender goes up in the equation, his sophistication and self-confidence go down accordingly. That was certainly my impression of Richard Speck. Though in his mid-twenties, his behavior level, even for a criminal, was late adolescent.

The warden wanted to show me one more thing before we left. In Joliet, as well as in other prisons, a psychological experiment was under way to see if soft pastel colors would decrease aggressiveness. A good deal of academic theory was behind this. They'd even put police weight-lifting champs in rooms painted pink or yellow and found they couldn't lift as much as they had before.

So the warden takes us to a room at the end of the cell block and says, "The rose-colored paint is supposed to take the aggression out of a violent offender. And if you put them in a room like this, they're supposed to get really calm and passive. Take a look inside this room, Douglas, and tell me what you see."

"I see there's not much paint on the walls," I observe.

He replies, "Yeah, that's right. See, the guys don't like these colors. They're peeling the paint off the wall, and they're eating it."

• • •

Jerry Brudos was a shoe fetishist. If that were as far as it went, there would have been no problem. But due to a variety of circumstances, including his punitive, domineering mother and his own compulsions, it went a lot further—from mildly strange all the way to deadly.

Jerome Henry Brudos was born in South Dakota in 1939 and grew up in California. As a young boy five years old, he found a pair of shiny high heels at a local dump. When he brought them home and tried them on, his mother, furious, told him to get rid of them. But he kept them, hidden, until his mother found out, took them away, burned them, and punished him. By the time he was sixteen, now living in Oregon, he was regularly breaking into neighborhood homes and stealing women's shoes and eventually underwear, which he would save and try on. The next year he was arrested for assaulting a girl he had lured into his car so he could get to see her naked. He was given several months of therapy at the state hospital in Salem, where he was not found to be dangerous. After high school, he did a brief stint in the Army before leaving on a psychological discharge. He was still breaking into houses, and stealing shoes and underwear—sometimes confronting the women he found there and choking them unconscious—when, out of a sense of obligation, he married the young woman with whom he had recently lost his virginity. He went to a vocational college and became an electronics technician.

Six years later, in 1968, now the father of two children and continuing his nighttime raids for souvenirs, Brudos answered the door to a nineteen-year-old named Linda Slawson, who had an appointment to sell encyclopedias and had come to the wrong house by mistake. Seizing this opportunity, he dragged her into the basement, and bludgeoned and strangled her. When she was dead, he undressed her and tried various of his collected outfits on the corpse. Before disposing of the body by sinking it in the Willamette River with a junked automobile transmission, he cut off the left foot, placed it in one of his prized high heels, and locked it in his freezer. He killed three more times over the next several months, cutting off breasts and making plastic molds of them. He was identified by various coeds he'd approached for dates using a similar story and was picked up when police staked out a supposed rendezvous site. He confessed and eventually pleaded guilty when it became clear an insanity defense wouldn't work.

Bob Ressler and I interviewed him in his permanent home at the Oregon State Penitentiary at Salem. He was heavyset and round-faced, polite and cooperative. But when I asked him specifics about the crimes, he said he'd blacked out because of hypoglycemia and didn't remember anything he might have done.

"You know, John, I get this attack of low blood sugar, and I could walk off the roof of a building and not know what I was doing."

Interestingly enough, when Brudos confessed to police, he remembered well enough to give them graphic details of the crimes and where the bodies and evidence could be found. He also inadvertently incriminated himself. He'd hung the body of one of his victims from a hook in his garage, clothed her in his favorite attire and shoes, then placed a mirror on the floor beneath her to see up her dress. While taking a picture, he'd unknowingly captured his own image in the photograph.

Despite his claims of hypoglycemic blackouts, Brudos showed many of the traits of an organized offender. This was tied in to the fantasy element he displayed from an early age. When he was a young teen living on the family farm, he fantasized about capturing girls in a tunnel where he would force them to do what he wanted. Once, he managed to trick a girl into the barn, then ordered her to undress so he could take her picture. We saw this type of behavior carry over into his adult offenses, yet as a young teenager, he was too naive and unsophisticated to think of anything other than photographing his naked victims. After the session in the barn, he locked the girl in the corncrib, then came back sometime later, wearing different clothes and with his hair combed differently, pretending to be Ed, Jerry's twin brother. He released the terrified girl, explaining that Jerry was undergoing intense therapy and begging her not to tell anyone lest he get in trouble and suffer another "setback."

What we see clearly in Jerome Brudos, along with this textbook escalation of activities, is a continual refinement of the fantasy. This is a much more significant finding than anything he could have told us directly. Even though a Kemper and a Brudos are so different in goals and modus operandi, we see in both—and so many of the others—an obsession with and "improvement" of the details from one crime to the next and one level of activity to the next. Kemper's victims of choice were beautiful coeds tied in his mind to his mother. The less sophisticated and intelligent Brudos was more content with victims of opportunity. But the obsession with detail was the same and took over both men's lives.

As an adult, Brudos made his wife, Darcie, dress in his fetishistic attire and submit to his photographic ritual, even though she was a straight, unadventuresome woman who was uncomfortable with this and scared of her husband. He had elaborate fantasies of constructing a torture suite but had to settle for his garage. In that garage was the freezer he kept locked so he could store his favorite body parts. When Darcie cooked meat for dinner, she had to tell Jerry what it was she wanted, and then he would bring it to her. She often complained to friends that it would be so much easier to look in the freezer herself and select a particular cut. Yet despite the inconvenience, she didn't think it odd enough to report. Or if she did, she was too afraid to do so.

Brudos was a near classic example of an offender who begins with innocuous oddities and escalates progressively—from found shoes to his sister's clothing to the possessions of other women. First he just steals from clotheslines, then he stalks women who are wearing high heels and breaks into empty houses, then gets bolder and is willing to confront the occupants. At first, merely putting on the clothing is enough, but eventually he wants more of a kick. Socially, he begins to ask girls to let him take pictures of them. Then, when one of them refuses to undress for him, he threatens her with a knife. He doesn't kill until a victim of opportunity happens to ring his doorbell. But once he's killed her and realizes the satisfaction, he's moved to do it again and again, each time stepping up his mutilation of the corpse.

I'm not meaning to suggest that every man attracted to stiletto heels or turned on by the thought of black lace bras and panties is destined for a life of crime. If that were true, most of us would be in prison. But as we see in Jerry Brudos, this kind of paraphilia can be degenerative, and it is also "situational." Let me give an example.

Some time ago, not far from where I lived, an elementary school principal reportedly had a thing for children's feet. He would play a game with them to see how long he could tickle their feet or toes. If they held out for a certain time, he would give them money. It came to parental attention when some of the kids were spending money at the mall they couldn't account for. When the principal was fired by the school district, many quarters of the community protested. He was a good-looking guy, he had a normal relationship with a steady girlfriend, and he was popular with children and parents alike. The teachers thought he was being railroaded. Even if he did have this thing for toes, it was essentially harmless. He'd never abused any of the children or tried to get them to undress. This is not the kind of person who's going to go out and abduct a child to feed his perversion.

I agreed with that assessment. The community was in no danger from him in that regard. I had met him and he was friendly and personable. But let's say during one of these games a little girl reacts badly, starts screaming or threatens to tell on him. In an instant of panic, he could end up killing the child simply because he doesn't know what else to do to manage the situation. When the school superintendent contacted my unit for advice, I told him I thought he had taken the right action in firing the man.

Around the same time, I was called down to the University of Virginia, where college girls were getting pushed to the ground and their clog-type shoes stolen in the melee. Fortunately, none of the women were badly hurt, and the local and campus police were treating the cases as something of a joke. I met with them and with the university administration, told them about Brudos and others I'd had experience with, and by the time I left I'd succeeded in my mission of putting the fear of God into them. The official attitude changed considerably after that, and I'm pleased to say there were no further incidents.

When I look at Jerry Brudos's criminal progression, I have to ask myself whether understanding and intervention at any of the earliest stages could have short-circuited the ultimate process.

In Ed Kemper, I felt I saw a serial killer manufactured by an emotionally harrowing childhood. I found Jerry Brudos's case somewhat more complex. Clearly, his particular paraphilia was with him from a very early age. He was a small child when he became fascinated by the pair of high heels he found in the junkyard. But part of his fascination could have been never having seen anything like them before. They were nothing like what his mother wore. Then, when she reacted so vociferously, they became forbidden fruit to him. Not too long after, he stole shoes belonging to his teacher. Yet when she found out, he was surprised by her reaction. Rather than reproving him, she was curious to know why he'd done this. So he was already getting mixed messages from adult women about what he was doing, and a presumably inborn urge was gradually being transformed into something sinister and far more deadly.

What would have happened had the dangerousness of his progression been recognized, and some productive means been tried to deal with his feelings? By the time of the first kill, it's way too late. But at any step along the way, could the process have been short-circuited? Through the study and my work since then, I've become very, very pessimistic about anything remotely akin to rehabilitation for most sexually motivated killers. If anything has a hope of working, it has to come at a much earlier stage, before they get to the point at which fantasy becomes reality.

When my sister, Arlene, was a teenager, my mom used to say she could tell a lot about the boys Arlene was going out with by asking them how they felt about their mothers. If the boy professed love and respect for his mother, that would probably reflect his relationships with other women in his life. If he thought of his mother as a bitch or whore or ball-buster, chances were pretty darn good he'd end up treating other women the same way.

From my experience, my mom's observation was right on the money. Ed Kemper cut a trail of destruction through Santa Cruz, California, before he finally worked up the nerve to kill the one woman he truly hated. Monte Rissell, who raped and murdered five women as a teenager in Alexandria, Virginia, told us that if he had been allowed to go with his father instead of his mother when their seriously troubled marriage broke up, he thought he'd be a lawyer now rather than a lifer at the Richmond Penitentiary, where we interviewed him.

With Monte Ralph Rissell, we were able to start piecing together more parts of the puzzle. At seven, Monte was the youngest of three children at the time of the divorce, and his mother uprooted them and moved to California, where she remarried and spent much of the time alone with her new husband, leaving the kids with little adult supervision. Monte started getting into trouble early—writing obscene graffiti at school, then drugs, then shooting a cousin with a BB gun after an argument. He claimed that his stepfather had given him the rifle and, after the impulsive shooting, smashed it apart and hit Monte repeatedly with the barrel.

When Monte was twelve, this second marriage broke apart and the family moved back to Virginia. Monte told us he thought he and his sister were responsible. From then on, his crime career escalated: driving without a license, burglary, car theft, then rape.

His transition to murder was very instructive. Still in high school, on probation and receiving psychiatric counseling as a provision of the probation, he receives a letter from his girlfriend. She's a year ahead of him in school and now away at college. The letter told Monte that their relationship was over. He promptly gets in his car and drives up to the college, where he spots the girl with a new boyfriend.

Rather than do anything overt or take his rage out on the person who caused it, he drives back home to Alexandria, fortifies himself with some beer and marijuana, and spends hours sitting in his car in the parking lot of his apartment complex ruminating.

Around two or three in the morning, he's still there when another car appears, driven by a single woman. On the spur of the moment, Rissell decides to get back what he's just lost. He goes up to the woman's car, pulls a handgun on her, and forces her to go with him to a secluded area near the complex.

Rissell was calm, deliberate, and precise as he recounted his actions to Bob Ressler and me. I'd checked his IQ beforehand, and it was above 120. I can't say I detected a lot of remorse or contrition—except for the rare offenders who turn themselves in or commit suicide, the remorse is primarily over getting caught and going to jail. But he didn't try to minimize his crimes and I did feel he was giving us an accurate account. And the behavior he had just described, and was about to describe, contained several key insights.

First of all, this incident takes place after a triggering event or incident—what we came to call a stressor. And we would see this pattern over and over again. Anything can be a triggering stressor; different things bother each of us. But the two most common ones, not surprisingly, are losing your job and losing your wife or girlfriend. (I use the feminine here because, as I've noted, virtually all of these killers are men, for reasons I'll speculate about later.)

As a result of studying people like Monte Rissell, we came to realize that these stressors are so much a part of the serial murder dynamic that when we see certain circumstances at a crime scene, we feel comfortable predicting exactly what the stressor was in the particular case. In Jud Ray's Alaskan murder case, which I mentioned in chapter 4, the timing and details of the triple homicide of a woman and her two young daughters led Jud to predict the killer had lost his girlfriend *and* his job. Both of these traumas had taken place. In fact, the girlfriend had dumped the subject for his boss, who had then fired him to get him out of the picture.

So on the night that he sees his girl with a college man, Monte Rissell commits his first murder. This is significant enough in itself. But exactly how and why it happens tells us even more.

It turns out by happenstance that Rissell's victim is a prostitute, which means two things: she's not going to have the same fear of sex with a stranger that someone outside the profession would; and though scared, she'll probably have a pretty good survival instinct. So when he's got her all alone and it's clear he intends to rape her at gunpoint, she tries to diffuse the situation by hiking up her skirt and asking her attacker how he likes it and what position he wants her in.

"She asked which way I wanted it," he told us.

But rather than making him gentler or more sensitive, this behavior on her part only enrages him. "It's like this bitch is trying to control things." She apparently faked two or three orgasms to placate him, but this made things worse. If she could "enjoy" this rape, it reinforced his feeling that women are whores. She became depersonalized, and it was easy to think about killing her.

Yet he did let another victim go when she told him she was caring for her father, who was suffering from cancer. Rissell's brother had had cancer, so he identified with her. She had become personalized to him, just the opposite of this prostitute, or the young nurse Richard Speck had attacked as she lay bound and facedown on the couch.

But this does point out why it is so difficult to give general advice on what to do in a rape situation. Depending on the personality of the rapist and his motivation for the crime, either going along or trying to talk your way out of being assaulted may be the best course of action. Or it may make things worse. Resisting or struggling with the so-called "power reassurance rapist" might stop him in his tracks. Resisting the "anger excitation rapist," unless the victim's strong enough or quick enough to get away from him, could get a victim killed. Trying to make the act seem pleasurable because the rapist is sexually inadequate isn't necessarily the best strategy. These are crimes of anger and hostility and the assertion of power. The sex is only incidental.

After the rape of the woman abducted from the parking lot, as angry as he is, Rissell hasn't yet decided what to do with his victim. But at this point she does what many of us would perceive to be the logical thing: she tries to run away. This makes him feel even more that she's controlling the situation, not him. As we quoted Rissell in an article on the study for the *American Journal of Psychiatry*: "She took off running down the ravine. That's when I grabbed her. I had her in an armlock. She was bigger than me. I started choking her . . . she stumbled . . . we rolled down the hill and into the water. I banged her head against the side of a rock and held her head underwater."

What we were learning was that the behavior of the victim is equally as important in analyzing the crime as the behavior of the subject. Was this a high- or low-risk victim? What did she say or do, and did that egg the subject on or pull him back? What was their encounter all about?

Rissell's victims of choice were merely close by—in and around his apartment complex. And once he had killed, that taboo was gone. He realized he could do it, enjoy it, and get away with it. If we'd been called into this case and were profiling an UNSUB, we would expect to see some experience in his background—some violent crime short of murder—which, in fact, there was. Quite frankly, what we probably would have gotten wrong, at least initially, was the age. At the time of this first kill, Rissell was barely nineteen. We would have expected a man in his mid- to late twenties.

But Rissell's case demonstrates that age is a relative concept in our work. In 1989, Gregg McCrary from my unit was called into a baffling series of prostitute murders in Rochester, New York. Working closely with Capt. Lynde Johnson and a first-rate police force, Gregg developed a detailed profile and suggested a strategy that ultimately led to the arrest and successful prosecution of Arthur Shawcross. When we reviewed the profile afterward, we found that Gregg had nailed him almost precisely—race, personality, type of job, home life, car, hobbies, familiarity with the area, relationship to the police; virtually everything except the age. Gregg had predicted a man in his late twenties to about thirty with some already established comfort level for murder. In fact, Shawcross was forty-five. It turned out he'd been in prison for fifteen years for the murder of two young children (like prostitutes and the elderly, children are vulnerable targets), which had essentially put him on hold. Within months of his parole, he picked up where he'd left off.

Just as Arthur Shawcross was on parole at the time of his murders, so was Monte Rissell. And like Ed Kemper, he was able to convince a psychiatrist he was making excellent progress while he was actually killing human beings. This is kind of a sick version of the old joke about how many psychiatrists it takes to change a lightbulb—the answer being just one, but only if the lightbulb *wants* to change. Psychiatrists and mental health professionals are accustomed to using self-reporting on the part of the subject to track his progress, and this assumes the patient wants to get "well." It has turned out to be incredibly easy to fool many psychiatrists, and most of the good ones will say that the only fairly reliable predictor of violence is a past history of violence. One of the things I hope we've accomplished with the criminal-personality study and our work since then is to make the mental health community aware of the limitations of self-reporting where criminal behavior is concerned. By his very nature, a serial killer or rapist is manipulative, narcissistic, and totally egocentric. He will tell a parole officer or prison psychiatrist whatever he or she wants to hear, whatever it will take to get out of prison or stay on the streets.

As Rissell described his subsequent kills to us, we saw a steady progression. He was annoyed by his second victim's barraging him with questions: "She wanted to know why I wanted to do this; why I picked her; didn't I have a girlfriend; what was my problem; what was I going to do."

She was driving the car at gunpoint, and like the first, she tried to escape. At that point, he realized he had to kill her, stabbing her repeatedly in the chest.

By the time of the third kill, it was all pretty easy. He'd learned from his previous experience and wouldn't let this victim talk to him; he had to keep her depersonalized. "I was thinking . . . I've killed two. I might as well kill this one, too."

At this point in the progression he released the woman caring for her father with cancer. But by the final two murders, his intention was well established. He drowned one and stabbed the other—between fifty and a hundred times by his own estimate.

Like virtually all the others, Rissell showed us that the fantasy was in place long before the actual rapes or murders began. We asked him where he'd gotten his ideas. They came from a number of places as it turned out, but one of them, he said, was reading about David Berkowitz.

David Berkowitz, known first as the ".44-Caliber Killer" and then as the "Son of Sam" after he began writing to newspapers during his reign of terror in New York City, was more of an assassin personality than a typical serial killer. Over almost exactly a year—from July 1976 to July 1977—six young men and women were killed and more were wounded, all parked in lovers' lanes, all shot in their cars with a powerful handgun.

Like a number of serial killers, Berkowitz was the product of an adopted family, which he didn't know until about the time he was in the Army. He'd wanted to be sent to Vietnam, but ended up in Korea, where he had his first sexual encounter, with a prostitute, and contracted gonorrhea. When he got out of the service and went back to New York City, he began hunting for his biological mother, whom he found living with her daughter—his sister—in Long Beach, Long Island. Much to his surprise and dismay, they wanted nothing to do with him. He'd been shy, insecure, and angry, and now he blossomed into a potential killer. He'd learned how to shoot in the Army. He went to Texas and procured a Charter Arms Bulldog—a .44-caliber handgun—a large, powerful weapon that made him feel bigger and more powerful. He went out into the city dumps of New York and practiced with this weapon, hitting small targets until he was a good shot. And then this low-level postal employee by day went on the hunt by night.

We interviewed Berkowitz in Attica State Prison, where he was serving twenty-five years to life for each of six killings after pleading guilty, though he later came to deny his crimes. He had been the victim of a near-fatal attack in prison in 1979, when his throat had been slashed from behind. The wound had required fifty-six stitches and the attacker was never identified. So we came to him unannounced, not wanting to place him in further jeopardy. With the warden's cooperation, we had filled out most of our written questionnaire in advance, so we were well prepped.

For this particular encounter, I brought along some visual aids. As I mentioned, my father had been a pressman in New York and head of the printers' union in Long Island and had supplied me with tabloids proclaiming the Son of Sam's exploits in large headlines.

I hold up the New York *Daily News*, then pass it across the table to him as I say, "David, a hundred years from now no one is going to remember Bob Ressler or John Douglas, but they will remember the Son of Sam. In fact, right now there's a case in Wichita, Kansas, a guy who's killed about half a dozen women and calling himself the BTK Strangler. That's 'bind, torture, kill.' And you know, he's writing letters and he's talking about you in those letters. He talks about David Berkowitz, the Son of Sam. He wants to be like you because you have this power. I wouldn't even be surprised if he writes you a letter in jail here."

Berkowitz is not what I would call a charismatic guy, and he was always searching for some bit of recognition or personal achievement. He had bright blue eyes that were always trying to pick out if someone was genuinely interested, or laughing at him. When he heard what I had to say, his eyes lit up.

"Now you never had a chance to testify in court," I continue, "so all the public knows about you is that you're one bad son of a bitch. But from doing these interviews, we know that there must be another side, a sensitive side, a side that was affected by your background. And we want you to have the opportunity to tell us about that."

He's pretty emotionally undemonstrative, but he speaks to us with little hesitation. He admits having started more than two thousand fires in the Brooklyn-Queens area, which he documented in meticulous diary notes. That's one way he resembles an assassin personality—a loner who indulges in this obsessive journal writing. Another is that he doesn't want to have any physical contact with the victim. He's not a rapist or fetishist. He's not looking for souvenirs. Whatever sexual charge he's getting is from the act of shooting itself.

The fires he set were mainly of the nuisance variety, such as in trash cans or abandoned buildings. Like a lot of arsonists, he would masturbate while watching the flames, then again when the fire department came to put them out. The fire-starting also fits in with the other two elements of the "homicidal triad": bed-wetting and cruelty to animals.

I always thought of the prison interviews as like panning for gold. The vast majority of what you get is going to be worthless pebbles, but if you get one real nugget out of it, the effort has been well worth it. And that was certainly the case with David Berkowitz.

What's very, very interesting to us is that as he's stalking these lovers' lane areas, rather than go to the driver's side of the car—most frequently the male side—which would represent the greater threat, he shifts around to the passenger side. This tells us that, as he's firing into that vehicle in a typical police stance, his hatred, his anger, is directed at the woman. The multiple shots, like multiple stab wounds, indicate the degree of that anger. The male is simply in the wrong place at the wrong time. There's probably never any eye contact between attacker and victim. Everything is done from a distance. He could possess his fantasy woman without ever having to personalize her.

Equally interesting, another golden nugget that has become part of our general awareness of serial killers, is that Berkowitz told us he was on the hunt nightly. When he could not find a victim of opportunity, a victim who was going to be at the wrong place at the wrong time, he would go back to areas where he'd been successful in the past. He would go back to a crime-scene area (many of the others went back to body-disposal areas), and the grave sites, and symbolically roll in the dirt and relive that fantasy over and over again.

This is the same reason why other serial killers take photographs or make videotapes of their crimes. Once the victim is dead and the body has been disposed of, they want to be able to relive the thrill, continue acting out the fantasy, do it again and again. Berkowitz didn't need the jewelry or the underwear or the body parts or any other souvenir. He told us that just going back was enough for him. He would then go back home, masturbate, and relive the fantasy.

We would use this insight to great effect. People in law enforcement had always speculated that killers returned to the scenes of their crimes, but couldn't prove it or explain exactly why they did. From subjects like Berkowitz, we were starting to discover that the speculation was true, though not always for the reasons we might have suspected. Remorse can certainly be one of them. But as Berkowitz showed us, there can be others. Once you understand why a particular type of criminal might revisit the scene, you can begin planning strategies to deal with him.

The Son of Sam name came from a crudely written note addressed to police captain Joseph Borelli, who later went on to become NYPD chief of detectives. It was found near the car of victims Alexander Esau and Valentina Suriani in the Bronx. Like the others, both were killed from point-blank range. The note read:

I am deeply hurt by your calling me a weman-hater. I am not. But i am a monster. I am the "son of Sam." I am a little brat.

When father Sam gets drunk he gets mean. He beats his family. Sometimes he ties me up to the back of the house. Other times he locks me in the garage. Sam loves to drink blood.

"Go out and kill," commands father Sam.

Behind our house some rest. Mostly young—raped and slaughtered—their blood drained—just bones now.

Pap Sam keeps me locked in the attic too. I can't get out but I look out the attic window and watch the world go by.

I feel like an outsider. I am on a different wavelength then everybody else—programmed too kill.

However, to stop me you must kill me. Attention all police: Shoot me first—shoot to kill or else keep out of my way or you will die!

Papa Sam is old now. He needs some blood to preserve his youth. He has had too many heart attacks. "Ugh, me hoot, it hurts, sonny boy."

I miss my pretty princess most of all. She's resting in our ladies house. But i'll see her soon.

I am the "monster"—"Beelzebub"—the chubby behemouth.

I love to hunt. Prowling the streets looking for fair game—tasty meat. The wemon of Queens are prettyist of all. I must be the water they drink. I live for the hunt—my life. Blood for papa.

Mr. Borelli, sir, I don't want to kill any more. No sur, no more but I must, "honour thy father."

I want to make love to the world. I love people. I don't belong on earth. Return me to yahoos.

To the people of Queens, I love you. And i want to wish all of you a happy Easter. May God bless you in this life and in the next. And for now I say goodbye and goodnight.

POLICE: Let me haunt you with these words:

I'll be back!

I'll be back!

To be interrpreted as—bang, bang, bang, bang—ugh!!

Yours in murder

Mr. Monster.

This insignificant nobody had become a national celebrity. More than a hundred detectives joined what came to be known as Task Force Omega. The wild, raving communications continued, including letters to newspapers and journalists such as columnist Jimmy Breslin. The city was in terror. At the post office, he told us, he got a real thrill overhearing people talking about the Son of Sam and not knowing they were in the same room with him.

The next attack took place in Bayside, Queens, but both the man and woman survived. Five days later, a couple in Brooklyn were not so lucky. Stacy Moskowitz was killed instantly. Robert Violante survived, but lost his sight from his wounds.

The Son of Sam was finally caught because he parked his Ford Galaxy too close to a fire hydrant the night of the final murder. A witness in the area remembered seeing an officer writing up a ticket, and when it was traced, it led to David Berkowitz. When confronted by police, he said simply, "Well, you got me."

After his arrest, Berkowitz explained that "Sam" referred to his neighbor, Sam Carr, whose black Labrador retriever, Harvey, was apparently a three-thousand-year-old demon who commanded David to kill. At one point, he actually shot the dog with a .22 pistol, but it survived. He was instantly labeled a paranoid schizophrenic by much of the psychiatric community, with all sorts of interpretations being given to his various letters. The "pretty princess" of his first letter was apparently one of his victims, Donna Lauria, whose soul Sam had promised him after her death.

What was most significant to me about the letters, more

than any of the content, is the way his handwriting changes. In the first letter, it is neat and orderly, then progressively degrades until it is almost illegible. The misspellings become more and more common. It is as if two different people had been writing the letters. I showed this to him. He hadn't even realized it. If I were profiling him, as soon as I saw the degradation of the handwriting, I would know he was vulnerable, prime to slip up, to make some petty mistake, like parking in front of a fire hydrant, that would help police catch him. That vulnerable point would be the time to launch some sort of proactive strategy.

The reason Berkowitz opened up to us, I believe, was because of the extensive homework we'd done on the case. Early on in the interview, we came to the topic of this three-thousand-year-old dog that made him do it. The psychiatric community had accepted the story as gospel and thought it explained his motivation. But I knew that that story hadn't actually emerged until after his arrest. It was his way out. So when he started spouting about this dog, I said simply, "Hey, David, knock off the bullshit. The dog had nothing to do with it."

He laughed and nodded and admitted I was right. We'd read several long psychological dissertations on the letters. One compared him to the character of Jerry in Edward Albee's play *The Zoo Story*. Another tried to pick up his psychopathology by analyzing the writing word by word. But David was throwing them all a curve, which they swung at and missed.

The simple fact is that David Berkowitz was angry about how he had been treated by his mother and other women in his life and felt inadequate around them. His fantasy of possessing them blossomed into a deadly reality. The important things to us were the details.

With Bob Ressler's skillful administration of the NIJ grant and Ann Burgess's compilation of the interviews, by 1983 we had completed a detailed study of thirty-six individuals. We also collected data from 118 of their victims, primarily women.

Out of the study came a system to better understand and classify violent offenders. For the first time, we could really begin to link what was going on in a perpetrator's mind to the evidence he left at a crime scene. That, in turn, helped us to hunt them more efficiently and catch and prosecute them more effectively. It began to address some of the age-old questions about insanity and "what type of person could do such a thing?"

In 1988, we expanded our conclusions into a book, entitled *Sexual Homicide: Patterns and Motives*, published by Lexington Books. At this writing, it is in its seventh printing. But regardless of how much we learned, as we admitted in our conclusion, "this study raises far more questions than it answers."

The journey into the mind of the violent offender remains an ongoing quest of discovery. Serial killers are, by definition, "successful" killers, who learn from their experience. We've just got to make sure we keep learning faster than they do.

8

The Killer Will Have
a Speech Impediment

Sometime in 1980 I saw an article in my local paper about an elderly woman who was sexually assaulted and severely beaten by an unknown intruder and left for dead, along with her two dogs, which had been stabbed to death. It looked to the police as though the offender had spent a fair amount of time at the scene. The community was stunned and outraged.

A couple of months later, coming back from a road trip, I happened to ask Pam if there had been any news on that case. She told me there hadn't been, and that there were no strong suspects. I commented that that was too bad, because from what I'd read and heard, it sounded like a solvable case. It wasn't a federal jurisdiction, and we hadn't been asked in, but just as a local resident, I decided to see if there was anything I could do.

I went down to the police station, introduced myself, told the chief what I did, and asked if I could talk to the detectives working the case. He accepted my offer graciously.

The lead detective's name was Dean Martin. I can't remember if I refrained from any Jerry Lewis jokes, but I probably didn't. He showed me the case files, including the crime-scene photos. This woman had really been pummeled. And as I studied the materials, I started getting a clear mental picture of the offender and the dynamics of the crime.

"Okay," I said to the detectives, who were politely, if somewhat skeptically, listening to me, "here's what I think." It's a sixteen- or seventeen-year-old high school kid. Whenever we see an old victim of a sexual assault, we look for a young offender, someone unsure of himself, without much or any experience. A victim any younger, stronger, or more challenging would be too intimidating to him. He'll be disheveled-looking, he'll have scruffy hair, generally poorly groomed. Now what happened on this particular night was his mother or father kicked him out of the house and he had no place to go. He's not going to go too far in this situation. Instead, he's going to look for the closest and easiest shelter he can find. He doesn't have the kind of relationship with any girl or other guys that he can just crash at their house until the storm at home blows over. But as he's out wandering, feeling miserable, powerless, and angry about it, he comes to this lady's house. He knows she lives alone, he's worked there in the past or done some odd jobs for her. He knows she isn't much of a threat.

So he breaks in, maybe she protests, maybe she starts yelling at him, maybe she's just terrified. Whatever her reaction, that both inflames and empowers him. He wants to show himself and the world what a man he is. He attempts sex with her, but he can't penetrate. So he beats the hell out of her, at a certain point deciding he'd better go all the way because she can identify him. He isn't wearing a mask; this has been an impulse crime, not a planned one. But she's so traumatized that even though she lives, she can't give the police any description.

After the attack, he's still got no place to go, and she certainly isn't threatening him, he knows she won't get any visitors at night, so he stays and eats and drinks, because by this point he's hungry.

I pause in my narrative and tell them there's someone who meets this description out there. If they can find him, they've got their offender.

One detective looks at another. One of them starts to smile. "Are you a psychic, Douglas?"

"No," I say, "but my job would be a lot easier if I were."

"Because we had a psychic, Beverly Newton, in here a couple of weeks ago, and she said just about the same things."

What's more, my description did fit someone who lived nearby, whom they'd briefly considered. After our meeting, they interviewed him again. There wasn't enough evidence to hold him, and they couldn't get a confession. Shortly after that, he left the area.

The chief and detectives wanted to know how, if I wasn't a psychic, I could come up with such a specific scenario. Part of the answer is that, by that time, I had seen enough cases of violent crime against all types of people, had correlated enough details with each one, and had interviewed enough violent offenders that I had a pattern in my mind of what sort of crime is committed by what sort of person. But, of course, if it were that straightforward, we could teach profiling from a manual or offer the police a computer program that could come up with a list of suspect characteristics for any set of inputs. And the fact of the matter is that while we use computers a lot in our work and they are capable of some impressive things, some other more complex things they simply can't do and may never be able to do. Profiling is like writing. You can give a computer all the rules of grammar and syntax and style, but it still can't write the book.

What I try to do with a case is to take in all the evidence I have to work with—the case reports, the crime-scene photos and descriptions, the victim statements or autopsy protocols—and then put myself mentally and emotionally in the head of the offender. I try to think as he does. Exactly how this happens, I'm not sure, any more than the novelists such as Tom Harris who've consulted me over the years can say exactly how their characters come to life. If there is a psychic component to this, I won't run away from it, though I regard it more in the realm of creative thinking.

Psychics can, on occasion, be helpful to a criminal investigation. I've seen it work. Some of them have the ability to focus subconsciously on particular subtle details at a scene and draw logical conclusions from them, just as I try to do and train my people to do. But I always advise investigators that a psychic should be a last resort as an investigative tool, and if you're going to use one, don't expose him or her to officers or detectives who know the details of the case. Because good psychics are proficient at picking up small, nonverbal clues, and the psychic could amaze you and establish credibility by giving back to you facts of the case you already know without necessarily having any particular insight into what you don't know but want to find out. In the Atlanta child murders, hundreds of psychics showed up in the city and offered their services to the police. They came up with all sorts of descriptions of killers and methods. As it turned out, none was even close.

Around the same time that I met with the local police, departments from around the San Francisco Bay area called me in on a series of murders in heavily wooded areas along hiking paths they had linked together and attributed to an UNSUB the press had dubbed the "Trailside Killer."

It had started in August of 1979 when Edda Kane, an athletic, forty-four-year-old bank executive, disappeared while on a solitary hike up the east peak of Mount Tamalpais, a beautiful mountain overlooking the Golden Gate Bridge and San Francisco Bay, which was known by the nickname the "Sleeping Lady." When Kane wasn't home by dark, her worried husband called the police. Her body was found by a search-team dog the next afternoon, naked except for one sock, facedown, in a kneeling position as if begging for her life. The medical examiner determined cause of death to be a single bullet to the back of the head. There was no evidence of sexual assault. The killer took three credit cards and $10 in cash, but left her wedding ring and other jewelry.

The following March, the body of twenty-three-year-old Barbara Schwartz was found in Mount Tamalpais Park.

She had been stabbed repeatedly in the chest, also apparently while kneeling. In October, twenty-six-year-old Anne Alderson didn't return from her jog around the fringes of the park. Her body was found the next afternoon with a bullet wound in the right side of her head. Unlike previous victims, Alderson was fully clothed, faceup, propped against a rock with only her right gold earring missing. The live-in caretaker on Mount Tamalpais, John Henry, said he had seen her sitting alone in the park's amphitheater on what was to be the last morning of her life, watching the sun come up. Two other witnesses had seen her less than half a mile from where Edda Kane's body had been found.

A promising suspect was Mark McDermand, whose invalid mother and schizophrenic brother had been found shot to death in their cabin on Mount Tamalpais. After eleven days as a fugitive, McDermand surrendered to Marin County detective Capt. Robert Gaddini. Detectives were able to link him to the murders of his own family, but while he was heavily armed, none of his guns matched the .44- or .38-caliber weapons used in the Trailside cases. And then the killings resumed.

In November, Shauna May, twenty-five, failed to meet up with two hiking companions in Point Reyes Park, a few miles north of San Francisco. Two days later, searchers found her body in a shallow grave near the decomposing corpse of another hiker, twenty-two-year-old Diana O'Connell, a New Yorker who had disappeared in the park a month before. Both women had been shot in the head. The same day, two other bodies were discovered in the park, identified as belonging to nineteen-year-old Richard Stowers and his eighteen-year-old fiancée, Cynthia Moreland, both of whom had been missing since mid-October. Investigators determined they had been killed the same long Columbus Day weekend as Anne Alderson.

The early murders had already sent terror through hikers in the area and prompted signs advising people, especially women, not to go into the woods alone. But with the discovery of four bodies in a single day, all hell broke loose. Marin County sheriff G. Albert Howenstein Jr. had collected several eyewitness accounts of people having seen the victims with strange men just before their deaths, but on certain key points, such as age and facial features, the descriptions conflicted with each other. This, by the way, isn't unusual even in a single murder, much less a multiple over several months. An unusual pair of bifocals was found at the Barbara Schwartz scene, which apparently belonged to the killer. Howenstein released information on the glasses and the prescription, sending out flyers to all the optometrists in the area. The frames were of apparent prison issue, so Captain Gaddini contacted the California State Department of Justice to try to identify all recently released offenders with a history of sex crimes against women. Various jurisdictions and agencies, including the FBI's San Francisco Field Office, were now actively working the case.

There was speculation in the press that the Trailside Killer might, in fact, be San Francisco's Zodiac Killer, who remained an UNSUB but who had been inactive since 1969. Perhaps Zodiac had been in prison for some other crime all this time and had been released by unknowing corrections officials. But unlike Zodiac, the Trailside Killer felt no need to taunt police or communicate with them.

Sheriff Howenstein brought in a psychologist from Napa, Dr. R. William Mathis, to analyze the case. Noting the ritualistic aspects of the cases, Dr. Mathis said he would expect the offender to keep souvenirs, and anyone identified as a suspect should be followed for a week before being arrested in the hope that he might lead police to the murder weapon or other evidence. As far as his appearance and behavioral characteristics, Mathis described a handsome man with a winning personality.

Working on Mathis's advice, Howenstein and Gaddini set various types of proactive traps, including having male park rangers pose as female hikers, but nothing was working. The public pressure on law enforcement was intense. The sheriff announced to the public that the killer lays in wait for his victims and puts them through psychological trauma before killing them, probably making them plead for their lives.

When the Bureau's San Rafael Resident Agency asked for assistance from Quantico, they'd originally contacted Roy Hazelwood, who was our chief expert on rape and violence against women. Roy is a sensitive, caring guy, and the case affected him deeply. I remember him describing it to me as we walked back to our office suite from the classroom building, where he had just finished teaching a National Academy class. I almost got the sense Roy felt personally responsible, as if the combined efforts of the FBI and about ten cooperating local agencies weren't enough; that *he* should be cracking the case and bringing the offender to justice.

Unlike me, Roy had full-time teaching responsibilities. I had given up most of my classroom work by this point and was the Behavioral Science Unit's only full-time profiler actively working cases. So Roy asked me to go out to San Francisco and give the police there some on-the-scene input.

As we've noted earlier, there is often resentment when the FBI comes into a case. Some of this is left over from the Hoover days, when it was often felt that the Bureau would just move in and take over the investigation of high-profile crimes. My unit can't come in unless we're asked by whichever agency has primary jurisdiction, be it a local police department or even the FBI itself. But in Trailside, the Marin County Sheriff's Department had brought in the Bureau early, and with the kind of play the cases were getting in the media, I frankly felt they welcomed someone like me to come in and take the heat off them, at least for a while.

At the sheriff's department offices, I reviewed all the

case materials and crime-scene photos. I was particularly interested in Marin detective sergeant Rich Keaton's observations that the murders all seemed to have taken place at secluded, heavily wooded sites with a thick canopy of foliage blocking out most of the sky. None of these areas was accessible by car, only by foot, involving at least a mile's hike. The scene of Anne Alderson's murder was reasonably close to a service road that represented a shortcut from the park amphitheater. This all strongly suggested to me that the killer was a local, intimately familiar with the area.

I gave my presentation in a large training room at the Marin County Sheriff's Department. Seats were banked in a semicircle, like a medical lecture hall. Of the fifty or sixty people in the room, about ten were FBI agents, the rest police officers and detectives. As I looked out over the heads of the audience, I noticed more than a few gray hairs—experienced veterans had been brought back from retirement to help catch this guy.

The first thing I did was challenge the profile that had already been given. I didn't think we were dealing with a good-looking, charming, sophisticated type. The multiple stabbings and blitz-style attacks from the rear told me we were dealing with an asocial type (though not necessarily antisocial) who'd be withdrawn, unsure of himself, and unable to engage his victims in conversation, develop a good line, or con or coax or trick them into doing what he wanted. The hikers were all physically fit. The blitz attack was a clear indication to me that the only way he could control his intended victim was to devastate her before she could respond.

These were not the crimes of someone who knew his victims. The sites were secluded and protected from view, which meant the killer essentially had as much time as he wanted to act out his fantasy with each victim. Yet he still felt the need for a blitz attack. There was no rape, just handling of the bodies after death; masturbation, probably, but no intercourse. The victims were a range of ages and physical types, unlike those of a glib, sophisticated killer such as Ted Bundy, most of whose victims conformed to a single image: pretty, college-age women with long, dark hair, parted in the middle. The Trailside Killer was nonpreferential, like a spider waiting for a bug to fly into his web. I told the assembled group of officers I expected this guy to have a bad background. I agreed with Captain Gaddini that he had spent time in jail. Priors might include rapes or, more likely, rape attempts, but no murders before this series. There would have been some precipitating stressor before it began. I certainly expected him to be white since all the victims were, and I thought he'd have some blue-collar mechanical or industrial job. Because of the efficiency of the murders and his success in evading the police thus far, I pegged his age at low to mid-thirties. I also thought he'd be pretty bright. If they ever tested his IQ, it would be well above normal. And if they looked into his background, they'd find a history of bed-wetting, fire-starting, and cruelty to animals, or at least two of the three.

"Another thing," I added after a pregnant pause, "the killer will have a speech impediment."

It wasn't hard to read the expressions or body language in the room. They were finally expressing what they'd probably been thinking all along: *this guy's full of shit!*

"What makes you say that?" one cop asked sarcastically. "The wounds look like a 'stutter stab' to you?" He grinned at his own "discovery" of a new method of killing.

No, I explained, it was a combination of inductive and deductive reasoning, considering just about every other factor in the cases; all of the factors I'd already been through. The secluded locations where he wasn't likely to come in contact with anyone else, the fact that none of the victims had been approached in a crowd or tricked into going along with him, the fact that he felt he had to rely on a blitz attack even in the middle of nowhere—all of this told me we were dealing with someone with some condition he felt awkward or ashamed about. Overpowering an unsuspecting victim and being able to dominate and control her was his way of overcoming this handicap.

It could be some other type of ailment or disability, I allowed. Psychologically or behaviorally speaking, it could be a very homely individual, someone with bad acne scarring, polio, a missing limb, anything like that. But with the kind of attack we'd seen, we had to rule out a missing limb or any serious crippling condition. And with all the various witness accounts and all of the people in the parks around the time of the murders, we would have expected to hear about someone with an obvious disfigurement. A speech impediment, on the other hand, was something that the UNSUB could easily feel ashamed of or uncomfortable with to the extent that it might limit normal social relationships, yet wouldn't "stand out" in a crowd. No one would know about it until he opened his mouth.

Giving this kind of guidance to a roomful of seasoned cops with a lot at stake and the press and public breathing down their necks is definitely a high ass-pucker situation, the kind I like to create for the people I'm interrogating but would just as soon avoid myself. You can't completely do that, though. You're always haunted by the thought so clearly stated by one of the detectives in the room that afternoon:

"What if you're wrong, Douglas?"

"I may be wrong about some things," I conceded as truthfully as I could. "I may miss the age. I may miss the occupation or the IQ. But I'm certainly not going to miss the race or the sex, and I'm not going to miss that he's blue collar. And in this particular case, I'm not going to miss that he has some kind of defect that really bothers him. Maybe it's not a speech impediment, but I think it is."

When I was finished, I couldn't tell how much of an impact I'd had or whether any of this had sunk in. But one cop did come up to me afterward and say, "I don't know whether you're right or wrong, John, but at least you gave the investigation some direction." That's always good to hear, though you tend to hold your breath until you see what that investigation ultimately turns up. I went back to Quantico and the combined Bay Area sheriff and police departments went about their work.

On March 29, the killer struck again, this time shooting a young couple in Henry Cowell Redwoods State Park near Santa Cruz. When he told Ellen Marie Hansen, a twenty-year-old sophomore at the University of California–Davis, that he was going to rape her, she protested, whereupon he opened fire with a .38 pistol, killing her outright and severely wounding Steven Haertle, whom he left for dead. But Haertle was able to provide a partial description of a man with crooked, yellow teeth. Police built on this with other witnesses and were able to tie such a man to a red, late-model foreign car, possibly a Fiat, though again, this description varied considerably from previous ones. Haertle thought the subject was in his fifties or sixties and balding. Ballistics linked these shootings to previous Trailside murders.

On May 1, pretty, blond, twenty-year-old Heather Roxanne Scaggs disappeared. She was a student at a printing trade school in San Jose, and her boyfriend, mother, and roommate all recalled she said she was going out with an industrial arts teacher at the school, David Carpenter, who had arranged for her to buy a car from a friend of his. Carpenter was fifty years of age, which was unusual for a crime of this type.

From that point on, things began falling into place and the net began closing. Carpenter drove a red Fiat with a dented tailpipe. This last detail was a piece of "hold-back" information the police hadn't let out previously.

David Carpenter should have been identified and caught before he actually was. The fact is, he was incredibly lucky and had also involved multiple police jurisdictions, which complicated the manhunt. He had an incarceration record for sex crimes. Ironically, the reason he didn't show up as a sex offender on state parole records was that he had been released by California to serve out a federal sentence, and though on the streets, he was still technically in federal custody. So he slipped through the cracks. Another irony was that Carpenter and his second victim, Barbara Schwartz, at whose murder scene his glasses had been found, shared the same optometrist! Unfortunately, he had not seen the flyer the sheriff's department circulated.

Other witnesses came forward, including an older woman who had recognized the composite drawing on television and said he had been the purser on a ship she and her children had taken to Japan twenty years before. The man had given her "the creeps" with the inappropriate attention he continually paid her young daughter.

And Peter Berest, the manager of the Glen Park Continental Savings and Loan branch in Daly City, recalled his pretty, sensitive, and trusting part-time teller, high school student Anna Kelly Menjivar, who had disappeared from her home late the previous December. Though she had not previously been linked to the Trailside slayings, her body had also been found in Mount Tamalpais Park. Berest remembered how kind and sweet Anna had been to the regular customer with a severe stutter whom Berest later learned had been arrested in 1960 for attacking a young woman at the Presidio, the Army installation at the north tip of San Francisco.

San Jose police and the FBI put Carpenter under surveillance and eventually arrested him. He turned out to be the product of a domineering and physically abusive mother, and at least an emotionally abusive father, a child of well above average intelligence who was picked on because of his severe stuttering. His childhood was also marked by chronic bed-wetting and cruelty to animals. In adult life, his anger and frustration turned into fits of unpredictable, violent rage and a seemingly unquenchable sex drive.

The first crime for which he was caught and served time, the attack on a woman with a knife and hammer in the Presidio, came following the birth of a child into an already strained marriage. During the brutal assault and shortly before, the victim reported, his terrible stutter was gone.

Because of all the requests that had been coming in from National Academy graduates, FBI director William Webster had given the Behavioral Science instructors official approval to offer psychological profiling consultation back in 1978. By the early 1980s the service had become extremely popular. I was working cases full-time, and instructors such as Bob Ressler and Roy Hazelwood were consulting as their teaching duties allowed. But despite the fact that we felt good about what we were doing and the results we thought we were achieving, no one at the top really knew for sure if this was an effective use of Bureau resources and manpower. So in 1981, the FBI's Institutional Research and Development Unit—then headed by Howard Teten, who had moved over from Behavioral Science—undertook the first in-depth cost-benefit study of what was then called simply the Psychological Profiling Program. Teten, whose informal consultations had begun the program almost by accident, was interested to see if it was really having any effect and if headquarters should continue it.

A questionnaire was developed and sent to our clients—officials and detectives at any law enforcement agency that had used our profiling services. These included city, county, and state police departments, sheriff's departments, FBI field offices, highway patrols, and state investigative agencies. While most of the requests had had to do with murder investigations, the R&D Unit also compiled data on our consultation in rapes, kidnappings, extortion, threats, child molestation, hostage situations, and accidental-death and suicide determination.

Profiling was still a hazy and hard-to-evaluate notion to

many people within the Bureau. A lot considered it witch-craft or black magic, and some of the rest thought of it as window dressing. So we knew that unless the study showed strong and verifiable successes, all of the nonteaching facets of the Behavioral Science Unit could go by the board.

We were therefore both gratified and relieved when the analysis came back in December 1981. Investigators from all over the country came through enthusiastically for us, urging that the program be continued. The final paragraph of the report's covering letter sums it up:

> The evaluation reveals that the program is actually more successful than any of us really realized. The Behavioral Science Unit is to be commended for their outstanding job.

The detectives generally agreed that the area in which we were the most helpful was in narrowing down lists of suspects and directing the investigation into a tighter focus. An example was the brutal and appallingly senseless killing of Francine Elveson in the Bronx in October 1979, not far from some of David Berkowitz's haunts. In fact there was concern on the part of NYPD that a Son of Sam devotee might be using his hero for inspiration. We teach the case at Quantico because it's a good model of just how we came up with a profile and how the police used it to push forward a baffling and long-unsolved murder.

Francine Elveson was a twenty-six-year-old teacher of handicapped children at a local day-care center. Weighing ninety pounds and standing less than five foot tall, she brought a rare empathy and sensitivity to her students, being mildly handicapped herself with kyphoscoliosis, or curvature of the spine. Shy and not very socially oriented, she lived with her parents in the Pelham Parkway House apartments.

She had left for work as usual at six-thirty in the morning. About eight-twenty, a fifteen-year-old boy who also lived in the building found her wallet in the stairwell between the third and fourth floors. He had no time to do anything with it and still be on time for school, so he kept it until he came home for lunch, then gave it to his father. The father went to the Elveson apartment a little before three that afternoon and gave the wallet to Francine's mother, who then called the day-care center to let Francine know her wallet had been found. Mrs. Elveson was told her daughter had not shown up for work that day. Instantly alarmed, she and her other daughter and a neighbor began a search of the building.

On the roof landing at the top of the stairwell, they came upon a sight of overwhelming horror. Francine's nude body had been severely beaten by blunt-force trauma, so severely that the medical examiner later found that her jaw, nose, and cheeks had been fractured and her teeth loosened. She had been spread-eagled and tied with her own belt and nylon stockings around her wrists and ankles, though the medical examiner determined she was already dead when that was done. Her nipples had been cut off after death and placed on her chest. Her underpants had been pulled over her head to cover her face, and bite marks were on her thighs and knees. The several lacerations on the body, all of them shallow, suggested a small penknife. Her umbrella and pen had been forced into her vagina, and her comb was placed in her pubic hair. Her earrings had been placed on the ground symmetrically on either side of her head. The cause of death was determined to be ligature strangulation with the strap of the victim's own pocketbook. On her thigh the killer had scrawled, "You can't stop me," and on her stomach he had written, "Fuck you," both with the pen that had been inserted into her vagina. The other significant feature of the scene was that the killer had defecated near the body and covered the excrement with some of Francine's clothing.

One of the things Mrs. Elveson told the police was that a

gold pendant in the form of the Hebrew letter *chai*, for good luck, was missing from around Francine's neck. When the mother described the shape of the pendant, detectives realized her body had been ceremonially positioned to replicate it.

Traces of semen were found on her body, but DNA typing was unknown to forensic science back in 1979. There were no defense wounds on the hands or blood traces or skin fragments under fingernails, which suggested there had been no struggle. The only tangible piece of forensic evidence was a single African American hair found on the body during the autopsy.

Upon examining the scene and establishing the known facts, homicide detectives determined that the initial attack took place as Francine walked down the stairs. After she was battered unconscious, she was carried up to the roof landing. The autopsy indicated that she hadn't been raped.

Because of its horrible nature, the case attracted a tremendous amount of public attention and media coverage. A police task force of twenty-six detectives was assembled, which questioned more than two thousand potential witnesses and suspects and checked on all known sex offenders in the New York City metropolitan area. But after a month, the investigation didn't seem to be going anywhere.

Figuring there was no harm in getting another opinion, New York Housing Authority detective Tom Foley and Lt. Joe D'Amico contacted us at Quantico. They came down, bringing files and reports, crime-scene photos, and autopsy protocols. Roy Hazelwood, Dick Ault, Tony Rider (who would go on to become chief of the Behavioral Science Unit), and I met with them in the executive dining room.

After going over all the evidence and case materials and trying to place myself in the shoes of both the victim and the attacker, I came up with a profile. I suggested that the police seek an average-looking white male between the ages of twenty-five and thirty-five, probably right around thirty, who would be disheveled in appearance, unemployed, and mainly nocturnal, live within a half mile of the building with his parents or older female relative, be single and have no relationships with women and no close friends, be a high school or college dropout with no military experience, have low self-esteem, and not own a car or hold a driver's license, who was currently or had been in a mental institution taking prescription medication, had attempted suicide by strangulation or asphyxia, was not a drug or alcohol abuser, and who would have a large collection of bondage and S&M pornography. This would be his first murder, in fact his first serious crime, but unless he was caught, not his last.

"You don't have to go far for this killer," I told the investigators. "And you've already talked to the guy." They would already have interviewed him and members of his family, since they lived in the area. Police would find him cooperative, probably overly so. He might even seek them out, injecting himself into the investigation to make sure it didn't get too close to him.

To a lot of people unfamiliar with our techniques, this seemed like a lot of hocus-pocus. But if you go through it methodically, you can begin to see how we come up with our impressions and recommendations.

The first thing we decided was that this was a crime of opportunity, a spontaneous event. Francine's parents told us that she sometimes took the elevator and sometimes walked the stairs. There was no way to predict what her preference would be on any given morning. If the killer had been lying in wait for her in the stairwell, he might have missed her altogether and, in any event, would likely have run into other people before seeing Francine.

Everything used in the attack and on the victim's body belonged to the victim. The killer had brought nothing to the scene, other than perhaps the small pocketknife. He had no weapons or rape kit. He had not stalked her or gone to the scene with the intention of committing the crime.

This, in turn, led us to the next conclusion. If the UNSUB

had not gone to the building with the intention of committing this crime, he must have been there for some other reason. And for him to have been there before 7 a.m. and to have run into Francine on the stairwell, he must have either lived in the building, worked there, or knew his way around pretty well. This could have meant a mailman or telephone company or Con Ed worker, though I thought that unlikely since we had no witness reports, and someone in that situation would not have been able to take the time he clearly spent with her. After the initial attack on the stairs, he knew he could take her up to the roof landing without much fear of being interrupted. Also, since no one in the building saw anything or anyone unusual, he must have fit in. Francine did not scream or struggle, so she probably knew him, at least by sight, and no one noticed anyone strange or menacing going into or out of the building that morning.

Because of the sexual nature of the attack, we felt confident we were dealing with a man in her general age range. We stated the range to be between twenty-five and thirty-five, probably right around the middle. I was willing to rule out the fifteen-year-old who found the wallet (as well as his forty-year-old father) based solely on this. Based on my experience, I could not imagine someone of that age treating the body this way. Even Monte Rissell, an extremely "precocious" serial rapist, had not behaved in this manner. This advanced a sexual fantasy would take years to develop. Also, the fifteen-year-old was black.

Even though the examination of the body had turned up the African American hair, I was convinced we were dealing with a white killer. Very rarely did we see this type of crime cross racial lines, and when we did, there was usually other evidence to substantiate it. There was none in this case, and I had seldom, if ever, seen this kind of mutilation from a black subject. A black former janitor in the building who had never returned his keys was considered a good suspect, but I didn't think it would be him both because of this behavioral consideration and the fact that some of the tenants would have been sure to notice him.

How did I account for that hair connecting the crime to a black UNSUB? the police wanted to know. I couldn't, which made me somewhat uncomfortable, but I was still sure enough I was right to stand by it.

This was a "high-risk" crime and a "low-risk" victim. She had no boyfriends, was neither a prostitute, a drug taker, a beautiful child in an open environment, nor was she in a bad neighborhood away from home. The building was about 50 percent black, 40 percent white, and 10 percent Hispanic. No other similar crimes had been reported here or anywhere else in the neighborhood. Any attacker could have chosen a much "safer" place to commit a sexual crime. This, combined with the lack of advance preparation, pointed to a disorganized offender.

A combination of other factors, taken together, gave me an even clearer picture of the type of person who had killed Francine Elveson. There had been rather horrible sexual mutilation and masturbation over the body, but no intercourse. The penetration with the umbrella and pen were acts of sexual substitution. Quite clearly, the adult male we were looking for was an insecure, sexually immature, and inadequate individual. The masturbation suggested this was the acting out of some ritual he had been fantasizing about for some time. The masturbatory fantasy would have been fueled by rough bondage and sadomasochistic pornography, also a hallmark of a sexually inadequate male. Remember, he had tied her up after unconsciousness or death. The choice of a small, physically frail victim who still had to be blitz-attacked and neutralized quickly before he could perpetrate his violent fantasies on her only confirmed this in my mind. Had he carried out his sadistic acts on a living, conscious victim, it would have been a different story as to personality. But as it was, he would have a lot of difficulty maintaining relationships with women. If he dated at all, which I doubted, he would seek out much younger women whom he'd have a better shot at dominating or controlling.

The fact that he had been hanging around the apartment building when other people like Francine were on their way to work told me he was not gainfully employed in a full-time job. If he had any job at all, it would be a part-time one, possibly at night, which didn't pay him much.

From that I concluded that he would not be able to live on his own. Unlike a lot of slicker types of killers, this guy would not be fully able to hide his weirdness from peers, which would mean he would not have many friends and wouldn't live with a roommate. He would probably be nocturnal and wouldn't care much about his appearance. Since he wouldn't be living with friends and could not afford a place of his own, he would be living with his parents, or more likely, I felt, a single parent or older female relative such as a sister or an aunt. He would not be able to afford an automobile, which meant he either took public transportation to the building, walked, or lived there. I didn't see him taking a bus to get there so early in the morning, which then suggested that he lived in the building or within, say, a half mile.

Then there was the placement of the various ritual objects—the severed nipples, the earrings, the positioning of the body itself. This type of compulsiveness amidst this frenzy of disorganized mayhem told me my prey had some deep psychological and psychiatric problems. I expected him to be on, or at least to have been on, some kind of prescription medication. That and the fact that the crime took place in early morning indicated that alcohol wasn't a factor with this person. Whatever his instability or psychosis was, it was getting worse and would have been noticeable to those around him. Previous suicide attempts, particularly involving asphyxiation—the method of killing he had used on Francine—were a good possibility. I was betting he either was, or had been, in a mental institution. I ruled out any military experience because of this and thought he would be either a high school or college dropout with a history of unfulfilled ambitions. I was reasonably sure this was a first murder for this guy, but if he got away with it, it wouldn't be his last. I didn't expect him to strike again right away. This crime would be enough to hold him for weeks or months. But eventually, when the circumstances were favorable and the victim of opportunity again presented herself, he would strike again. His messages written on the body told me that much.

His placing the victim in the degrading, ritualistic posture told me he didn't have much remorse about the crime. Had her body been covered, I might have thought that placing her underpants over her face was a sign that he was somewhat sorry and wanted to leave her with some dignity, but that was negated by the exposure of the body. So the covered face was more in the line of depersonalizing and degrading her than any act of concern.

Interestingly, he did use her clothing to cover up his own feces. Had he defecated at the scene and left it exposed, this could have been interpreted as part of his ritual fantasy or a further sign of contempt for this victim in particular or for women in general. But the fact that he covered it indicated either that he was there a long time and had no place else to go or couldn't control his nerves or both. Based on previous experience, I thought his inability to refrain from defecating at the scene might also be the result of medication.

After receiving the profile, the police went back over their extensive suspect and interview list. They tossed out one known former sex offender who was now married with children. The preliminary cut-down had twenty-two names on it, and of these, one stood out as fitting the profile closely.

His name was Carmine Calabro. A thirty-year-old, white unemployed actor, he lived off and on with his widowed father in the Elvesons' building, also on the fourth floor.

He was unmarried and reportedly had trouble maintaining relationships with women. A high school dropout, he had no military experience. When police searched his room, they found an extensive collection of bondage and S&M pornography. He did have a history of suicide attempts by hanging and asphyxia—both before and after the Elveson murder.

But he had an alibi. As I'd predicted, the police had interviewed his father, as they had every other tenant in the building. Mr. Calabro had told them that Carmine was an in-patient resident at a local mental hospital undergoing treatment for depression. This was why the police had ruled him out earlier.

But armed with the profile description, they immediately went back to work on him and quickly determined how lax security was at that particular institution. They were then able to establish conclusively that Carmine had been absent without leave—he had simply walked out—the evening before Francine Elveson's murder.

Thirteen months after the murder, Carmine Calabro was arrested and police got a dental impression from him. Three forensic dentists then confirmed that his teeth matched the bite marks on Francine's body. This was to be key evidence in the trial, at which Calabro pleaded not guilty, and which ended with a murder conviction and a sentence of twenty-five years to life.

The African American hair, by the way, turned out to be unrelated. The medical examiner's office did a careful procedural investigation and discovered that the body bag used to transport Francine Elveson's body to the morgue had previously been used for a black male victim and had not been properly cleaned out between uses. But this does go to show that forensic evidence on its own can be misleading, and if it doesn't fit the investigator's overall impression of the case, it should be looked at carefully before being accepted as proof.

This case was very gratifying to us, made even more

gratifying by the fact that we had made believers out of the people we worked with in New York, among the sharpest and most sophisticated law enforcement people in the business. For an April 1983 article about the profiling program in *Psychology Today*, Lieutenant D'Amico said, "They had him so right that I asked the FBI why they hadn't given us his phone number, too."

After that article appeared, Calabro wrote to us from the Clinton Correctional Facility in Dannemora, New York, even though his name and Elveson's name never appeared in the article. In a rambling letter with poor grammar and spelling, he generally had complimentary things to say about the FBI and NYPD, reasserted his innocence, grouped himself together with David Berkowitz and George Metesky, the Mad Bomber, and wrote, "I am not contradicting your profile of the killer in this case, as a matter of fact, on two points, I sincerely believe you are correct."

He went on to ask if we had been informed of the presence of hair evidence on the body, which he thought might exculpate (my word, not his) him. Then, curiously, he went on to ask when we came up with the profile and whether we had all the evidence. If we had all the evidence, then he intended to let the matter rest, though if we didn't, he would write us again.

I thought this letter might be an opening to allow us to include Calabro in our study. So in July 1983, Bill Hagmaier and Rosanne Russo, one of the first woman agents in the Behavioral Science Unit, went up to Clinton to interview Calabro. They described him as being nervous but polite and cooperative, just as he had been with the police. He focused quite heavily on his innocence and the upcoming appeal, stating that he had been unfairly convicted on the bite-mark evidence. As a result, he had had all of his teeth removed so that "they cannot accuse me again" and proudly displayed his empty mouth. Other than that, the interview was in many ways a rehash of his letter, though Hagmaier and Russo said he seemed quite interested in what they were doing and didn't want them to leave. Even in prison, he remained a loner.

There is no doubt in my mind that Carmine Calabro is deeply psychologically disturbed. Nothing about his case, his background, or our communication with him indicates anything approaching normalcy. At the same time, I still believe that like most disturbed individuals he understood the difference between right and wrong. Having these bizarre and deranged fantasies is not a crime. Making the willful choice to act upon them to the harm of others most certainly is.

9

Walking in the Shoes

By this time in the early 1980s I was handling upward of 150 cases a year and was on the road an equal number of days. I was starting to feel like Lucille Ball trying to get ahead of the conveyor belt in the famous *I Love Lucy* candy factory skit—the more stuff that came at me, the more frantically I had to scramble to keep from falling behind. Actually getting ahead of the game so I could take a moment to breathe was out of the question.

As our work and results became known, requests for assistance were pouring in from all over the United States and many foreign countries. Like a triage officer in an emergency room, I had to start prioritizing cases. Rape-murders where there appeared to be a threat of further loss of life got my most immediate attention.

With cold cases or those where the UNSUB didn't seem to be active, I'd ask the police why they'd called us in. Sometimes the victim's family would be pressuring them for a solution. That was certainly understandable and my heart always went out to them, but I couldn't afford to spend precious time on an analysis that was just going to be shelved by the locals without any action.

With active cases, it was interesting to note where they came from. In the early days of the program, anything from one of the most major departments—say, NYPD or LAPD—would arouse my suspicion as to why they'd come to our unit in Quantico at all. Sometimes it was a jurisdictional feud with the FBI, such as who gets the surveillance films, who'll do the interrogation, and who'll prosecute a series of bank robberies. Or it could have been that the case was a political hot button and the locals just wanted someone else to catch the flak. All of these considerations went into my decision on how to respond to a request for assistance, because I knew all of them would help determine whether that particular case was going to get solved.

Initially, I had provided written analyses. As the caseload increased exponentially, though, I didn't have time for that any longer. I would take notes as I examined a file. Then, when I spoke to the local investigator—either in person or on the phone—I would go over my notes and recall the case. Normally, the cops would take copious notes of their own on what I was telling them. On those rare occasions when a cop was in the same room with me, if he would just listen without writing anything down, I would quickly lose patience, tell him it was his case, not mine, and if he wanted our help, he'd better get his ass in gear and work as hard as I was.

I'd done enough of these that, like a doctor, I knew how long each "office visit" should take. By the time I'd reviewed the case, I knew whether or not I could help, so I wanted to focus on the crime-scene analysis and victimology right away. Why was this victim selected over all other potential victims? How was he or she murdered? From those two questions, you can begin to address the ultimate question: who?

Like Sherlock Holmes, I had quickly come to realize that the more ordinary and routine the crime, the less behavioral evidence there was to work with. I couldn't be much help on street holdups. They're too common, the behavior is too mundane, and therefore the suspect pool is enormous. Likewise, a single gunshot or stab wound presents a more difficult scenario than multiple wounds, an outdoor case is more challenging than an indoor one, a single high-risk victim such as a prostitute doesn't give us as much information as a series.

The first thing I'd look at was the medical examiner's report to learn the nature and type of wounds, the cause of death, whether there was any sexual assault, and if so, what kind. The quality of medical examiner work varied wildly throughout the thousands of police jurisdictions around the country. Some of them were real forensic pathologists and their work was first-rate. For example, when Dr. James Luke was medical examiner of Washington, D.C., we could always count on complete, detailed, and accurate protocols. Since his retirement from that job, Dr. Luke has been a valued consultant to my unit at Quantico. On the other hand, I saw situations in small towns down South where the coroner was the local funeral director. His idea of a postmortem exam would be to show up at the scene, kick the body, and say, "Yep, that boy's sure dead."

After I'd gone through the body-related findings, I'd read the preliminary police report. When the first officer arrived, what did he see? From that point on, it's possible the scene was altered, either by him or someone on the investigative team. It was important to me to be able to visualize the scene as closely as possible to how the offender left it. If it wasn't the way it had been, I wanted to know that. For example, if there was a pillow on the victim's face, who put it there? Was it there when the officer arrived? Did a family member who found the body do it for the sake of dignity? Or was there some other explanation? Finally, I'd look at the crime-scene photos and try to complete the picture in my mind.

Photographs weren't always of the best quality, particularly back when most departments were still shooting in black and white. So I'd also ask for a schematic drawing of the crime scene with all directions and footprints noted. If detectives had something particular they wanted me to look at, I asked them to write it on the back of the photo, so I wouldn't be influenced by someone else's observation in my first pass-through. By the same token, if they had a particular suspect at the top of their list, I didn't want to know, or I asked them to send it to me in a sealed envelope so I could be objective in my own analysis.

It was also important to try to figure out if anything had been taken from the victim or removed from the crime scene. Generally, it was clear if cash or valuables or prominent jewelry was taken, each of which would help point to the offender's motive. Other items are not always so easy to track.

When an officer or detective would tell me that nothing was taken, I'd ask, "How do you know? Do you mean to tell me that if I took a bra or a single pair of panties from your wife's or girlfriend's drawer, you'd be able to tell? Because if so, you're a sick puppy." Something as subtle as a barrette or lock of hair could be missing, and that would be difficult to trace. The mere fact that nothing *appeared* to be missing was never a definitive finding in my mind. And when we'd eventually catch an offender and search his premises, we'd often find surprise souvenirs.

It was clear from early on that a lot of folks, both inside the Bureau and out, really didn't understand what we were all about. This was brought home to me during a two-week homicide school Bob Ressler and I were teaching in New York in 1981. There were about a hundred detectives, mainly from NYPD but also from jurisdictions all over the New York metropolitan area.

One morning, before the class on profiling began, I'm at the front of the room setting up the large, three-quarter-inch Sony VCR we used in those days. This obviously overworked, clearly burnt-out detective with pale, bloodshot eyes wanders by me and says, "You're into this profiling stuff, huh?"

"Yeah, that's right," I answer, turning to the boxy VCR. "In fact, this is the profiling machine right here."

He looks at me skeptically, the way seasoned detectives do when dealing with a suspect, but he stays with me.

"Give me your hand," I say. "I'll show you how it works."

Tentatively, he gives me his hand. On a three-quarter-inch VCR, the tape cassette slot is pretty large. I take his hand, put it in the tape slot, and turn some dials. Meanwhile, Ressler's somewhere else in the room, preparing his material. He overhears me and is ready to come over, thinking I'm about to get punched out.

But the guy just says, "So what's my profile?"

I say, "Why don't you wait for the class. You'll see how it works."

Fortunately for me, the guy must have figured out during class what was going on as I explained the profiling process and used the VCR for its real purpose: to demonstrate! And he wasn't waiting for me at the end. But the point of this story is that I've always wished it were that easy to come up with a usable profile. Not only can you not stick a hand (or any other body part) in a machine and come up with a profile, for years computer experts have been working with law enforcement officials to develop programs that would replicate the logical processes we go through. So far, they haven't come up with much.

The fact of the matter is, profiling and crime-scene analysis is a lot more than simply inputting data and crunching it through. To be a good profiler, you have to be able to evaluate a wide range of evidence and data. But you also have to be able to walk in the shoes of both the offender and the victim.

You have to be able to re-create the crime scene in your head. You need to know as much as you can about the victim so that you can imagine how she might have reacted. You have to be able to put yourself in her place as the attacker threatens her with a gun or a knife, a rock, his fists, or whatever. You have to be able to feel her fear as he approaches her. You have to be able to feel her pain as he rapes her or beats her or cuts her. You have to try to imagine what she was going through when he tortured her for his sexual gratification. You have to understand what it's like to scream in terror and agony, realizing that it won't help, that it won't get him to stop. You have to know what it was like. And that is a heavy burden to have to carry, especially when the victim is a child or elderly.

When the director and cast of *The Silence of the Lambs* came to Quantico to prepare for filming, I brought Scott Glenn, who played Jack Crawford—the special agent some say was based on me—into my office. Glenn was a pretty liberal guy who had strong feelings on rehabilitation, redemption, and the fundamental goodness of people. I showed him some of the gruesome crime-scene photos we worked with every day. I let him experience recordings made by killers while they were torturing their victims. I made him listen to one of two teenage girls in Los Angeles being tortured to death in the back of a van by two thrill-seeking killers who had recently been let out of prison.

Glenn wept as he listened to the tapes. He said to me, "I had no idea there were people out there who could do anything like this." An intelligent, compassionate father with two girls of his own, Glenn said that after seeing and hearing what he did in my office, he could no longer oppose the death penalty: "The experience in Quantico changed my mind about that for all time."

But just as difficult, I have to put myself in the position of the attacker, to think as he thinks, to plan along with him, to understand and feel his gratification in this one moment out of his life in which his pent-up fantasies come true and he is finally in control, completely able to manipulate and dominate another human being. I have to walk in that killer's shoes, too.

The two men torturing and killing the teenage girls in the van were named Lawrence Bittaker and Roy Norris. They even had a nickname for their van: Murder Mac. They met while serving time at the California Men's Colony at San Luis Obispo. Bittaker was serving time for assault with a deadly weapon. Norris was a convicted rapist. When they discovered their mutual interest in dominating and hurting young women, they realized they were soul mates. And when they were both paroled in 1979, they got together in a Los Angeles motel and laid plans to kidnap, rape, torture, and kill one girl of appropriate age for each teen year, thirteen through nineteen. They had already successfully carried out their plans against five girls when one managed to escape from them after her rape and go to the police.

Norris, the less dominant of the two, eventually caved in to police examination, confessed, and in exchange for immunity from the death sentence, agreed to finger the even more sadistic and aggressive Bittaker. He led police to the various body sites. One, already skeletonized from the California sun, had an ice pick still protruding from the ear.

What is notable about this case, aside from the heart-rending tragedy of these promising lives snuffed out and the utter depravity of torturing young girls, in Norris's words, "for fun," is the different behavioral dynamic when two offenders are involved in the same crime. Generally, what we see is one more dominant and one more compliant partner, and often one more organized and one less organized. Serial killers are inadequate types to begin with, and the ones who need partners to carry out their work are the most inadequate of all.

As horrible as their crimes were (and Lawrence Bittaker is among the most loathsome and repugnant individuals I have ever come across), they are not, unfortunately, unique. Like Bittaker and Norris, James Russell Odom and James Clayton Lawson Jr. met in prison. It was the mid-1970s and they were both doing time for rape at Atascadero State Mental Hospital in California. Looking back at their records, I would consider Russell Odom a psychopath and Clay Lawson more of a schizophrenic. While at Atascadero, Clay evocatively described to Russell his plans for what he would like to do when he was let out. This included capturing women, cutting off their breasts, removing their ovaries, and sticking knives into their vaginas. He said he was inspired by Charles Manson and his followers. Lawson made it clear that sexual intercourse was not part of his plan. He did not consider this part of "doing his thing."

Odom, on the other hand, considered intercourse very much his thing and, as soon as he was released, drove his 1974 powder-blue Volkswagen Beetle cross-country to Columbia, South Carolina, where Lawson was working as a pipe fitter and living with his parents after parole. (VW Beetles, as I've noted, seemed to be the car of choice for serial killers—as well as FBI agents without savings—at that time.) Odom thought that with their related but separate interests, they could make a good team and each do his own thing.

Within a few days of Odom's arrival, the two of them go out looking for a victim in the 1974 Ford Comet belonging to Lawson's father. They stop at a 7-Eleven on U.S. Highway 1 and spot a young woman they like working behind the counter. But too many people are around, so they leave and go to a porno movie.

I think it's important to underscore here that when they realized they couldn't stage a successful abduction without being resisted or at least witnessed, they left without having committed their intended crime. Both men were mentally ill, and in Lawson's case, a pretty good argument could be made for criminal insanity. *Yet when circumstances did not favor the success of their crime, they refrained from committing it.* They were not under such a compulsion that they were *compelled* to act. So I will say it again for the record: in my opinion and based on my experience, the mere presence of a mental disorder does not let an offender off the hook. Unless he is completely delusional and does not comprehend his actions in the real world, he *chooses* whether or not to hurt someone else. And the truly bonkers ones are easy to catch. Serial killers are not.

The next night after their first hunt, Odom and Lawson go to a drive-in movie theater. When the show is over, sometime after midnight, they drive back to the 7-Eleven. They go in and buy a few small items—a chocolate milk, a bag of peanuts, a pickle. This time, they're the only ones in the store, so they abduct the young female store clerk with Odom's .22-caliber handgun. Lawson has a .32 pistol in his pocket. When the police arrive later on, after being called by a customer who notices the store is unattended, they find that the cash register has not been touched, the woman's pocketbook is behind the counter, and nothing of value has been taken.

The two men drive to a secluded spot. Odom orders her to undress completely, then rapes her in the backseat of the car. Meanwhile, Lawson is standing outside by the driver's door, telling Odom to hurry up and give him his turn. After about five minutes, Odom ejaculates, buckles his pants, and gets out of the car so Lawson can take his place.

Odom walks away from the car, he says, to throw up. Lawson later claims that Odom told him, "We had to get rid of her," even though Lawson had elicited a promise from her that she wouldn't tell if they let her go. At any rate, about five minutes later, Odom hears the woman scream from the car and yell, "Oh, my throat!" When he returns, Lawson has cut her throat and is mutilating her naked body with a knife he'd bought from the 7-Eleven the previous night.

The next day, as the two of them are in Odom's VW, getting rid of the victim's clothing that they had wrapped into two bundles, Lawson tells him he had tried to cannibalize the woman's sexual organs after the attack, but it had made him sick.

The horribly mutilated body was discovered in plain view, and the killers were arrested within a few days of the murder. Russell Odom, scared for his life, readily admitted the rape but denied he had taken part in the murder.

In his statement to police, Clay Lawson made it clear

he had had no intercourse with the victim: "I did not rape the girl. I only wanted to destroy her." This is a guy who chewed chalk in the courtroom during his trial.

They were tried separately. Odom received life plus forty years for rape, unlawful weapon possession, and accessory before and after the fact to murder. Lawson was convicted of first-degree murder and was electrocuted on May 18, 1976.

Like Bittaker and Norris, this case is characterized by a mixed presentation of behavior—and therefore behavioral evidence—because of the participation of two distinct personalities. The bodily mutilation is a sign of a disorganized personality type, while the finding of semen in the victim's vagina strongly points to an organized personality. We taught the Odom and Lawson case at Quantico, and it was in the back of my mind when I got a call from Chief John Reeder of the Logan Township, Pennsylvania, Police Department. It was early in my career as a profiler. Reeder was a National Academy graduate, and through Special Agent Dale Frye of the FBI's resident agency in Johnstown, he and Blair County district attorney Oliver E. Mattas Jr. asked for help in solving the rape, murder, and mutilation of a young woman named Betty Jane Shade.

The facts presented to me were these:

About a year earlier, on May 29, 1979, this twenty-two-year-old woman was walking home from her baby-sitting job at about 10:15 p.m. Four days later, a man who stated he was out on a nature walk stumbled upon her badly mutilated but well-preserved body in an illegal garbage dump site on top of Wopsononock Mountain, near Altoona. Her long blond hair had been cut off and was hanging on a nearby tree. County coroner Charles R. Burkey told the local newspaper it was the "most gruesome" death he had ever seen. He found that Betty Jane Shade had been sexually assaulted, her jaw fractured, her eyes blackened, the body with numerous stab wounds. The cause of death was a severe blow to the head, and postmortem mutilation included numerous stab wounds, the removal of both breasts, and an incision from the victim's vagina to rectum.

Although the partially undigested contents of her stomach indicated she had been killed soon after she disappeared, her body was too well preserved to have been at the dump site for four days. There was no larvae infestation or trauma from animals that one would normally expect. The police had also been investigating complaints of illegal dumping at the mountainous site, so they would have found the body themselves had it been there earlier.

I reviewed all of the case materials Reeder sent me and came up with a profile, which I related during a lengthy telephone conference. During this conference, I tried to educate the police about the principles of profiling and the kinds of things we look for. I thought they should be looking for a white male, aged seventeen to twenty-five, though I noted that if he lived way the hell out in the sticks, he could be older because his social development would be slower. He would be thin or wiry, a loner, not exactly a whiz kid in high school, introverted, probably into pornography. The childhood background would be classic—a dysfunctional, broken family with an absent father and a domineering, overly protective mother. She might have given him the impression that all women are bad except for her. The UNSUB would therefore fear women and not be able to deal with them, which was why he had to render her unconscious or powerless so quickly.

He knew her very well. That was clear from the severe facial trauma. He had a tremendous amount of anger and sought to depersonalize her, through the face, breast, and genital mutilation. The removal of the hair said something else to me. While this could also be thought of as an attempt at depersonalization, I knew from victimology that Shade was a neat, meticulous individual and was proud of her well-groomed, well-cared-for hair. So the cutting off of the hair was an insult, a degrading gesture. And this also hinted at someone who knew her very well. Yet there was no sign of sadistic abuse or torture before death as there had been with Bittaker and Norris. This was not someone who derived his sexual satisfaction from inflicting pain.

I told the police not to look for the "used-car salesman type down the street with the outgoing personality." If this guy was employed at all, it would be menial; a janitorial or blue-collar job. Anyone who would leave the body at that sort of dump site had to have a menial job or something that involved dirt or grime. The time of the abduction, the missing breasts, the obvious moving of the body, and the revisiting the final dump site, all told me he'd be mainly nocturnal. I expected him to visit the cemetery, maybe go to the funeral, to twist things around in his mind until he was convinced he had had a "normal" relationship with Betty Jane. For that reason, I thought a polygraph would be virtually useless even after they had a suspect. The chances were strong he would live somewhere between her home and where she was seen leaving work at her baby-sitting job.

Though they didn't have anything solid enough for an arrest, the police told me they had two suspects they considered strong. One was her live-in boyfriend and self-described fiancé, Charles F. Soult Jr., known as Butch. He would certainly have to be strongly considered. But the police were very high on the other one: the man who found the body and whose story didn't quite add up. He was a machinist for the railroad, out on disability. He said he'd been out on a nature walk but had found the body at an obvious trash dump. An elderly man out walking his dog said he had seen this individual urinating at the scene. He was dressed inappropriately for a long hike, and though it had been raining, he was completely dry. He lived within four blocks of Betty Jane Shade's house, and had tried unsuccessfully to pick her up on several occasions. He was nervous in his encounters with the police and said he had been afraid to report the body because he didn't want to be blamed for the crime. This is a typical excuse by a subject who comes forward proactively to inject himself into the investigation and tries to deflect suspicion from himself. He was a beer drinker and heavy smoker, certainly strong enough to kill and dispose of the body himself. He had a history of antisocial behavior. On the night of the murder, he and his wife claimed to be home watching television by themselves, which provided them with no solid alibi. I told the police that someone like this would contact an attorney and be uncooperative from then on. That was exactly what had happened with him, they reported. He'd gotten a lawyer and refused a polygraph.

All of this sounded pretty promising. But what bothered me most was that he was married with two children and living with his wife. This wouldn't have been his style. If a married guy had done the murder, he would have a lot of sadistic rage toward women. He would draw out the killing, abuse her more before death, but not mutilate her afterward. He was also thirty, which struck me as being on the high side.

Soult looked like a stronger choice to me. He fit virtually all of the profile elements. His parents had separated when he was young. His mother was a domineering woman, overly involved in her son's life. At twenty-six, he was inept with women. He told police he had had just two sexual encounters in his life, both with an older woman who made fun of him because he couldn't get it up. He said he and Betty Jane were very much in love and engaged to be married, though she dated and had sexual relationships with other men. I felt sure that if she were still alive, she'd tell a completely different story. At her funeral, he said he wanted to dig up the coffin and climb in there with her. And when interviewed by the police, he had cried incessantly over the loss of Betty Jane.

Butch Soult and his brother, Mike, worked as trash haulers, the police said.

"Jesus, this sounds pretty good," I replied.

They had access to the dump site, reason to know about it and go there, and a means of transporting the body.

But as much as I liked Butch as a suspect, two things bothered me. First, as I'd expected, he was kind of a little twerp who wasn't much bigger than Shade. I didn't think he was capable of moving the body or arranging it into the froglike position with the legs spread and bent at the knees in which it was found. Second, semen was found in the victim's vagina, indicative of a traditional rape. I would not have been surprised to find semen on the body, in her under-pants or other clothing, but not this. Like David Berkowitz, this guy would be a masturbator, but not a rapist. He had to get his sexual satisfaction indirectly. It didn't add up.

This was a mixed organized-disorganized presentation, in many ways similar to the murder of Francine Elveson in New York, with the same early blitz attack, facial disfigure-ment, and genital mutilation. Whereas Elveson's nipples had been cut off, Shade's entire breasts had been removed.

But in the New York case, the larger Carmine Calabro had carried the tiny victim a couple of floors up and left her. And the ejaculation had all been masturbatory.

Keeping the lessons from Odom and Lawson in mind, I thought there was only one logical possibility. I believed it was likely Butch Soult had met Betty Jane on the street after she left her job, they got into an argument, he beat her up and probably rendered her unconscious, then transported her to a secluded location. I also believed he could have struck the blow that killed her, cut off her hair, mutilated her body, and kept the breasts as souvenirs. But between the time she was first attacked and the time she was killed, she had been raped, and I didn't think a disorganized, sexually inadequate, mother-dominated young man such as Soult was capable of that. And I didn't think he had moved the body by himself.

Butch's brother, Mike, was the logical second suspect.

He came from the same background and had the same job. He had spent some time in a mental institution, and had a record of violence, behavior problems, and poor anger control. The main difference was he was married, though their mother was so domineering in his life as well. The night Betty Jane Shade was abducted, Mike's wife had been in the hospital having a baby. Her pregnancy was a major stressor, plus it had deprived him of a sexual release. It made perfect sense that after the attack, the panicked Butch had called his brother, who had raped the young woman while Butch looked on, then, after the murder, had helped him dispose of the body.

I told the police an indirect, nonthreatening approach would be best. Unfortunately, they had already interviewed Butch several times and polygraphed him. As I knew it would, the exam showed no deceit on his part, but inappropriate emotional reactions. I thought the best approach now would be to focus on Mike, hammering home that all he did was have sex with Shade and help dispose of her body, but that if he didn't cooperate at this point, he would be in as much hot water as his brother.

This tactic paid off. Both brothers—and their sister, Cathy Wiesinger, who claimed to be Betty Jane's best friend—were arrested. Cathy, according to Mike, had been in on the body disposal as well.

So what happened? I believe Butch had been trying to have sex with this sexually attractive, sexually experienced woman, but couldn't. His resentment built up until it didn't take much to set him off. After he attacked Shade, he panicked and called in his brother. But his anger built even further when Mike could have sex with her and he couldn't. His anger continued, and four days later he mutilated the body, giving him "the final word."

One of the victim's breasts was recovered. Mike told police that Butch kept the other one, which didn't surprise me. Wherever he hid it, it was never found.

Charles "Butch" Soult was convicted of first-degree murder and Mike, following a plea arrangement, was sent to a mental institution. Chief Reeder commented publicly that we were directly instrumental in developing the investigation and obtaining statements from the perpetrators. We, in turn, were fortunate to have a local partner like him who had been trained in our methods and understood the collaborative process between police and Quantico.

Because of this cooperation, we were able to take out a killer and his accomplice before they had a chance to kill again. Chief Reeder and his men and women went back to the business of keeping the peace in Logan Township, Pennsylvania. And I went back to my 150-odd other active cases, hoping I'd learned something that would help me in at least one of them to walk in the shoes of both perpetrator and victim.

10

Everybody Has a Rock

One evening years before, when I was back home after my ill-fated college experience in Montana, I was having dinner with my parents at a pizza and beer place in Uniondale, Long Island, called Coldstream. Just as I took a bite out of my slice of everything-with-extra-cheese, my mother—out of the blue—said, "John, have you ever had sexual relations with a woman?"

I swallow hard, trying to gulp down what I had just bitten off. This isn't the kind of question nineteen- or twenty-year-old kids are used to being asked by their mothers in the mid-1960s. I turn to my father for some sign of support, but he's stone-faced. He'd been caught as much off-guard as I had.

"Well, have you?" she persists. She wasn't a Holmes for nothing.

"Uh . . . yeah, Mom. I have."

I see this look of revulsion come over my mother's face. "Well, who was she?" she demands.

"Ah . . . Well . . ." I've sort of lost the healthy appetite I'd come into the place with. "Actually, there've been several."

I don't tell her one had been in her mid-teens in a home for unwed mothers in Bozeman. But you'd have thought I just told her where I'd hidden the bodies after I'd dismembered them, and it had been right in their basement. "Who is going to have you as a husband now?" she laments.

Again I turn to my unusually silent father. *Come on, Dad, help me out!*

"Oh, I don't know, Dolores. It's not a big deal these days."

"It's always been a 'big deal,' Jack," she counters, then

turns back to me. "What would happen, John, if your future bride someday asked you whether you had had relations with another woman before you met her?"

I pause in mid-bite. "Well, Mom, I would tell her the truth."

"No, don't say that," my father pipes up.

"What do you mean, Jack?" my mother asks. *Okay, Dad, let's see you get out of this one.*

The interrogation session ended in an uneasy stalemate. I'm not sure if I got anything out of the encounter. I either told Pam of my past or she suspected it. At any rate, she did agree to marry me, despite my mother's fears. But when I thought back to that grilling from my perspective as a federal law enforcement official, profiler, and expert on criminal behavior and psychology, an important realization did dawn on me. Even if I'd had all the training and analytical experience that I have now, I still wouldn't have handled my mother's inquisition any better!

Because she'd gotten to me on a vulnerable point of truth.

I'll give you another example. Ever since I became the FBI's chief profiler, I personally selected and trained all of the other profilers. For that reason, I've enjoyed a particularly close and cooperative relationship with all the men and women who've been on my team. Most of them have become stars in their own right. But if I could ever be said to have had a true disciple among them, it would be Greg Cooper. Greg left a prestigious job as chief of police in a town in Utah while still in his early thirties and joined the FBI after hearing Ken Lanning and Bill Hagmaier speak at a law enforcement seminar. He distinguished himself in the Seattle Field Office, but always had the dream of coming to Quantico to work in Behavioral Science. He had requested and studied all of my profiling and analysis of the Green River Killer, and when I flew out to Seattle to appear on a viewer-participation television special called *Manhunt Live*, Greg volunteered to be my chauffeur and guide. When I became chief of the reorganized Investigative Support Unit, Greg was working in an FBI resident agency in Orange County, California, and living in Laguna Niguel. I brought him back to Quantico, where he became an outstanding performer.

When he first came into the unit, Greg was assigned to share an underground, windowless office with Jana Monroe, a former police officer and homicide detective in California before she became a special agent who, among her many other fine qualities, happens to be a smashingly attractive blond. In other words, she puts it all together. Now, not too many men would find this a hardship assignment, but Greg happens to be a devout Mormon, a very straight and devoted family man with five lovely children and a stunning wife named Rhonda, to whom it was a major sacrifice to move from their sunny California paradise to sleepy, hot, and humid Virginia. Every time she asked about his office mate, Greg would hem and haw and try to change the subject.

Finally, about six months after he'd been on the job for us, Greg brings Rhonda to the unit Christmas party. I'm not there because I'm working a case out of town, but the naturally vivacious Jana is. And typical for her in a party situation, she's wearing a subtle, understated, short, and form-fitting bright red dress with a plunging neckline.

When I get back, Jim Wright, the unit's second-in-command who has taken over for me as profiling program manager, tells me there were real fireworks between Rhonda and Greg after the party. She's none too happy about his spending his days in such close confines with a beautiful, tough, charming agent who knows her way around a firing range and dance floor with equal facility.

So I have my secretary get Greg out of a meeting and tell him I want to see him right away. He gets to my office looking somewhat concerned. He's only been here six months, this unit has been his dream, and he really wants to make good.

Life on the farm. How I spent my summers in high school; posing with one of my early clients.
(photo by Jack Douglas)

The big game against Wantaugh High—the first time I really tried to apply "psychological profiling" against an opponent. I am easy to spot on the Hempstead bench—wearing the Hannibal Lecter–like face mask, having broken my nose in a previous game.
(photo by Jack Douglas)

A portrait of the agent as a young man. My first trip back home after joining the Bureau, posing with my badge and one of the new suits my father bought me. Note also the FBI regulation haircut. This was a rare moment of smiling on this trip. I spent most of the Christmas 1970 vacation memorizing the manual of Bureau communications for Assistant Director Joe Casper.   (photo by Jack Douglas)

Graduation from the 107th Session of the FBI National Academy, December 16, 1976.
From left to right: me, Pam, FBI Director Clarence Kelley, my mother Dolores,
and my father Jack.   (FBI photo)

Milwaukee. A photo used in SWAT and hostage-rescue training showing positions at the moment
Joe Del Campo fired the shot that ended the Jacob Cohen murder-hostage drama.

(FBI training photo)

The first generation, January 1978. Just seven months after I joined the Behavioral Science Unit in Quantico, I posed with some of the living legends. From left to right: Bob Ressler; Tom O'Malley, who taught sociology; me; Dick Harper, who also taught sociology; Jim Reese, the profiler who went on to become our expert on stress; Dick Ault and Howard Teten, who taught applied criminology and began the FBI's profiling program.   (FBI photo)

The next generation, June 1995. The Investigative Support Unit. From left to right: Steve Mardigian, Pete Smerick, Clint Van Zandt, Jana Monroe, Jud Ray, me (kneeling), Jim Wright, Greg Cooper, Gregg McCrary. Not pictured are Larry Ankrom, Steve Etter, Bill Hagmaier, and Tom Salp.

(photo by Mark Olshaker)

Special Agent John Conway and I interview Edmund Kemper at Vacaville.

Wayne D. Williams, during his 1982 murder trial in the Atlanta child murders case.
I advised Assistant D.A. Jack Mallard on what would be the best strategy for bringing out a side
of the personality Williams managed to keep hidden from the jury.

(AP/Wide World Photo)

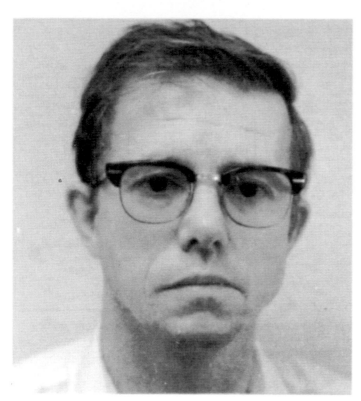

Robert Hansen, the Anchorage, Alaska, baker, who graduated from hunting game to hunting local prostitutes he'd abducted and set loose in the woods.

(Alaska State Troopers photo)

The trophy room of Robert Hansen showing his take before he escalated into human game.

(Alaska State Troopers photo)

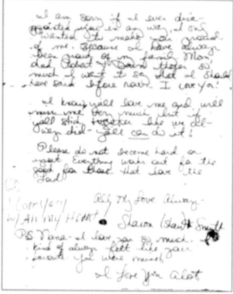

The "Last Will and Testament" of seventeen-year-old Shari Faye Smith—probably the greatest and most moving testament of courage, faith, and character I have seen in my twenty-five years in law enforcement.

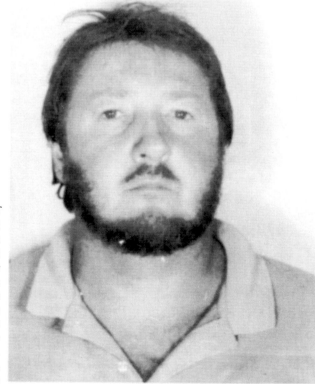

Larry Gene Bell, convicted of killing Shari Faye Smith and Debra May Helmick in South Carolina. When I interrogated him in Lexington County Sheriff Jim Metts's office, he denied that "the Larry Gene Bell sitting here" could have committed such crimes, but admitted that "the bad Larry Gene Bell" could have.

(Lexington County, South Carolina, Sheriff's Department photo)

A typical case consultation. Gregg McCrary presents details of the series of prostitute murders in Rochester, New York, to colleagues in the Investigative Support Unit. This investigation and McCrary's proactive strategies helped Rochester and New York State police find and arrest Arthur Shawcross, who was tried and convicted of ten of the murders. From left to right are Jim Wright, Gregg McCrary, me, and Steve Etter.　(photo by Mark Olshaker)

In organizing our rigorous training program for new members of the Investigative Support Unit, we received the generous cooperation of some outstanding forensic and law enforcement organizations. Here, Jud Ray and I present a plaque of appreciation to Lt. Donald Stephenson, Commanding Officer of the New York Police Department Crime Scene Unit, for the department's help in training our people on-scene.　(New York Police Department photo)

An example of a proactive technique. In certain types of cases, after developing the profile, we will often "go public" through the local media, hoping that someone will recognize the description of the UNSUB and come forward.

(*The Fairfax Journal*)

I look up from my desk and say, "Close the door, Greg. Sit down." He does, even more disturbed by my tone of voice. "I just got off the phone with Rhonda," I continue. "I understand you've had some problems."

"You just got off the phone with Rhonda?" He's not even looking at me. He's staring straight at the call-director phone on my desk.

"Look, Greg," I said in my most soothing counselor tones, "I'd like to cover for you, but when you and Jana go on the road together, I can't make any special provisions. This is something you're going to have to deal with on your own. Rhonda obviously knows what's going on between you and Jana and—"

"Nothing's going on between me and Jana!" he splutters.

"I know there are a lot of stresses in this job. But you've got a beautiful, terrific wife, nice kids. Don't throw it all away."

"It's not what you think, John. It's not what she thinks. You have to believe me." And all the time he's still staring at that telephone, maybe thinking if he concentrates hard enough, he's going to be able to burn it right through the desk. He's broken out in a cold sweat. I can see the carotid artery pounding in his neck. He's heading south fast.

So at that point I let up. "Look at you, you miserable wretch!" I grin triumphantly. "You call yourself an interrogator?" At the time he was preparing a chapter on interrogation for the *Crime Classification Manual*. "Have you done anything to be guilty about?"

"No, John. I swear!"

"And look! You're putty in my hands! You're completely innocent. You're a former chief of police. You're an experienced interrogator. And yet I was able to play you like a yo-yo. So what do you have to say for yourself?"

At that particular time, as the sweat of relief rolled off his balding head, he didn't have anything to say for himself, but he got the point. I knew I could jerk him around like that because it had been done to me with equal success and could be again if the situation arose.

We're all vulnerable. It doesn't matter how much you know, how experienced you are, how many suspect interrogations you've handled successfully. It doesn't matter if you understand the technique. Each of us can be gotten to—if you can just figure out where and how we're vulnerable.

I'd learned this during one of my earliest cases as a profiler, and I put it to use many times thereafter—not only in demonstrations to my own team. It was the first time I actually "staged" an interrogation.

In December 1979, Special Agent Robert Leary from the Rome, Georgia, Resident Agency called with the details of a particularly horrible case and asked me to give it my top priority. The week before, Mary Frances Stoner, a pretty and outgoing twelve-year-old girl in Adairsville, about a half-hour from Rome, had disappeared after being dropped off by the school bus at the driveway to her house, approximately a hundred yards back from the road. Her body was later found about ten miles away in a wooded lovers' lane area by a young couple who noticed the bright yellow coat over her head. They contacted police and did not disturb the scene, a critical consideration. The cause of death was determined to be blunt-force trauma to the head. Postmortem examination detected skull fracturing consistent with a large rock. (There's a bloodstained one right near her head in the crime-scene photos.) Marks on the neck also indicated manual strangulation from the rear.

Before I looked at the case materials, I wanted to know as much as possible about the victim. No one had anything other than wonderful things to say about Mary Frances. She was described as friendly to everyone, gregarious, and charming. She was sweet and innocent, a drum majorette in the school band who often wore her uniform to school. She was a cute twelve-year-old who looked twelve, rather than trying to look eighteen. She wasn't promiscuous, she'd never been involved with drugs or alcohol. The autopsy clearly indicated she'd been a virgin when raped. All in all, she was what we would characterize as a low-risk victim taken from a low-risk setting.

After being briefed, listening to Leary, and studying the files and crime-scene photos, I jotted down the following half-page note:

Profile
   Sex—m
   Race—w
   Age—mid-twenties–late twenties
   Marital—married: problems or divorced
   Military—dishonorable, medical
   Occupation—blue collar: electrician, plumber
   IQ—average–above average
   Education—H.S. at most; dropout
   Criminal Record—arson, rape
   Personality—confident, cocky, passed polygraph
   Color Vehicle—black or blue
   Interrogate—direct, projection

This was a rape of opportunity, and the murder had not been planned or intended. The disheveled appearance of the clothing on the body indicated that Mary Frances had been forced to undress, then was allowed to redress hurriedly after the rape. I could see from the photos that one shoe was untied, and the report noted bleeding in her panties. No debris was on her back, behind, or feet, which suggested she was raped in a car, not on the wooded ground where her body was found.

Looking intently at the rather routine crime-scene photos, I began to understand what had happened. I could imagine the whole thing.

Because of her youth, as well as her outgoing and trusting nature, Mary Frances would have been easily approachable in so nonthreatening an environment as the school bus stop. The UNSUB probably coaxed her up to his car, then grabbed her or forced her in with a knife or gun. The remoteness of the area in which her body was found indicated that he knew the region well and knew he wouldn't be disturbed there.

From the abduction scene I could tell this wasn't a planned crime, but rather one that took form as he drove past. Just as in the Odom and Lawson case, had anyone else happened upon the scene at the right time, the crime wouldn't have gone forward. Because of the young girl's cuteness and sunny disposition, in his own mind the fantasy-fueled offender had made over her innocent friendliness into promiscuity and the desire to play sexually with him.

Of course, in actuality, nothing could have been further from the truth. Once he assaulted her, she would have been terrified, in severe pain, crying out for help, and begging for her life. The fantasy he'd been nurturing for years was one thing, but the reality wasn't pretty. He'd lost control of the situation with this little girl and realized he was in one hell of a mess.

At this point, he realizes the only way out for him is to kill her. But since she's in fear for her life, controlling her is much more difficult than he'd imagined. So to make it easier on himself, to make her more cooperative and compliant, he tells her to get dressed quickly and he'll let her go—either he'll let her run away or maybe he'll tie her to a tree and leave the scene himself.

But as soon as she turns her back on him, he comes up behind her and strangles her. He's probably able to render her unconscious, but strangulation requires a lot of upper-body strength. He wasn't able to control her before, and he can't finish the job. He drags her under a tree, picks up the nearest large rock he can find, and drops it down on her head three or four times, killing her.

I didn't feel the offender knew Mary Frances well, but

they had seen each other around town enough for her to have recognized him and for him to have formed fantasies about her. He'd probably seen her going to school in her little majorette uniform.

I knew from the placement of the coat over her head that our UNSUB didn't feel good about the crime. I also knew that time was against the police. In this type of crime and with this type of intelligent, organized offender, the longer he had to think about it, rationalize it, and justify it as the victim's fault, the more difficult it would be to get a confession. Even if he were polygraphed, the results would be inconclusive at best. And as soon as he felt the heat was off and he wouldn't arouse suspicion by leaving, he'd be off to another part of the country where he'd be difficult to trace and where some other little girl would be in danger.

To me, the UNSUB was clearly from the area and the police had almost assuredly interviewed him already. He'd be cooperative but cocky, and if the police accused him, he wouldn't break. I told them a crime with this degree of sophistication would not be a first, although there was a good chance this was his first murder. His blue or black car would be several years old because he could not afford a newer one, but it would be functional and well maintained. Everything in it would be in place. From my experience, orderly, compulsive people like that generally favored darker cars.

After hearing all this, one of the officers on the phone said, "You just described a guy we released as a suspect in the case." He was still a suspect in another crime and he fit the profile to a T. His name was Darrell Gene Devier, a white male, twenty-four years of age, who'd been married and divorced twice and who was currently living with his first ex-wife. He was a tree-limb trimmer in Rome, Georgia, where he was a strong suspect in the rape of a thirteen-year-old girl, but had never been charged. He had joined the Army after his first divorce but had gone AWOL and was discharged after seven months. He drove a three-year-old black Ford Pinto that was well maintained. He admitted to having been arrested as a juvenile for possession of a Molotov cocktail. He dropped out of school after eighth grade, but IQ tests listed a range of 100 to 110.

He had been interviewed to see if he had seen or heard anything, since he'd been trimming trees on the Stoners' street for the power company for about two weeks before Mary Frances's abduction. The police told me he was scheduled for a polygraph that very day.

That wouldn't be a good idea, I told them. They wouldn't get anything out of the exam, and it would only reinforce the suspect's ability to cope with the interrogation process. At that time, we didn't have a lot of field experience with interrogation, but from the prison interviews and the ongoing serial-killer study, I felt that I knew what I was talking about. Sure enough, when they called me back the next day, they told me the lie detector had been inconclusive.

Now that he knows he can beat the box, there's only one way to get him, I said. Stage the interrogation at the police station at night. The suspect will feel more comfortable initially, making him more vulnerable to questioning. This will also give him a message about your seriousness and dedication. He knows there isn't an arbitrary break point like lunch or dinner, and he knows he's not going to be hung out as a media trophy if he caves in. Have the local police and the FBI's Atlanta Field Office carry out the interrogation together to show a united front and to imply that the full weight of the government of the United States is against him. Pile up stacks of file folders on tables in front of him with his name on them, even if they're just full of blank pages.

Most important: without saying anything about it, place the bloody rock on a low table at a forty-five-degree angle to his line of sight so that he'll have to turn his head to look at it. Closely observe all his nonverbal cues—his behavior, respiration, perspiration, carotid pulse. If he is the killer, he will not be able to ignore that rock, even though you haven't mentioned it or explained its significance.

What we needed to create was what I call the "high ass-pucker factor." I actually used the Stoner case as a laboratory for my theories. Many of the techniques we refined later had their experimental origins here.

He won't confess, I continued. Georgia is a capital-punishment state, and even if he's only sent to prison, his rap as a child molester could get his ass raped the first time he takes a shower. All of the other prisoners will be gunning for this guy.

Use low, mysterious lighting and have no more than two officers or agents in the interview environment at one time, preferably one from the FBI and one from the Adairsville PD. What you've got to do is imply that you understand the subject, understand what was going through his mind and the stresses he was under. No matter how disgusting it feels to you, you're going to have to project the blame onto the victim. Imply that she seduced him. Ask if she led him on, if she turned on him, if she threatened him with blackmail. Give him a face-saving scenario. Give him a way of explaining his actions.

The other thing I knew from all the cases I'd seen is that in blunt-force-trauma or knife homicides, it's difficult for the attacker to avoid getting at least traces of the victim's blood on him. It's common enough that you can use it. When he starts to waffle, even slightly, I said, look him straight in the eye and tell him the most disturbing part of the whole case is the known fact that he got Mary's blood on him.

"We know you got blood on you, Gene; on your hands, on your clothing. The question for us isn't 'Did you do it?' We know you did. The question is 'Why?' We think we know why and we understand. All you have to do is tell us if we're right."

And that was exactly how it went down. They bring

Devier in. He looks instantly at the rock, starts perspiring and breathing heavily. His body language is completely different from the previous interviews: tentative, defensive. The interrogators project blame and responsibility onto the girl, and when he looks as if he's going with it, they bring up the blood. This really upsets him. You can often tell you've got the right guy if he shuts up and starts listening intently as you speak. An innocent guy will yell and scream. And even if a guilty guy yells and screams to make you think he's innocent, you can tell the difference.

He admits to the rape and agrees with the interrogator that she threatened him. Bob Leary tells him they know he didn't plan on killing her. If he had, he would have used something more efficient than the rock. In the end, he confesses to the murder and to the rape in Rome the previous year. Darrell Gene Devier was tried for the rape and murder of Mary Frances Stoner, convicted, and sentenced to death. He was executed in the Georgia electric chair on May 18, 1995, almost sixteen years after the murder and his arrest; that's almost four more years than Mary Frances had on earth.

The key to this type of interrogation, I found, is to be creative; to use your imagination. I had to ask myself, "What would get to me if I were the one who did it?" We're all vulnerable. It's going to be a different thing for each of us. In my case, with my sloppy bookkeeping, my SAC could probably call me in, have me see one of my expense vouchers on his desk, and make me sweat. But there's always something.

Everybody has a rock.

The lessons learned in the Devier case can have applications far beyond the sick world of sexual murder. Whether it's embezzlement, public corruption, a mob investigation, a fencing scheme, or a corrupt union you have to penetrate, it doesn't matter; the principles are going to be the same. What I would advise in any of these types of cases would be to target whomever you deem to be the "weakest link," figure out a way to bring him in and let him see what he's up against, then win his cooperation in going after the others.

In any kind of conspiracy case, this is a critical issue. What you want to do is flip one guy to be a government witness, then watch the whole house of cards come tumbling down. The choice of whom to approach first is so important because if you pick the wrong guy and then can't flip him, he's going to tip off everyone else and you're back at square one.

Let's say we're investigating a big-city public corruption case in which we suspect eight or ten people are involved from one particular agency. And let's say the number one or two man in the agency is the best "catch." But when we profile the guy, we find that he has his personal act together despite the corruption. He isn't a boozer or a womanizer; in fact, he's a strong family man—no illnesses, no money problems, no obvious vulnerabilities. If he's approached by the FBI, there's a good chance he'd simply deny everything, tell us to go to hell, and alert the others.

The way you get to someone like this is to go through the smaller fish, just as with organized crime. As we go through all the records, maybe one candidate will stand out from the rest for our purposes. He isn't a higher-up, but a clerk who fixes all the paperwork. He's been at his job for twenty years, so everything he has is invested in it. He has financial and medical problems, both of which provide strong vulnerabilities.

Next comes the choice of who is "cast" to lead the interrogation. My preference is usually for someone a little older and more authoritative than the subject, a sharp dresser with a commanding appearance, someone who can be friendly and outgoing and make the subject relax, but become absolutely serious and directed as soon as circumstances call for it.

If there's a holiday coming up in the next few weeks, or perhaps the subject's birthday or anniversary, I advise postponing the interrogation to take advantage of that. If you get him in the room and he realizes that, if he doesn't cooperate, this might be the last holiday season he'll be spending with his family, that can give you some added leverage.

"Staging" can be just as effective in dealing with a non-violent offender as it was in the Stoner murder case. For any large or ongoing investigation, I suggest concentrating all of your materials into one place, whether or not this was actually done for the case. For example, if you take over a conference room for your "task force," gathering all your agents, staff, and case files together, you'll be showing your subject just how serious you are. If you can "decorate" the walls with, say, blowups of surveillance photos and other signs of just how wide-ranging and official this ongoing investigation is, the point will be driven home all the more forcefully. A couple of video monitors playing tapes of your targets in the act are icing on the cake.

Among my personal favorite touches are wall charts showing the penalties each person would face if convicted. There's nothing terribly profound about this, but it does tend to keep the pressure on the subject and remind him of the stakes. I want to get that "ass-pucker factor" as intense as I can.

I've always found that the late-night or early-morning hours are often the best time to conduct an interrogation. People tend to be more relaxed and at the same time more vulnerable. Again, if you and your guys are working through the night, you immediately send the message that this case is a big deal and you are very committed to it. Another practical consideration of a nighttime interrogation in any conspiracy case is that your subject should not be seen by any of the others. If he thinks he's been "made," then there's not going to be any deal.

The basis of any successful deal is going to be the truth and an appeal to your subject's reason and common sense. All the staging does is call attention to the key elements. If I were conducting the interrogation of our representative sub-ject in the public corruption case, I might call him at home late at night and say something like, "Sir, it's very important that I talk to you tonight. FBI agents are walking up to your door even as we speak." I would stress that he wasn't under arrest and didn't have to go with the agents. But I'd strongly suggest that he accompany them downtown because he might not have another chance. There would be no need to Mirandize him at this point because he isn't being charged with anything.

Once he arrived at the office, I'd let him cool his heels a while. When the other football team has to make a long-yardage field goal on the last play to win the game, you call a time-out to give their kicker time to think about it. Anyone who's had to wait to see the doctor before an important ap-pointment knows how effective this can be.

Once he was ushered into my office, I'd close the door, trying to seem warm and friendly, very understanding, everything man-to-man. I'd call the guy by name. "I want to make sure you understand you're not under arrest," I'd reiterate. "You're free to leave any time you want and my men will drive you back home. But I think you should listen to what I have to say. This could be the most important date in your life."

I might have him say the date with me to make sure we're on the same wavelength.

"I also want you to know that we're aware of your medi-cal history and we have a nurse on stand-by." This would be true. One of the reasons we targeted this guy was because of this particular vulnerability.

Now we start talking turkey. I would stress that the FBI realizes he's a little fish, that he's been underpaid for what he's done, and that he's not really the one we want the most. "Right now, as you can see, we're interviewing many of the people involved in this case. The ship is going down; no question about it. You can go down with it or you can reach up for the third time before drowning and grab for a life preserver. We know you've been used, manipulated, taken advantage of by others much more powerful than you. We have a U.S. attorney standing by to offer a real deal if you want to take it."

As a parting shot, I would stress, "Remember, this is the only time we'll be able to make you this offer. I've got twenty agents working this case. We can go out and arrest everyone if we have to. Don't you think someone will roll if you don't? And then you'll go down with the ship. If you want to go down with the big guys, that's your choice. But tonight is the last time we'll be able to talk like this. Will you cooperate?"

If he does—and it really is in his best interests if he does—then we Mirandize him and let him contact an attorney. But as a good-faith gesture, I'd probably ask him to get on the phone and arrange a meeting with one of the other players. You don't want him having second thoughts and backing out. Once you've got your first guy's commitment, the rest of the pieces start falling into place.

The reason this works so effectively, even if you understand our complete approach in advance, is because it's mutually beneficial to the investigator and the targeted subject. It's based on truth and tailored to the subject's life and situation and emotional needs. Even knowing how it was staged for maximum impact, if I were the subject presented with this deal, I'd take it, because it does represent my best chance. The strategy behind this type of interrogation is the same as the one I developed for the Stoner murder case. I keep thinking to myself, "What would get to me?"

Because everybody has a rock.

Gary Trapnell, the armed robber and airplane hijacker I interviewed at the federal prison in Marion, Illinois, is just about as intelligent and insightful as any criminal I've studied. He's the one who was so confident in his own abilities that he assured me he could fool any prison psychiatrist into believing he had any given mental condition I specified. He was also confident that if he were out of prison, he'd be able to evade the law.

"You just can't catch me," he asserted.

"Okay, Gary," I said hypothetically, "You're out. And you're smart enough to know you have to break off all contact with family members to keep away from the feds.

"Now I know your father was a high-ranking, decorated military officer. You really loved and respected him. You wanted to be like him. And your crime spree began when he died."

I could see from his facial reaction that I was on to something; that I'd hit a nerve.

"Your dad is buried in Arlington National Cemetery. So suppose I have agents staking out his grave around Christmas, on his birthday, and the anniversary of the date he died?"

In spite of himself, Trapnell broke out into a sardonic smile. "You got me!" he announced.

Again, the reason this occurred to me was because I tried to put myself in his place; I tried to figure out what would get to me. And my experience tells me that there is a way to get to everyone, if you can only figure out what it is.

In my own case, it might be something similar to what I would have used on Trapnell; that is, a particular date might be the emotional trigger.

My sister Arlene had a beautiful blonde daughter named Kim. She was born on my birthday, June 18, and I always felt a special bond with her. When she was sixteen, Kim died in her sleep. We were never able to find out the exact cause. To compound the pain and joy of her memory, it happens that my eldest daughter, Erika—now college age— looks very much like Kim. I'm sure that Arlene never sees Erika without seeing Kim in her mind, picturing what Kim would have grown up to become. My mother feels the same way.

If I were to target *me*, for instance, I'd plan the approach right before my birthday. I'm emotionally up, looking forward to the celebration with my family. But I'm also thinking about my niece, Kim—the birthday we shared, how much she resembles Erika—and I'm going to be feeling vulnerable. If I happen to see photographs of the two girls on the wall, I'm likely to come even more unglued.

It doesn't matter that I know what the overall strategy is in approaching me. It doesn't matter that I'm the one who came up with it. If the triggering stressor is a legitimate, valid concern, it will have a good chance of working. This one could be mine. Yours would be something else and we'd have to try to figure out in advance what it would be. But there would be something.

Because everybody has a rock.

11

Atlanta

In the winter of 1981, Atlanta was a city under siege.

It had begun quietly a year and a half earlier, almost unnoticed. Before it was over—if in fact it will ever be over—it had become one of the largest and perhaps one of the most publicized manhunts in American history, politicizing a town and polarizing a nation, every step of the investigation steeped in bitter controversy.

On July 28, 1979, police responded to a complaint of a foul odor in the woods off Niskey Lake Road and discovered the body of thirteen-year-old Alfred Evans. He'd been missing for three days. While examining the site, police discovered another body about fifty feet away—this one partially decomposed—belonging to fourteen-year-old Edward Smith, who had disappeared four days before Alfred. Both boys were black. The medical examiner determined that Alfred Evans had probably been strangled, while Edward Smith had definitely been shot with a .22-caliber weapon.

On November 8, the body of nine-year-old Yusef Bell was discovered in an abandoned school. He had been missing since late October and had also been strangled. Eight days later, fourteen-year-old Milton Harvey's body was found near Redwine Road and Desert Drive in the East Point section of Atlanta. He had been reported missing in early September, and as with Alfred Evans, no definite cause of death could be determined. Both of these children were also black. But there wasn't enough similar evidence to attach any particular significance. Unfortunately, in a city the size of Atlanta, children disappear all the time. Some of them are found dead.

On the morning of March 5, 1980, a twelve-year-old girl named Angel Lanier set out for school but never arrived. Five days later her body was found, bound and gagged with an electrical cord, on the side of a road. She was fully clothed, including her underwear, but another pair of panties had been stuffed in her mouth. Cause of death was determined to be ligature strangulation. The medical examiner found no evidence of sexual assault.

Eleven-year-old Jeffrey Mathis disappeared on March 12. At this point, the Atlanta Police Department still hadn't made anything out of six black children either missing or turning up dead. There were as many differences as similarities among the cases, and they hadn't seriously considered the possibility that some or all of them might be related.

But other people had. On April 15, Yusef Bell's mother, Camille, aligned with other parents of missing and slain black children and announced the formation of the Committee to Stop Children's Murders. They pleaded for official help and recognition of what they saw going on around them. This wasn't supposed to be happening in Atlanta, the cosmopolitan capital of the New South. This was a city on the move, the town supposedly "too busy to hate," which boasted a black mayor in Maynard Jackson and a black public safety commissioner in Lee Brown.

The horrors didn't stop. On May 19, fourteen-year-old Eric Middlebrook was found murdered about a quarter mile from his home. Death was caused by blunt-force trauma to the head. On June 9, twelve-year-old Christopher Richardson disappeared. And on June 22, the second young girl, eight-year-old LaTonya Wilson, was abducted from her bedroom in the early hours of a Sunday morning. Two days later, ten-year-old Aaron Wyche's body was found beneath a bridge in DeKalb County. He died of asphyxia and a broken neck. Anthony "Tony" Carter, nine, was found behind a warehouse on Wells Street on July 6, facedown in the grass, dead of multiple stab wounds. From the absence of blood at the scene, it was clear his body had been moved from another location.

The pattern could no longer be ignored. Public Safety Commissioner Brown set up the Missing and Murdered Task Force, which would ultimately include more than fifty members. Yet on it went. Earl Terrell, ten, was reported missing on July 31 off Redwine Road, near where Milton Harvey's body had been found. And when twelve-year-old Clifford Jones was found dead by ligature strangulation in an alley off Hollywood Road, the police finally accepted a connection and stated that the investigation would now be conducted under the assumption that the murders of black children were related.

Up until this point, the FBI had no jurisdiction to enter a case that for all its hideous enormity remained a series of local crimes. A break came with Earl Terrell's disappearance. His family had received several telephone calls demanding a ransom for the safe return of their son. The caller indicated that Earl had been taken to Alabama. The presumed crossing of state lines brought the federal kidnapping statute into effect and allowed the FBI to investigate. But it soon became clear that the ransom calls had been a hoax. Hopes faded for Earl's life and the FBI had to back out.

Another boy, eleven-year-old Darron Glass, was reported missing on September 16. Mayor Maynard Jackson asked the White House for help—specifically, to have the FBI conduct a major investigation into the Atlanta child murders and disappearances. With jurisdiction still very much an issue, Att. Gen. Griffin Bell ordered the FBI to begin an investigation of whether the children who had not been found were being held in violation of the federal kidnapping statute; in other words, was there an interstate character to the crimes? As an added responsibility, the Atlanta Field Office was charged with determining if the cases were, in fact, linked. In effect but not in so many words, the Bureau was given the message: solve the cases and find the killer, as quickly as possible.

The media, of course, had seized on the frenzy. The growing gallery of young black faces published regularly in the newspapers became a proclamation of collective municipal guilt. Was this a conspiracy to commit genocide on the black population, targeting its most vulnerable members? Was this the Klan or Nazi Party or some other hate group set to make its stand a decade and a half after the major civil rights legislation? Was this simply one crazed individual with a personal mission to kill young children? This last possibility seemed the least likely. These kids were falling victim at an incredibly rapid rate. And while to date, the overwhelming majority of serial killers had been white, almost never did they hunt outside their own race. Serial murder is a personal crime, not a political one.

But this did give the FBI another possible legitimacy in the case. If the interstate kidnapping angle didn't pan out, we were still charged with determining if this fit the 44 Classification: violation of federal civil rights.

By the time Roy Hazelwood and I went down to Atlanta, there were sixteen cases with no end in sight. By then the Bureau's involvement had an official case name: ATKID, also designated Major Case 30, though there was little public fanfare when the FBI came in. The Atlanta police didn't want anyone stealing their show, and the FBI's Atlanta Field Office didn't want to create expectations they might not be able to meet.

Roy Hazelwood was the logical choice to join me in Atlanta. Of all the Behavioral Science Unit instructors, Roy was doing the most profiling, teaching the National Academy course on interpersonal violence and taking on many of the rape cases that came to the unit. Our primary goals were to determine for ourselves if the cases were linked, and if so, was there a conspiracy?

We reviewed the voluminous case files—crime-scene photos, descriptions of what each child was wearing when found, statements from witnesses in the area, autopsy protocols. We interviewed family members of the children to see if there was a common victimology. The police drove us around the neighborhoods where the children had disappeared and took us to each of the body dump sites.

Without talking over our impressions with each other, Roy and I both took psychometric tests, administered by a forensic psychologist, which we filled out as if each of us were the killer. The test involved motivation, background, and family life—the types of things we'd put into a profile. The doctor who administered the test was amazed that our results were nearly identical.

And what we had to say wasn't aimed at winning any popularity contests.

First, we didn't think these were Klan-type hate crimes. Second, we were almost positive the offender was black. And third, while many of the deaths and disappearances were related, not all of them were.

The Georgia Bureau of Investigation had received several tips about Ku Klux Klan involvement, but we discounted them. If you study hate crimes going all the way back to the early days of the nation, you find that they tend to be highly public, highly symbolic acts. A lynching is intended to make a public statement and create a public display. Such a crime or other racial murder is an act of terrorism, and for it to have an effect, it must be highly visible. Ku Klux Klansmen don't wear white sheets to fade into the woodwork. If a hate group had targeted black children throughout the Atlanta area, it wouldn't have been content to let months go by before the police and the public figured out something was going on. We would have expected bodies strung up on Main Street, USA, and the message would have been none too subtle. We didn't see any of that type of behavior in these cases.

The body dump sites were in predominantly or exclusively black areas of the city. A white individual, much less a white group, could not have prowled these neighborhoods without being noticed. The police had canvassed extensively and had no reports of whites near any of the children or dump sites. These areas had street activity around the clock, so even under the cover of night, a white man could not have been around there completely unnoticed. This also fit in with our experience that sexual killers tend to target their own race. Even though there was no clear evidence of sexual molestation, these crimes definitely fit a sexual pattern.

There was a strong link among many of the victims. They were young and outgoing and streetwise, but inexperienced and rather naive about the world beyond their neighborhood. We felt this was the type of child who would be susceptible to a come-on or ruse or con from the right individual. That individual would have to have a car, since the children were taken away from the abduction sites. And we felt he would have to have some aura of adult authority. Many of these kids lived in conditions of obvious poverty. In some of the houses we found no electricity or running water.

Because of that and the children's relative lack of sophistication, I didn't think it would take much of a lure. To test this, we had Atlanta undercover officers go into these areas, often posing as workmen, and offer a child five dollars to come with him to do some job. They tried it with black officers and with white officers and it didn't seem to matter. These kids were so desperate for survival, they'd do just about anything for five dollars. It wasn't going to take someone all that sharp to get to them. The one other thing the experiment showed was that white men were noticed in these neighborhoods.

But as I said, while we did find a strong linkage, it didn't seem to apply to all the cases. After carefully evaluating the victims and the circumstances, I didn't think the two girls had been killed by the primary offender, or even by the same person as each other. The manner of LaTonya Wilson's abduction from her bedroom was too specialized. Of the boys,

I thought most of the "soft kills"—the strangulations—were related, not necessarily all the unknown causes of death. And other aspects of the evidence led us to believe we weren't dealing with a single killer. Strong evidence in a couple of the cases suggested the killer had been a member of the victim's family, but when FBI director William Webster announced this publicly, he was slam-dunked by the press. Aside from the obvious political problems with such a statement, any case separated from the Missing and Murdered list made that family ineligible to receive any of the funds that were starting to be contributed by groups and individuals around the country.

Even though we felt more than one person was responsible, we felt we were dealing with one particular individual who was on a tear, and he would keep killing until he was found. Roy and I profiled a black male, single, between the ages of twenty-five and twenty-nine. He would be a police buff, drive a police-type vehicle, and somewhere along the way he would insinuate himself into the investigation. He would have a police-type dog, either a German shepherd or a Doberman. He would not have a girlfriend, he would be sexually attracted to the young boys, but we weren't seeing any signs of rape or other overt sexual abuse. This, I thought, spoke to his sexual inadequacy. He would have some kind of ruse or con with these kids. I was betting on something having to do with music or performing. He would have a good line, but he couldn't produce. At some point early in each relationship, the kid would reject him, or he would at least perceive it that way, and he would feel compelled to kill.

Atlanta PD checked all known pedophiles and sexual "priors," eventually getting down to a list of about fifteen hundred possible suspects. Police officers and FBI agents visited schools, interviewing children to see if any of them had been approached by adult males and hadn't told their parents or the police. And they rode buses, passing out flyers with the missing children's photos, asking if anybody had seen them, particularly in the company of men. They had undercover officers hanging out at gay bars trying to overhear conversations and pick up leads.

Not everyone agreed with us. And not everyone was happy to have us down there. At one of the crime scenes in an abandoned apartment house, one black cop came up to me and said, "You're Douglas, aren't you?"

"Yeah, that's right."

"I saw your profile. It's a piece of shit." I wasn't sure whether he was actually evaluating my work or pointing up the newspapers' frequent claim that there were no black serial killers. This wasn't exactly true. We had had cases of black serial killers of both prostitutes and members of their own families, but not much in the way of stranger murders, and none with the modus operandi we were seeing here.

"Look, I don't have to be here," I said. "I didn't ask to come." At any rate, the frustration level was high. Everyone involved wanted the case solved, but everyone wanted to crack it himself. As was often true, Roy and I knew we were down there to take some of the flak and be blamed if everything hit the fan.

Aside from the Klan conspiracy scenario, all kinds of theories were floating around, some more bizarre than others. Various children were found missing various articles of clothing, but none identical. Was this killer outfitting his own mannequin at home the way Ed Gein had tried collecting sections of women's skin? On the later kills, was the UNSUB evolving by leaving bodies more out in the open? Or was it possible the original UNSUB had committed suicide and a copycat had taken over for him?

To me, the first real break came when I was back in Quantico. A call had come in to the police department in Conyers, a small town about twenty miles from Atlanta. They thought they might finally have a lead. I listened to the tape in Larry Monroe's office, along with Dr. Park Dietz.

Before becoming Behavioral Science Unit chief, Monroe had been one of the outstanding instructors at Quantico. Like Ann Burgess, Park Dietz had been brought to the unit by Roy Hazelwood. He was at Harvard at the time and just starting to get a reputation in law enforcement circles. Now based in California, Park is probably the foremost forensic psychiatrist in the country and a frequent consultant to our unit.

The caller on the tape professed to be the Atlanta child killer and mentioned the name of the most recent known victim. He was obviously white, sounded like a typical redneck, and promised he was "going to kill more of these nigger kids." He also named a particular spot along Sigmon Road in Rockdale County where police could find another body.

I remember the excitement in the room, which I'm afraid I squelched. "This is not the killer," I declared, "but you have to catch him because he'll keep calling and be a pain in the ass and a distracting force as long as he's out there."

Despite the police excitement, I felt confident I was right about this jerk. I'd had a similar situation shortly before this when Bob Ressler and I had been over in England to teach a course at Bramshill, the British police academy (and their equivalent to Quantico) about an hour outside London. England was in the midst of the Yorkshire Ripper murders. The killer, who apparently patterned himself after the Whitechapel murderer of late Victorian times, was bludgeoning and stabbing women up north, mostly prostitutes. There had been eight deaths so far. Three more women had managed to escape, but could provide no description. The age-range estimates ran from early teens to late fifties. Like Atlanta, all of England was gripped in terror. It was the largest manhunt in British history. The police would ultimately conduct nearly a quarter million individual interviews throughout the country.

Police departments and newspapers had received letters

from "Jack the Ripper," confessing to the crimes. Then a two-minute tape cassette arrived in the mail to Chief Inspector George Oldfield, taunting the police and promising to strike again. As in the Atlanta case, this seemed to be the big breakthrough. The tape was copied and played throughout the country—on television and radio, on toll-free telephone lines, over the PA at soccer matches—to see if anyone could recognize the voice.

We had been told that John Domaille was at Bramshill while we were there. He's a big-shot cop and the lead investigator on the Ripper cases. He's told that these two profiling guys from the FBI are here and maybe we should get together. So after class, Bob and I are sitting alone in the academy pub when this guy comes in, is recognized by someone at the bar, and goes over and starts talking to him. We can read his nonverbals and know he's making fun of the blokes from the U.S. I say to Ressler, "I bet that's him."

Sure enough, we're pointed out to him, he and the other guys come over to our table, and he introduces himself. I say, "I noticed you didn't bring any files with you."

He starts making excuses about how complicated a case this is and it would be difficult to bring us up to speed in a short amount of time and such like that.

"Fine," I reply. "We've got plenty of cases of our own. I'd just as soon sit here and drink."

This take-it-or-leave-it approach gets the Brits interested. One of them asks what we would need to profile a case. I tell him to start by just describing the scenes. He tells me that the UNSUB seems to get the women in a vulnerable position and then blitzes them with a knife or hammer. He mutilates them after death. The voice on the tape was pretty articulate and sophisticated for a prostitute killer. So I say, "Based on the crime scenes you've described and this audiotape I heard back in the States, that's not the Ripper. You're wasting your time with that."

I explained that the killer he was looking for would not

communicate with the police. He'd be an almost invisible loner in his late twenties or early thirties with a pathological hatred of women, a school dropout, and possibly a truck driver since he seemed to get around quite a bit. His killing of prostitutes was his attempt to punish women in general.

Despite the fortune of time and resources they'd spent on getting this tape out, Domaille said, "You know, I was worried about that," and later changed the course of his investigation. When thirty-five-year-old truck driver Peter Sutcliffe was arrested on a fluke on January 2, 1981—in the midst of the Atlanta horrors—and was proved to be the Ripper, he bore little resemblance to the one who had made and sent the tape. The impostor turned out to be a retired policeman who had a grudge to settle with Inspector Oldfield.

After listening to the Georgia tape, I spoke to the Conyers and Atlanta police and, off the top of my head, came up with a scenario I thought would take out this impostor. Like the Ripper's, this guy's tone was taunting and superior. "From the tone of his voice and what he's saying, he thinks you're all dumb shits," I said, "so let's use this."

I advised them to play as dumb as he thought they were. Go to Sigmon Road but search the *opposite* side of the street; miss him completely. He'll be watching and maybe you'll get lucky and grab him right there. If not, he'll at least call and tell you what idiots you are, that you're looking in the wrong place. Park Dietz loves this, assimilating this off-the-cuff field stuff into his academic knowledge.

The police make a very public show of looking for this body, screw up the directions, and sure enough, the guy calls back to tell them how stupid they are. They're ready with the trap and trace and get this older redneck right in his house. Just to make sure he's not on the level, they search the right area of Sigmon Road, but of course there's no body.

The Conyers incident wasn't the only red herring in this case. Large investigations often have a fair number of them, and Atlanta was no exception. Close to the road, in the woods near where the earliest skeletonized remains were found, detectives discovered a girlie magazine with semen on some of the pages. The FBI lab was able to lift latent fingerprints and from that get an ID. It's a white male who drives a van and he's an exterminator. The psychological symbolism, of course, is perfect. For this type of sociopath, it's only one small step from exterminating bugs to exterminating black children. We already know that many serial killers return to crime scenes and dump sites. The police speculate that he pulls along the side of the road in his car, looks out over his conquest, and masturbates as he recalls the thrill of the hunt and kill.

This development works its way up to the director of the FBI, to the attorney general, all the way to the White House. All of them are anxiously waiting to make the announcement that we've got the Atlanta child killer. A press release is being prepared. But a couple of things bother me. For one thing, he's white. For another, he's happily married. I figure there must be another reason why this guy was there.

They bring him in for questioning. He denies everything. They show him the magazine with semen stuck to the pages. They tell him they've got his prints on it. Okay, he admits, I was driving along and I threw it out of the car. This doesn't make any sense, either. He's driving along, one hand on the wheel, the other hand on himself, and he manages to throw this thing out of a car so that it lands in the woods? He'd have to have an arm like Johnny Unitas.

Realizing this is a serious jam he's in, he admits that his wife is pregnant, due any day, and he hasn't had sex in months. Rather than even think of cheating on this woman he loves, who's about to bear his child, he went down to the 7-Eleven, bought this magazine, then thought he'd go out into these isolated woods on his lunch hour and gain some relief.

My heart went out to this guy. Nothing is sacred! He

figures he'll go off where he won't bother anybody, mind his own business, and now even the president of the United States knows he was jacking off in the woods!

When they caught the impostor in Conyers, I thought that would be that; at least we'd been able to get this racist ass out of the way so the police could concentrate on their investigation. But I hadn't factored one thing in properly, and that was the active role of the press. Since then, I've made sure never to commit that oversight again.

One thing I had realized was that, at a certain point, the vast media attention the child murders were getting became a satisfaction to the killer in its own right. What I hadn't counted on was that he would be *reacting specifically* to media reports.

What happened was the press was so hungry for any possible break in the case that they heavily covered the police search along Sigmon Road, which came up empty. But soon afterward, another body *is* found in open view along Sigmon Road in Rockdale County: that of fifteen-year-old Terry Pue.

To me, this is an incredibly significant development and the beginning of the strategy for how to catch the killer. What it means is, he's closely following the press and reacting to what they're reporting. He knows the police aren't going to find a body on Sigmon Road because he didn't put one there. But now he's showing how superior he is, how he can manipulate the press and the police. He's showing his arrogance and contempt. He *can* dump a body along Sigmon Road if he wants to! He's broken his pattern and driven twenty or thirty miles just to play this game. We know he's watching, so let's see if we can use that to manipulate his behavior.

Had I known this or considered the possibility beforehand, I would have thought about staking out the general area along Sigmon Road. But it was too late for that now. We had to look forward and see what we could do.

I had several ideas. Frank Sinatra and Sammy Davis Jr. were coming to Atlanta to give a benefit concert at the Omni to raise money for families of the victims. The event was receiving tremendous coverage, and I was absolutely certain the killer would be there. The challenge was, how to pick him out of twenty-odd thousand people?

Roy Hazelwood and I had profiled a police buff. That could be the key. "Let's give him a free ticket," I suggested.

As usual, the police and Atlanta Field Office agents looked at me as if I were crazy. So I explained. We'll advertise that because so many people are expected, additional security guards will be needed. We'll offer minimum wage, require that each applicant must have his own vehicle (since we knew our guy had one), and those with some kind of background or experience with law enforcement will be given preference. We have the screening interviews at the Omni, using hidden closed-circuit television. We'll eliminate the groups we don't care about—women, older people, etc.—and concentrate mainly on young black men. Each one will fill out an application, on which we'll have them list experience such as ambulance driving, whether they've ever applied for a police or security job before, all the things that will help us qualify our suspect. We can probably get down to a group of maybe ten or twelve individuals that we can then cross-check against the other evidence.

This idea went right up the line to the assistant attorney general. The problem is, anytime you have a large organization working on anything that isn't right out of the book, "analysis paralysis" can set in. By the time my strategy was finally approved, it was the day before the concert and the feeble attempt to recruit "security guards" at that point was too little, too late.

I had another scheme. I wanted to have wooden crosses made up, about a foot high. Some would be given to families, others would be placed at crime scenes as memorials. One large one could be erected at a church in collective memory of the children. Once this was publicized, I knew the killer would visit some of the sites, particularly the remote ones. He might even try to take one of the crosses. If we had key sites surveilled, I thought we'd have a good chance of nabbing him.

But it took the Bureau weeks to okay the plan. Then there was a turf war over who got to make the crosses—should it be the FBI exhibit section in Washington, the carpentry shop at Quantico, or should the Atlanta Field Office contract it out? The crosses did eventually get made, but by the time they were usable, events in the case had overtaken us.

By February, the city was about out of control. Psychics were swarming around, all giving their own "profiles," many dramatically contradicting each other. The press was jumping on any possibility, quoting anyone remotely related to the case who would talk. The next victim to turn up after Terry Pue's body was found along Sigmon Road was twelve-year-old Patrick Baltazar, off Buford Highway in DeKalb County. Like Terry Pue, he had been strangled. At that time, someone in the medical examiner's office announced that hair and fibers found on Patrick Baltazar's body matched those found on five of the previous victims. These were among the ones I had linked together as having the same killer. The announcement of the forensic findings received wide-scale coverage.

And something clicked with me. *He's going to start dumping bodies in the river.* Now he knows they're getting hair and fiber. One previous body, that of Patrick Rogers, had been found on the Cobb County side of the Chattahoochee River in December, a victim of blunt-force trauma to the head. But Patrick was fifteen, five foot nine, and 145 pounds, a school dropout who had been in trouble with the law. The police were not considering his case related. Whether he was or not, though, I felt the killer would come to the river now, where the water would wash away any trace evidence.

We've got to start surveilling the rivers, I said, particularly the Chattahoochee, the major waterway that forms the
northwestern boundary of the city with neighboring Cobb
County. But several police jurisdictions were involved, one
for each county, as well as the FBI, and no one could take
overall charge. By the time a joint surveillance operation
composed of FBI and Homicide Task Force personnel was
organized and approved, it was already into April.

But in the meantime, I wasn't surprised when the next
body found—thirteen-year-old Curtis Walker—showed up
in the South River. The next two—Timmie Hill, thirteen,
and Eddie Duncan, the oldest at twenty-one—appeared
within a day of each other in the Chattahoochee. Unlike
the previous victims, most of whom had been found fully
clothed, these three bodies had been stripped to their underwear, another way of removing hair and fiber.

Weeks went by with the surveillance teams in place,
watching bridges and potential dump sites along the river.
But nothing was happening. It was clear the authorities were
losing faith and felt as if they were getting nowhere. With
no clear progress being made, the operation was scheduled
to be shut down at the 6 a.m. shift change on May 22.

At about 2:30 that very morning, a police academy
recruit named Bob Campbell was on his final surveillance
shift on the bank of the Chattahoochee beneath the Jackson
Parkway Bridge. He saw a car drive across and apparently
stop briefly in the middle.

"I just heard a loud splash!" he reported tensely into
his walkie-talkie. He directed his flashlight into the water
and saw the ripples. The car turned around and came back
across the bridge where a stakeout car followed it and then
pulled it over. It was a 1970 Chevy station wagon and the
driver was a short, curly-haired, twenty-three-year-old,
very light black man named Wayne Bertram Williams. He
was cordial and cooperative. He claimed to be a music pro-
moter and said he lived with his parents. Police questioned

him and looked into his car before letting him go. But they didn't lose track of him.

Two days later, the nude body of twenty-seven-year-old Nathaniel Cater surfaced downstream, not far from where the body of Jimmy Ray Payne, twenty-one, had been found a month earlier. There wasn't enough evidence to arrest Williams and get a search warrant, but he was put under "bumper lock" surveillance.

He soon became aware of the police following him and led them on wild-goose chases throughout the city. He even drove to Safety Commissioner Lee Brown's home and started honking his horn. He had a darkroom in his house, and before a warrant could be obtained, he was observed burning photographs in his backyard. He also washed out the car.

Wayne Williams fit our profile in every key respect, including his ownership of a German shepherd. He was a police buff who had been arrested some years earlier for impersonating a law officer. After that, he had driven a surplus police vehicle and used police scanners to get to crime scenes to take pictures. In retrospect, several witnesses recalled seeing him along Sigmon Road when the police were reacting to the phone tip and searching for the nonexistent body. He had been taking photographs there, which he offered to the police. We also found out that he had, indeed, attended the benefit concert at the Omni.

Without arresting him, the FBI asked him to come to the office, where he was cooperative and didn't ask for an attorney. From reports I received, I didn't feel that the interrogation had been properly planned or organized. It had been too heavy-handed and direct. And I thought he was reachable at that point. After the interview, I was told he hung around the office and acted as if he still wanted to talk about police and FBI stuff. But when he left that day, I knew they would never get a confession out of him. He agreed to a polygraph, which proved inconclusive. Later, when police and FBI agents got a warrant and searched the house he shared with his retired-schoolteacher parents, they found books that showed how to beat a lie detector.

That warrant was obtained on June 3. Despite Williams's having washed out the car, police found hair and fiber linking him with about twelve of the murders, the exact ones I had profiled as being done by the same killer.

The evidence was compelling. Not only did they get fibers linking the bodies to Williams's room and house and car, Larry Peterson of the Georgia State Crime Lab matched fibers from clothing some of the victims had worn on occasions prior to their disappearance. In other words, there was a connection to Williams before some of the murders.

On June 21, Wayne B. Williams was arrested for the murder of Nathaniel Cater. The investigation into the other deaths continued. Bob Ressler and I were at the Hampton Inn, near Newport News, Virginia, speaking before a meeting of the Southern States Correctional Association, when the arrest was announced. I was just back from England and the Yorkshire Ripper case, and I was talking about my work on serial murder. Back in March, *People* magazine had run a story about Ressler and me and that we were tracking the Atlanta killer. In the article, which headquarters had directed us to cooperate with, I'd given elements of the profile, particularly our opinion that the UNSUB was black. The story had gotten a lot of attention nationally. So when I took questions from this audience of more than five hundred people, someone asked my opinion of the Williams arrest.

I gave some of the background on the case and our involvement with it and how we had come up with the profile. I said he fit the profile and added carefully that if it did turn out to be him, I thought he "looked pretty good for a good percentage of the killings."

I didn't know the questioner was a reporter, though I'm sure I would have answered the same even if I had. The next day I was quoted in the *Newport News–Hampton Daily*

Press as saying, "He looks pretty good for a good percentage of the killings," leaving out my critically important qualifying statement before that.

The story hit the news wire, and the next day I was being quoted all over the country, on all the network news programs, in all the major newspapers, including a story in the *Atlanta Constitution* with the headline "FBI Man: Williams May Have Slain Many."

I was getting calls from everywhere. There were television cameras in the hotel lobby and in the hallway outside my room. Ressler and I had to climb down the fire escape to get out.

Back at headquarters, the shit was hitting the fan. It looked like an FBI agent intimately involved with the case had declared Wayne Williams guilty without a trial. Driving back to Quantico, I tried to explain to Unit Chief Larry Monroe on the mobile telephone what had really happened. He and the assistant director, Jim McKenzie, tried to help me out and run interference with OPR, the FBI's Office of Professional Responsibility.

I remember I was sitting in the upper floor of the library at Quantico where I used to go to write my profiles in peace and quiet. It also had the advantage of windows to look out of, unlike our subterranean offices. Monroe and McKenzie came up to talk to me. They were both big supporters of mine. I was the only one doing profiling full-time, I was completely burnt out from running all over the place, Atlanta had been a huge emotional drain, and the thanks I got for all of it was the threat of a censure for this statement that was picked up out of context by the media.

We had scored a major triumph for the art of profiling and criminal investigative analysis with this case. Our evaluation of the UNSUB and what he would do next was right on the money. Everyone was watching us, from the White House on down. I had stuck my neck way out, and if I'd screwed up or been wrong, the program would have died.

We'd always been told that this job was high risk, high gain. With tears in my eyes, I told Monroe and McKenzie I saw it as "high risk, no fucking gain." I said it just wasn't worth it and threw my case folders down on the table. Jim McKenzie said I was probably right, but they just wanted to help me.

When I went to headquarters to appear before OPR, the first thing I had to do was sign a waiver of my rights. Upholding justice in the outside world and practicing it inside are not necessarily the same thing. The first thing they did was whip out the *People* magazine. Jackie Onassis was on the cover.

"Weren't you warned about doing interviews like this?"

No, I said, the interview had been approved. And at the convention, I was talking about our serial killer research in general when someone brought up the Wayne Williams case. I was careful about the way I phrased my reply. I couldn't help the way it was reported.

They raked me over the coals for four hours. I had to write out a statement, going over the newspaper reports and what had happened item by item. And when I was finished, they told me nothing and gave me no feedback on what was going to happen to me. I felt as if I'd given the Bureau so much of myself without any reinforcement, sacrificed so many other things, taken so much time away from my family, and now I faced the prospect of being censured, being "on the bricks" without pay for some period of time, or losing my job altogether. For the next several weeks, I literally didn't want to get out of bed in the morning.

That was when my father, Jack, wrote me a letter. In it, he talked about the time he'd been laid off from his job with the *Brooklyn Eagle*. He, too, had been depressed. He'd been working hard, doing a good job, but also felt he had no control over his life. He explained how he had learned to face what life throws at you and to regroup his inner resources to fight another day. I carried that letter around with me in my briefcase for a long time, long after this incident was over.

After five months, OPR decided to censure me, asserting that I had been warned after the *People* article not to talk to the press about pending investigations. The letter of censure came from Director Webster himself.

But as pissed off as I was, I didn't have much time to stew about it unless I was prepared to quit altogether, and whatever my feelings about the organization were at that time, the work itself was too important to me. I still had on-going cases all over the United States, and the Wayne Williams trial was coming up. It was time to fight another day.

The Wayne Williams trial began in January 1982 after six days of jury selection. The panel they ended up with was predominantly black, nine women and three men. Although we felt he was good for at least twelve of the child killings, Williams was being tried on only two murder counts—Nathaniel Cater and Jimmy Ray Payne. Ironically, both of these young men had been in their twenties.

Williams was represented by a high-profile legal defense team from Jackson, Mississippi—Jim Kitchens and Al Binder—and a woman from Atlanta, Mary Welcome. Some of the key members of the prosecution were Fulton County assistant district attorneys Gordon Miller and Jack Mallard. Because of my work on the investigative phase of the case, the district attorney's office asked me to come down and advise them as the trial progressed. For most of the proceedings, I sat directly behind the prosecution table.

If the trial were held today, I would be able to testify as to MO, signature aspects, and case linkage, as I have in many others. And if there was a conviction, during the penalty phase I could give a professional opinion on the defendant's dangerousness in the future. But back in 1982, what we did hadn't yet been recognized by the courts, so I could only advise on strategy.

Much of the prosecution's case rested on about seven

hundred pieces of hair and fiber evidence, meticulously analyzed by Larry Peterson and Special Agent Hal Deadman, an expert from the FBI lab in Washington. Even though Williams was charged only with the two murders, Georgia criminal procedure allowed the state to bring in other linked cases, something that couldn't be done in Mississippi and that the defense didn't seem prepared for. The problem for the prosecution was that Williams was mild-mannered, controlled, well-spoken, and friendly. With his thick glasses, soft features, and delicate hands, he looked more like the Pillsbury Doughboy than a serial killer of children. He had taken to issuing press releases about how he was not guilty and how his arrest was purely racial in nature. Just before the trial began, he said in an interview, "I would compare the FBI to the Keystone Kops and the Atlanta police to *Car 54, Where Are You?*"

No one on the prosecution side had any hopes that Williams would take the stand, but I thought he might. From his behavior during the crimes and this type of public statement, I thought he was arrogant and self-confident enough to think he could manipulate the trial the way he had manipulated the public, the press, and the police.

In a closed meeting between the two sides held in Judge Clarence Cooper's chambers, Al Binder said they were bringing in a prominent forensic psychologist from Phoenix named Michael Brad Bayless to testify that Williams didn't fit the profile and was incapable of the murders. Dr. Bayless had conducted three separate interview examinations with Williams.

"Fine," Gordon Miller replied. "You bring him in and we'll bring in as rebuttal witness an FBI agent who's predicted everything that's happened so far in this case."

"Shit, we want to meet him," Binder said. Miller told him I'd been sitting behind the prosecution table for most of the trial.

But I did meet with both sides. We used the jury room.

I explained my background to the defense and told them if they had any problems with my being an FBI agent or not being a doctor, I could get a psychiatrist we worked with, such as Park Dietz, to study the case, and I felt confident he would testify to the same things.

Binder and his associates seemed fascinated by what I had to say. They were cordial and respectful, and Binder even told me his son wanted to be an FBI agent.

As it turned out, Bayless never did testify. The week after the trial ended, he told reporters for the *Atlanta Journal* and *Atlanta Constitution* newspapers that he believed Williams was emotionally capable of murder, that he had an "inadequate personality," and that, in his opinion, the motive in the murders was "power and an obsessive need for control." He said that Williams "wanted me to do one of two things, and that was to change my report and not say certain things, or not testify." He asserted that one of the key problems for the defense was Williams's insistence on controlling everything himself.

I found this all extremely interesting, in no small part because it dovetailed so well with the profile Roy Hazelwood and I had come up with. But during the trial I found another incident equally interesting.

Like most of the out-of-town participants, I was staying at the Marriott downtown near the courthouse. One night, I was eating alone in the dining room when this distinguished-looking black man in his mid-forties comes up to my table and introduces himself as Dr. Brad Bayless. I tell him I know who he is and why he's here. He asks if he can sit down.

I tell him I think it's a bad idea that we're seen together if he's going to be testifying for the defense tomorrow. But Bayless says he isn't concerned about that, sits down, and asks me what I know about him and his background, which turns out to be quite a lot. I give him one of my minilectures on criminal psychology and comment that if he testifies the

way the defense wants him to, he's going to embarrass himself and his profession. When he leaves the table, he shakes
my hand and says he'd really like to come to Quantico and
take our courses. I kind of wink and say we'll see how you
do on the stand tomorrow.

The next day in court, lo and behold, I find out Dr.
Bayless has gone back to Arizona without testifying. At
the bench, Binder is complaining about the "power of the
prosecution" and how they're scaring off his expert witnesses. I hadn't set out to do that, if that's what happened,
but I certainly wasn't going to back away when the chance
fell in my lap. But what really happened, I think, was that
Dr. Bayless had too much integrity not to call it as he saw
it or to let himself be used by either side for their own
purposes.

During the prosecution's case, Hal Deadman and Larry
Peterson had done a masterful job with the hair and fiber
evidence, but it was extremely complex stuff and by its very
nature, not a very theatrical presentation; all about how
this carpet fiber twists in this direction and that carpet fiber
twists in the other direction. Ultimately, they matched fibers
from all twelve victims to Williams's violet and green bed-
spread, connected most of them to the carpet in Williams's
bedroom, about half to the carpet in the living room, the
same number to his 1970 Chevrolet, and in all but one case
were able to make a connection to hair from the defendant's
German shepherd, Sheba.

When it was the defense's turn, they had a handsome
and charming Kennedy look-alike from Kansas who smiled
a lot at the jury come in to rebut Deadman's testimony. At
the end of the session, when the prosecution team met to go
over what had happened that day, everyone was laughing
about how this good-looking guy from Kansas had not been
at all convincing.

They came to me. "What do you think, John?"

I'd been watching the jury. I said, "Let me tell you something: you guys are losing the case." They were shocked and it was the last thing they wanted to hear.

"You may not think he was convincing," I explained, "but the jurors believe him." I knew what Hal Deadman was talking about and I still found it difficult going. The defense witnesses may have been overly simplistic, but they were much easier to follow.

They were gracious enough not to tell me I was full of shit, but, incisive profiler that I am, I realized I wasn't wanted here. I had a big backlog of cases waiting for me and I was preparing for the Mary Frances Stoner murder trial. All this time on the road was starting to take its personal toll, too. I was having marital problems based on my lack of involvement with the family, I wasn't getting the exercise I thought I needed, I was stressed all the time. I called Larry Monroe at Quantico and told him I was coming back home.

No sooner do I get back to National Airport and drive home than I receive a message saying the prosecution's had second thoughts. They're starting to think some of the things I said may, in fact, be happening. They want me to come back to Atlanta to help them examine the defense witnesses.

So two days later I fly back again. Now they're much more open, asking for advice. And the big surprise to all of them is that Wayne Williams decides to take the stand, which I'd predicted. He's examined by his attorney, Al Binder, who has a deep, resonant voice. The way he hunches over as he asks questions, he looks like a shark, which is why he has the nickname Jaws.

He keeps making the same point to the jury. "Look at him! Does he look like a serial killer? Look at him. Get up, Wayne," he says, telling him to hold out his hands. "Look how soft his hands are. Do you think he would have the strength to kill someone, to strangle someone with these hands?"

Binder put Williams on the stand the middle of one day and kept him on all the next day. And Williams did a tremendous job for himself, just as he must have known he would. He was totally believable as the innocent victim of an embarrassed, racially biased system that needed a suspect fast and had found one.

So the next question for the prosecution was, how are we going to cross-examine him? Assistant District Attorney Jack Mallard has the ticket. He's the one on the spot. He has a low, slow voice and a mellifluous southern accent.

I didn't have any formal training in courtroom procedure or examination of witnesses, but I had an instinct for what it would take. It was really all based on the idea of "walking in the shoes." I asked myself, what would be upsetting to me? And the answer I came up with was to be questioned by someone who just knew I was guilty, regardless of what I tried to make him believe.

I said to Mallard, "Remember the old TV show *This Is Your Life*?" You've got to do that with him. You've got to keep him on the stand as long as you can, you've got to break him down. Because he's an overcontrolled, rigid personality, he's an obsessive-compulsive. And to get to that rigidity, you have to keep the pressure on him, sustain the tension by going through every aspect of his life, even stuff that doesn't seem to mean anything, like where he went to school. Just keep it up. Then, when you've worn him down, you have to physically touch him, just like Al Binder did. What's good for the defense is good for the prosecution. Move in close, violate his space, and catch him off guard. Before the defense has the opportunity to object, ask him in a low voice, "Did you panic, Wayne, when you killed these kids?"

And when the time comes, that's just what Mallard does. For the first several hours of cross-examination, he can't rattle Williams. He catches him up in a number of glaring inconsistencies, but it's the same calm, "How could it possibly be me?" Williams. The gray-haired, gray-suited Mallard methodically goes through his whole life, then at the right time, he goes in close, puts his hand on Williams's arm, and in a low, methodical south-Georgia drawl says, "What was it like, Wayne? What was it like when you wrapped your fingers around the victim's throat? Did you panic? Did you panic?"

And in a weak voice of his own, Williams says, "No."

Then he catches himself. He flies into a rage. He points his finger at me and screams, "You're trying your best to make me fit that FBI profile, and I'm not going to help you do it!"

The defense goes ballistic. Williams goes nuts, ranting about "FBI goons" and calling the prosecution team "fools." But that was the turning point of the trial. Jury members later said so themselves. They stared with their mouths open. For the first time, they had seen the other side of Wayne Williams. They could see the metamorphosis before their eyes. They could understand the violence of which he was capable. Mallard winked at me, then went back to hammering Williams on the stand.

After his eruption in open court like that, I knew that he knew his only chance was to get back some of the sympathy he'd built up throughout the trial. I tapped Mallard on the shoulder and said, "You watch, Jack. One week from today, Wayne's going to get sick." I don't know why I picked the one-week time frame, but exactly one week later, the trial was interrupted and Williams was rushed to the hospital with stomach pains. They found nothing wrong with him and released him.

In her statement to the jury, Williams's attorney Mary Welcome held up a thimble and asked them, "Are you going to let a thimbleful of evidence convict this man?" She held up a piece of green carpet from her office, saying how common it was. How can you convict a man because he has green carpet?

So that day, some other agents and I went to her law firm.

We walked in, went into her office while she wasn't there, and pulled up some carpet fibers. We brought them back and had the experts put them under the microscope and gave the evidence to the prosecution, demonstrating that the fibers from her carpet were completely different from the fibers in the carpet in the Williams home.

On February 27, 1982, after eleven hours of deliberation, the jury returned a guilty verdict in both murders. Wayne B. Williams was sentenced to two consecutive life terms, which he is serving in the Valdosta Correctional Institution in south Georgia. He still maintains his innocence, and the controversy surrounding Williams has never died down or gone away. If he does ever manage to win a new trial, I am confident the result will be the same.

Despite what his supporters maintain, I believe the forensic and behavioral evidence points conclusively to Wayne Williams as the killer of eleven young men in Atlanta. Despite what his detractors and accusers maintain, I believe there is no strong evidence linking him to all or even most of the deaths and disappearances of children in that city between 1979 and 1981. Despite what some people would like to believe, young black and white children continue to die mysteriously in Atlanta and other cities. We have an idea who did some of the others. It isn't a single offender and the truth isn't pleasant. So far, though, there's been neither the evidence nor the public will to seek indictments.

I got a number of complimentary letters and citations as a result of my work on the Wayne Williams case, including ones from the Fulton County District Attorney's Office saying I had come up with the effective cross-examination strategy, and one from John Glover, SAC of the Atlanta Field Office, summarizing the entire ATKID investigation. One of the most moving and appreciated came from Al Binder, the lead defense attorney, who wrote to say how impressed he was by the job we had done on the case.

These came in just about the time the letter of censure

did. Jim McKenzie, very upset about this turn of events, had put me in for an incentive award, not only for the Williams case, but for five other cases I'd contributed to.

It came through in May. So now I had a letter of commendation from the director to go with my letter of censure on the same case. It said, in part, that "through your talent, dedication to duty, and professionalism, you have indeed enhanced the Bureau's fine reputation throughout the Nation, and you may be certain that your valuable services are truly appreciated." A "substantial" cash award of $250 accompanied the commendation, which I figured worked out to about a nickel an hour. I promptly donated the money to the Navy Relief Fund for the benefit of the families of men and women who had died in service to their country.

If we were faced with a case like the Atlanta child murders today, I'd like to think we could get to the killer significantly sooner, before the trail of death and suffering was so appallingly long. We would all be much more efficient about coordinating our efforts. Our proactive techniques are more sophisticated and based on far more real-world experience. We would know how to stage the interrogation for maximum effect. We would plan better for the search warrant and get it before critical evidence could be destroyed.

But whatever mistakes we made, the ATKID case was a decisive turning point for our unit. We put ourselves on the map, proved the value of what we could do, and in the process achieved instant credibility throughout the law enforcement community worldwide and helped put another killer behind bars.

High risk, high gain.

12

One of Our Own

Judson Ray is one of the living legends at Quantico. He very nearly wasn't. In February of 1982, while he was working ATKID as a special agent in the Atlanta Field Office, his wife tried to have him killed.

We first became aware of each other, though we didn't meet, during the "Forces of Evil" case in early 1978. A serial killer dubbed the "Stocking Strangler" had assaulted six elderly women in Columbus, Georgia, after breaking into their homes, strangling each of them with their own nylon stockings. All of the victims were white, and forensic evidence the medical examiner found on some of the bodies suggested the strangler was black.

Then the chief of police received an alarming letter, written on U.S. Army stationery, claiming to be from a group of seven people calling itself the Forces of Evil. The letter made mention of the belief that the Stocking Strangler was black and threatened to kill a black woman in retaliation if he was not caught by June 1, or "1 June," as the writer or writers stated it. They claimed already to have abducted a woman named Gail Jackson. If the "S-Strangler" was not caught by "1 Sept," "the victims will double." The letter suggested that the military stationery had been stolen and that the group originated in Chicago.

This development represented everyone's worst nightmare. A brutal killer stalking Columbus was horrible enough. An organized and murderous vigilante reaction to it could tear the community apart.

Other letters followed, upping the ante with a further

demand for a $10,000 ransom, as the police searched franti-
cally but without success for any of these seven white men.
Gail Jackson was a prostitute, well known around the bars
that serviced Fort Benning. And she was indeed missing.

Jud Ray was a shift commander in the Columbus Police
Department. As an Army Vietnam veteran and a black police officer who had worked his way up through the ranks,
he was acutely aware that the community would not heal
until these twin threats of the Stocking Strangler and the
Forces of Evil organization were neutralized. With no progress in the investigation despite all the time and effort that
had gone into it, his cop instincts told him they had to be
looking for the wrong people in the wrong way. He tried to
keep up on law enforcement developments around the country and had heard about the profiling program in Quantico.
He suggested that the department contact the Behavioral
Science Unit and see what we made of the case.

On March 31, we were asked through the Georgia Bureau
of Investigation to analyze the case. Despite what the original letter had stated, we were all pretty sure the connection
to the Army and Fort Benning was not a casual one. Bob
Ressler, who had been a military policeman before he joined
the Bureau, took the lead.

Within three days we had returned our report. We felt
there was no evidence this self-styled Forces of Evil was
composed of seven white men. In fact, we didn't believe it
was composed of any white men. It would be a lone black
male, trying to divert attention away from himself and the
fact that he had already murdered Gail Jackson. From his
military usage of dates (e.g., "1 June") and his reference to
meters rather than feet or yards, it was clear he was in the
military. The letters were almost illiterate, ruling out an officer, who would have had a better education. From his own
experience, Bob felt he would likely be either an artillery-
man or a military policeman, twenty-five to thirty years of
age. He would already have killed two other women, prob-

ably also prostitutes—that's what his reference to "the victims will double" was all about—and we thought there was some chance he might be the Stocking Strangler as well.

When our profile was circulated around Fort Benning and the bars and nightclubs the victim was known to frequent, the Army and Columbus police quickly came up with the name of William H. Hance, a black, twenty-six-year-old specialist four assigned to an artillery unit at the fort. He confessed to the murders of Gail Jackson, Irene Thirkield, and another woman, an Army private named Karen Hickman, at Fort Benning the previous fall. He admitted that he had made up the Forces of Evil to throw police off his track.

The actual Stocking Strangler was identified from a photograph by a witness at one of the scenes as Carlton Gary, a twenty-seven-year-old black man who was born and raised in Columbus. He was captured after a series of restaurant holdups, but escaped, and was not recaptured until May 1984. Both Hance and Gary were convicted and sentenced to die for their crimes.

After the community settled back to normal, Jud Ray took a leave of absence to run a program at the University of Georgia that recruited minorities and women into law enforcement careers. Once this project was over, he planned to go back to police work. But with his military and investigative background, not to mention the fact that he was black and at this time the Bureau desperately needed to establish itself as an equal-opportunity employer, he accepted an offer from the FBI. I first met him casually when he was at Quantico for new-agent training. He was then assigned to the Atlanta Field Office, where his experience and knowledge of the local area and people was considered a tremendous asset.

We next met late in 1981 when I was down in Atlanta for ATKID. Like everyone else in the field office, Jud was deeply involved in the investigation. Each agent was part of a team working five ATKID cases, and Jud was working an intense schedule.

He was also under tremendous pressure from another source. His marriage, shaky for some time, was breaking up. His wife had been drinking heavily, verbally abusing him, acting erratically. "I didn't even know this woman anymore," he said. Finally, one Sunday evening, he'd given her an ultimatum: either she had to change her ways and get help or he was going to take their two daughters—ages eighteen months and eight years—and leave.

Much to his surprise, Jud did begin seeing positive signs. She became more attentive to him and the girls. "I saw an abrupt change in her personality. She quit boozing," he recalled. "She started doting over me. For the first time in thirteen years of marriage, she got up in the morning to make me breakfast. Suddenly, she'd become all the things I wanted her to be."

But then he added, "I should have known this was too good to be true. And that's something I would lecture to police afterward. If your spouse suddenly shows you a radical change of behavior—negatively or positively—you ought to be suspicious right away."

What was happening was that Jud's wife had already decided to have him killed and was buying time until she could make the arrangements. If she pulled it off successfully, she would be able to avoid the trauma and humiliation of an ugly divorce, keep the two kids herself, and collect on a quarter-million-dollar life insurance policy. Far better to be the grieving and well-off widow of a murdered law officer than a divorced woman alone in the world.

Unbeknownst to Jud, two men had been watching his moves and habits for several days. They waited outside his apartment building in the morning and followed him on I-20 into Atlanta every day. They were looking for the opportunity to get him defenseless, so the hit could be accomplished efficiently and a getaway made without witnesses.

But they quickly realized they had a problem. Jud had been a law officer long enough that the first rule a cop learns was instinctive to him: keep your gun hand free. No matter where the two would-be shooters tracked him, he always seemed to have his right hand ready to go for his gun.

They went back to Mrs. Ray and told her the problem. They wanted to take him out in the parking lot outside the apartment, but Jud would be able to get to at least one of them before they could finish him off. She had to do something about that free right hand.

Not letting a detail like this stand in her way, she got a travel coffee cup and suggested Jud take it to work with him every morning. "For thirteen years, she never made me or the girls breakfast, and now she was trying to get me to take that damn coffee cup with me."

But he resisted. After all these years, he just couldn't get used to the idea of driving with his left hand on the wheel and his right hand occupied with a coffee cup. This was in the days before cup holders were commonplace in cars. Had they been, this story might have had a completely different outcome.

The gunmen came back to Mrs. Ray. "We can't take him in the parking lot," one of them reported. "We've got to take him inside."

So the hit was scheduled for early February. Mrs. Ray had taken the two girls out for the evening and Jud was home alone. The shooters come to the building, down the hall, and up to the apartment door, where they ring the bell. The only problem is, they have the wrong apartment number. When a white man comes to the door, the two guys ask where the black man is who lives there. Innocently, he tells them they have the wrong apartment. Mr. Ray lives over there.

But now the shooters have been seen by this neighbor. If there's a hit tonight, there's no way he's not going to remember two black men asking where Jud Ray lives when the police question him. So they leave.

Later, Mrs. Ray comes back home assuming the job's

been done. Hesitantly, she looks around, then crawls into the bedroom, mentally preparing for the 911 call she's going to make, saying something terrible has happened to her husband.

She gets to the bedroom and sees Jud lying there on the bed. She's still creeping around. He turns over and says, "What the hell are you doing?" whereupon she freaks out and runs to the bathroom.

But in the following days her good behavior continues and Jud thinks she's really turned around. As naive as he thinks this was in retrospect, after many rocky years in a relationship, there is such an overwhelming desire to believe things truly have gotten better.

It's two weeks later—February 21, 1981. Jud is now working the murder of Patrick Baltazar. It's potentially a big break in the ATKID investigation because hair and fiber found on the twelve-year-old's body appear to match specimens found on previous victims of the child killer.

That night, Jud's wife makes him an Italian dinner. What he doesn't know is that she's heavily laced the spaghetti sauce with phenobarbital. As planned, she takes the two girls with her and goes to visit her aunt.

Later on, Jud's home alone in the bedroom. He thinks he hears something coming from the front of the apartment. The light in the hallway changes, goes dim. Someone's unscrewed the lightbulb in his older daughter's bedroom. Then he hears muffled voices down the hall. What's happened is that the first shooter's lost his nerve. The two of them are discussing what to do now. He doesn't know how they've gotten in, but it doesn't matter at the moment. They're here.

"Who is it?" Jud calls out.

Suddenly, a shot rips out, but it misses him. Jud dives for the floor, but a second bullet hits him in the left arm. It's still dark. He's trying to hide behind the king-size bed.

"Who is this?" he calls out. "What do you want?"

A third shot hits the bed, close to him. In his mind, he's

going through this intuitive survival drill, trying to figure out what kind of gun it is. If it's a Smith & Wesson, they've got three shots left. If it's a Colt, they've only got two.

"Hey, man!" he yells. "What's wrong? Why're you trying to kill me? Take what you want and get out. I haven't seen you. Just don't kill me."

There's no reply. But now Jud can see him, silhouetted against the moonlight.

You're going to die tonight, Jud acknowledges to himself. No way you're going to get out of this. But you know what it's like. You don't want detectives walking in here tomorrow and saying, "This poor bastard, never put up a fight. He just let them come in and execute him." Jud resolves that when the detectives see the scene, they're going to know he fucking fought this guy.

The first thing he's got to do is get to his gun, which is on the floor on the other side of the bed. But a king-size bed represents a lot of real estate to cover when there's someone trying to kill you.

Then he hears, "Don't move, you motherfucker!"

In the darkness, he climbs back up and begins inching toward the edge of the bed and his gun.

He gets closer, agonizingly slowly, but he needs more leverage to make the final move effectively.

When he's got all four fingers gripping the edge, he whirls off onto the floor, but lands with his right hand under his chest. And since he's been shot in his left arm, he doesn't have enough power in his left hand to reach for the gun.

Just then, the shooter jumps on the bed. He shoots Jud at point-blank range.

He feels as if he's just been kicked by a mule. Something inside him seems to collapse on itself. He doesn't know the technical details at the time, but the bullet has gone through his back, knocked out his right lung, penetrated the third intercostal space between his ribs, and ripped out the front of his chest into his right hand, which he's still lying on.

The shooter jumps down off the bed, stands over him, feels his pulse. "There, you motherfucker!" he declares, and walks out.

Jud's in shock. He's lying on the floor hyperventilating. He doesn't know where he is or what's happening to him.

Then he realizes, he must be back in combat in Vietnam. He can smell the smoke, see the muzzle blasts. But he can't breathe. He thinks, "Maybe I'm not really in Nam. Maybe I'm just dreaming I am. But if I'm dreaming, why is it so hard to breathe?"

He struggles to get up. He staggers over to the television and turns it on. Maybe that'll tell him if he's dreaming. Johnny Carson and the *Tonight* show come on. He reaches out and touches the screen, trying to tell if it's real, leaving a streak of wet blood across the glass.

He needs to get some water. He makes his way to the bathroom, turns on the tap, and tries to cup the water in his hand. That's when he sees the bullet embedded in his right hand and the blood streaming from his chest. Now he knows what's happened to him. He goes back out into the bedroom, lies down at the foot of the bed, and waits to die.

But he's been a cop too long. He can't let himself go this quietly. When the detectives come the next day, they've got to see that he struggled. He gets up again, makes his way to the phone, and dials O. When the operator comes on, he gasps for air, tells her that he's an FBI agent and that he's been shot. Immediately, she puts him through to the DeKalb County Police Department.

A young female officer comes on the line. Jud tells her that he's FBI and he's been shot. But he can barely get the words out. He's been drugged, he's lost a lot of blood, his speech is slurred.

"What do you mean, you're FBI?" she challenges. Jud hears her yell to her sergeant that there's some drunk on the line claiming he's with the FBI. What does the sergeant want her to do? The sergeant tells her she can hang up.

Then the operator breaks in, telling them he's for real and that they've got to send emergency help immediately. She won't let them off until they agree.

"That operator saved my life," Jud told me later.

He passed out when she broke in and didn't regain consciousness until the emergency medical team was putting the oxygen mask over his face. "Don't prepare him for shock," he hears the team leader say. "He's not going to make it."

But they take him to DeKalb General Hospital, where there's a thoracic surgeon on duty. And as he's lying there on the gurney in the emergency room, as the doctors frantically try to save his life, he knows.

With the clarity that comes from a close encounter with death, he's saying to himself, "This isn't a reprisal. I've put a lot of people in jail, but they couldn't get that close. The only person who could get that close to me is someone that I trusted implicitly."

When he comes out of surgery and is taken to the intensive care unit, the Atlanta SAC, John Glover, is there. Glover has been bearing the weight of ATKID for months, and now this. Like the dead children and like Jud, Glover is also black, one of the highest-ranking blacks in the Bureau. He feels enormously for Jud.

"Find my wife," Jud whispers to him. "Make her tell you what happened."

Glover thinks Jud's still delirious, but the doctor says no—he's conscious and alert.

Jud spends twenty-one days in the hospital, his hospital room under armed guard since no one knows who these shooters are or whether they're coming back to finish him off. Meanwhile, his case is going nowhere. His wife expresses shock and dismay over what happened and thanks God he wasn't killed. If only she'd been there that night.

In the office, a team of agents are tracking down leads. Jud's been a cop for a long time. He could have a lot of enemies. Once it's clear he's going to recover, the question is phrased in a lighter vein, in terms of the popular TV series *Dallas*: "Who shot J.R.?"

It's a couple of months before he can get his routine back to normal. He finally tackles the stack of bills that have been piling up since the attack. He moans as he faces a Southern Bell telephone bill for more than $300. But as he starts going through it, he begins putting the case together in his mind.

The next day, he comes into the office and says he thinks this phone bill is the key. As the victim, he's not supposed to be working his own case, but his colleagues listen.

Listed on the bill are a bunch of calls back to Columbus. From the phone company, they get the name and address that go with the number. Jud doesn't even know this guy. So he and several other agents get in the car and drive the hundred miles down to Columbus. Their destination is the home of a preacher, who, Jud decides, is actually more of a snake oil salesman.

The FBI agents lean on him, but he denies having anything to do with the attempted murder. The agents aren't going to let him off easily. This is one of our own, they tell him, and we're going to get the person or persons who did this.

Then the story begins to emerge. This preacher is known around Columbus as a man who can "get things done." Mrs. Ray had approached him to do the job back in October, but he says he told her he wouldn't do it.

She answers that she'll find someone who will and asks to use the phone, saying she'll pay him back for the long-distance calls. The preacher tells the agents she called back to an old neighbor in Atlanta who'd been in the Army in Vietnam the same time as Jud and knew his way around a gun. She tells him, "We've got to get this thing done!"

And to top it all off, the preacher claims, "Mrs. Ray stiffed me for the phone calls."

The agents get in the car and drive back to Atlanta,

where they confront the former neighbor. Under grilling, he admits Mrs. Ray asked him about a contract killing, but he swears he had no idea it was Jud she was trying to get.

Anyway, he says he told her he didn't know anybody who did that sort of thing and put her in touch with his brother-in-law, who might. The brother-in-law, in turn, introduces her to another guy, who agrees to take on the job and hires two other men to be the shooters.

Mrs. Ray, the former neighbor's brother-in-law, the man who took the contract, and the two shooters are all indicted. The former neighbor is named an unindicted coconspirator. The five charged are found guilty of attempted murder, conspiracy, and burglary. They each get a ten-year sentence, the most the judge can give them.

I would see Jud from time to time in relation to ATKID. Before long, he began seeking me out. Since I wasn't one of his colleagues in the office but knew what the stress of the job was all about and could understand what he'd been through and continued to go through, I guess he felt he could talk to me. In addition to all the other feelings that go with such a thing, he told me he found the public airing of his domestic situation very painful and embarrassing.

With all Jud suffered, the Bureau wanted to do whatever was best for him and thought that transferring him to another field office far from Atlanta would help him recover. But after talking with Jud and sharing his feelings, I didn't think so. I thought he should stay where he was for a while.

I went in and spoke to John Glover, the SAC in Atlanta. I said, "If you transfer him, you're eliminating the support system he has right here in this office. He needs to stay here. Let him spend a year getting his children settled again and close to the aunt who helped raise him." I suggested that if he was going to go anywhere, it should be to the Columbus Resident Agency, since he'd been a cop there and still knew most of the force.

They did keep him in the Atlanta-Columbus area, where

he began to get his life back in order. Then he moved to the New York Field Office, where his main job was foreign counterintelligence. He also became one of the office's profile coordinators—the liaison between the local police and my unit at Quantico.

When slots became available in the unit, we brought Jud on, along with Roseanne Russo, also from New York, and Jim Wright, from the Washington Field Office, who had spent more than a year working the John Hinckley case and trial. Roseanne eventually left the unit for the Washington Field Office and foreign counterintelligence. Jud and Jim both became distinguished and internationally known members of the team and close friends of mine. When I became unit chief, Jim Wright took over from me as manager of the profiling program.

Jud claimed to have been shocked that we picked him. But he'd been an outstanding coordinator in New York, and because of his strong law enforcement background, he worked out right from the beginning. He was a quick learner and extremely analytical. As a police officer, he'd seen these cases from the "trenches" and brought that perspective to them.

When it would come up in a teaching situation, Jud wouldn't be afraid to mention the attempt on his life and its repercussions. He even had a tape recording of his emergency telephone call, which he would sometimes play for a class. But he couldn't stand to be in the room. He would step outside until it was over.

I told him, "Jud, this is a tremendous thing." I explained that so many of the elements at the scene—the footprints, the blood on the television—would have been misleading or nonsensical. Now we were beginning to understand how seemingly irrational elements can have a rational explanation. "If you work this case up," I told him, "it could be an extremely valuable teaching tool."

He did that, and it became one of the most interesting

and informative cases we taught. And it became a catharsis for him: "I found it quite a personal revelation. In the
process of preparing to teach, I'd go down an alleyway I'd
never ventured into before. Every time you talk about it to
people you can trust, you explore another alley. Contract
spouse killings and attempts happen more frequently in this
country than we'd like to believe. And the family is often so
embarrassed that no one will talk about it." Watching Jud
teach this case has been among my most moving experiences as an Academy instructor. And I know I'm not alone.
Eventually, he got to the point where he would stay and
listen when the emergency tape was played.

By the time Jud became part of my unit, I had already
done a fair amount of research on postoffense behavior. It
had become clear to me that no matter how hard he tries,
much of what the offender does after the crime is beyond
his conscious control. As a result of his own case, Jud became very interested in the issue of *pre*offense behavior. For
a while, we had understood the importance of precipitating
stressors as distinct events leading to the commission of a
crime. But Jud expanded the unit's horizons considerably
and demonstrated how important it is to focus on the behavior and interpersonal actions before a crime takes place. A
radical or even subtle but significant change in a partner's
behavior can mean that he or she has already begun to
plan for a change in the status quo. If the husband or wife
becomes unexpectedly calm or much more friendly and accepting than before, it can mean he or she has already come
to regard that change as inevitable or imminent.

Contract spouse killings are difficult to investigate. The
survivor has laid the emotional groundwork well. The only
way to crack these cases is to get someone to talk, and you
have to understand the dynamics of the situation and what
really happened to be authoritative in this. As much as the re-
arrangement of a crime scene can lead the police in the wrong
direction, a spouse's preoffense behavior is a form of staging.

More than anything else, Jud's case is an object lesson for us on how you can misinterpret behavior at a crime scene. If Jud had died, we would have come to some wrong conclusions.

One of the first things a rookie cop is taught is not to contaminate a crime scene. But by his own barely conscious actions, veteran cop and special agent that he was, Jud inadvertently contaminated his own crime scene. We would have interpreted all of the footprints and evidence of his movement to have been a burglary that went bad—that the intruders had walked him around the room, forcing him to tell them where particular items were hidden. The blood on the TV screen would have suggested that Jud had been lying in bed watching television when he'd been surprised and immediately shot.

The most important consideration, as Jud told me, was that "if I had died, I'm absolutely convinced she would have gotten away with it. It was well planned and her actions had prepped everyone in the neighborhood. She would have been completely believable as the grieving spouse."

As I said, Jud and I became close friends; he's probably the closest thing to a brother I have ever had. I used to joke that he would make sure to play the tape for me right around performance-rating time, to assure the full measure of my sympathy. Fortunately, though, that was never necessary. Jud Ray's record speaks for itself. He is now chief of the International Training Unit, where his skill and experience will benefit a new generation of agents and policemen and policewomen. But wherever he goes, he will always be one of our own and one of the best—one of the few law officers around to survive an attempt on his life through character and sheer force of will, and then to bring the culprits to justice himself.

13

The Most Dangerous Game

In 1924, the author Richard Connell wrote a short story entitled "The Most Dangerous Game." It was about a big-game
hunter named General Zaroff who had tired of pursuing animals and had begun hunting a much more challenging and
intelligent prey: human beings. It's still a popular story. My
daughter Lauren read it recently in school.

As far as we know, until about 1980, Connell's tale remained in the realm of fiction. But its status changed with a
mild-mannered baker in Anchorage, Alaska, named Robert
Hansen.

We didn't profile Hansen or devise a strategy to identify
and catch him according to our usual procedure. In September 1983, by the time my unit was called in, Alaska state
troopers had already identified Hansen as a murder suspect.
But they weren't sure of the extent of his crimes, or whether
such an unlikely individual, a respectable family man and
pillar of the community, was capable of the terrible things
of which he was being accused.

What had happened was this:

The previous June 13, a young woman had run frantically to an Anchorage police officer. She had a pair of
handcuffs dangling from one wrist and told an extraordinary
story. She was a seventeen-year-old prostitute who'd been
approached on the street by a short, pockmarked man with
red hair who had offered her $200 for oral sex in his car. She
said that while she was performing, he slipped a handcuff
on her wrist and pulled out a gun, then drove her to his
house in the fashionable Muldoon area of the city. No one

else was home. He told her that if she cooperated and did what he asked, he would not hurt her. But then he forced her to strip naked, raped her, and inflicted severe pain by biting her nipples and thrusting a hammer into her vagina. While he still had her handcuffed to a pole in his basement and immobilized, he slept for several hours. When he awoke, he told her that he liked her so much that he was going to fly her in his private airplane out to his cabin in the woods, where they'd have sex again and then he'd fly her back to Anchorage, where he would free her.

But she knew the chances of that were pretty remote. He had raped and assaulted her and hadn't done anything to hide his identity. If he got her into that cabin, she would be in real trouble. At the airport, while her kidnapper was loading supplies into the plane, she managed to escape. She ran as fast as she could looking for help. That was when she found the policeman.

From the description she gave, her kidnapper appeared to be Robert Hansen. He was in his mid-forties, had grown up in Iowa, and had been in the Anchorage area for seventeen years, where he ran a successful bakery and was considered a prominent member of the community. He was married, with a daughter and a son. The police drove her to Hansen's house in Muldoon, which she said was where she'd been tortured. They took her to the airport and she identified the Piper Super Cub that belonged to Robert Hansen.

The police then went to Hansen and confronted him with the young woman's charges. He responded with outrage, saying he had never met her, and asserted that because of his prominence, she was obviously trying to shake him down for money. The very idea was ridiculous. "You can't rape a prostitute, can you?" he said to police.

And he had an alibi for the night in question. His wife and two children were in Europe for the summer, and he was home having dinner with two business associates. He gave their names and they corroborated his story. Police had no evidence on him—just the young woman's word—so he wasn't arrested or charged.

But though they lacked proof, both the Anchorage police and Alaska state troopers office smelled smoke and knew a fire was out there somewhere. Back in 1980, construction workers had been excavating on Eklutna Road when they came upon the partial remains of a woman. Her body had been partly eaten by bears and bore the signs of having been stabbed to death and buried in a shallow grave. Known only as "Eklutna Annie," she had never been identified and her killer had never been caught.

Later in the year, the body of Joanne Messina was discovered in a gravel pit near Seward. Then, in September 1982, hunters near the Knik River found the body of twenty-three-year-old Sherry Morrow in a shallow grave. She was a topless dancer who'd been missing since the previous November. She'd been shot three times. Shell casings found at the scene identified the bullets as coming from a .223 Ruger Mini-14, a high-powered hunting rifle. Unfortunately, it was a common weapon in Alaska, so it would have been difficult to track down and interview every hunter who owned one. But one peculiar aspect to the case was that no bullet holes were in her clothing, indicating she must have been naked when shot.

Almost exactly a year later another body was discovered in a shallow grave along the bank of the Knik. This time it was Paula Golding, an out-of-work secretary who had rather desperately taken a job in a topless bar to make ends meet. She had also been shot with a Ruger Mini-14. She'd gone missing in April, and since then the seventeen-year-old prostitute had been abducted and escaped. Now, with Golding to add to the list of unsolved crimes, the Criminal Investigation Bureau of the Alaska state troopers office decided they'd better follow up on Mr. Hansen.

Even though the police had a suspect before I heard about him, I wanted to make sure my judgment wouldn't be clouded by the investigative work already done. So before I let them give me the specifics on their man during our first phone conference, I said, "First tell me about the crimes and let me tell you about the guy."

They described the unsolved murders and the details of the young woman's story. I described a scenario and an individual they said sounded very much like their suspect, down to the stuttering. Then they told me about Hansen, his job and family, his position in the community, his reputation as an outstanding game hunter. Did this sound like the kind of guy who could be capable of these crimes?

He sure did, I told them. The problem was, while they had a lot of secondhand information, they just didn't have physical evidence to charge him. The only way to get him off the street, which they were extremely anxious to do, was to get a confession. They asked me to come on-scene and help them develop their case.

In a sense, this was the opposite of what we normally do in that we were working from a known subject, trying to determine whether his background, personality, and behavior fit a set of crimes.

I brought along Jim Horn, who had recently joined my unit from the Boulder, Colorado, Resident Agency. We'd gone through new-agents training together back in the old days, and when I finally got authorization for four agents to work with me, I'd asked Jim to come back to Quantico. Along with Jim Reese, Jim Horn is now one of the two top stress-management experts in the Bureau, a critical function in our line of work. But in 1983, this was one of his first cases on the behavioral side.

Getting to Anchorage was one of the more exciting and least pleasurable business trips I've had. It ended up with a red-eye, white-knuckle flight over water. When we arrived, the police picked us up and took us to our hotel. On the way, we passed some of the bars where the victims had worked. It was too cold most of the time for hookers to work outside, so they made their business connections in the bars, which were open practically twenty-four hours a day. They closed for maybe an hour to clean up and sweep out the drunks. At the time, largely as a result of the huge transient population that came in for the construction of the oil pipeline, Alaska had among the highest rates in the country of suicide, alcoholism, and venereal disease. It had very much become the modern version of our Wild West frontier.

I found the entire atmosphere very strange. There appeared to be an ongoing conflict between the native people and those who had come from "the lower forty-eight." You had all these macho men walking around with big tattoos and looking as if they'd come straight out of a Marlboro ad. With the great distances people had to travel, it seemed as though almost everyone had an airplane, so Hansen wasn't unusual in that respect.

What was significant to us about this case was that it was the first time profiling was used to support a search warrant. We began analyzing everything we knew about the crimes and about Robert Hansen.

As far as victimology was concerned, the known victims had been prostitutes or topless dancers. They were part of a great crop of available victims who traveled up and down the West Coast. Because they were so transient, and because prostitutes are not in the habit of reporting their whereabouts to the police, it was difficult to know if anything had happened to any one of them until a body turned up. This was exactly the same problem the police and FBI faced with the Green River Killer down in Washington State. So the choice of victims was highly significant. The murderer was targeting only women who would not be missed.

We didn't know everything about Hansen's background, but what we did know fit into a pattern. He was short and slight, heavily pockmarked, and spoke with a severe stutter. I surmised that he had had severe skin problems as a teenager and, between that and the speech impediment, was probably teased or shunned by his peers, particularly girls. So his self-esteem would have been low. That might also have been why he moved to Alaska—the idea of a new start in a new frontier. And, psychologically speaking, abusing prostitutes is a pretty standard way of getting back at women in general.

I also made much of the fact that Hansen was known as a proficient hunter. He had made a local reputation for himself by taking down a wild Dall sheep with a crossbow while hunting in the Kuskokwim Mountains. I don't mean to imply that most hunters are inadequate types, but in my experience, if you have an inadequate type to begin with, one of the ways he might try to compensate is by hunting or playing around with guns or knives. The severe stutter reminded me of David Carpenter, San Francisco's "Trailside Killer." As in Carpenter's case, I was betting that Hansen's speech problem disappeared when he felt most dominant and in control.

Putting this all together, even though this was a scenario we'd never seen before, I was beginning to get an image of what I thought was going on. Prostitutes and "exotic dancers" had been found dead in remote wooded areas of gunshot wounds suggestive of those made with a hunting rifle. In at least one case, the shots had been fired at an undressed body. The seventeen-year-old who said she had escaped claimed Robert Hansen wanted to fly her to his cabin in the woods. Hansen had packed his wife and children off to Europe for the summer and was home alone.

It was my belief that, like General Zaroff in "The Most Dangerous Game," Robert Hansen had tired of elk and bear and Dall sheep and turned his attention to a more interesting prey. Zaroff explained that he used captured sailors who shipwrecked on the intentionally unmarked rocks in the channel leading to his island: "I hunt the scum of the earth—sailors from tramp ships—a thoroughbred horse or hound is worth more than a score of them."

Hansen, I was surmising, regarded prostitutes in much

the same way. They were people he could regard as lower and more worthless than himself. And he wouldn't need the gift of gab to get one to come with him. He would pick her up, make her his prisoner, fly her out into the wilderness, strip her naked, let her loose, then hunt her down with a gun or knife.

His MO wouldn't have started this way. He would have started simply by killing the early ones, then using the plane to fly their bodies far away. These were crimes of anger. He would have gotten off on having his victims beg for their lives. Being a hunter, at a certain point it would have occurred to him that he could combine these various activities by flying them out into the wilderness alive, then hunting them down for sport and further sexual gratification. This would have been the ultimate control. And it would have become addictive. He would want to do it again and again.

And this led me to the details of the search warrant. What they wanted from Jim and me was an affidavit they could take to court explaining what profiling was all about, what we would expect to find in the search, and our rationale for being able to say so.

Unlike a common criminal or someone whose gun is an interchangeable tool, Hansen's hunting rifle would be important to him. Therefore, I predicted the rifle would be somewhere in his house, though not in open view. It would be in a crawl space, behind paneling or a false wall, hidden in the attic; someplace like that.

I also predicted our guy would be a "saver," though not entirely for the normal reasons. A lot of sexual killers take souvenirs from their victims and give them to the women in their lives as a sign of dominance and a way of being able to relive the experience. But Hansen couldn't very well put a woman's head on the wall the way he would a big-game animal's, so I thought it likely he would take some other kind of trophy. Since there was no evidence of human mutilation on the bodies, I expected him to have taken jewelry, which he would have given to his wife or daughter, making up a story about where the piece came from. He didn't appear to have kept the victims' underwear or any other item we could account for, but he might have kept small photographs or something else from a wallet. And from my experience with this type of personality, I thought we might find a journal or list documenting his exploits.

The next order of business was cracking his alibi. It was no big deal for his two business associates to say they were with him the night in question if nothing was at stake for them. If we could create some high stakes, however, that could change things. Anchorage police got the district attorney to authorize a grand jury to investigate the abduction and assault of the young prostitute who had identified Hansen. The businessmen were then approached by the police and asked to give their stories again. Only this time they were informed that if they were found to be lying to the grand jury, they'd each be facing hard time.

As we'd anticipated, that was enough to break things open. Both men admitted they had not been with Hansen that night, that he'd asked them to help him out of what he characterized as an awkward situation.

So Hansen was arrested on charges of kidnapping and rape. A search warrant of his home was immediately executed. There police found the Ruger Mini-14 rifle. Ballistics tests matched it to the shell casings found near the bodies. As we'd figured, Hansen had a well-outfitted trophy room where he watched television, full of animal heads, walrus tusks, horns and antlers, mounted birds, and skins on the floor. Under the floorboards in the attic they found more weapons, and various cheap items of jewelry belonging to the victims. One of these was a Timex watch. He had given other items to his wife and daughter. They also found a driver's license and other ID cards from some of the dead women. They didn't come across a journal, but they did find the equivalent: an aviation map marked with where he had left various bodies.

All of this evidence, of course, was enough to make a case to nail him. But without the warrant, we wouldn't have had it. And the only way we could get a warrant in this instance was to demonstrate to a judge's satisfaction that there was sufficient *behavioral* evidence to justify a search. We have successfully aided in search-warrant affidavits leading to arrests many times since then, perhaps most notably in the Delaware case of Steven Pennell, the "I-40 Killer," who was executed in 1992 for torturing and killing women he picked up in his specially outfitted van.

By the time Anchorage police and Alaska state troopers actually interrogated Robert Hansen in February 1984, I was home recovering from my collapse in Seattle. Roy Hazelwood, who was heroically covering for me while still handling all his own work, coached the police on interview techniques.

As he had when police first confronted him with the abduction charge, Hansen denied everything. He pointed to his happy home life and his success in business. At first he claimed that the reason shells from his rifle had been found at various sites was that he had been there and practiced his shooting. Apparently, the presence of dead bodies at each of the locations was merely coincidental. But eventually, faced with a mountain of evidence and the prospect of an angry prosecutor seeking the death penalty if he didn't come clean, he admitted to the murders.

In trying to rationalize and justify himself, he claimed that he only wanted oral sex from the prostitutes he picked up—something he didn't feel he should ask from his proper, respectable wife. If the hooker satisfied him, he said, that would be that. The ones who didn't comply—who tried to control the situation—those were the ones he punished.

In this way, Hansen's behavior mirrored what we learned in our prison interview with Monte Rissell. Both Hansen and Rissell were inadequate types with bad backgrounds. The women who received the worst of Rissell's wrath were the ones who tried to feign friendship or enjoyment to placate him. What they didn't realize was that for this type of individual, the power and domination of the situation is everything.

Hansen also asserted that thirty to forty prostitutes had gone with him willingly in his plane and that he had brought them back alive. I found this proposition hard to believe. The class of prostitutes Hansen picked up are in business to turn a quick trick and move on to the next customer. If they've been in the business for any time, they're generally pretty good assessors of people. They're not willingly going to take a plane ride into the country with some john they've just met. If they made a mistake with him, it would be in letting him convince them to come with him to his house. Once he got them inside, it was too late.

Like his fictional counterpart, General Zaroff, Hansen stated that he hunted and killed only a certain class of people. He would never consider hurting a "decent" woman, but felt that prostitutes and topless or nude dancers were fair game. "I'm not saying I hate all women, I don't . . . but I guess prostitutes are women I'm putting down as lower than myself. . . . It's like it was a game, they had to pitch the ball before I could bat."

Once he started his hunting, the killing became anticlimactic. "The excitement," Hansen told interrogators, "was in the stalking."

He confirmed our suspicions about his background. He had grown up in Pocahontas, Iowa, where his father was a baker. Robert was a shoplifter as a child, and long after he reached adulthood and could afford to buy what he wanted, he still stole for the thrill of it. His trouble with girls started in high school, he said. He resented the fact that his stuttering and bad acne kept people away from him. "Because I looked and talked like a freak, every time I looked at a girl she would turn away." He had an uneventful stint in the Army, then married when he was twenty-two. There followed a string of arson and burglary convictions, separation and divorce from his wife, and remarriage. He moved to Alaska upon his second wife's graduation from college. There he could make a new start. But his troubles with the law continued for several more years, including repeated assault charges against women who apparently rejected his advances. Interestingly, like so many of the others, he drove a VW Beetle at the time.

On February 27, 1984, Hansen pled guilty to four counts of murder, one of rape, one of kidnapping, and assorted theft and weapons charges. He was sentenced to 499 years in prison.

One of the questions we'd had to answer in the Hansen case before police knew how to proceed was whether all of the noted prostitute and topless-dancer deaths in Anchorage had been or could have been committed by the same individual. This is often a critical issue in criminal investigative analysis. Just about the time the body of Robert Hansen's first victim was discovered in Alaska, I'd been called by the Buffalo, New York, Police Department to evaluate a string of vicious, apparently racially hate-based murders.

On September 22, 1980, a fourteen-year-old boy named Glenn Dunn was shot and killed in the parking lot of a supermarket. Witnesses described the gunman as a young white male. The next day Harold Green, thirty-two, was shot at a fast-food restaurant in suburban Cheektowaga. That same night, thirty-year-old Emmanuel Thomas was killed in front of his own house, in the same neighborhood as the previous day's murder. And the next day another man, Joseph McCoy, was killed in Niagara Falls.

As far as anyone could tell, only two factors linked these senseless murders. All the victims were black men. And all had been killed by .22-caliber bullets, prompting the press to bestow an instant title: the ".22-Caliber Killer."

Racial tension ran high in Buffalo. Many in the black community felt helpless and accused the police of doing nothing to protect them. In some ways it seemed to mirror the horror taking place in Atlanta. And as so often happens in these situations, things didn't immediately get better. They got worse.

On October 8, a seventy-one-year-old black taxi driver named Parler Edwards was found in the trunk of his cab in suburban Amherst with his heart cut out. The next day, another black taxi driver, forty-year-old Ernest Jones, was found on the bank of the Niagara River with his heart torn out of his chest. His cab, covered with blood, was found a couple of miles away within the Buffalo city limits. The day after that, a Friday, a white man roughly matching the description of the .22-Caliber Killer entered the hospital room of thirty-seven-year-old Collin Cole, announced, "I hate niggers," and proceeded to strangle the patient. Only a nurse's arrival caused the intruder to flee and saved Cole from death.

The community was in an uproar. Public officials were concerned a wide-scale reaction from black activist groups might be imminent. At the request of Buffalo SAC Richard Bretzing, I came up that weekend. Bretzing is a very proper, solid guy, a real family man and a key member of the FBI's so-called Mormon Mafia. I'll never forget, he had a sign in his office saying something to the effect of, "If a man fails at home, he fails in his life."

As I always try to do, I looked first at the victimology. As the police had suggested, there really weren't any significant common denominators between the six victims except their race and, I felt, being unfortunate enough to be in the wrong place at the wrong time. Quite clearly, the .22-caliber shootings were all done by the same individual. These were mission-oriented, assassin-style killings. The only evident psychopathology in these crimes was a pathological hatred of blacks. Everything else about them was detached and removed.

I could see this individual joining hate groups, or even groups with positive goals or values such as a church and convincing himself he was contributing to them. For this reason, I could see him joining the military, but he would have been discharged early in his career for psychological reasons or failure to adjust to military life. This would be a rational and organized individual, and his prejudiced delusional system would be orderly and "logical" within itself.

The other two crimes, the horrifying attacks on the taxi drivers, also were racially based, but in these cases, I did not feel we were dealing with the same offender. These crimes were the work of a disorganized, pathologically disoriented person, possibly hallucinatory and in all probability a diagnosed paranoid schizophrenic. To me, the crime scenes reflected rage, overcontrol, and overkill. For the four shootings and two eviscerations to have been perpetrated by the same individual would have meant a severe personality disintegration between the murders of Joseph McCoy and that of Parler Edwards less than two weeks later. This didn't square with the incident in the hospital—if that person was, in fact, the .22-Caliber Killer—plus my instinct and experience told me that the heart remover's sick fantasies had been building for a long time, several years at least. Robbery wasn't a motive in either set of killings, but while the first four represented a quick hit and get the hell out, the crime scenes of the last two clearly showed that the offender took a lot of time at the site. If these six crimes were related, it was more likely to me that the psycho who cut out the hearts might have been triggered by the racist who had already gone about assassinating blacks in the community.

Then, on December 22, in midtown Manhattan, four blacks and one Hispanic were knifed to death over a thirteen-hour period by the "Midtown Slasher." Two other black victims narrowly escaped being killed. On December 29 and 30, the slasher apparently struck again upstate, stabbing and killing thirty-one-year-old Roger Adams in Buffalo and twenty-six-year-old Wendell Barnes in Rochester.

In the next three days, three other black men in Buffalo survived similar attacks.

Now I couldn't assure police that the .22-Caliber Killer was also the Midtown Slasher or the man who had committed this last set of crimes. But what I could say with conviction was that it was the *same type of individual*. They all had the racist element, and all were committed in a blitz-assassination style.

The .22-Caliber case broke in two steps over the next several months. In January, Army private Joseph Christopher, age twenty-five, was arrested at Fort Benning, Georgia (where three years before William Hance had tried to play the racist card in the "Forces of Evil" murders), charged with slashing a black fellow soldier. A search of his old house near Buffalo turned up a large store of .22-caliber ammunition and a sawed-off rifle. Christopher had just enlisted the previous November and was on leave from Fort Benning during the times of the Buffalo and Manhattan murders.

While in the Confinement Center at Fort Benning, he told Capt. Aldrich Johnson, the officer in charge, that he did "that thing in Buffalo." He was charged with the Buffalo shootings and some of the stabbings. He was convicted, and after some back-and-forth wrangling about his mental competence, was sentenced to sixty years to life. Capt. Matthew Levine, the psychiatrist who examined Christopher at Martin Army Hospital, said he was amazed by how closely Christopher fit the .22-Caliber Killer profile. As the profile had predicted, the subject did not adjust well to military life.

Christopher neither admitted nor denied the murders of the two taxi drivers. He wasn't charged with them and they don't fit into the pattern of the others, from either a *modus operandi* or *signature* perspective. Both of these are extremely important concepts in criminal investigative analysis, and I have spent many hours on the witness stands of courtrooms throughout the country trying to get judges and juries to understand the distinction between them.

Modus operandi—MO—is learned behavior. It's what the perpetrator does to commit the crime. It is dynamic—that is, it can change. Signature, a term I coined to distinguish it from MO, *is what the perpetrator has to do to fulfill himself*. It is static; it does not change.

For example, you wouldn't expect a juvenile to keep committing crimes the same way as he grows up unless he gets it perfect the first time. But if he gets away with one, he'll learn from it and get better and better at it. That's why we say that MO is dynamic. On the other hand, if this guy is committing crimes so that, say, he can dominate or inflict pain on or provoke begging and pleading from a victim, that's a signature. It's something that expresses the killer's personality. It's something he needs to do.

In many states, the only way prosecutors can link crimes is by MO, which I believe we've shown is an archaic method. In the Christopher case, a defense attorney could easily make the argument that the Buffalo .22-caliber shootings and the Manhattan midtown slashings showed a markedly different modus operandi. And he'd be right. But the signature is similar—a propensity to randomly assassinate black men fueled by racial hatred.

The shootings and the eviscerations, on the other hand, show me a markedly different signature. The individual who cut out the hearts, while still possessing a related underlying motivation, has a ritualized, obsessive-compulsive signature. Each type needs something out of the crime, but each one needs something different.

The differences between MO and signature can be subtle. Take the case of a bank robber in Texas who made all of his captives undress, posed them in sexual positions, and took photographs of them. That's his signature. It was not necessary or helpful to the commission of a bank robbery. In fact, it kept him there longer and therefore placed him in greater jeopardy of being caught. Yet it was something he clearly felt a need to do.

Then there was a bank robber in Grand Rapids, Michigan. I flew out to provide on-site consultation in the case. This guy also made everyone in the bank undress, but he didn't take pictures. He did it so the witnesses would be so preoccupied and embarrassed that they wouldn't be looking at him and so couldn't make a positive ID later on. This was a means toward successfully robbing the bank. This was MO.

Signature analysis played a significant role in the 1989 trial of Steven Pennell in Delaware, in whose case we'd prepared the affidavit leading to the search warrant. Steve Mardigian from my unit worked closely with the combined task force of New Castle County and Delaware state police, producing a profile that allowed police to narrow their focus and come up with a proactive strategy to nail the killer.

Prostitutes had been found strangled with their skulls fractured along Interstates 40 and 13. The bodies had clearly been sexually abused and tortured. Steve's profile was very accurate. He said the offender would be a white male in his late twenties to early thirties, employed in one of the construction trades. He would drive a van with high mileage, cruise excessively looking for victims, exhibit a macho image, have an ongoing relationship with a wife or girlfriend, but enjoy dominating women. He would bring his weapons of choice with him and destroy evidence afterward. He would be familiar with the area and choose his disposal sites accordingly. He would be emotionally flat during the crimes and would kill again and again until caught.

Steven B. Pennell was a thirty-one-year-old white male who worked as an electrician, drove a van with high mileage, cruised excessively looking for victims, exhibited a macho image, was married but enjoyed dominating women, had a carefully prepared "rape kit" in his van, attempted to destroy evidence when he knew the police were onto him, was familiar with the area, and chose his disposal sites accordingly. He was emotionally flat during the crimes and killed repeatedly until caught.

He was located when Mardigian suggested using a decoy female cop posing as a hooker. For two months Officer Renee C. Lano walked the highways, always looking for a man in a van to pull up who matched the profile's description. They were particularly interested in the van's carpeting. Blue fibers consistent with automobile carpeting had been found on one of the victims. If a van did stop, Lano was under strict orders not to get in—even though she was wired, that could have been a death sentence—but to find out as much as she could. When a guy matching the traits finally did stop, she engaged him in conversation and haggled extensively about the price for her services through the opened passenger door. As soon as she noticed the blue carpeting, she began admiring the van, and as they talked, she began casually scraping up carpet fibers with her fingernails. The FBI laboratory would confirm that they matched the previous samples.

At Pennell's trial, I was called in to testify about the signature aspects of the case. The defense was trying to show that it was unlikely these crimes were all committed by the same individual because so many details of the modus operandi varied. I made it clear that regardless of the MO, the common denominator in each of the murders was physical, sexual, and emotional torture. In some cases the murderer had used pliers to squeeze his victims' breasts and cut their nipples. He had bound others at the wrists and ankles, cut them on the legs, whipped or beaten their buttocks, or hit them with a hammer. So, though the methods of torture varied—the MO, if you will—the signature was the pleasure he received out of inflicting pain and hearing his victims' anguished screams. This wasn't necessary to accomplish the murder. It was necessary for him to get what he wanted to out of the crime.

Even if Steven Pennell were still alive and reading this, he would not be able to change his behavior in future crimes. He might be able to devise different or more ingenious methods of torturing women. But he would not be able to refrain from the torture itself.

Fortunately for all of us, as I mentioned, the State of Delaware had the good judgment and decency to execute Pennell by lethal injection on March 14, 1992.

One of our landmark cases in the use of signature analysis was the 1991 trial of George Russell Jr., charged with the bludgeoning and strangulation murder of three white women in Seattle—Mary Anne Pohlreich, Andrea Levine, and Carol Marie Beethe—the year before. Steve Etter from my unit did the profiling, then I went out to testify. In these cases, the prosecution knew it could not get a conviction based on a single murder. Police had the most compelling evidence in the Pohlreich killing and felt it would shore up the other two cases. So the key was tying all three together.

Russell wasn't the type you'd think of for these heinous crimes. Though having a long record as a petty thief, he was a handsome black man in his thirties, well spoken and charming, with a wide circle of friends and acquaintances. Even the local Mercer Island police who'd run him in on many charges in the past couldn't believe he would commit murder.

By 1990, it was still unusual to see sexually based homicide between races, but as society loosened up and became more tolerant, we were beginning to see race as less of an issue. This would be particularly true for a cooler, more sophisticated type like Russell. He regularly dated both black and white women and had friends in both races.

The strategic focal point came when Public Defender Miriam Schwartz made a pretrial motion before King County Superior Court judge Patricia Aitken to have the cases severed from each other and tried separately, based on the premise that the three murders were not committed by the same offender. The prosecutors, Rebecca Roe and Jeff Baird, asked me to explain how the crimes were all linked.

I mentioned the blitz-style MO attack in each one. Since

the three killings happened over a seven-week period, I would not expect the offender to change his MO unless something had gone wrong in one case and he felt a need to improve upon it. But more compelling was the signature aspect.

All three women had been left naked and posed provocatively and degradingly. The sexual content of the posed scene escalated from one to the next. The first was posed with hands clasped and legs crossed at the ankles and left near a sewer grate and trash Dumpster. The second was posed on a bed with a pillow over her head, her legs bent out to each side, a rifle inserted into her vagina, and red high heels on her feet. The final one was posed spread-eagled on her bed with a dildo in her mouth and the second *Joy of Sex* book placed under her left arm.

The blitz attacks were necessary to kill these women. The degrading posing was not.

I explained the difference between posing and staging. Staging, I said, appears in crimes where the offender is trying to throw off the investigation by making the police believe that something happened other than what did, such as when a rapist tries to make his intrusion look like a routine burglary. That would be an aspect of MO. Posing, on the other hand, would be signature.

"We don't get that many cases of posing," I testified at the hearing, "treating the victim like a prop to leave a specific message. . . . These are crimes of anger, crimes of power. It's the thrill of the hunt, it is the thrill of the kill, and it is the thrill afterwards of how that subject leaves that victim and how he's basically beating the system."

I felt confident in saying, "The probability is extremely high that it was a single suspect." Bob Keppel, the chief criminal investigator with the state attorney general's office and a veteran of the Green River Task Force, testified along with me, saying that of more than a thousand murder cases he'd examined, only about ten had included posing, and none had all of the elements of these three.

At this point, we weren't saying that Russell was the offender; all we were saying was that whoever did one did all three.

The defense planned to bring in an expert to refute what I had to say, to testify that I was wrong on signature and that these three crimes were not committed by the same individual. Ironically, that person was my longtime FBI colleague and serial-killer study partner, Robert Ressler, retired from the Bureau but still consulting in the field.

I thought this was a pretty tight and compelling case for anyone as experienced in profiling and crime-scene analysis as both Bob and I were, and so I was extremely surprised that he would be willing to come out on the other side and testify for severance of the cases. To put it bluntly, I felt he was out-and-out wrong. But as we've all admitted many times, what we do is far from an exact science, so he was certainly entitled to his opinion. Bob and I have since come out on opposite sides of a number of issues, perhaps most noticeably as to whether Jeffrey Dahmer was insane. Bob sided with the defense that he was. I agreed with Park Dietz, who testified for the prosecution, that he was not.

I was therefore even more surprised when Bob said he had other commitments and never showed up for the Russell pretrial hearing, and instead sent another retired agent, Russ Vorpagel. Russ is a bright guy. He was a chess champion who could play against ten opponents at once. But profiling wasn't his main specialty, and I thought the facts were against him. He endured a pretty hard time from Rebecca Roe when she cross-examined him after he disputed my opinion. At the end of the hearing, Judge Aitken ruled that based on the signature evidence Keppel and I had presented regarding the likelihood of a single offender in all three cases, they could be tried together.

I testified on signature again during the trial itself, refuting the multiple-killer theory the defense had put forth. In the Carol Beethe murder, defense attorney Schwartz suggested that her boyfriend had both the opportunity and the motive. We always study spouses or lovers in sexual homicides, and it was my firm opinion that this was a sexually motivated "stranger" homicide.

In the end, a jury of six men and six women deliberated four days and found George Waterfield Russell Jr., guilty of one count of first-degree murder and two counts of aggravated first-degree murder. He was sentenced to life imprisonment without possibility of parole and sent to the state's maximum-security penitentiary at Walla Walla.

This was my first time back in Seattle since my collapse and coma there. It was good to be back and have a hand in solving a case after the intense frustrations of Green River. I went back to Swedish Hospital and was pleased to see they still had the plaque I'd given them in thanks. I went back to the Hilton Hotel to see if I could remember anything, but I couldn't. I suspect that that was just too much trauma for my mind to consciously process. And anyway, after all the time I'd put in on the road for so many years, hotel rooms all blend together.

We have now developed signature analysis to the point that we testify routinely in serial-murder trials, not only I but other profilers who've taken up my interest as well, most notably Larry Ankrom and Greg Cooper.

In 1993, Greg Cooper played a major role in obtaining twin first-degree murder convictions against Gregory Mosely, who had raped, beaten, and stabbed two women in two separate jurisdictions in North Carolina. Like the related crimes in the Russell trial, it would have been difficult for either jurisdiction to successfully convict on its own. Both had to have testimony linking the cases, and after studying the crime-scene photos and case files, Greg felt he could give it.

The key to signature analysis in the Mosely cases, Greg decided, was overkill. Both victims were lonely, single, mildly handicapped women in their early twenties who had attended the same country-western nightclub, where they had been abducted a couple of months apart. Both had been severely beaten. You might say beaten to death, except for the fact that they were also strangled manually and by ligature; one had been stabbed twelve times, and there was evidence of vaginal and anal penetration. There was forensic evidence in one case, including DNA from semen linking the crime to Mosely. Both rape-torture murders had been committed in secluded areas and the bodies dumped at isolated, remote sites.

Greg testified at the first trial that the signature behavioral evidence indicated an inadequate personality who was a sexual sadist. His inadequacy was clear from his choice of victims. His sadism was even clearer from what he did to them. Unlike many of the inadequate, disorganized types, this one didn't kill them before mutilating their bodies. He wanted to be in total physical and emotional control. He wanted to be the author of their pain and enjoy the response his cruelty provoked.

Through his testimony in the first case, Greg helped enable the prosecution to introduce the second murder. Mosely was convicted and sentenced to death. In the second trial nine months later, Greg was able to do the same thing, achieving another conviction and death sentence.

The first time he testified, Greg and Mosely locked eyes as Greg described Mosely's personality to the packed courtroom. Greg could tell by the grim expression on Mosely's face that he was thinking, "How the hell could you know that?" The pressure was intense. If Greg had been unsuccessful, the case would have been thrown out and the second case could have been weakened beyond salvage.

When Mosely first saw Greg at his second trial, he muttered to his police escorts, "That's the son of a bitch who's gonna try to get me again!"

Traditionally, to get a successful prosecution and conviction in a murder case, you've needed conclusive forensic evidence, eyewitness accounts or a confession, or good, strong circumstantial evidence. Now, from our work in behavioral profiling from crime scenes and signature analysis, there is another arrow in the police's and prosecution's quiver. In and of itself, it's not usually enough to convict. But taken together with one or more of the other elements, it can often link various crimes together and be just what is needed to put a case over the top.

Serial killers play a most dangerous game. The more we understand the way they play, the more we can stack the odds against them.

14

Who Killed the All-American Girl?

Who killed the all-American girl?

That was the haunting question that had hung over the small town of Wood River, Illinois, for four years. Among many others, it obsessed Inspector Alva Busch of the state police, and it obsessed Don Weber, the state's attorney for Madison County.

The evening of Tuesday, June 20, 1978, Karla Brown and her fiancé, Mark Fair, threw a party with plenty of beer and music for the friends who had helped them move into their new home at 979 Acton Avenue in Wood River. It was a single-story, white, wooden-sided house on a tree-lined street, with slender round columns flanking the front door, and they had spent the last two weeks getting this typical starter home into move-in shape. It represented an exciting new beginning for the twenty-three-year-old Karla and twenty-seven-year-old Mark. They'd been going together for five years when Mark had finally made it clear he'd gotten over his male hesitancy and was ready to make the real commitment. With Karla finishing up her degree at a local college and Mark working as an apprentice electrician, their future was bright.

Despite the years of putting off the big question, Mark Fair knew how fortunate he was to have Karla as his intended wife. Karla Lou Brown was the embodiment of the all-American girl. Less than five foot tall, she had wavy blond hair, a knockout figure, and a beauty queen's smile. She had been the ideal of the boys and the envy of the other girls at Roxana High School, where everyone remembered her as a pert, peppy cheerleader. Her closest friends knew a sensitive, introspective dimension went along with the charming, flirty public side. They knew she was devoted to Mark, who was strong, athletically built, and more than a foot taller than she. Together, Karla and Mark made a terrific couple.

After the party Tuesday night they went back to their apartment in East Alton to pack up the remaining boxes. They hoped to be ready to actually move in and sleep in the new place the next night.

Wednesday morning, after Mark left for his job with Camp Electric and Heating Company, Karla went over to Acton Avenue, where she would organize and straighten until Mark got off work about four-thirty. They were excited about spending the night there.

When Mark finished work, he went over to the house of his friend Tom Fiegenbaum, who lived on the same block as Mark's parents and had agreed to help him move a large and unusual A-frame doghouse from the parents' backyard.

They got to Acton Avenue about five-thirty, and as Tom backed his truck down the driveway, Mark went to get Karla. He couldn't find her, which meant she'd probably run out to get something she needed for the house, but he noticed the back door was unlocked. This bothered him. She was going to have to be careful about that sort of thing.

Mark brought Tom in to show him the house. After showing him the main floor, Mark led him into the kitchen and down the stairs to the basement. When he reached the bottom stair, he didn't like what he saw. Several small tables were overturned. Things seemed to be in a mess, despite the fact that he and Karla had organized everything the night before. Something was spilled on the sofa and the floor.

"What's happening here?" Mark asked rhetorically. As he turned to go back upstairs to try to find Karla, he saw through the door to the laundry room.

There was Karla, on her knees and bent forward, wearing a sweater but naked from the waist down, her hands tied behind her back with electrical cord, her head stuffed into a ten-gallon, drum-like barrel filled with water. The barrel was one of the ones he and Karla had used for moving clothes. And the sweater, which had been packed in one of the barrels, was one she wore only in winter.

"Oh my God! Karla!" Mark screamed as he and Tom raced over. Mark pulled her head from the barrel and laid her back on the floor. Her face was puffy and blue, with a deep cut across her forehead and another on her jawline. Her eyes were open, but it was obvious she was dead.

Mark collapsed in grief. He asked Tom to find something to cover her with, and after Tom came back with a red blanket, they called the police.

When Officer David George of the Wood River Police Department arrived a few minutes later, Mark and Tom were outside the front door waiting for him. They led the officer down to the basement and showed him the scene. Throughout the encounter, Mark was barely able to contain himself. "Oh, God, Karla," he kept repeating.

This kind of horror wasn't supposed to happen in Wood River, a quiet community about fifteen minutes from St. Louis. Before long, all the top cops were there to see what was going on, including thirty-nine-year-old chief of police, Ralph Skinner.

Karla showed signs of severe blunt-force trauma to the head, possibly from the upset TV tray stand in the room. Two socks were tied around her neck, and the autopsy would conclude that she had died by strangulation and was already dead by the time her head was submerged in the drum of water.

As much of a focus as this murder scene was, problems dogged the police right from the beginning. Illinois State Police inspector Alva Busch, an experienced crime-scene technician, couldn't get the flash attachment for his camera to work. Bill Redfern, who had taken the call at the police station from Tom Fiegenbaum, fortunately brought a camera and took crime-scene photos but at the time happened to have only black-and-white film in his camera. Another problem was all the people who had been at the house helping the couple move. That was a lot of potential fresh latent fingerprints legitimately at the scene. Selecting out others would be difficult if not impossible.

Some elements appeared to be possible clues, but made no sense. Most notable of these was a glass coffee carafe stuck up in the rafters in the basement. Just before spotting it, police had noted the carafe missing from the machine in the kitchen. No one, including Mark, had any logical explanation for why it was where it was, and its role in the murder, if any, wasn't clear. Alva Busch managed to lift a few latent prints from the glass surface, but they didn't turn out to be complete enough to use.

In the days following the murder, police combed the neighborhood, talking to anyone who might possibly have seen anyone. The next-door neighbor, Paul Main, said that on the day of the murder, he was on his front porch much of the afternoon with his friend John Prante. Prante recalled being at Main's house briefly that morning, just after applying for a job at a local oil refinery, but said he left early to apply for other jobs. The night before the murder, Main, Prante, and a third friend had watched Karla, Mark, and the gang helping them move. All three of them said they had hoped to be invited to the moving-in party since Main was a neighbor and the other friend had known Karla casually in high school. But they had never been asked to join in. The closest they got was when the friend called to Karla from across the driveway.

The neighbor across the street, an elderly woman named Edna Vancil, remembered seeing a red car with a white roof parked in front of 979 the day of the murder. Bob Lewis, one of the people at the party, said he had seen Karla on the driveway talking to a "rough-looking," long-haired guy next door who had pointed to Karla and called her by name. That would have been Paul Main's friend.

"You've got a good memory. It's been a long time," Lewis heard Karla reply. He said he then told Mark Fair about the encounter, suggesting that if those were the kinds of people they were living next to, he'd better be careful until he got to know them better. Mark didn't seem concerned and said that Karla knew the long-haired guy from high school and that he was just visiting Paul Main.

Another woman was driving down the street, taking her grandson to the dentist. She and the child saw a man and a woman talking on the driveway, but even when she was questioned under hypnosis, her description wasn't much.

The police talked to many of Karla's girlfriends, trying to find out if anyone had a grudge against her, perhaps a spurned boyfriend. But all of them said Karla was well liked and had no enemies that they knew of.

One woman, Karla's former roommate, did have an idea, though. Karla's father had died when she was young, and her mother, Jo Ellen, had married Joe Sheppard Sr., from whom she was now divorced. The roommate reported that Karla had not gotten along with Sheppard, who had hit her and was always coming on to her friends. He had to be considered a suspect. He had come over the night of the murder and barraged the police with questions. As I've noted, it's not unusual for a killer to approach the police or otherwise inject himself into the investigation. But there was no evidence linking Sheppard to the crime.

The other person who had to be examined closely was Mark Fair. Along with Tom Fiegenbaum, he had found the body, he had access to the house, he was the closest person to the victim. As I noted with regard to the George Russell case, the spouse or lover always has to be considered. But Mark was at work for the electrical contractor when the murder would have taken place; a number of people had seen him and talked to him. And there was no question in anyone's mind—the police, Karla's friends, her family— that his grief was genuine and profound.

As the investigation geared up, the police polygraphed many of the people they had interviewed, people who could have had contact with Karla shortly before her death. Mark, Tom, and Joe Sheppard passed without any ambiguity. No one really failed. The closest was Paul Main, a man of marginal intellect who had been at home next door that afternoon. Though he claimed John Prante had been with him on his porch and could vouch for him that he hadn't left, Prante himself—who passed his polygraph exam—acknowledged that he had left in the morning to look for work and therefore couldn't say where Main had been during that time. But even though Main's polygraph was questionable and he remained a suspect, as with everyone else nothing tied him directly to the crime.

The trauma of Karla Brown's murder affected Wood River deeply. It remained a wound that wouldn't heal. Both the local and state police had interviewed everyone they could find, had followed up every possible lead. Yet frustratingly, they appeared no closer to a solution. Months went by. Then it was a year. Then two. It was particularly tough on Karla's sister Donna Judson. With her husband, Terry, they seemed involved on almost a daily basis. Karla's mother and her other sister, Connie Dykstra, were unable to face that kind of intense involvement and had less contact with the authorities working on the case.

It was also tough on Don Weber, the state's attorney responsible for Madison County, which contained Wood River. He had been an assistant prosecutor at the time of the murder. A combination of tough prosecutor and deeply sensitive man, Weber desperately wanted to show the public that the kind of outrage perpetrated on Karla would not be tolerated in his district. He was practically obsessed with bringing her killer to justice. Following his election in November 1980 to the top post of state's attorney, he promptly reactivated the case.

The other one who just couldn't let the case rest, no matter how long it dragged on without progress, was the state crime-scene investigator, Alva Busch. There are always a couple of cases in a cop's career that won't let go. And it turned out to be through Busch that this one finally got a critical push forward.

In June of 1980, a full two years after Karla's killing, Busch was in Albuquerque, New Mexico, to testify in a murder trial in a case in which he'd processed a stolen car in Illinois. While waiting for the pretrial motions to be completed, he attended a presentation at the sheriff's department given by Dr. Homer Campbell, an expert from the University of Arizona in the computer enhancement of photographs.

"Hey, Doc," Busch said to him at the end of the presentation, "have I got a case for you." Dr. Campbell agreed to examine the crime-scene and autopsy photos to see if he could help determine exactly the type of instrument or weapon that had been used on Karla. Busch copied and sent all the relevant pictures to Campbell.

That the photos were only black and white didn't make the job any easier, but Campbell was able to do a careful analysis with his sophisticated equipment. Through computer enhancement, he could essentially turn the photos inside out and he was able to report several things. The deep gashes were made by a claw hammer, and the cuts on the chin and forehead had come from the wheels of the over-turned TV tray table. But what he told Busch next turned the case completely around and sent it off in a new direction.

"What about the bite marks? Do you guys have any suspects in the bite marks on her neck?"

"What bite marks?" was all Busch could think to say into the phone.

Campbell told him that while the images he'd managed to raise weren't the best, they definitely showed bite marks on Karla's neck, clear enough that if a suspect was identified, they could get a good comparison. One in particular didn't overlap any of the other wounds or marks on the skin.

Unlike anything else they had so far, bite marks were good, solid evidence, practically the same as fingerprints. A comparison of Ted Bundy's teeth with bite marks found on the buttocks of a murder victim in the Chi Omega sorority house at Florida State University had helped convict the notorious serial killer. Campbell had been a prosecution witness at Bundy's trial. (On the morning of January 24, 1989, after extensive interviews and conversations with Bill Hagmaier from our unit, Bundy was put to death in the Florida electric chair. No one will ever know for certain how many young lives he took.)

Once the Illinois police had Dr. Campbell's bite-mark images, they began refocusing on some of their original possibilities, most notably the neighbor Paul Main. But after police obtained a bite sample from Main, Campbell couldn't match it to the crime-scene and autopsy photographs. They made an attempt to locate Main's friend John Prante to see if he would finger Main with this added information, but they couldn't find him.

There were other attempts at a solution, including bringing in a well-known Illinois psychic, who, without knowing any of the details of the case, said, "I hear water dripping." To the police, this was a clear reference to the discovery of Karla's body. But beyond the fact that the killer lived near railroad tracks (most people do in Madison County), the psychic didn't offer much help.

Even with the knowledge of the bite marks, little progress was being made in the case. In July of 1981, Don Weber and four of his staff members attended a seminar in New York on forensic science in criminal investigations as part of setting up his new administration as state's attorney. Knowing Weber would be there, Dr. Campbell suggested he bring the Brown case photos and show them to Dr. Lowell

Levine, a forensic odontologist from New York University, who was speaking at the seminar. Levine studied the photos but, after agreeing with Campbell that certain of the wounds were definitely bite marks, said he could not make a definitive match. He suggested that they exhume Karla's body, commenting that "a casket is cold storage for evidence." I didn't know Levine personally, but I certainly did by reputation. He had done the analysis in the Francine Elveson case in New York. (He must have done a pretty damn good job, too, since when Bill Hagmaier and Roseanne Russo went to interview Carmine Calabro at the Clinton Correctional Facility, he'd had all his teeth removed to avoid incriminating himself in the appeal. Dr. Levine went on to head up the forensic science unit for New York State.)

In March of 1982, Weber and two state police investigators attended the annual training session for the St. Louis Metropolitan Major Case Squad. I was at the meeting, giving an overview of personality profiling and crime-scene analysis to the large gathering. While I don't personally remember the encounter, Weber describes in his fascinating study of the case, *Silent Witness* (with Charles Bosworth Jr.), that he and his colleagues came up to me after my presentation and asked if what I had just described could be used in their case. I apparently told them to call me at my office when I got back to Quantico and that I'd be happy to help them however I could.

Upon his return, Weber learned that Rick White of the Wood River police had also been at the session and had independently concluded that this would be a good approach in the Brown investigation. White contacted me and we arranged for him to come to Quantico with the crime-scene photos and to let me analyze them on the spot and give my reactions. Weber was too involved in cases being prepared for trial to come himself, but he assigned Assistant State's Attorney Keith Jensen in his place, along with White, Alva Busch, and Randy Rushing, one of the state police officials who'd been with him in St. Louis. The four of them drove over eight hundred miles to Quantico in an unmarked cruiser. The then-current Wood River police chief, Don Greer, was on vacation in Florida, but flew up to Washington to attend the meeting, too.

We met in the conference room. The four investigators had spent much of the drive organizing their thoughts and theories to present to me; they could not have known that I liked to come to my own conclusions before being influenced by anyone else's ideas. We hit it off well, though. Unlike many situations in which we've been brought in for political reasons or to cover someone's ass, these guys were here because they'd simply refused to give up. They really wanted to be here and were genuinely anxious for anything I could do to steer them in the right direction.

I hit it off particularly well with Alva Busch, who shared my difficulty with authority. Like me, he was known to piss off a lot of people with his outspokenness. In fact, Don Weber had had to threaten to call in all his political markers for Busch to be allowed to make the trip to Quantico.

I requested the crime-scene photos and spent several minutes poring over them. I asked a few questions to orient myself, then said, "Are you ready? You might want to record this."

The first thing I told them was my experience told me that when bodies ended up in water inside a house—a bath or shower or a container—the object was not to wash away clues or evidence, as we were seeing in Atlanta, but to "stage" the crime to look like something other than what it actually was. Then I said that they had already undoubtedly interviewed the killer. He was in the neighborhood or immediate vicinity. This kind of crime is almost always a neighborhood or household crime. People don't travel long distances to commit them. If he got blood on him, which he most certainly did, he had to be able to go someplace close by to clean it off and get rid of his bloody clothing. Our guy was comfortable in the situation and knew he wouldn't be disturbed, either because he knew Karla well or had been observing her enough to know her and Mark's habits. Since you've talked to him, he has been cooperative with your investigation. That way, he feels he can keep control of the situation.

He didn't go to Karla's house that afternoon with the plan of killing her. The killing was an afterthought. If he'd planned it, he would have brought his weapons and implements (his "rape kit") with him. Instead, we have manual strangulation and blunt-force trauma, demonstrating a spontaneous act of anger or desperation in reaction to her rejection of him. Manipulation, domination, and control are the watchwords of the rapist. He'd probably gone over to the house offering to help her move in. Karla was known as a friendly sort, and since she knew this guy in some way, she probably let him in. What he wanted from her was sex, some sort of a relationship. When she resisted or he realized he was in over his head, he—like Mary Frances Stoner's killer in South Carolina—decided the only way to save himself was to kill her. And even at that point, he probably panicked and had second thoughts. There was water on the floor and on the sofa. After he strangled her, he might very well have splashed water on her face to try to revive her. When that didn't work, he would have had to deal with her wet face, so he dragged her across the floor and pushed her head in the tub to make it look like some bizarre or kinky ritual; in other words, to draw attention away from what had actually happened. The head in the tub of water had a secondary significance as well. She had rejected him. Now he could degrade her. As in so many other cases, the more an offender does at a scene, even if it's an attempt to throw the police off the scent, the more clues and behavioral evidence he gives you to work with.

This guy is in his mid- to late twenties, I said, and this is not the work of someone who has experience killing. His staging was poor and shows he's never tried to do it before.

However, he does have an explosive, assaultive personality, so he could have committed lesser crimes. If he's ever been married, he's recently been separated or divorced or is having marital discord. Like so many of these guys, this one is a real loser with a poor self-image. He may come across as confident, but deep down, he is extremely inadequate.

He is of average intelligence and IQ, went no further than high school, and his use of wire to bind her suggests shop training or one of the vocational trades. Once the investigation was launched, you would find him changing residences and/or jobs, and once the heat was off and he wouldn't create any suspicion, he might very well leave town. He'd also be turning heavily to drugs or alcohol or cigarettes to relieve his tension. In fact, alcohol could have played some role in the crime itself. This was a bold move for this particular guy. He may have been drinking beforehand, which would have lowered his inhibition, though he wouldn't be drunk, because then he wouldn't have done so much on the scene postoffense.

He'd be having difficulty sleeping, he would have a problem with his sex life, and you'd find him becoming more and more nocturnal. If he had a regular job, he would have missed a lot of work as the investigation geared up. He would change his appearance, too. If he had a beard and long hair at the time of the killing, he would have shaved them. If he was clean-shaven, he would have grown a beard. You're not looking for a preppie type, though. He's naturally scruffy and unkempt, and any attempt to keep himself orderly will be an obvious manifestation of overcontrol. He will find this effort physically and mentally exhausting.

As to automobile, in this case I fell back on my old killer standby—a Volkswagen Beetle. It would be old and not terribly well maintained; red or orange.

This is someone who will be following the police investigation closely in the media, and he will be taking his leads from them. If the chief of police has publicly announced that there have been no new leads, that's going to give him a mechanism to cope. He could easily have passed a polygraph; a lot of killers do. The next phase of the investigation has to have as its goal to begin to shake him up.

There can be a lot of stressors. Every year in June he could become more nervous. The same could happen around Karla's birthday. He's probably been out to visit Karla's grave at Calvary Hill Cemetery. He may have sent flowers or asked her directly for forgiveness.

So the next thing you've got to do, I said, is to announce a new and promising lead, something that will appear to get the case back on the front burner. Continuously advertise and publicize this. Keep that "ass-pucker factor" as intense as possible. Mention that you've brought an FBI profiler into the case and that what he's telling you fits in perfectly with the new evidence you've developed.

At that point they told me of Dr. Levine's recommendation to exhume the body and wanted to know what I thought about it. I told them it was a terrific idea, and the more public hoopla leading up to it, the better. Weber should go on television beforehand and announce that if the body is still in good shape and the new examination turns up the evidence they expect, they will be close to solving the murder. In a sense, what they would be conveying to the killer is that they were "resurrecting" Karla, bringing her back from the grave, to bear witness in her own murder.

The digging up of the body will be a tremendous stressor to him. I want Weber to state publicly that if it takes another twenty years, he's going to solve this case. Your offender is going to be concerned and inquisitive. He'll be asking a lot of questions. He may even call the police directly! Make sure you videotape or photograph everyone who shows up at the cemetery; he may be there. He's going to be in a lot of suspense about what shape the body is in. And when you finally announce how pleased you are with its condition, that's going to send him farther over the edge. At the same time, he'll become even more of a loner, isolating himself from whatever friends he has. This will be the time to start listening to people in bars and places like that to see if any of the regulars are displaying markedly changed behavior. He may recently have joined a church or taken up religion as a means to cope. And while you're putting all this stress on him, there should be a comment in the paper from one of the cops—it could even be from me—that sounds almost empathic. We should say we know what he's going through, that he did not intend to kill her and has been carrying this huge weight on his shoulders all these years.

I went on to outline an interrogation strategy similar to what had worked in the Stoner case. The important thing was that once a suspect had been identified, he shouldn't be arrested right away but left to stew for a week or so, then you'd want to get him to confess before arresting him. The more facts you have at your disposal, the more things you can say, like, "We know you carried her from here to here" or "We know about the water," the better shot you'll have. An object that had a material role in the murder (such as the rock in the Stoner case) would be good to have in the room.

After hearing my impressions, my five visitors seemed to take what I had said to heart. They asked how I could tell all that just by hearing routine details of the case and looking at photographs. I'm not sure of the answer to that, though Ann Burgess has noted that I'm a visual person and like to work first from what I can look at. She says, and it's probably true, that I have a tendency in consultations to say "I see" rather than "I think." Part of it probably has to do with not being able to be on-scene most of the time, so I've got to re-create the environment within my head. Often, when police would call me back several years after I'd analyzed a case for them, I could recall it and what I'd said about the UNSUB if they would just describe the crime scene to me.

The investigators from Illinois said that from what I told them, two of their many interviewees still looked like strong suspects—Paul Main and his friend John Prante. Both had been next door that day, and at least one of them, Prante, had been drinking beer. Their stories had never quite squared with each other, which could have been the result of their low intelligence and drinking, or could have meant that one or both of them were lying. Prante had done better than Main on the polygraph, but they both fit the profile well. In fact, in some ways Prante fit better. He had been more cooperative with the police, and after the heat had died down, he had left town as I predicted the killer would, only to return later on.

I said that the campaign I had outlined could be used against both of them. In fact, since I thought whoever had done it felt periodic guilt and remorse, a bit of extra flair might involve having a woman portray Karla and call each of them in the middle of the night, sobbing and asking, "Why? Why? Why?" This should coincide with articles in the paper about what an all-American girl Karla had been and how tragic it was that she had been cut down in her prime. I've always gone for the theatrical touch.

Once the campaign had been on for about a week or ten days, the police could see if either Main or Prante was reacting in the way I'd said the killer would. If one of them was, then the next step would be to use informants—friends, acquaintances, work associates—to try to draw comments or a confession out of him.

The exhumation of the body on June 1, 1982, was handled just the way I'd hoped, with Lowell Levine on the scene, a lot of television and press coverage, and appropriately solemn and optimistic statements from Weber. I've found that in smaller towns it's a lot easier to get the kind of cooperation you need from journalists than it is in big cities, where they're much more apt to feel you're trying to manipulate them or tell them what to print. I see it more as a cooperative effort between the press and law enforcement that shouldn't compromise the integrity of either. I've never asked a newspaper or TV reporter to lie or produce a false or incomplete story. But on many occasions, I have given out the information I needed to have an UNSUB read and react to. When reporters are cooperative with me, I'm cooperative with them. And in certain cases, when they've been particularly cooperative, I've given them exclusives when the inside story could finally be told.

Fortunately, Karla's body was in amazingly well-preserved condition. The new autopsy was performed by Dr. Mary Case, an assistant medical examiner for the city of St. Louis. Unlike in the first postmortem, Dr. Case determined that the cause of death was drowning. She also found a skull fracture. Most important, they got the bite-mark evidence they needed.

The organized publicity campaign continued in earnest. Tom O'Connor of the state police and Wayne Watson of the Financial Fraud and Forgery Unit interviewed Main at his house, ostensibly about public-aid payments he was receiving that he was possibly ineligible for. They led him into a discussion of Karla Brown's murder. While he wouldn't confess and denied any involvement in the crime, he had definitely been closely following the publicity and had some inside information. For example, Watson mentioned that Main had left out Acton Avenue on his list of previous addresses. He said he had been trying to forget because of bad memories of the cops hassling him about the neighbor girl who got killed there.

Watson said, "She's the one who was shot, strangled, and drowned in a fifty-gallon barrel."

"No, no! Not shot, not shot!" Main replied emphatically.

Just around the time of the exhumation, a man named Martin Higdon went to the Wood River police and said he'd gone to high school with Karla Brown and that all of the current publicity had led to discussions at work. He thought the police should know that a woman he worked with claimed that at a party not long after the murder, a man said he had been at Karla's house on the day she was killed.

O'Connor and Rick White interviewed the woman, whose name was Vicki White (no relation). She confirmed the story, saying she and her husband, Mark, had been at a party at Spencer and Roxanne Bond's house, where she'd spoken to a man she'd known at Lewis and Clark Community College. The man said he had been at Karla's house the day of the murder. He mentioned where she had been found and that she had been bitten on her shoulder. He was going to have to leave town because he thought he would be considered a prime suspect. At the time, she'd discounted this as idle talk.

His name was John Prante.

How could he have known about the bite marks so soon after the murder when the police didn't know about them until two years later? O'Connor and White asked each other. They then interviewed the party's host, Spencer Bond, who had the same recollection as Vicki and Mark White. Bond also mentioned that Main had given him details about how Karla was found. The question was whether Main had gotten the information from Prante, or vice versa. Though Prante had done better on the polygraph, Weber and the police didn't think Main was bold enough to have carried out such a crime or smart enough to have set up Prante.

Bond had recently seen Prante, driving his old red Volkswagen Minibus. Though I'd gotten the color and make right, I'd missed out on the model. But this, in itself, was significant. About this time, we were starting to see a shift in vehicle of preference to vans. Bittaker and Norris used one. Steven Pennell used one. Unlike a car, in the back of a van you can do whatever you want and not be seen. You have, in effect, a mobile murder site.

I was not surprised to hear that John Prante had grown a beard since the murder. Bond agreed to wear a wire while he spoke to Prante about the case. While Prante didn't admit the killing, he revealed how closely he fit the profile. He had studied welding at Lewis and Clark. He had left town after the murder. He had been divorced and had trouble with women. He was extremely curious about the investigation.

Thursday, June 3, Weber's office secured a court order compelling Prante to submit to a dental impression the next day. Chief Don Greer told him they were trying to tie up loose ends, and if he didn't match, they could eliminate him as a suspect.

After leaving the dentist's office, Prante called Weber, just as I figured he would. He wanted to know what was going on with the investigation. Weber had the presence of mind to get his assistant Keith Jensen on the line at the same time, just to make sure Weber couldn't later be knocked out of the case as a potential witness. In talking with Weber, Prante contradicted his earlier story about when he'd been at Paul Main's house. As I predicted, he appeared cooperative.

The police got more information from a second wired exchange between Bond and Prante, then even more from a taped conversation between Bond and Main. Prante told Bond he was up to several packs of cigarettes a day. Main went so far as to suggest that perhaps Karla had set Prante off by rejecting his sexual advances. That led to another police interview with Main, in which he stated that he believed Prante was responsible for the murder, though he recanted after a private conversation with Prante.

The following Tuesday, Weber, Rushing, and Greer flew to Long Island to see Dr. Levine. They gave him the new autopsy photographs and three sets of dental impressions— Main's, those of another long-standing suspect, and Prante's. Levine eliminated the first two right away. He couldn't say with scientific certainty that only Prante's teeth out of the whole world would match up, but they did—perfectly.

Paul Main was arrested and charged with obstructing justice. Prante was charged with murder and burglary with intent to commit rape. He went to trial in June of 1983. In July, he was found guilty and sentenced to seventy-five years in prison.

It had taken four years, but through the combined efforts of many dedicated people, a killer was finally brought to justice. I was particularly pleased and gratified to receive a copy of a letter Assistant State's Attorney Keith Jensen sent to FBI director William Webster. In it he wrote, "The community finally feels safe, and the family feels justice has been done, none of which could have happened without John Douglas. While he is an extremely busy man, I feel his efforts should not go unnoticed. I extend my sincere thanks and wish that there were more John Douglases available with the competency, capacity, and ability to assist as he did."

These were kind words indeed. Fortunately, though, the previous January I had been able to make my case to Jim McKenzie, the assistant director of the Academy, that we did need "more John Douglases." In turn, he'd managed to sell headquarters, even though it meant stealing bodies from other programs. That was how I got Bill Hagmaier, Jim Horn, Blaine McIlwaine, and Ron Walker in the first go-round, then Jim Wright and Jud Ray in the second. As time soon told, they all made sizable contributions.

Despite everyone's best efforts, some cases, like Karla Brown's, take years to close. Others just as complex can be solved in a matter of days or weeks if everything breaks right.

When a stenographer named Donna Lynn Vetter in one of the FBI's southwestern field offices was raped and murdered in her ground-floor apartment one night, Roy Hazelwood and Jim Wright were given an unambiguous order from the Director's Office: get down there immediately and solve the case. By that time, we had divided the country into regions. This one fell in Jim's territory.

The message had to be loud and clear: you don't get away with killing FBI personnel, and we'll do whatever we have to to make sure. At two the next afternoon, an FBI Hostage Rescue Team helicopter carried the two agents and their hastily packed bags from Quantico to Andrews Air Force Base in Maryland, where they boarded a Bureau jet. Upon landing, they went immediately to the crime scene, which had been held intact for them by the local police.

Vetter was a white, twenty-two-year-old woman who'd grown up on a farm, and even though she'd worked for the Bureau for more than two years, she'd moved to the city only eight months before. Naive to the dangers of urban life, she'd taken an apartment in an industrial, predominantly black and Hispanic area. The resident manager was cognizant of security considerations. She had installed a white porch-type lightbulb—instead of the regular yellow one—over the door of each apartment where a single female tenant lived, so that her staff and the security guards would pay special attention. The system was not made public. But for all its good intentions, the code would have been quickly transparent to even the most casual snooper.

Police had been called shortly after 11 p.m. when one of the other residents noticed the apartment's window screen had been ripped out and called the complex's security guard. The victim's nude body, beaten about the face and bearing multiple stab wounds, was covered with blood. The autopsy showed she had been raped.

The assailant forced entry through the front window, knocking over a large potted plant on his way in. The telephone cord had been unplugged from the wall. Large, hideous bloodstains were on the dining-room carpet and kitchen floor, where the main attack seemed to have taken place. One stain where the body had lain looked eerily like a life-size angel, her wings spread as if in flight. The blood tracks indicated the victim was then dragged into the living room. From the defense wounds on the body, it seemed that she had gone for a kitchen knife, but he had grabbed it and turned it on her.

Vetter's bloodstained clothing was found by the emergency medical team at the edge of the kitchen floor near the cabinets. Her shorts and panties were rolled, indicating they'd been removed by the attacker while she was lying on the floor. When police arrived at the scene, the lights in the apartment were off. They speculated that the offender had probably turned them off to delay discovery after he left.

From everything they learned from coworkers, family, and neighbors, the young woman was shy, honest, and devout. She had grown up in a strict and solid religious environment, and she took her religion seriously. She wasn't in any way glamorous and seemed to have little, if any, social life, either with men or her coworkers, who described her as conscientious and hardworking but "different." This probably had a lot to do with her lack of sophistication and sheltered upbringing. No one suggested any kind of illicit behavior or hanging around with the "wrong kind." No drugs, alcohol, cigarettes, or birth control pills were in her apartment. Her parents were absolutely convinced of her chastity and said they thought she would do anything to protect her virginity.

After studying the scene, that was what Roy and Jim concluded had happened. While there was blood all over the place, one particular bloodstain aroused their special interest. It was right outside the bathroom door. Inside the bathroom, they noticed urine but no tissue in the bowl of the unflushed toilet.

This gave them an immediate sense of what had taken place between the intruder and the victim. She must have been in the bathroom when she heard the break-in. She got up without taking the time to flush and went out to see what was going on. As soon as she passed through the bathroom door, he hit her hard in the face, essentially trying to neutralize her. Jim and Roy found the murder weapon, a kitchen knife, hidden under a seat cushion in the living room.

The murder weapon itself told them something—that the UNSUB had not broken into the apartment with the intention of murder. And the fact that nothing of value was taken suggested he had come with intentions other than burglary. The evidence suggested he was there to rape. Had he been there to murder, rather than spend time with her, there would have been no reason to unplug the phone. The easy access of the apartment, the victim's plainness, his blitzing her before he'd even said a word to her, all pointed to an angry, macho type with low intelligence and no social skills or confidence in his ability to control someone else through words. Unless he completely controlled this unthreatening victim right from the beginning, he knew he couldn't succeed in his goal.

What he hadn't counted on was how fiercely this shy, quiet woman would resist. Everything in her background told the profilers that this was exactly what she would do to defend her honor. But the attacker wouldn't have known. The more she fought him, the more he was in danger of losing control, and the more his rage grew. With the Karla Brown case, another rape that turned to murder, I felt the assailant's rage was secondary to his need to "deal with" the mess he'd created. In this killing, it looked as if the rage and need to deal with the victim had equal importance. The anger in this case was sustained rather than momentary. The drag marks showed that after he attacked her in the kitchen, he dragged her into another room where he raped her, bleeding and dying.

Roy and Jim began preparing their profile the very evening they arrived. They were looking for a man between twenty and twenty-seven years of age. Normally, in a sexually based or lust murder, if the victim was white, you would expect the offender to be white, too. But the agents firmly believed this had started out as a rape, and so the "rules" of rape applied. This was a predominantly black and Hispanic apartment complex and neighborhood, with a high incidence in the area of white women being raped by black men, so there was a very strong chance the killer was probably black.

They didn't think the UNSUB would be married, but he could have been living in a financially dependent or exploitive relationship with someone. Any woman who had a relationship with him would be younger, less experienced, or in some way easy to influence. He would not be involved with anyone he found challenging or in any way intimidating. While he would be of fairly low intelligence and have an unspectacular record in school (where he'd probably been a behavior problem), he would be streetwise and able to take care of himself in a fight. He would want to seem macho and tough to those around him, and he would wear the best clothing he could afford. Likewise, he would be athletic and try to stay in good condition.

He would live within walking distance of the scene, in a lower-income rental unit. He'd have some menial job and would be in frequent conflict with coworkers or authority figures. Because of his explosive temper, he wouldn't have been in the military, or if he had, he would have been discharged. The agents didn't think he had killed before, but would have burglarized and assaulted. Roy Hazelwood, one of the leading experts on rape and crimes against women, believed strongly that he had a past history of rape or sexual assault.

They predicted his postoffense behavior, which in many ways mirrored that of Karla Brown's killer, including absence from work, heavier drinking, weight loss, and a change in appearance. Most important, they felt that this type of individual would mention his crime or confide in a family member or close associate. And that could be the key to a proactive strategy for catching him.

Since they knew the UNSUB would be following the news, Roy and Jim decided to make their profile public, submitting for interviews with the local press. The only significant detail they withheld was the racial factor. In case they were wrong, they didn't want to lead the investigation astray and misdirect potential leads.

But what they did make as public as possible was their belief that whomever the UNSUB had talked to about the murder was in grave danger him—or her—self, now that he or she knew this incriminating information. If you recognize yourself in this situation, they urged, please contact authorities before it's too late. Within two and a half weeks, the offender's armed-robbery partner called the police. The subject was apprehended, and based on a matchup of palm prints found at the murder scene, he was charged.

When we went over the profile afterward, we found that Jim and Roy had been right on the money. The offender was a twenty-two-year-old black male who lived four blocks from the crime scene. He was single, lived with, and was financially dependent on, his sister. At the time of the murder he was on probation for rape. He was tried, found guilty, and sentenced to death. His execution was carried out only recently.

I've often told my people that we should be like the Lone Ranger, riding into town, helping to bring about justice, then quietly riding out again.

Who were those masked men? They left this silver bullet behind.

Them? Oh, they were from Quantico.

In this particular case, Jim and Roy rode out of town quietly. They had been rushed down in a private Bureau jet. When their work was done, they flew home tourist class, crammed in with happy vacationers and screaming kids in the back of a commercial flight. But we knew what they'd done, and so did all the recipients of the "silver bullets" they had left behind.

15

Hurting the Ones We Love

Going over case files in his windowless office at Quantico one day, Gregg McCrary got a phone call from one of the police departments in his region. It was one of those anguishing cases you seem to hear about all too often.

A young single mother was leaving her garden apartment complex to go shopping with her two-year-old son. Just before she got into her car, she suddenly developed stomach cramps, so she turned around, hurried back across the parking lot, and went into a rest room just inside the apartment building's back door. It was a safe, friendly neighborhood where everyone knew everyone else, and she gave her little boy strict instructions to stay inside the building and play quietly until she came out.

I'm sure you've already anticipated what happened next. It's about forty-five minutes before she's finished in the bathroom. She comes out and the child isn't in the hall. Not yet alarmed, she goes outside and looks around, figuring he's just wandered off a little, even though the weather is chilly and brisk.

But then she sees it: one of her little boy's knit mittens, lying on the pavement of the parking lot and no sign of him anywhere. Now she panics.

She rushes back to her apartment and immediately dials 911. Frantically, she tells the emergency operator that her child's been kidnapped. The police arrive quickly and comb the area looking for clues. By this time the young woman is hysterical.

The news media picks up the story. She goes before the

microphones and pleads to whoever took her son to bring him back. As sympathetic as the police are, they want to cover their bases, so they quietly administer a polygraph, which she passes. They know that in any child abduction, time is of the essence, which is why they call Gregg.

He hears the scenario and listens to a recording of the 911 call. There's something about it he doesn't like. Then there's a new development. The agonized woman receives a small parcel in the mail. It has no return address, no note or communication enclosed—just the matching mitten to the one she found in the parking lot. The woman goes to pieces.

But now Gregg knows. He tells the police the little boy is dead and that his mother killed him.

How do you know? the police press him. Children get snatched away by perverts all the time. How do you know this isn't one of those cases?

So Gregg explains. First, there was the scenario itself. No one is more fearful of a child getting snatched away by a pervert than a mother. Is it logical that she would leave her son unattended for that long a period? If she had to be in the bathroom for an extended time, wouldn't she have taken him in with her or made some other makeshift arrangement? It's possible that it happened the way she said, but then you start compounding the factors.

On the 911 tape, she distinctly says that someone "kidnapped" her child. It's been Gregg's experience that parents will do almost anything to psychologically deny such a horrible situation. In the heat of hysterical emotion, you might expect to hear her say he was missing, he ran off, she doesn't know where he is, or something like that. For her to use the word *kidnap* at this stage suggests she is already thinking ahead in the scenario that will play out.

The tearful plea before the news media is certainly not incriminating in itself, though we are now all haunted by the image of Susan Smith in South Carolina pleading for the safe return of her two young sons. Generally, parents we see doing this are completely on the level. But the problem is that this kind of public display tends to legitimize the few who aren't.

What capped it for Gregg, though, was the return of the mitten. Basically, children are abducted for one of three reasons: they're taken by kidnappers for profit; they're taken by child molesters for sexual gratification; and they're taken by pathetic, lonely, unstable people who desperately want a child of their own. The kidnapper will have to communicate with the family, either by phone or written message, to set out his demand. The other two types want nothing at all to do with the family. None of the three merely send back an artifact to let the family know the child was taken. The family already knows that. If there is to be some proof of the legitimacy of the crime, it will accompany a demand; otherwise, it's meaningless.

What Gregg decided the mother had done was to stage a kidnapping according to her perception of what a real one would be like. Unfortunately for her, she had no idea of the actual dynamics of this type of crime, and so she blew it.

Quite clearly, she had reasons for what she had done and could therefore convince herself that she had done nothing wrong. That was why she passed the polygraph. But Gregg wasn't satisfied with that. He brought in an experienced FBI polygraph expert and had her retested, this time with the knowledge that she was a suspect. And this time the results were completely different. After some directed questioning, she admitted having murdered her child and led police to the body.

Her motive was the common one, the one Gregg had suspected all along. She was a young single mother, missing out on all the fun of her late teens and early twenties because she was saddled with this child. She had met a man who wanted to intensify their involvement and start a new family of their own. But he had made it clear that there was no room in their life together for this kid.

What is significant about this type of case is, had the police come upon the body without having had the child reported missing, Gregg would still have come to the same conclusion. The child was found buried in the woods in his snowsuit, wrapped in a blanket, then completely covered with a thick plastic bag. A kidnapper or child molester would not have taken this much care to make him warm and "comfortable," or to try to shelter the body from the elements. While many murder scenes show obvious and prolonged rage, and dump sites often show contempt and hostility, the hallmarks of this burial were love and guilt.

The human race has a long history of hurting the ones we love or should love. In fact, during Alan Burgess's first television interview after becoming Behavioral Science Unit chief, he stated, "We've had violence for generations and generations, going all the way back to Bible days when *Cain shot Abel.*" Fortunately, the reporters didn't seem to catch his reinterpretation of the world's first murder weapon.

One of the major cases of nineteenth-century England involved allegations of intrafamily violence. In 1860, Scotland Yard inspector Jonathan Whicher went to the town of Frome in Somerset on the murder of a baby named Francis Kent, from a prominent family in the area. The local police were convinced the child had been killed by Gypsies, but after investigating, Whicher became convinced that the actual culprit was Francis's sixteen-year-old sister, Constance. Because of the family's stature and the very idea that a teenage girl could possibly kill her baby brother, Whicher's evidence was overruled in court and Constance was acquitted of the charges he had brought against her.

A huge public reaction against Whicher forced him to resign from Scotland Yard. For years, he worked on his own to prove he'd been right and that this young woman was a murderess. Eventually, bankruptcy and poor health made him abandon his quest for the truth—a year before Constance Kent confessed to the crime. She was tried again and sentenced to life in prison. Three years later, Wilkie Collins based his groundbreaking detective novel, *The Moonstone*, on the Kent case.

The key to many murders of and by loved ones or family members is staging. Anyone that close to the victim has to do something to draw suspicion away from himself or herself. One of the earliest examples I worked on was the murder of Linda Haney Dover in Cartersville, Georgia, the day after Christmas in 1980.

Though she and her husband, Larry, were separated, they remained on reasonably cordial terms. The five-foot-two, 120-pound, twenty-seven-year-old Linda regularly came over to the house they used to share to clean for him. In fact, that's what she was doing that Friday, December 26. Larry, meanwhile, took their young son out for a day in the park.

When the two of them return from their outing in the afternoon, Linda's no longer there. But instead of finding a clean, straight house, Larry sees the bedroom is a mess. Sheets and pillows are pulled off the bed, dresser drawers are half-open, clothing is strewn around, and red stains that look like blood are on the carpet. Larry instantly calls the police, who rush over and search the house, inside and out.

They find Linda's body wrapped in the comforter from the bedroom, with only her head exposed, in the outside crawl space under the house. As they unwrap the blanket, they see that her shirt and bra have been pushed up above her breasts, her jeans are around her knees, and her panties have been pulled down to just below her pubic area. There is blunt-force trauma to the head and face and multiple stab wounds, which appear to the officers to have been made after the bra was pushed up. They believe the weapon to be a knife from an open kitchen drawer, but they can't find it (and never do). The crime scene indicates that she had been assaulted initially in a bedroom, then her body was moved outside and into the crawl space. Blood drops on her thighs show that the killer had handled and positioned her.

Nothing in her background made Linda Dover a particularly high-risk victim. Though she was separated from Larry, she wasn't involved in any other relationships. The only unusual stress factors would be the holiday time of year and whatever led up to the disintegration of her marriage.

Based on the crime-scene photos and the information the Cartersville police sent me, I told them the UNSUB would be one of two types. Quite possibly, he would be a young and inexperienced, inadequate loner who lived nearby and essentially stumbled into this crime of opportunity. Police mentioned after I said this that they'd been having problems with a neighborhood thug, whom many of the residents were afraid of.

But the crime had too many staging elements, which made me lean toward the second type: someone who knew the victim well and therefore wanted to divert attention from himself. The only reason a killer would have felt the need to hide the body on the premises was what we classify as a "personal cause homicide." The trauma to the face and neck seemed highly personal, too.

I told them I felt this UNSUB was intelligent but only educated through high school and had a job requiring physical strength. He would have a history of assaultive behavior and a low frustration level. He would be moody, unable to accept defeat, and was probably depressed for one reason or another at the time of the murder, most likely from money problems.

The staging had its own internal logic and rationale. Whoever had brutalized Linda did not want to leave her body out in the open where another family member—particularly her son—might find it. That's why he took the time to wrap her in the blanket and move her to the crawl space. He wanted to make this look like a sex crime—hence the raising of the bra and exposure of the genital area—though there was no evidence of rape or sexual assault. He thought he had to do this, but still felt uncomfortable with police seeing her bare genitals and breasts, so he covered them with the blanket.

I said the offender would be overly cooperative and concerned at first, but would turn arrogant and hostile when challenged on his alibi. His postoffense behavior might include increased drinking or drug use, or perhaps a turn toward religion. He would have changed his appearance, maybe even changed jobs and moved out of the area. I told the police to look for a total reversal in behavior and personality.

"The way he is today is nothing like the way he was prior to the homicide," I said.

What I didn't know was that, at the time the Cartersville police requested the profile from me, they had already charged Larry Bruce Dover with his wife's murder and wanted to make sure they were on the right track. This really ticked me off for several reasons. For one, I had more active cases than I could handle. But more importantly, this put the Bureau in what could potentially be an uncomfortable position. Fortunately for all concerned, the profile turned out to be a perfect match. As I explained to the Director and the Atlanta SAC, if it hadn't been so accurate, a skillful attorney might have been able to subpoena me as a defense witness and force me to say that my "expert" profile pointed away from the defendant in certain areas. From that point on, I learned always to ask police if they had a suspect, even though I didn't want to know in advance who it was.

But at least justice was served in this case. On September 3, 1981, Larry Bruce Dover was convicted of the murder of Linda Haney Dover and sentenced to life behind bars.

A variation on the theme of domestic staging came with the murder of Elizabeth Jayne Wolsieffer, known as Betty, in 1986.

Just after seven on the morning of Saturday, August 30, police in Wilkes-Barre, Pennsylvania, were called to 75

Birch Street, the home of a popular dentist and his family. Upon arriving about five minutes later, Officers Dale Minnick and Anthony George encountered thirty-three-year-old Dr. Edward Glen Wolsieffer, who was lying on the floor, the victim of an attempted strangulation and a blow to the head. His brother, Neil, was there with him. Neil explained that he lived across the street, had been called by his brother, and had rushed over. Glen had been stunned and disoriented and said Neil's was the only phone number he could remember. As soon as Neil got here, he had been the one who called the police.

The men said that Glen's thirty-two-year-old wife, Betty, and their five-year-old daughter, Danielle, were upstairs. Every time Neil started to go up to check on them, Glen had felt faint or begun moaning again, so neither of them had been upstairs yet. Glen told Neil he was afraid an intruder was still in the house.

Officers Minnick and George search the house. They don't find an intruder, but they come upon Betty dead in the master bedroom. She's on her side, lying on the floor next to the bed with her head toward the foot of the bed. From the bruises on her neck, the drying foam around her mouth, and the bluish coloring of her bruised face, it appears she's been manually strangled. The bedsheets are stained with blood, but her face seems to have been cleaned off. She's clad only in her nightgown, which has been pushed up to her waist.

Danielle is asleep and unharmed in the next bedroom. When she wakes up, she tells the police she didn't hear anything—no sounds of breaking in or fighting or any commotion.

Without describing the scene upstairs, Minnick and George come back down and ask Dr. Wolsieffer what happened. He says he was awakened just as it was getting light by a noise that sounded like someone breaking into the house. He got his handgun from the night table and went to investigate without waking Betty.

As he neared the bedroom door, he saw a large man at the top of the stairs. The man didn't seem to spot him, and he followed him downstairs, but then lost him and started looking around the first floor for him.

Suddenly, he was attacked from behind with some kind of cord or ligature, but he was able to drop his gun and slip his hand in before it could tighten around his throat. Glen then kicked back, hitting the man in the groin and causing him to loosen his grip. Before Glen could turn around, though, he was struck in the head from behind and blacked out. When he awoke sometime later, he called his brother.

Dr. Wolsieffer's visible injuries don't appear serious to the police or the paramedics they've called to the scene—a contusion on the back of the head, pink marks on the back of the neck, small scratches on the left side of his ribs and chest. But they don't want to take chances, so they have him taken to the emergency room. He doesn't look too bad to the doctor there, either, but he admits him based on the dentist's report of having been unconscious.

From the beginning, the police were suspicious of Wolsieffer's story. It didn't seem logical that an intruder would enter the home from a second-story window in daylight. Outside, they found an old ladder leading to the open window of the back bedroom the intruder allegedly used as his entrance. But the ladder was so rickety, it didn't look as if it could support the weight of even an average-size person. It was leaning against the side of the house with the rungs facing the wrong direction. The ladder had made no indentations in the soft ground to indicate that any weight had been placed on it, nor were there any markings on the aluminum gutters it was resting against. And no dew or grass was on the rungs or roof near the window as there should have been had someone used it that morning.

There were also contradictory indicators inside the house. Nothing of value appeared to have been taken, not even any jewelry that would have been apparent in the bedroom.

And if the intruder intended to kill, why would he leave an unconscious man with a gun nearby downstairs and go back upstairs to kill, but not sexually assault, his wife?

Two points were especially disturbing. If Glen had been choked to the point of passing out, why were there no marks on the front of his neck? And the most unfathomable part of all: neither Glen nor his brother, Neil, had gone upstairs to check on Betty and Danielle.

To further fuzz things up, Dr. Wolsieffer's story evolved as time went on. His description of the intruder grew more explicit as he recalled more details. The man wore a dark sweatshirt, a stocking mask, and had a mustache, Wolsieffer said. He contradicted himself on several points. He told family members he'd been out late Friday night but talked to his wife before going to sleep. He had told police that he never awakened her. Initially, he had reported that about $1,300 had been taken from a desk drawer, but later took that back when police found a deposit slip for the money. When police tried to question him after they arrived on the emergency call, he seemed only barely conscious and practically incoherent, yet when told at the hospital of his wife's death, he referenced having heard the police call for the coroner.

As long as the investigation continued, Glen Wolsieffer came up with newer and more elaborate scenarios to explain the attack. Eventually, the number of intruders grew to two. He had admitted having an affair with a former dental assistant but told police he had ended it a year ago. Yet later he conceded that he'd just seen—and had sex with—the woman a few days before the murder. And he'd neglected to tell police about another affair he was having at the same time with a married woman.

Betty Wolsieffer's friends told police that as much as she loved her husband and had tried to make things work, she was tired of his behavior, particularly the late Friday nights, which had become a regularity. Days before she was killed, she had told a friend she was going to "take a stand" if Glen stayed out late again the coming Friday.

Following the initial interviews at his home and the hospital, Glen refused to talk to police on the advice of his lawyer. So they focused on his brother, Neil. His story of that morning seemed almost as strange as Glen's. He refused a polygraph, saying he had heard they were often inaccurate and he feared a damaging result. After repeated requests by the police, Betty's family, and pressure from the media to cooperate in the investigation, Neil scheduled an interview with police at the courthouse in October.

At about 10:15 a.m., fifteen minutes past the scheduled time for the interview, Neil was killed in a head-on collision between his small Honda and a Mack truck. He was actually traveling away from the courthouse when hit. The coroner's inquest ruled his death a suicide, though it later appeared he may have overshot the turn and was nervously trying to get back. We may never know for sure.

More than a year after the murder, the Wilkes-Barre police had assembled a large amount of circumstantial evidence pointing to Glen Wolsieffer as his wife's killer, but they had no hard evidence and so no proof with which to charge him. His fingerprints and hair were found at the crime scene, but it was his own bedroom, so that didn't say much. Police theorized that any ligature or bloody clothes he may have worn could have been disposed of in a nearby river prior to Glen's call to his brother. Their only hope for an arrest and conviction lay in bolstering their case with an expert opinion that the crime was committed by someone who knew the victim personally and had staged the crime scene.

In January of 1988, the Wilkes-Barre police asked me to provide an analysis of the crime. After reviewing the by-then voluminous material, I concluded rather quickly that the murder was indeed committed by someone who knew the victim well and staged the crime scene to cover that up. Since the police already had a suspect, I didn't want to generate our normal profile, or point the finger directly at the husband, but I tried to give the police some ammunition to help them support an arrest.

A daylight, weekend break-in in that neighborhood, into a home with two cars parked in the driveway, was an extremely high-risk crime against low-risk victims. A burglary scenario was highly improbable.

It was totally inconsistent with everything we'd seen during our years of research and case consultation throughout the world that an intruder would enter a second-story window and immediately head downstairs without checking rooms on the second floor.

There was no evidence that an intruder had brought any weapons with him, which made an intended homicide scenario highly improbable. Mrs. Wolsieffer was not sexually violated, which made an intended-rape-gone-bad scenario equally improbable. And there was no evidence of even an attempt to take anything, which was another reason that an intended-burglary scenario was improbable. This narrowed down the potential motives considerably.

The method of death—manual strangulation—is a personal-type crime. It is not a method a stranger is going to choose, particularly one who has planned enough and made the effort to break in.

The police continued methodically and meticulously building their case. Although they were convinced as to who the murderer was, their evidence was still circumstantial and had to hold up in court. In the meantime, Glen Wolsieffer moved to Falls Church, Virginia, outside Washington, D.C., and set up a dental practice there. Late in 1989, an arrest warrant and affidavit of probable cause was prepared, referencing my report. On November 3, 1989, thirty-eight months after the murder, a team of state, county, and local police came down to Virginia and arrested Wolsieffer in his dental office.

He told one of the arresting officers, "It happened too fast. We got into it. Everything was a blur." Later, he claimed he was talking about the attack on him by the intruder(s), not the murder of his wife.

Though I'd already been qualified at that time as a crime-scene analysis expert in several states, the defense referred to me as a "voodoo man" for the way I came up with my interpretations, and the judge ultimately ruled that I couldn't testify. Still, the prosecution was able to incorporate what I'd told them. Combined with the thorough police work, they were able to secure a conviction for murder in the third degree.

There were many red flags in the Wolsieffer case—the rickety and wrongly positioned ladder, the staging of a sex crime without any evidence of sexual assault, the inconsistency of the choking wounds, the seeming lack of concern evidenced by not checking on the wife and child, the fact that the child was never awakened by any noise. But the most prominent red flag of all was the utter illogic of the supposed intruder's actions and behavior. Anyone breaking into a house to commit a crime, any crime, is going to first concern himself with the greatest threat—in this case the six-foot-two, two-hundred-pound armed man of the house—and only secondarily with the lesser threat, the unarmed woman.

An investigator always has to have his antennae up for these inconsistencies. Perhaps because we've seen so many of these cases, we're always acutely aware of going beyond what people say to try to figure out what the behavior really shows.

In some ways we're like actors preparing for a role. The actor sees the words written on the page of the script, but what he wants to act is the "subtext"—what the scene is really about.

One of the clearest examples of that is the 1989 murder of Carol Stuart and the severe wounding of her husband,

Charles, in Boston. Before it was done, the case became a cause célèbre and threatened to tear the community apart.

One night as the couple was driving home through Roxbury from a natural-childbirth class, they were apparently attacked by a large black man while their car was stopped at a light. He shot Carol, thirty, and then went after twenty-nine-year-old Charles, who sustained serious abdominal injuries requiring sixteen hours of surgery. Though doctors at Brigham and Women's Hospital worked feverishly to save Carol, she died within hours. Their baby boy, Christopher, was delivered at the same time by cesarean section but died within a few weeks. Charles was still recuperating in the hospital at the time of Carol's large and publicized funeral.

The Boston police sprang into action, rounding up every black man they could find who matched Charles's description of the attacker. Finally, he picked one out of a lineup.

But shortly thereafter, his story began to unravel. His brother Matthew doubted there had been a robbery at all when he was called upon to help Charles dispose of a bag containing the supposedly stolen items. The day after the district attorney announced he was charging Charles Stuart with the murder, Charles committed suicide by jumping off a bridge.

The black community was understandably outraged by the accusation he had made, just as they were six years later when Susan Smith falsely claimed a black man had kidnapped her two children. In the Smith case, however, the local sheriff in South Carolina went out of his way to diffuse the problem. Cooperating with the media and federal authorities (such as our own agent, Jim Wright), he got to the truth in a matter of days.

It didn't work out so efficiently in the Stuart case, though I feel it could have had police clearly analyzed what Stuart had told them and weighed it against what appeared to have happened at the scene. Not everyone will go to such lengths to stage a crime—that is, to shoot yourself that seriously.

But just as in the Wolsieffer case, if a supposed offender strikes out at the lesser threat first—in most cases the women—there has to be a reason. In any robbery situation, the robber will *always* attempt to neutralize the most formidable foe first. If the greater threat is not taken out first, there has to be another reason. With "Son of Sam" David Berkowitz, he shot the women first, and in most cases more seriously, because they were his target. The man was just in the wrong place at the wrong time.

The problem posed by staged crimes for any of us in the law enforcement field is that you can easily become emotionally involved with the victims and survivors. If someone is in obvious distress, we obviously want to believe him. If he's a halfway decent actor, if the crime appears legitimate on the surface, there's a tendency to look no further. Like doctors, we can empathize with the victims, but we're doing no one any favors if we lose our objectivity.

What kind of person could have done such a thing?

As painful as the answer to that question might sometimes be, that's what we're here to find out.

16

"God Wants You to Join Shari Faye"

Shari Faye Smith, a beautiful and vivacious high school senior, was abducted as she stopped at the mailbox in front of her family's house near Columbia, South Carolina. She was coming home from a nearby shopping center where she'd met her steady boyfriend, Richard. It was 3:38 p.m. on a warm and sunny May 31, 1985, two days before Shari was scheduled to sing the national anthem at the Lexington High School graduation.

Only minutes later, her father, Robert, found her car at the head of the long driveway to the house. The door was open, the motor was running, and Shari's purse was lying on the seat. Panic-stricken, he immediately called the Lexington County Sheriff's Department.

Things like this just didn't happen in Columbia, a proud and peaceful community that seemed to embody the very notion of "family values." How could this pretty, outgoing young blonde disappear from in front of her own home, and what kind of person could be involved in such a thing? Sheriff Jim Metts didn't know. But he did sense he had a crisis on his hands. The first thing he did was to organize what became the largest manhunt in South Carolina history. Law enforcement officers from state agencies and neighboring counties came in to help, assisted by more than a thousand civilian volunteers. The second thing Metts did was to quietly rule out as a suspect Robert Smith, who had publicly begged for the return of his daughter. In any instance of a disappearance or possible crime against such a low-risk victim, spouse, parents, and close family members always have to be considered.

The anguished Smith family waited for some word, any word, even a ransom demand. Then they got a phone call. A man with a strangely distorted voice claimed he had Shari captive.

"So you'll know this is not a hoax, Shari had on a black-and-yellow bathing suit beneath her shirt and shorts."

Shari's mother, Hilda, pleaded with him, making sure he knew Shari was diabetic and needed regular nourishment, water, and medication. The caller made no ransom demands, saying only, "You'll get a letter later today." The family and the law officers became even more alarmed.

Metts's next move reflected his background and training. Both he and Undersheriff Lewis McCarty were graduates of the FBI's National Academy and had an excellent relationship with the Bureau. Without hesitation, Metts called both Robert Ivey, SAC of the Columbia, South Carolina, Field Office, and my unit in Quantico. I was unavailable, but he got a quick and sympathetic response from Agents Jim Wright and Ron Walker. Analyzing the circumstances of the abduction, photos of the scene, and reports of the telephone call, the two agents agreed they were dealing with a sophisticated and extremely dangerous man, that Shari's life was very much in jeopardy. They were afraid the young woman could already be dead and that the subject would soon feel the compulsion to commit another such crime. They surmised that what had probably happened was that the kidnapper had seen Shari and her boyfriend, Richard, kissing at the local shopping center and had followed her home afterward. Her bad luck was to stop at the mailbox. Had she not stopped or had there been cars driving by on the street, the crime would never have happened. The sheriff's department set up recording equipment at the Smith home in hopes of further communication.

Then came a critical and extremely distressing piece of evidence. In all my years in law enforcement, with all of the horrible, almost unbelievable things I've seen, I have to say that this is about the most heart wrenching. It was a two-page, handwritten letter to the family from Shari. Written down the left side in capital letters was the phrase "GOD IS LOVE."

As excruciating as I still find reading this letter, it is such an extraordinary documentation of the character and courage of this young woman that I want to reprint it in full:

6/1/85   3:10 AM   I LOVE ya'll

Last Will & Testament

I Love you mommy, daddy, Robert, Dawn, & Richard and everyone else and all the other friends and relatives. I'll be with my father now, so please, please don't worry! Just remember my witty personality & great special times we all shared together. Please don't ever let this ruin your lives just keep living one day at a time for Jesus. Some good will come out of this. My thoughts will always be with & in *you!* (casket closed) I love you all so *damn* much. Sorry dad, I had to cuss for once! Jesus forgive me. Richard sweetie—I really did & *always* will love you & treasure our special moments. I ask one thing though. Accept Jesus as your personal savior. My family has been the greatest influence of my life. Sorry about the cruise money. Some day please go in my place.

I am sorry if I ever disappointed you in any way, I only wanted to make you proud of me because I have always been proud of my family. Mom, dad, Robert & Dawn there's so much I want to say that I should have said before now. I love you!

I know y'all love me and will miss me very much, but if y'all stick together like we always did—y'all *can* do it!

Please do not become hard or upset. Everything works out for the good for those that love the Lord.

All My Love Always—

I Love Y'all
w/All My Heart!   Sharon (Shari) Smith

P.S. Nana—I love you so much. I kind of always felt like your favorite.
You were mine!

I Love You Alot

Sheriff Metts sent the pages to the crime lab at SLED— the South Carolina Law Enforcement Division—for paper and fingerprint analysis. Reading a copy of the letter at Quantico, we were reasonably sure the kidnapping had turned into a murder. Yet the close-knit Smith family, whose religious faith was so movingly reflected in Shari's writing, clung to hope. And on the afternoon of June 3, Hilda Smith got a brief call asking if the letter had arrived.

"Do you believe me now?"

"Well, I'm not really sure I believe you because I haven't had any word from Shari and I need to know that Shari is well."

"You'll know in two or three days," the caller said ominously.

But then he called back that evening, saying that Shari was alive and implying he would release her soon. Several of the caller's statements, however, told us otherwise:

"I want to tell you one other thing. Shari is now a part of me. Physically, mentally, emotionally, spiritually. Our souls are now one."

When Mrs. Smith asked for assurance her daughter was well, he said, "Shari is protected and . . . she is a part of me now and God looks after all of us."

Ultimately, all of the calls were traced to public phones in the area, but in those days, "trap and trace" required keeping the caller on the phone for about fifteen minutes, and that was never possible. But the recording system had been set up, and copies of the tapes were rushed to us by the FBI field office. As Wright, Walker, and I listened to each recording, we were struck by Mrs. Smith's strength and control in talking with this monster. It was clear where Shari had gotten it from.

Hoping there would be more calls, Metts asked us how he should advise the family to deal with them. Jim Wright told him they should try to react very much like a police negotiator handling a hostage situation. That is, listen carefully, restate anything of possible importance the caller said to make sure they understood his message, try to get him to react and reveal more about himself and his agenda. This could have several benefits. First, it might keep the call going long enough for a successful trap and trace. And second, it might "reassure" the caller that he was getting a sympathetic hearing and encourage him into more contact.

Needless to say, this degree of controlled performance is a tall order to a horrified and grief-stricken family. But the Smiths were amazing in their ability to pull it off, getting us important information.

The kidnapper called the next night, this time speaking to Shari's twenty-one-year-old sister, Dawn. It had been four days since Shari disappeared. He gave Dawn details about the kidnapping, saying he had stopped his car when he saw her at the mailbox, appeared friendly, and took a couple of photographs of her, then forced her into his car at gunpoint. Through this and other conversations, he veered back and forth between being outwardly friendly, cruelly matter-of-fact, and vaguely regretful that the whole thing "got out of hand."

He continued his narrative: "Okay, four fifty-eight a.m.— no, I'm sorry. Hold on a minute. Three-ten a.m., Saturday, the first of June, uh, she handwrote what you received. Four fifty-eight, Saturday, the first of June, we became one soul."

"Became one soul," Dawn repeated.

"What does that mean?" Hilda asked in the background.

"No questions now," the caller stated.

But we knew what he meant, despite his assurance that "blessings are near," and that Shari would be returned the following evening. He even told Dawn to have an ambulance standing by.

"You will receive instructions where to find us."

For us in Quantico, the most significant part of the taped conversation was his comment on the time: 4:58, then going back to 3:10 a.m. This was confirmed for us by the grim call Hilda answered at noon the next day:

"Listen carefully. Take Highway 378 west to traffic circle. Take Prosperity exit, go one and a half miles, turn right at sign Moose Lodge Number 103, go one-quarter mile, turn left at white-framed building, go to backyard, six feet beyond we're waiting. God chose us." Then he hung up.

Sheriff Metts played back the recording, which led him directly to Shari Smith's body, eighteen miles away in neighboring Saluda County. She was wearing the yellow top and white shorts she'd last been seen in, but the decomposition of the body told the sheriff and medical examiner she'd been dead for several days—since 4:58 on the morning of June 1, we were pretty sure. The condition of the body, in fact, made it impossible to determine the method of killing or whether Shari had been sexually assaulted.

But Jim Wright, Ron Walker, and I were convinced her murderer had strung the family along with hopes for her return just long enough for critical forensic evidence to degrade. The sticky residue of duct tape was on Shari's face and hair, but the tape itself had been removed—further indication of planning and organization. They don't generally start out this well organized, which indicated to us an intelligent, somewhat older individual who was returning to the body dump site for some type of sexual gratification. Only when the body had decomposed to the point where a "relationship" was no longer possible would he stop going back there.

The abduction itself, in the middle of the afternoon in a rural, residential area, required a certain degree of finesse and sophistication. We pegged his age at late twenties to early thirties, and I definitely leaned toward the higher end. From the easy cruelty of the mind games he was playing with the family, we agreed among ourselves he'd probably been married early—briefly and unsuccessfully. At present, he'd either be living alone or with his parents. We expected some kind of criminal record—assaults on women, or at least obscene phone calls. If he had any murder priors, it would be children or young girls. Unlike a lot of serial killers, this guy wouldn't go after prostitutes; he'd be too intimidated by them.

The precise directions and the self-correction about time gave us other important insights. The directions had been carefully thought out and written down. He had gone back to the scene several times and had done exacting measurements. When he called the family, he had been reading from a script! He understood that he had to get his message out and get off the phone as soon as possible. Several times on the phone, he'd lost his place when interrupted and had to begin again. Whoever he was, he was rigid and orderly, meticulous and obsessively neat. He would take notes compulsively and keep lists on everything, and if he lost his place in his notes, he would lose his train of thought as well. We knew he had to have driven to and from the abduction site in front of Shari's home. I guessed from the personality that his car would be clean and well maintained, three years old or newer. All in all, a mixed presentation of someone whose outward arrogance and contempt for the whole stupid world out there conflicted continually with deep-seated insecurity and feelings of inadequacy.

In this type of case, the crime scene becomes psychologically part of the killing. The geography of the crime also suggested a local man, probably someone who had lived in the area for most or all of his life. For the things he wanted to do with Shari, then with her body, he would need time alone in a secluded area where he knew he would not be disturbed. Only a local would know where those areas would be.

The Signal Analysis Unit of the FBI Engineering Section told us the caller's voice distortion was accomplished by something they called a variable speed control device. Teletype requests for assistance on tracking down manufacturers and retail outlets went out to field offices throughout the country. We decided from this report that the UNSUB had some sort of background in electronics, and possible employment in the home construction or remodeling field.

The next day, as Bob Smith was making final arrangements with the funeral home for the burial of his younger daughter, the killer called again, this time collect, and demanded to speak to Dawn. He said he would be turning himself in the following morning, and that the photographs he had taken of Shari at the mailbox were in the mail to the Smith family. He self-pityingly asked Dawn for the family's forgiveness and prayers. He also implied that instead of turning himself in, he was considering committing suicide, lamenting again how "this thing got out of hand and all I wanted to do was make love to Dawn. I've been watching her for a couple of—"

"To who?" Dawn interrupted.

"To—I'm sorry, to Shari," he corrected himself. "And I watched her a couple of weeks, and, uh, it just got out of hand."

This was the first of several instances in which he would confuse the two sisters, not a difficult thing to do since both girls were pretty, outgoing blondes who looked strikingly alike. Dawn's picture had been in the newspaper and on television, and whatever appealed to him about Shari probably applied to Dawn as well. Listening to the recordings, it was impossible not to be sickened by this sadistic and monumentally self-indulgent performance. But I knew at that point—as cold and calculating as it may sound—that Dawn could serve as bait to catch the killer.

In a call the same day to a local television anchorman, Charlie Keyes, he reiterated his intention to turn himself in, saying he wanted the popular Keyes to serve as a "medium" and promising him an exclusive interview. Keyes listened, but wisely remained detached and promised the caller nothing.

First of all, I told Lewis McCarty on the phone, he has no intention of surrendering. He isn't going to kill himself, either. He told Dawn he was a "family friend," and he's just psychopathic enough to want the Smiths to understand and empathize with him. We did not believe he knew the family; this was just part of his fantasy of being close to and loved by Shari. He is totally narcissistic, and the longer this goes on, I counseled McCarty, the more reaction he gets from the family, the more comfortable and into the whole experience he becomes. And he will kill again, someone very much like Shari if he can find someone like that, another victim of opportunity if he can't. The underlying theme of everything he does is power, manipulation, domination, and control.

On the evening of the day of Shari's funeral, he called again and spoke to Dawn. In a particularly perverse action, he had the operator tell Dawn it was a collect call from Shari. Once again he claimed he was going to turn himself in, then went into a horribly casual and banal description of her death:

"So, from about two in the morning from the time she

actually knew until she died at four fifty-eight, we talked a lot and everything and she picked the time. She said she was ready to depart, God was ready to accept her as an angel."

He described having sex with her and said that he'd given her a choice of death—shooting, drug overdose, or suffocation. He said she'd chosen the last one and he'd suffocated her with duct tape over her nose and mouth.

"Why did you have to kill her?" Dawn tearfully demanded.

"It got out of hand. I got scared because, ah, only God knows, Dawn. I don't know why. God forgive me for this. I hope and I got to straighten it out or he'll send me to hell and I'll be there the rest of my life, but I'm not going to be in prison or the electric chair."

Both Dawn and her mother pleaded with the caller to turn himself over to God, rather than kill himself. In my unit, we were pretty damn sure he had no intention of doing either.

Two weeks to the day after Shari Smith was kidnapped, Debra May Helmick was abducted from the yard in front of her parents' trailer home in Richland County, twenty-four miles from the Smith home. Her father was inside the house at the time, just twenty feet away. A neighbor saw someone pull up in a car, get out and speak with Debra, then suddenly grab her, yank her into the car, and speed off. The neighbor and Mr. Helmick immediately took off after the car, but lost it. Like Shari, Debra was a pretty, blue-eyed blonde. Unlike Shari, she was only nine years old.

Sheriff Metts launched another intense effort to find her. Meanwhile, things were starting to get to me. When you do the kind of work my unit and I do for a living, you have to maintain some degree of distance and objectivity from the case materials and subject matter. Otherwise, you go crazy. And as difficult as that had been in the Smith case so far, this latest horrible development made that all but impossible. Little Debra Helmick was only nine—the same age as my daughter Erika, also a blue-eyed blonde. My second girl, Lauren, was just barely five. Aside from the horrible, gnawing sensation of, "This could have been my child," there is that understandable feeling of wanting to handcuff your kids to your wrist and never let them out of your sight. When you see what I've seen, not actually doing that—giving your children the space and freedom they need to live—is a constant emotional struggle.

Despite the difference in the Smith and Helmick girls' ages, the timing, circumstances, and modus operandi indicated we were likely dealing with the same offender. I know that both the sheriff's department and my unit agreed on that. So with somber acceptance of the probability that they now officially had a serial killer on their hands, Lewis McCarty flew up to Quantico and brought all of the case materials with him.

Walker and Wright reviewed all the decisions that had led to the profile and all of the advice they had given. With the added information from the new crime, they saw no reason to change their evaluation.

Despite the voice disguise, our UNSUB was almost assuredly white. These were both sexually based crimes perpetrated by an insecure and inadequate adult male. Both victims were white, and we had found it unusual to see this kind of crime cross racial lines. He would be outwardly shy and polite, have a poor self-image, and would probably be heavyset or overweight, not attractive to women. We told McCarty we would expect our man to be displaying even more compulsive behavior now. Close associates would notice some weight loss, he might be drinking heavily, not shaving regularly, and he would be eager to talk about the murder. Someone this meticulous would be following television reports avidly and collecting newspaper clippings. He would also collect pornography, with a particular emphasis on bondage and sadomasochism. He would now be thoroughly enjoying his celebrity, his sense of power over his victims and the community, his ability to manipulate the grieving Smith family. As I'd feared, when he couldn't get a victim who matched his fantasies and desires, he went for the most vulnerable victim of opportunity. Because of Shari's age, she had at least been reasonably approachable. But if he really thought about it, we didn't think our guy would feel particularly good about Debra Helmick, so we didn't expect any phone calls to her family.

McCarty went home with a twenty-two-point list of conclusions and characteristics about the subject. When he got back, he said he told Metts, "I know the man. Now all we have to find out is his name."

As gratifying as his faith in us was, things are seldom so simple. Combined state law enforcement agencies and the Columbia Field Office combed the area, looking for any trace of Debra. But there was no communication, no demands, no fresh evidence. Up in Quantico, we waited for word, trying to prepare ourselves for whatever happened. The empathy you feel for the family of a missing child is almost unbearable. At both SAC Ivey's and Sheriff Metts's request, I packed my bags and flew down to Columbia to give on-scene assistance in what promised to be a breaking case. I brought Ron Walker with me. It was the first trip we'd made together since he and Blaine McIlwain had saved my life in Seattle.

Lew McCarty met us at the airport, and we wasted no time, familiarizing ourselves with the various scenes. McCarty drove us to each of the abduction sites. It was hot and humid, even by our Virginia standards. There were no overt signs of struggle in front of either home. The Smith body dump site was just that—the murder had clearly taken place elsewhere. But seeing the locations, I was more convinced than ever that our UNSUB had to know the area intimately, and even though several of the calls to the Smiths had been long distance, he had to be a local.

There was a meeting at the sheriff's department for

the key people on the case. Sheriff Metts had a large and impressive office—about thirty feet long with twelve-foot-high ceilings, and walls completely covered with plaques and certificates and memorabilia; everything he'd ever done in his life was up on those walls, from testimonials for solving murders to appreciation from the Girl Scouts. He sat behind his massive desk with the rest of us—Ron and me, Bob Ivey, and Lew McCarty—in a semicircle around him.

"He's stopped calling the Smiths," Metts lamented.

"I'll get him to call again," I said.

I told them the profile should provide a valuable aid in the police investigation, but I thought we also needed to try to force him quickly into the open and explained some of the proactive techniques I had in mind. I asked if there was a local newspaper reporter who'd cooperate with us. It wasn't a question of censorship or giving him or her direct orders what to write, but it had to be someone sympathetic with what we were trying to accomplish who wouldn't be all hot to break our backs, as so many journalists seem to be.

Metts suggested Margaret O'Shea from the *Columbia State* newspaper. She agreed to come to the office, where Ron and I tried to educate her about the criminal personality and how we thought this individual would react.

He would be closely following the press, we told her, especially any story featuring Dawn. We knew from our research that these types often went back to the crime scenes or grave sites of their victims. I told her that with the right type of story, I thought we could entice him into the open and trap him. At the very least, we hoped we could get him to start calling again. I told her we had had close cooperation from members of the press in the Tylenol poisonings, and that had served as a model of the way we wanted things to be.

O'Shea agreed to give us the kind of coverage we wanted. McCarty then took me to meet the Smiths and explain what I wanted them to do. What I had in mind, essentially, was using Dawn to bait our trap. Robert Smith was extremely nervous about this, not wanting to place his remaining daughter in jeopardy. As concerned as I was about this ploy, I felt it represented our best shot and tried to reassure Mr. Smith that Shari's killer was a coward and would not come after Dawn amidst such intense publicity and scrutiny. And having studied the phone recordings, I was convinced Dawn was smart and courageous enough to do what I wanted her to.

Dawn took me into Shari's room, which they had left intact from the last time she was there. As you might expect, this is common among families who've lost a child suddenly and tragically. The first thing that struck me was Shari's collection of stuffed koala bears—all shapes and sizes and colors. Dawn said the collection was important to Shari, and all her friends knew that.

I spent a long time in the room, trying to get a feel for Shari as she must have been. Her killer was definitely catchable. We just had to make the right choices. After some time, I picked up a tiny koala, the kind whose arms open and close as you squeeze its shoulders. I explained to the family that in a few days—just enough time to get full newspaper coverage—we would hold a memorial service at Shari's grave at Lexington Memorial Cemetery, during which Dawn would attach the stuffed animal to a bouquet of flowers. I thought we had a good chance of drawing the killer to the service, and an even better chance of having him return to the scene after the ceremony was over to take the koala as a tangible souvenir of Shari.

Margaret O'Shea understood just the kind of press we needed and had the paper send a photographer to the service. Since there was no gravestone yet, we'd had a white wooden lectern constructed with Shari's picture laminated to the front. In turn, the family members stood at the grave and offered prayers for Shari and Debra. Then Dawn held up Shari's little koala and attached it by the arms to the stem of a rose from one of the bouquets that had been sent to the cemetery. Altogether, it was an extremely emotional and moving experience. While the Smiths spoke and a group of photographers took pictures for the local press, Metts's men quietly took down license numbers of all cars passing by. The one thing that bothered me was that the grave site was so close to the road. I thought such an unsecluded spot might intimidate the perpetrator from coming up close and also allow him to see what he wanted from the road. But we could do nothing about that.

Pictures appeared in the paper the next day. Shari's killer didn't come for the koala bear that night as we'd hoped. I think the proximity to the road did scare him. But he did call again. Shortly after midnight, Dawn answered the phone for another collect call "from Shari Faye Smith." After establishing that it was, in fact, Dawn on the line, and making sure that "you know this isn't a hoax, correct?" he made his most chilling pronouncement thus far:

"Okay, you know, God wants you to join Shari Faye. It's just a matter of time. This month, next month, this year, next year. You can't be protected all the time." Then he asked her if she had heard about Debra May Helmick.

"Uh, no."

"The ten-year-old? H-E-L-M-I-C-K?"

"Uh, Richland County?"

"Yeah."

"Uh-huh."

"Okay, listen carefully. Go One north . . . well, One west, turn left at Peach Festival Road or Bill's Grill, go three and a half miles through Gilbert, turn right, last dirt road before you come to stop sign at Two Notch Road, go through chain and No Trespassing sign, go fifty yards, and to the left, go ten yards. Debra May is waiting. God forgive us all."

He was getting bolder and cockier, no longer using the voice-altering device. Despite the overt threat against her life, Dawn did her best to hold him on the line as long as possible, brilliantly keeping her wits about her and demanding the pictures of her sister he'd promised were coming but which had never arrived.

"Apparently the FBI must have them," he said defensively, acknowledging his understanding of our role in the case.

"No, sir," Dawn shot back, "because when they have something, we get it, too, you know. Are you going to send them?"

"Oh, yes," he replied noncommittally.

"I think you're jerking me around because you said they were coming and they're not here."

We were getting closer, but the responsibility of having placed Dawn in more danger was weighing heavily on me. While Ron and I helped the local authorities, the technicians at the SLED laboratories in Columbia were subjecting their only piece of hard evidence—Shari's last will and testament—to every imaginable test. It had been written on lined paper from a legal pad, which gave one analyst an idea.

Using a device called an Esta machine, which can detect almost microscopically slight impressions made on the paper from sheets that had been higher up in the pad, he detected a partial grocery list and what seemed to be a string of numbers. Eventually, he was able to make out nine numerals of a ten-number sequence: 205-837-13_8.

The area code for Alabama is 205, and 837 is a Huntsville exchange. Working with Southern Bell's Security Division, SLED went through all ten possible phone numbers in Huntsville, then cross-checked to see if any of them related back to the Columbia–Lexington County region. One of them had received multiple calls from a residence just fifteen miles from the Smith home, several weeks before Shari was kidnapped. This was the biggest lead yet. According to municipal records, the house belonged to a middle-aged couple, Ellis and Sharon Sheppard.

Armed with this information, McCarty took several

deputies and raced to the Sheppard home. Its occupants were cordial and friendly, but other than that the fifty-odd-year-old Ellis was an electrician, nothing about him fit our profile. The Sheppards had been happily married for many years and had none of the background we had predicted in the killer. They acknowledged making the calls to Huntsville, where their son was stationed in the Army, but said they had been out of town when both horrible murders had been committed. After such a promising forensic lead, it was a disappointing outcome.

But McCarty had spent considerable time working with us and had faith that the profile was accurate. He described it to the Sheppards, then asked them if they knew anyone who might fit it.

They looked at each other in a moment of instant recognition. That would be Larry Gene Bell, they agreed.

Under McCarty's careful questioning, they proceeded to tell the undersheriff all about Bell. He was in his early thirties—divorced with a son who lived with his ex-wife, shy and heavyset, he worked for Ellis doing electrical wiring at various houses and other odd jobs. Meticulous and organized, he had house-sat for them the six weeks they'd been away, after which he'd gone back to live with his parents, with whom he'd been staying. Sharon Sheppard recalled writing their son's phone number on a writing pad for Gene, as they called him, in case anything came up with the house while Gene was there. And now that they thought about it, when he'd picked them up at the airport, all he'd wanted to talk about was the kidnapping and murder of the Smith girl. They had been surprised by his appearance when they saw him: he had lost weight, was unshaven, and seemed highly agitated.

McCarty asked Mr. Sheppard if he had a gun. He kept a loaded .38 pistol at home for protection, Ellis replied. McCarty asked to see it, and Ellis obligingly took him to where he kept the weapon. But it wasn't there. The two men looked all over the house and finally found it—under the mattress of the bed Gene had slept on. It had been fired and was currently jammed. Also under the mattress was a copy of *Hustler* magazine, showing a beautiful blonde in bondage in a crucified position. And when McCarty played a portion of one of the telephone calls to Dawn, Ellis was sure it was Larry Gene Bell's voice he was listening to: "No doubt about it."

At about two a.m., Ron Walker knocked on my door and got me out of bed. He'd just gotten a call from McCarty, who told us about Larry Gene Bell and asked us to come to the office right away. We all matched up the evidence and the profile. It was uncanny how accurately he fit. This looked like a bull's-eye. Sheriff's photos showed a car registered to Bell on the road near the grave site, but the driver had not gotten out.

Metts planned to have Bell arrested as he left for work in the morning and wanted advice from me on how to conduct the interrogation. Behind the office was a trailer the department had obtained in a drug raid that they used as an auxiliary office. At my suggestion, they quickly turned it into a "task force" headquarters for the case. They put case photographs and maps of the crime scenes on the walls and stacked the desks high with folders and case materials. I told them to man the trailer with busy-looking cops to give the impression of a tremendous amount of evidence amassed against the killer.

Getting a confession would be difficult, we warned them. South Carolina was a capital punishment state, and at the very least, the guy would expect a long prison term doing hard time as a child molester and killer—not exactly the optimum circumstances for someone who values his life and bodily integrity. The best hope, I felt, would be some face-saving scenario—either trying to put some of the blame on the victims themselves, as offensive as that would be to the interrogators, or getting him to explain himself away with an insanity defense. Accused people with no other way out often jump at this, even though, statistically, juries rarely go for it.

Sheriff's deputies arrested Larry Gene Bell early in the morning as he left his parents' home for work. Jim Metts carefully watched his face as he was brought into the "task force" trailer. "It was like a whitewash came over his face," the sheriff reported. "It put him in the proper psychological perspective." He was Mirandized and waived his rights, agreeing to talk to the investigators.

The officers went at him most of the day while Ron and I waited in Metts's office, receiving bulletins on the progress and coaching them on what to do next. Meanwhile, deputies armed with a search warrant were examining Bell's home. As we could have predicted, his shoes were lined up perfectly under his bed, his desk was meticulously arranged, even the tools in the trunk of his three-year-old, well-maintained car were arranged just so. On his desk they found directions to his parents' house written out in precisely the same manner as the directions he'd given to the Smith and Helmick body dump sites. They found more bondage and S&M pornography as we'd expected. Technicians found hairs on his bed that would match up with Shari's, and the commemorative stamp used to mail her last will and testament matched a sheet in his desk drawer. And when his photograph was subsequently shown on the TV news, the witness to Debra Helmick's abduction recognized him immediately.

His background quickly emerged. As we'd predicted, he had been involved in various sexual incidents since childhood, which had finally gotten out of hand when he was twenty-six and tried to force a nineteen-year-old married woman into his car at knifepoint. To avoid going to prison, he had agreed to psychiatric counseling, but quit after two sessions. Five months later he tried to force a college girl into his car at gunpoint. He received a five-year prison term and was paroled after twenty-one months. While on probation, he made more than eighty obscene phone calls to a ten-year-old girl. He pleaded guilty and only got more probation.

But back at the trailer, Bell wasn't talking. He denied any involvement with the crimes, admitting only that he had been interested in them. Even after they played the tapes for him, he was unresponsive. After about six hours, he said he wanted to talk to Sheriff Metts personally. Metts came in and again advised him of his rights, but he wouldn't confess to anything.

So, late in the afternoon, Ron and I are still in the sheriff's office when Metts and District Attorney Don Meyers (called the county solicitor in South Carolina) come in with Bell. He's fat and soft and reminds me of the Pillsbury Doughboy. Ron and I are both surprised, and Meyers says to Bell in his Carolina accent, "Do you know who these boys are? These boys are from the F-B-I. You know, they did a profile and it fits you right down to a tee! Now these boys want to talk to you for a little bit." They put him on this white sofa against the wall, then they both go out, leaving us alone with Bell.

I'm sitting on the edge of the coffee table directly in front of Bell. Ron is standing behind me. I'm still wearing what I'd left the motel in long before daybreak, which is a white shirt and practically matching white trousers. I call it my Harry Belafonte outfit, but in this context, in the white room with the white sofa, I look kind of clinical; almost otherworldly.

I start giving Bell some of the background on our serial-killer study and make it clear to him that from our research, I understand perfectly the motivation of the individual responsible for these homicides. I tell him he may have been denying the crimes all day because he's trying to repress thoughts he doesn't feel good about.

I say, "Going into the penitentiaries and interviewing all these subjects, one of the things we've found is that the truth almost never gets out about the background of the person. And generally when a crime like this happens, it's like a nightmare to the person who commits it. They're going through so many precipitating stressors in their life— financial problems, marital problems, or problems with a girlfriend." And as I'm saying this, he's nodding as if he's got all these problems.

Then I say, "The problem for us, Larry, is that when you go to court, your attorney probably isn't going to want you to take the stand, and you'll never have the opportunity to explain yourself. All they'll know about you is the bad side of you, nothing good about you, just that you're a cold-blooded killer. And as I say, we've found that very often when people do this kind of thing, it is like a nightmare, and when they wake up the next morning, they can't believe they've actually committed this crime."

All the time I'm talking, Bell is still nodding his head in agreement.

I don't ask him outright at that point if he did the murders, because I know if I phrase it that way, I'll get a denial. So I lean in close and say to him, "When did you first start feeling bad about the crime, Larry?"

And he says, "When I saw a photograph and read a newspaper article about the family praying in the cemetery."

Then I say, "Larry, as you're sitting here now, did you do this thing? Could you have done it?" In this type of setting, we try to stay away from accusatory or inflammatory words like *kill*, *crime*, and *murder*.

He looks up at me with tears in his eyes and says, "All I know is that the Larry Gene Bell sitting here couldn't have done this, but the bad Larry Gene Bell could have."

I knew that that was as close as we would come to a confession. But Don Meyers wanted us to try one more thing, and I agreed with him. He thought if Bell were confronted face-to-face by Shari's mother and sister, we might get an instantaneous reaction from him.

Hilda and Dawn agree to this, and I prepare them for what I want them to say and how I want them to act. So then we're in Metts's office. He's sitting behind his huge desk, Ron Walker and I are on either side of the room, forming a triangle. They bring in Bell and sit him in the middle, facing the door. Then they bring in Hilda and Dawn and tell Bell to say something. He keeps his head down, as if he can't bring himself to look at them.

But as I've instructed her, Dawn looks him straight in the eye and says, "It's you! I know it's you. I recognize your voice."

He doesn't deny it, but neither does he admit it. He starts giving them back all the stuff I'd given him to get him to talk. He says the Larry Gene Bell sitting here couldn't have done it and all the other bullshit. I'm still hoping he'll seize on the possibility of an insanity defense and spill his guts out to them.

This goes on awhile. Mrs. Smith keeps asking him questions, trying to bring him out. Inside, I'm sure everyone is sick to their stomachs having to listen to this.

Then suddenly, I have this flash. I wonder if Dawn or Hilda is armed. Were they checked out to see if they had a gun, because I don't remember anyone doing this. So the whole time now, I'm sitting on the edge of my seat, practically bouncing on the balls of my feet, ready to grab a gun and disarm either of them if one starts reaching into a purse. I know what I'd want to do in a situation like this if it were my child, and a lot of other parents feel the same way. This is the perfect opportunity to kill this guy, and no jury in the world would convict them.

Fortunately, Dawn and Hilda had not tried to smuggle in a weapon. They had more restraint and faith in the system than I might have had, but Ron checked afterward, and they hadn't been searched.

• • •

Larry Gene Bell stood trial for the murder of Shari Faye Smith late the following January. Because of the huge amount of publicity, the venue was changed to Berkeley County, near Charleston. Don Meyers asked me to testify as an expert witness about the profile and how it was developed, and about my interrogation of the defendant.

Bell didn't take the stand and never again admitted any blame. What he'd said to me in Sheriff Metts's office was the closest he ever came. He spent most of the trial taking copious, compulsive notes on the same kind of legal pad that Shari Smith's last will and testament had been written on. Yet the state's case was pretty convincing. After almost a month of testimony, the jury needed only forty-seven minutes to return the verdict of guilty of kidnapping and first-degree murder. Four days later, upon the further deliberation and recommendation of the jury, he was sentenced to death by electrocution. He was tried separately for the kidnapping and murder of Debra May Helmick. That jury didn't need much longer to come up with the same verdict and punishment.

From my perspective, the Larry Gene Bell case was an example of law enforcement at its best. There was tremendous cooperation between many county, state, and federal agencies; sensitive and energetic local leadership; two heroic families; and a perfect symbiosis between profiling and crime analysis and traditional police and forensic techniques. Working together, all of these factors stopped an increasingly dangerous serial killer early in his potential career. I'd like it to be a model for future investigations.

Dawn Smith went on to do impressive things with her life. The year after the trial, she won the title of Miss South Carolina and was a runner-up in the Miss America pageant. She married and pursued her musical ambitions and became a country and gospel singer. I see her on television from time to time.

As of this writing, Larry Gene Bell remains on death row at the South Carolina Central Correctional Facility where he keeps his cell remarkably neat and orderly. Police believe he is responsible for a number of other murders of girls and young women in both North and South Carolina. As far as I'm concerned, based on my research and experience, there is no possibility of rehabilitating this type of individual. If he is ever let out, he will kill again. And for those who argue that such a long stay on death row constitutes cruel and unusual punishment, I might agree with them up to a point. Delaying imposition of the ultimate penalty is cruel and unusual—to the Smith and Helmick families, the many who knew and loved these two girls, and all the rest of us who want to see justice done.

17

Anyone Can Be a Victim

On June 1, 1989, a fisherman in his boat spotted three "floaters" in Florida's Tampa Bay. He contacted the Coast Guard and the St. Petersburg police, who removed the badly decomposed bodies from the water. They were all female, hogtied with a combination of yellow plastic rope and regular white rope. All three were weighted down with fifty-pound cinder blocks tied around the neck. These blocks were of a two-hole variety rather than the more common three-hole type. Silver duct tape covered the mouths and, from residue, appeared to have covered the eyes when they were dropped in the water, and all three were wearing T-shirts and bathing-suit tops. The suit bottoms were missing, suggesting some sexual nature to the crime, though the state of the bodies in the water didn't allow for any forensic determination of sexual assault.

From a car found near the shore, the three bodies were identified as Joan Rogers, thirty-eight, and her two daughters, seventeen-year-old Michelle and fifteen-year-old Christie. They lived on a farm in Ohio, and this was their first real vacation. They had already been to Disney World and were now staying at the Days Inn in St. Petersburg before returning home. Mr. Rogers didn't feel he could spare the time away from the farm and hadn't accompanied his wife and daughters.

Examination of the dead women's stomach contents, correlated with interviews from restaurant workers at the Day's Inn, fixed the time of death to have been about forty-eight hours previously. The only tangible piece of forensic evidence was a scribbled note found in the car giving directions from the Days Inn to the spot where the car was found. On the other side were directions and a drawn map from Dale Mabry, a busy commercial street in St. Petersburg, to the hotel.

The case instantly became a major news event, involving the police departments of St. Petersburg and Tampa and the Hillsborough County Sheriff's Department. Fear among the public was high. If these three innocent tourists from Ohio can be killed like this, everyone reasoned, then anyone can be a victim.

Police tried to follow up on the note, matching the handwriting against that of hotel employees and people in shops and offices around the area on Dale Mabry where the directions began. But they came up with nothing. The brutal, sexual nature of the killings, however, was alarming and indicative. The Hillsborough Sheriff's Office contacted the FBI's Tampa Field Office, saying, "We may have a serial case." Still, the combined work of the three police jurisdictions and the FBI produced no significant progress.

Jana Monroe was an agent in the Tampa Field Office. Before coming to the Bureau, she'd been a police officer and then a homicide detective in California. In September 1990, after Jim Wright and I interviewed her for an opening in the unit, we requested her reassignment to Quantico. Jana had been a profile coordinator in the field office, and once she joined the unit, Rogers became one of the first cases she did for us.

Representatives of the St. Pete police flew up to Quantico and presented the case to Jana, Larry Ankrom, Steve Etter, Bill Hagmaier, and Steve Mardigian. They then developed a profile, which described a white man in his mid-thirties to mid-forties; in a blue-collar, home maintenance–type occupation; poorly educated; with a history of sexual and physical assault and precipitating stressors immediately prior to the murder. As soon as the heat was off the investigation, he would have left the area, but like John Prante in the Karla Brown case, he might later have returned.

The agents were confident of the profile, but it didn't lead to an arrest. Little progress was being made. They needed a more proactive approach, so Jana went on *Unsolved Mysteries*, one of the nationally syndicated television programs that often have good results in locating and identifying UNSUBs. Thousands of leads were generated after Jana's appearance and description of the crime, but still, none of them panned out.

If one thing doesn't work, I always tell my people, you try something else, even if it's never been tried before. And that's what Jana did. The note of scribbled directions seemed to be the one item linking the victims to the killer, but so far it hadn't been very useful. Since the case was well known in the Tampa–St. Pete community, she came up with the idea of blowing it up on billboards to see if anyone recognized the handwriting. It's accepted in law enforcement circles that most people will not recognize handwriting outside their immediate family and close friends, but Jana figured someone might well come forward, particularly if the subject had been abusive and a spouse or partner was looking for a reason to turn him in.

Several local businessmen donated billboard space, and the note was reproduced for all to see. Within a couple of days, three separate individuals who had never met each other called the police and identified the handwriting as belonging to Oba Chandler, a white male in his mid-forties. An unlicensed aluminum-siding installer, he had been sued by each of these three people when their newly installed siding had come loose after the first heavy rain. They were so sure of the ID because each had a handwritten copy of his legal response to their charges.

In addition to the age and profession, he fit the profile in other key areas. He had a previous record of property crimes, assault and battery, and sexual assault. He had moved out of the immediate area after the heat was off, though he hadn't felt a need to leave the region. The precipitating stressor was that his current wife had just delivered a baby he didn't want.

And, as often happens once you can do something to break a case open, another victim came forward after hearing the details of the murder. A woman and her girlfriend had met a man matching Chandler's description who wanted them to come out with him on his boat in Tampa Bay. The girlfriend had a bad feeling about the whole thing and had refused, so this woman went alone.

When they were out in the middle of the bay, he tried to rape her. When she tried to resist, he'd warned her, "Don't scream or I'm going to put duct tape on your mouth, tie you to a cinder block, and drown you!"

Oba Chandler was arrested, tried, and found guilty of the first-degree murder of Joan, Michelle, and Christie Rogers. He was sentenced to death.

His victims were ordinary, trusting people whose selection was almost random. Sometimes the selection is completely random, proving the frightening assertion that anyone *can* be a victim. And in situations like these, as in the Rogers case, proactive techniques become all-important.

In late 1982, people were dying suddenly and mysteriously in the Chicago area. Before long, Chicago police came up with a connection between the deaths and isolated the cause: the victims had all taken Tylenol capsules laced with cyanide. Once the capsule broke down in the stomach, death followed quickly.

Ed Hagarty, the Chicago SAC, asked me to come into the investigation. I'd never worked a product-tampering case, but as I thought about it, I figured that much of what I'd learned from the prison interviews and experience with a variety of other types of offenders should apply here, too. In FBI code, the case became known as "Tymurs."

The primary problem facing the investigators was the

random nature of the poisonings. Since the offender neither targeted a specific victim nor was present at the crime
scene, the type of analysis we normally did wouldn't reveal
anything directly.

The homicides were apparently motiveless—that is,
they weren't motivated by any of the traditional, recogniz-
able motives such as love, jealousy, greed, or revenge. The
poisoner could be targeting the manufacturer, Johnson &
Johnson, any of the stores selling the product, one or more
of the victims, or society in general.

I saw these poisonings as the same type of act as a random bombing or throwing rocks down from an overpass
onto cars below. In all of these crimes, the offender never
sees the face of his victim. I pictured this offender—much
like David Berkowitz shooting into darkened cars—as more
concerned with acting out his anger than with targeting a
particular type of victim. If this type of subject were ever
made to see the faces of his victims, he might have second
thoughts or show some remorse.

Given the ready comparison with other random, cowardly crimes, I felt I had an understanding of what the
UNSUB would be like. Even though we were dealing with
a different type of crime, in many ways the profile was a
familiar one. Our research had shown us that subjects who
kill indiscriminately without seeking publicity tend to be
motivated primarily by anger. I believed this guy would
have periods of severe depression and would be an inadequate, hopeless type who would have experienced failure
throughout his life in school, jobs, relationships.

Statistically, the subject would probably fit the assassin
mold—a white male in his late twenties to early thirties, a
nocturnal loner. He would have gone to victims' homes or
visited grave sites, possibly leaving something significant
there. I expected him to be employed in some position as
close to power and authority as he could come, such as ambulance driver, security guard, store detective, or auxiliary

policeman. And he would probably have some military experience, either Army or Marines.

I thought he'd have had psychiatric treatment in the past and have been on prescription drugs to control his problem. His car would be at least five years old, not well maintained but representing strength and power, such as the Ford model favored by police departments. Near the time of the first poisoning—around September 28 or 29—he would have experienced a precipitating stressor for which he may have blamed society in general, fueling his anger. And once the case became public, he would discuss it with whoever would listen to him in bars, drugstores, and with police. The power these crimes represented was a major boost for his ego, which indicated he might keep a diary or scrapbook of media coverage.

I told the police it was also likely he'd written to people in positions of power—the president, the director of the FBI, the governor, the mayor—to complain about perceived wrongs against him. In early letters, he would have signed his name. As time passed without what he considered an appropriate response from anyone, he grew angry over being ignored. These random killings could be his way of getting back at all those who didn't take him seriously.

Finally, I warned against reading too much into the selection of Tylenol as the means of poisoning. This was a crude, sloppy operation. Tylenol was a common drug and the capsules were easy to open. It was at least as likely that he liked the packaging as that he had any particular grudge against Johnson & Johnson.

As with serial bombers, arsonists, and other such cases, in a large city like Chicago many people would fit the general profile. Therefore, like the Rogers case, it was more important to focus on proactive techniques. The police had to keep pressure on the subject and not let him cope. One of the ways they could do this was by issuing only positive statements. At the same time, I warned them not to provoke him by calling him a madman, which, unfortunately, was already happening.

More important than that, though, would be to encourage the press to print articles humanizing the victims, since the very nature of the crime tended to dehumanize them in the UNSUB's mind. In particular, I thought he might begin to feel some guilt if forced to confront the human face of a twelve-year-old girl who had died, and we might be able to get to him through that.

As a variation on what we'd tried in Atlanta and in the Shari Smith case, I suggested holding a nighttime vigil at the grave sites of some of the victims, which I thought the UNSUB might attend. Recognizing that the subject probably didn't feel good about himself, I also advised giving heavy press to anniversaries associated with the crimes.

I thought we could encourage him to visit specific stores in the way we'd been able to "direct" bank robbers in Milwaukee and Detroit to hold up specific bank branches where we were waiting for them. For example, the police could leak information about steps being taken to protect customers at one particular store. I thought the guy might feel compelled to visit that store to see firsthand the effects of his actions. A variation on that would be to publish an article about an arrogant store manager who would publicly state how confident he was in his establishment's security and that it would be impossible for the Tylenol poisoner to tamper with any product on his shelves. Another version of this ploy would be to have police and FBI agents respond to a "hot tip" at a particular store, with attendant publicity. This would turn out to be a false alarm. But the police official would then state for the cameras that his department's intelligence capability is so efficient that the unknown subject decided against planting the poisoned Tylenol. This should provide him with an indirect challenge he might find difficult to pass up.

We could put forth a bleeding-heart psychiatrist who

would give an interview professing great support for the subject, categorizing him as a victim of society and thereby providing him with a face-saving scenario. The subject would be expected to call or drive by the doctor's office, where we'd be ready to trap and trace.

And I thought that if officials set up a volunteer civilian task force to help the police with all the phoned-in tips, the subject would likely volunteer to help man it. Had we been able to set up something like that in Atlanta, I think we would have seen Wayne Williams. Ted Bundy, in his time, had volunteered at a Seattle rape crisis center.

There is always some squeamishness on the part of law enforcement about cooperating too closely with—or using—the media. This has come up a number of times in my career. Back in the early 1980s, when the profiling program was relatively new, I was called up to headquarters to meet with the Criminal Investigation Division and Bureau legal counsel to explain some of my proactive techniques.

"John, you don't lie to the press, do you?"

I gave them a recent example of how a successful proactive approach to the media had worked. In San Diego, a young woman's body was found in the hills, strangled and raped, with a dog collar and leash around her neck. Her car was found along one of the highways. Apparently, she had run out of gas and her killer had picked her up—either as a Good Samaritan or forcibly—and had driven her up to where she was found.

I suggested to the police that they release information to the press in a particular order. First, they should describe the crime and our crime analysis. Second, they should emphasize the full thrust of FBI involvement with state and local authorities and that "if it takes us twenty years, we're going to get this guy!" And third, on a busy road like that where a young woman was broken down, someone had to have seen something. I wanted the third story to say that there had been reports of someone or something suspicious around the time of her abduction and that the police were asking the public to come forward with information.

My reasoning here was that if the killer thought someone might have seen him at some point (which they probably did), then he would think he had to neutralize that with the police, to explain and legitimize his presence on the scene. He would come forward and say something to the effect of, "I drove by and saw she was stuck. I pulled over and asked if I could help, but she said she was okay, so I drove off."

Now, police do seek help from the public all the time through the media. But too often they don't consider it a proactive technique. I wonder how many times offenders have come forward who slipped through their fingers because they didn't know what to look for. By the way, this is not to imply that genuine witnesses need have any fear of coming forward with their stories. You will not become a suspect, but you may very well help lead to the arrest of one.

In the San Diego case, the technique worked just as I had outlined it. The UNSUB injected himself into the investigation and was caught.

"Okay, Douglas, we see your point," the FBI headquarters staff responded begrudgingly. "Just keep us informed whenever you think you're going to use this approach." Anything new or innovative can be scary to a bureaucracy.

I hoped that in one way or another, the press could help bring forth the Tylenol poisoner. Bob Greene, the popular syndicated columnist of the *Chicago Tribune*, met with the police and FBI. He then wrote a moving article about twelve-year-old Mary Kellerman, the poisoner's youngest victim and the only child of a couple unable to have more children. As the story appeared, police and FBI agents were ready with surveillance on her home and the grave. I think most of the people involved thought this was bullshit, that guilt-ridden and/or happily reminiscing killers don't actually return to grave sites. But I urged them to give it a week.

I was still in Chicago when the police staked out the cemetery, and I knew I'd face their ire if they didn't come up with anything. Stakeouts are boring, uncomfortable work under the best of circumstances. They're even worse in a graveyard at night.

The first night, nothing happens. It's peaceful and quiet. But sometime during the second night, the surveillance team thinks they hear something. They approach the grave, being careful to stay out of sight. They hear the voice of a man just about the age the profile predicted.

The man is tearful, apparently on the verge of sobbing. "I'm sorry," he pleads. "I didn't mean it. It was an accident!" He begs the dead girl to forgive him.

Holy shit, they're thinking, Douglas must be right. They pounce on him.

But wait a minute! The name he uses isn't Mary.

This guy is scared out of his wits. And when the police finally get a close look, they see he's standing in front of the grave *next* to Mary's!

It turns out that buried next to Mary Kellerman is the victim of an unsolved automobile hit-and-run, and her unwitting killer has come back to confess his crime.

Four or five years later, Chicago PD used the same ploy with an unsolved murder. Spearheaded by FBI training coordinator Bob Sagowski, they began giving information to newspapers around the time of the anniversary of the murder. When police apprehended the murderer at the grave, he commented simply, "I wondered what took you so long."

We didn't catch the Tylenol poisoner this way. We didn't catch a murderer at all. A suspect was apprehended and convicted on extortion charges linked to the murders, though there wasn't sufficient evidence to try him for the murders themselves. He fit the profile, but had been out of the Chicago area when police conducted the cemetery stakeout. After his incarceration, however, no more poisonings were reported.

Of course, since there was no trial, we can't say with any legal certainty that this was our man. But it is clear that a certain percentage of the perpetrators of unsolved serial murders are actually caught, unbeknownst to the officers and detectives investigating the cases. When an active killer suddenly stops, there are three strong explanations aside from his simple decision to retire. The first is that he's committed suicide, which can be true for certain personality types. The second is that he's left the area and is actually plying his trade somewhere else. With the FBI's VICAP (Violent Criminal Apprehension Program) computer base, we're working to prevent that from happening by giving the thousands of police jurisdictions around the country the ability to share information easily with one another. The third explanation is that the killer has been picked up for some other offense—generally burglary or robbery or assault—and is serving time on the lesser charge without authorities having connected him to his most grievous offenses.

Since the Tylenol case, there have been numerous product tampering incidents, although most have been motivated by more traditional drives. In domestic cases, for example, a spouse's murder may be staged to look like product tampering. In evaluating this type of case, police should consider the number of incidents reported, whether they're localized or scattered, whether the product was consumed in close proximity to where it was apparently tampered with, and what the relationship has been between the victim and the individual reporting the crime. As in any other suspected personal-cause homicide, they should look for a history of conflict and gather all the information they can on pre- and postoffense behavior.

A crime that may appear on its surface to have had no particular intended victim may actually have had a specific target. And what seems to be a crime of general anger and frustration may actually involve a motive as traditional as wanting to get cleanly out of a marriage or a desire to collect insurance or an inheritance. After the Tylenol publicity, a wife knocked off her husband using poisoned Tylenol, figuring it would be attributed to the original killer. The staging was obvious and the details different enough so that no one was fooled. In these cases, forensic evidence also usually links the offender. For example, labs can analyze the source of cyanide or other poisons.

This same type of analysis makes it relatively easy for investigators to recognize when someone has altered a product with the intent to sue for money damages, such as placing a dead mouse in a jar of spaghetti sauce, a rat in a soda can, or a needle in a bag of snack food. Companies often want to settle quickly to avoid bad publicity and stay out of court. But forensic science has now evolved to the point where if the company strongly suspects product tampering, refuses to settle, and brings the case to the FBI, the odds are high that the tamperer will be found out and charged. In the same way, a good investigator will recognize acts of staged heroism—orchestrated scenarios created by an individual to get recognition from his or her peers or the public.

The Tylenol case, for all its horror, was something of an anomaly. It didn't seem to be primarily an extortion. For an extortionist to succeed, he must first establish that he has the capability to make good on his threat. Extortionists who threaten product tampering, therefore, will typically alter one bottle or package of the product, mark it in some way, and deliver a warning in a phone call or a note. The Tylenol poisoner, on the other hand, didn't begin with threats. He jumped right into killing.

By extortionist standards, he wasn't sophisticated. Based on the crude nature of the tampering (after these murders, Johnson & Johnson spent a fortune developing effective tamper-resistant packaging), I knew this guy wasn't highly organized. But of those who do make threats, some of the same guidelines can be used as would apply to a political-threat analysis to determine whether the threatener is actually dangerous and capable of carrying out his announced intention.

The same is true of bombers. If a bomb threat is made, it is always taken seriously. But quickly, so that society doesn't grind to a halt, authorities must determine whether the threat is real. Bombers and extortionists typically use the word *we* in their communications to imply a large group watching from the shadows. The fact is, though, most of these people are suspicious loners who don't trust others.

Bombers tend to fall into one of three categories. There are power-motivated bombers attracted to the destruction. There are mission-oriented bombers attracted to the thrill of designing, making, and placing the devices. And there are technician types who get gratification from the brilliance and cleverness of their actual design and construction. As far as motives, they range from extortion to labor disputes, revenge, even suicide.

Our research into bombers shows a repeating general profile. They're usually white males, the age being determined by the victim or target. They're of at least average intelligence, often quite above, though underachievers. They're neat, orderly, and meticulous, careful planners, nonconfrontational, nonathletic, cowardly, inadequate personalities. The profile comes from assessing the target or victim and the type of device (is it more explosive or incendiary, for instance), much as we profile a serial killer from a crime scene. We would consider the risk factors associated with both the victim and the offender, whether the victim was random or intended, how accessible he or she was, what time of day the attack occurred, the method of conveyance (such as through the mail), as well as any unique qualities or idiosyncrasies in the components or workmanship of the bomb.

Early in my profiling career I developed the first profile on the now-famous Unabomber (from the FBI code name Unabom), who got his nickname by targeting universities and professors.

We learn most about bombers from their communications. By the time Unabomber decided to communicate at length with the public through his letters to newspapers and multithousand-word manifesto, he had left a trail of three deaths and twenty-three injuries in a seventeen-year career. Among other feats, he managed temporarily to slow down the entire commercial airline industry through his promise of a bomb coming out of Los Angeles International Airport.

Like most bombers, he referred to a group (the "FC" or "Freedom Club") as responsible for his terrorism. Still, there is little doubt he is the type of loner I described.

The profile has been widely published by now and I've seen no reason to alter my judgment. Unfortunately, despite Dr. Brussel's groundbreaking work on the Metesky "Mad Bomber" case, when Unabomber first struck, law enforcement wasn't as sct up to use our type of analysis as they are now. Most of these guys are catchable early in their careers. The first and second crimes are the most significant in terms of behavior, location, and target, before they start perfecting what they do and moving around the country. As the years go on, they also expand their ideologies beyond the simple and elemental grudges against society that get them going in the first place. I think that had we been where we are now with profiling in 1979, Unabomber might have been caught years earlier.

Much of the time, bomb threats are a means of extortion, directed against an individual or a specific group. In the mid-1970s, a bomb threat was phoned in to the president of a bank in Texas.

In a long, complicated script, the caller says that a few days before when Southwest Bell sent technicians to the bank, it was actually his people. They planted a bomb that he can set off with a microwave switch, but he won't do it if the president complies with his demands.

Now comes the most chilling part. He says he has the president's wife, Louise. She drives a Cadillac, goes here in the morning, then here, et cetera, et cetera. Panicked, the president has his secretary call his home on another line because he knows his wife should be there. But no one answers. Now he's become a believer.

Then the caller makes his money demand: used bills—tens through hundreds. Don't contact the police, we can easily recognize their unmarked cars. Tell your secretary you'll be leaving the bank for about forty-five minutes. Don't contact anyone. Just before you leave, flash the lights in your office on and off three times. My group will be watching for this signal. Leave the money in your car, parked by the side of the road at a specific heavily trafficked area, leave the motor running and the parking lights on.

Now, in this particular case, there was no bomb and no abduction, merely a clever con man targeting the most likely victim. Everything about this scenario has a purpose. His timing was based on when the phone company had actually been working in the bank, so that he could cast them as his bomb planters. Everyone knows the phone company does technical work that no one understands or pays much attention to, so it's quite believable that they could have been impostors.

Knowing the bank president would call home for his wife, the extortionist had called her that morning, claiming to be from Southwest Bell, saying they had received a number of complaints about obscene phone calls in her neighborhood and they were trying to track the caller—so between noon and twelve forty-five today, don't pick up the phone if it rings; we'll be running a trap and trace.

The instruction about leaving the money in the car with the lights on and the motor running is perhaps the most ingenious part of the plan. The president thinks the lights are part of the signal, but in fact, they're part of the caller's escape system. Despite the warning not to contact the police, the extortionist knows the victim will probably involve them anyway, and the most dangerous phase for the offender is always the money exchange, when he presumes the police will be watching. Under this scenario, if the offender is unfortunate enough to be nabbed by the police in the car, he can say he was walking down this busy street, saw a car with lights on and the motor running, and decided to be a Good Samaritan and turn them off. If the police grab him at that point, they've got nothing. Even if they grab him with the money, since he's already established a legitimate reason to be in the car, he can say he found the bag sitting there on the seat and was going to turn it in'to the police.

For the extortionist, this is a percentage game. He's got his script written out and all he has to do is fill in the details. If today's targeted victim doesn't go for it, he'll try it on another the next day. Eventually, one of them is going to bite, and he'll end up with a nice piece of change for his efforts without actually having to kidnap or bomb anyone. In these cases, the script is generally a good piece of evidence since the offender will keep it, knowing it will be useful for future jobs. Because the one thing he knows is that with a few simple advance arrangements, anyone can be his victim.

Once authorities were finally onto his tricks, he was apprehended, tried, and convicted. He turned out to be a former disc jockey who had decided to put his gift of gab to more short-term advantage.

What's the difference between this type of individual and one who actually does kidnap? They're both in it for profit, so neither one wants to expose himself to the victim any more than necessary because killing is not part of the aim. The big difference is that the true kidnapper will generally need someone to help carry out his scheme, and while the simple extortionist is basically a clever con man, the kidnapper is a sociopath. Killing the victim is not his intention, but he is clearly willing to do so to fulfill his goals.

Steve Mardigian participated in the case of an Exxon Corporation vice president who was abducted in front of his home in New Jersey and held for ransom. In the struggle, he was shot in the arm by accident. The kidnappers—a former company security guard and his wife—went ahead with the abduction and held the wounded man (who had a heart condition) in a box, where he died. The reason for the box—or its equivalent—is so that the abductors can have as little contact with the victim as possible and not have to personalize him. In this case, the kidnappers professed regret at the outcome and a sense of desperation that led them to the crime in the first place. But they did it, and they carried it out step-by-step without hesitation. They were willing to have someone else die for their selfish purposes, and that is one of the definitions of sociopathic behavior.

As terrifying as it is, unlike certain other serious crimes, kidnapping is such a difficult act to get away with that an investigator really has to evaluate it carefully and with a skeptical eye, looking closely at victimology and preoffense behavior. And, while acknowledging that anyone can be a victim, the investigator has to be able to answer the question: why this particular victim?

A couple of years ago, I got an urgent call one night at home. A detective in Oregon proceeded to tell me the story of a young woman who went to school in his district. She was being stalked, but neither she nor anyone else could discover the identity of the stalker. She would see the stalker in the woods, but by the time her father or boyfriend went out to look, he was gone. He would call the house, but never when anyone else was home. The girl was turning into a basket case. After several unnerving weeks of this, she was at a restaurant with her boyfriend. She left the table to go to the ladies' room. While leaving the rest room, she was grabbed and quickly dragged out to the parking lot, where her assailant savagely stuck a gun barrel into her vagina, threatened to kill her if she went to the police, then let her go. She was emotionally traumatized and couldn't provide a good description.

Now, apparently, she'd been abducted as she left the library one night. Her car was found in the parking lot. There had been no communication and things were beginning to look pretty grim.

I asked the detective to tell me about the victim. She was a beautiful girl who'd always done well in school. But last year she'd had a baby and had had some problems with her family, particularly her father, about support. Her grades had been going to hell lately, especially after the stalking began.

I said not to say anything to the father just yet in case I was wrong and the young woman ended up dead, but this sounded to me like a hoax. Who would stalk her? She had a steady boyfriend and no recent breakups. Generally, when a noncelebrity is stalked, it is by someone who knows that person in one way or another. Stalkers aren't that good or careful at what they do. If she saw the stalker, her father and boyfriend should not have missed him each time. No one else ever got the phone calls. And when police put a trap and trace on the line, the calls suddenly stopped. It also happened that the kidnapping took place right before final exams—not at all a coincidental finding.

The proactive strategy, I suggested, would be to have the father be interviewed by the media, emphasize the positiveness of their relationship, say how much he loves her and wants her back, appealing to the kidnapper to let her go. If I was right, she should turn up a day or two later, banged up and dirty with a story about how she was abducted, abused, and thrown out of a car on the side of a road.

This is what happened. She was pretty banged up and filthy with a story of abduction. I said that the interrogation—in this case in the form of a debriefing—should focus on what we really believed had happened. It should not be accusatory, but acknowledge that she was having a lot of trouble with her parents; going through a lot of stress, trauma, and pain; was panicked by exams; and needed a face-saving way out. She should be told that she didn't need punishment, what she needed was counseling and understanding, and that she would get it. Once that was made clear, she confessed to the hoax.

This is one of those cases you sweat, though. If you're wrong, the consequences are horrible, because when stalking is for real, it can be a terrifying and, too often, deadly crime.

Most often, whether we're talking about the stalking of a celebrity or an ordinary person, the stalking begins with love or admiration. John Hinckley "loved" Jodie Foster and wanted her to return his love. However, she was a beautiful movie star going to Yale and he was an inadequate nobody. He believed he had to do something to equalize the situation and impress her. And what could be more "impressive" than the historic act of assassinating the president of the United States? In his more lucid moments, he must have realized that his dream of the two of them living happily ever after together wasn't going to come about. But through his act, he did achieve one of his goals. He became famous, and in a perverse way, he would be forever connected to Foster in the public mind.

As with most of these cases, there was an immediate stressor with Hinckley. Around the time he shot President Reagan his father had given him an ultimatum about getting a job and supporting himself on his own.

Secret Service agent Ken Baker conducted a prison interview with Mark David Chapman, the assassin of John Lennon. Chapman felt a strong connection to the former Beatle and, on a superficial level, tried to emulate him. He collected all of Lennon's songs and even went through a string of Asian girlfriends, to imitate Lennon's marriage to Yoko Ono. But as happens with many of these types, eventually he reached a point where his inadequacy was overwhelming. He could no longer deal with the disparity between himself and his hero and so had to kill him. Chillingly, one of the things that moved Hinckley to commit his crime and become famous (*notorious* is actually a much better word) was the example of Chapman.

I interviewed Arthur Bremer, who stalked and then attempted to assassinate Alabama governor George Wallace in Maryland while he was running for president, leaving Wallace paralyzed and in chronic pain for life. Bremer didn't hate Wallace. Prior to the shooting, he'd stalked President Nixon for several weeks but couldn't get close enough to him. He just got desperate to do something to show the world his worth, and Wallace was approachable, essentially another victim in the wrong place at the wrong time.

The cases of stalking that have turned to assassination are alarming in their number. In the case of political figures, there is the construct of a "cause" for the killing, although this is virtually always a cover for a deeply inadequate nobody who wants to be a somebody. In the case of movie stars and celebrities like John Lennon, even that excuse is meaningless. Among the most tragic of the cases is the murder of twenty-one-year-old Rebecca Schaeffer in front of her Los Angeles apartment in 1989. The beautiful and talented young actress, who had become widely known as Pam Dawber's younger sister on the television series *My Sister Sam*, was shot once, as she answered the front door, by Robert John Bardo, an unemployed nineteen-year-old from Tucson whose most recent job had been as janitor in a Jack in the Box. Like Chapman, Bardo had begun as an adoring fan. His adoration had grown into obsession, and if he couldn't then have a "normal" relationship with her, he would have to "possess" her in another way.

As we all know by now, stalking targets are not limited to the famous. There are, of course, frequent cases of people being stalked by former spouses or lovers. The deadly stage is reached when the stalker finally thinks, "If I can't have her (or him), no one else can either." But Jim Wright, our unit's most experienced specialist on stalking and among the leading experts on the subject in law enforcement, points out that anyone who deals with the public, particularly women, may be vulnerable to stalkers. In other words, the object of a stalker's desire need not be on television or the movie screen. She might be a waitress at the restaurant down the block or a teller at the local bank. Or she could even work in the same store or business.

That was what happened to Kris Welles, a young woman who worked for Conlans Furniture Company in Missoula, Montana. Kris was efficient and well respected and worked her way up in the company first to sales manager and then, in 1985, to overall manager.

At the same time Kris worked in the office, a man named Wayne Nance worked in the warehouse. He tended to keep to himself, but he seemed to like Kris, and she was always cordial and friendly to him. Still, Wayne's personality blew hot and cold, and the temper she perceived just beneath the surface scared her. No one had any complaints with Wayne's work habits, though. Day in and day out, he consistently worked the hardest of anyone in the warehouse.

What neither Kris nor her husband, Doug, a local gun dealer, knew was that Wayne Nance was obsessed with her. He watched her all the time and kept a cardboard box filled with souvenirs of her—snapshots, notes she had written at the office, anything that belonged to her.

The other thing neither the Welleses nor the Missoula police knew was that Wayne Nance was a killer. In 1974, he had sexually molested and stabbed a five-year-old girl. It was later discovered he had also bound, gagged, and shot several adult women, including the mother of his best friend. Alarmingly, all of this had taken place in counties neighboring where he now lived. Yet even in sparsely populated Montana, one police jurisdiction had no idea of the criminal activity recorded in another jurisdiction.

Kris Welles didn't know any of this until the night Nance broke into her and Doug's home outside of town. They had a female golden retriever, but the dog put up no resistance to him. Armed with a handgun, he shot Doug, tied him up in the basement, then forced Kris upstairs into the bedroom where he tied her to the bed so he could rape her. She obviously knew him well and he made no attempt to hide his identity.

Meanwhile, in the basement, Doug had managed to wriggle free from his bonds. Weak and on the verge of unconsciousness from pain and loss of blood, he staggered over to a table where a rifle loader from his store was set up. He managed to feed one round into the rifle, then mustering all his remaining strength, he pulled himself slowly and agonizingly up the basement stairs. As quietly as he could, he made his way up the stairs to the second floor, and in the hallway, his eyes blurring, he took aim for his one shot at Nance.

He had to get him before Nance saw him and went for his own gun. Nance was unhurt and had more shots available. Doug would be no match for him.

He squeezed the trigger. He hit Nance, knocking him backward. But then Nance got up again and started coming for him. The shot hadn't been deadly enough. Nance kept coming for him toward the staircase. There was nowhere to go and Doug couldn't leave Kris alone there, so he did the only thing he could. He charged forward at Nance, using his empty rifle as a club. He kept hammering at the powerful Nance until Kris could get herself free and help him.

To this day, the Welles case remains one of the few on record in which intended victims of a serial killer were actually able to fight back and kill their attacker in self-defense. Their story is a miraculous one, and we have had them out several times to speak to classes at Quantico. This unassuming couple have been able to give us rare insight from the perspective of victims who became heroes. Having been to hell and back that night, they are amazingly warm, sensitive, and "together" people.

At the end of one of their presentations at Quantico, a

police officer in the class asked them, "If Wayne Nance had lived and there was no death penalty—that is, if he were still sharing the earth with you—would you both be as mentally sound as you are now?"

They turned and looked at each other and then silently agreed on their response. "Almost definitely not," said Doug Welles.

18

Battle of the Shrinks

What kind of person could have done such a thing?

During our serial-killer study, Bob Ressler and I were in Joliet, Illinois, where we'd just interviewed Richard Speck. I was back in my hotel room that evening and was watching CBS news when I saw Dan Rather interviewing another killer, named Thomas Vanda, who also happened to be incarcerated at Joliet Penitentiary. Vanda was in for killing a woman through multiple stab wounds. He'd been in and out of mental institutions for much of his life, and every time he'd been "cured" and let out, he would commit another crime. Before the murder for which he was now doing time, he'd killed once before.

I called Ressler and said we had to talk to him while we were here. From the televised interview, I could tell he was the perfect inadequate type. He could as easily have been an arsonist as a killer. Or, if he had the tools and skills, he could have been a bomber.

We went back to the prison the next day and Vanda agreed to see us. He was curious as to what we were doing there, and he didn't get many visitors. Before the interview, we went over his file.

Vanda was white, about five foot nine, and in his mid-twenties. He had a soft, inappropriate affect and smiled a lot. Even while smiling, he still had "the look"—eyes darting back and forth all the time, nervous twitches, hand-rubbing. You wouldn't comfortably turn your back on this guy. The first thing he wanted to know was how I thought he looked on TV. When I told him he looked good, he laughed and loosened up. Among the things he told us was that he had joined a Bible study group in prison and thought it had helped him a lot. It may very well have. But I've seen a lot of inmates nearing parole-board appearances join religious groups to show they're on the right path to be released.

You could argue about whether this guy belonged in a maximum security prison or a secure mental hospital, but after the interview, I went to see the staff psychiatrist who treated him. I asked him how Vanda was doing.

The psychiatrist, who was around fifty, gave me a positive response, saying Vanda was "responding very nicely to medication and therapy." The psychiatrist mentioned the Bible study group as one example and said Vanda could be ready for parole if this progress continued.

I asked him if he knew the specifics of what Vanda had done. "No, I don't want to know," he replied. "I don't have the time, with all the inmates I have to deal with here." And, he added, he didn't want to unfairly influence his relationship with the patient.

"Well, Doctor, let me tell you what Thomas Vanda did," I insist. Before he can protest, I went on to relate how this asocial, loner-type personality joins a church group, and how, after a meeting when everyone else is gone, he propositions the young woman who hosted the meeting. She turns him down and Vanda doesn't take the rejection real well. Guys like that generally don't. He knocks her down, goes to her kitchen, comes back with a knife, and stabs her numerous times. Then, as she's on the floor dying, he inserts his penis into an open wound in her abdomen and ejaculates.

I've got to say, I find this amazing. She's like a rag doll at this point. Her body is warm, she's bleeding, he's got to be getting blood on himself. He can't even depersonalize her. And yet he's able to get an erection and get it off. So you'll understand why I insist this is a crime of anger, not sex. What's going through his mind is not sex—it's anger and rage.

This, by the way, is why it doesn't do any good to castrate repeat rapists—as satisfying and fulfilling as the idea may be to some of us. The problem is, it doesn't stop them, either physically or emotionally. Rape is definitely a crime of anger. If you cut someone's balls off, you're going to have one angry man.

I finished my story about Vanda. "You're disgusting, Douglas!" the psychiatrist declared. "Get out of my office!"

"I'm disgusting?" I countered. "You're gonna be in a position to make a recommendation that Thomas Vanda is responding to therapy and could be freed, and you don't know who in the hell you're talking to when you're dealing with these inmates. How are you supposed to understand them if you haven't taken the time to look at the crime-scene photos or reports, to go over the autopsy protocols? Have you looked at the way the crime was committed? Do you know if it was planned? Do you understand the behavior leading up to it? Do you know how he left the crime scene? Do you know if he tried to get away with it? Did he try to establish an alibi? *How in the hell do you know if he's dangerous or not?*"

He didn't have an answer and I don't think I made a convert that day, but this is something I feel strongly about. It's the basis of what we do in my unit. The dilemma, as I've stated many times before, is that much of psychiatric therapy is based on self-reporting. A patient coming to a therapist under normal circumstances has a vested interest in revealing his true thoughts and feelings. A convict desirous of early release, on the other hand, has a vested interest in telling the therapist what he wants to hear. And to the extent that the therapist takes that report at face value without correlating it with other information about the subject, that can be a real failing of the system. Ed Kemper and Monte Rissell, to name but two, were in therapy while they were committing their crimes, and both managed to remain undetected. In fact, both showed "progress" to their therapists.

The problem as I see it is that you get young psychiatrists and psychologists and social workers who are idealistic, having been taught at their universities that they really can make a difference. Then they come up against these guys in prison, and they want to feel that they've changed them. Often, they don't understand that in trying to assess these convicts, they're actually assessing individuals who themselves are expert in assessing people! In a short time, the convict will know if the doctor has done his or her homework, and if not, he'll be able to downplay the crime and its impact on victims. Few criminals will willingly give out the nitty-gritty details to someone who doesn't already have them. That's why complete preparation was so critical in our prison interviews.

As with Thomas Vanda's doctor, people in the helping professions often don't want to be prejudiced by knowing the gory details of what the criminal did. But as I always tell my classes, if you want to understand Picasso, you have to study his art. If you want to understand the criminal personality, you have to study his crime.

The difference is, the mental-health professionals start with the personality and infer behavior from that perspective. My people and I start with the behavior and infer the personality from *that* perspective.

There are, of course, varying perspectives on the issue of criminal responsibility. Dr. Stanton Samenow is a psychologist who collaborated with the late psychiatrist Dr. Samuel Yochelson on a pioneering study at St. Elizabeth's Hospital in Washington, D.C., about criminal behavior. After years of firsthand research that gradually stripped away most of his preconceived notions, Samenow concluded in his penetrating and insightful book, *Inside the Criminal Mind*, that "criminals think differently from responsible people." Criminal behavior, Samenow believes, is not so much a question of mental illness as character defect.

Dr. Park Dietz, who works with us frequently, has stated,

"None of the serial killers that I've had the occasion to study or examine has been legally insane, but none has been normal, either. They've all been people who've got mental disorders. But despite their mental disorders, which have to do with their sexual interests and their character, they've been people who knew what they were doing, knew what they were doing was wrong, but chose to do it anyway."

It's important to keep in mind here that insanity is a legal concept, not a medical or psychiatric term. It doesn't mean someone is or is not "sick." It has to do with whether that person is or is not responsible for his or her actions.

Now, if you believe that someone like Thomas Vanda is insane, fine. I think a case can be made for that. But once we've carefully examined the data, I think we have to face that whatever the Thomas Vandas of the world have, it may not be curable. If we accepted that, they wouldn't be let out so fast to keep doing what they do over and over again. Remember, this murder wasn't his first.

There has been a lot of talk lately about the concept of criminal insanity, and this talk isn't new. It goes back at least hundreds of years in Anglo-American jurisprudence, to William Lambard's *Eirenarcha*, or "Of the Office of the Justices of Peace" of the 1500s.

The first organized statement of insanity as a defense against criminal charges is the M'Naghten Rule of 1843, named after Daniel M'Naghten (sometimes spelled Mc-Naughten or McNaghten), who tried to kill British prime minister Sir Robert Peel and did manage to shoot Peel's private secretary. Peel, by the way, was responsible for organizing London's police force. To this day, London cops are still referred to as bobbies in his honor.

After M'Naghten was acquitted, public outrage was so great that the lord chief justice was called before the House of Lords to explain the logic. The basic elements state that a defendant is not guilty if his mental condition deprived him of the ability to know the wrongfulness of his actions or understand their nature and quality; in other words, did he know the difference between right and wrong?

The insanity doctrine evolved over the years into what was often referred to as the "irresistible impulse test," which stated that a defendant was not guilty if, because of mental illness, he was unable to control his actions or conform his conduct to the law.

It received a major overhaul in 1954 with Judge David Bazelon's Court of Appeals ruling in *Durham* v. *United States*, which held that a defendant is not criminally responsible if his crime was the "product of mental disease or defect," and if he would not have committed the crime but for that disease or defect.

Durham, which gave such broad latitude and wasn't primarily concerned with appreciating the difference between right and wrong, wasn't terribly popular with law enforcement personnel and many judges and prosecutors. In 1972, in another Court of Appeals case, *United States* v. *Brawner*, it was abandoned in favor of the American Law Institute (or ALI) Model Penal Code Test, which hearkened back to M'Naghten and irresistible impulse in saying that the mental defect had to make the defendant lack substantial capacity to appreciate the wrongfulness of his conduct or conform his conduct to the requirement of the law. In one form or another, the ALI Test has enjoyed increasing popularity among courts as time goes on.

But along with this discussion, which often degrades into a speculation on how many angels can dance on the head of a pin, I think we have to deal with a more basic concept. And that is *dangerousness*.

One of the classic confrontations in the ongoing battle of the shrinks was the serial-murder trial of Arthur J. Shawcross in Rochester, New York, in 1990. Shawcross had been accused of the murders of a string of local prostitutes and street people whose bodies had turned up in the wooded areas in and around the Genesee River gorge. The murders had gone on for nearly a year. The later bodies had also been mutilated after death.

After doing a detailed—and, as it turned out, highly accurate—profile, Gregg McCrary studied the UNSUB's developing behavior. When police discovered a body that had been mutilated, Gregg realized that the killer was going back to the dump sites to spend time with his prey. He then urged police to comb the woods to locate the body of one of the still-missing women. If they could do that, then secretly stake out the site, Gregg was sure they would eventually find the killer there.

As it happened, after several days of aerial surveillance, New York State Police did find a body in Salmon Creek along State Route 31. At the same time, Inspector John McCaffrey noticed a man in a car parked on a low bridge spanning the water. State and city police were called in to follow him. The man they picked up was Arthur Shawcross.

Under interrogation from a team led by Dennis Blythe of the State Police and Leonard Boriello of the Rochester Police Department, Shawcross confessed to several of the crimes. The key issue at his intensely covered ten-count murder trial was whether or not he was insane at the time of the killings.

The defense brought in Dr. Dorothy Lewis, a well-known psychiatrist at Bellevue Hospital in New York, who had done important work on the effects of violence on children. Lewis had become convinced that most, if not all, violent criminal behavior resulted from a combination of childhood abuse or trauma and some kind of physical or organic condition, such as epilepsy, an injury, or some kind of lesion, cyst, or tumor. There is, of course, the case of Charles Whitman, the twenty-five-year-old engineering student who climbed to the top of the clock tower at the University of Texas at Austin in 1966 and opened fire on passersby below. Before police could surround the tower and kill him ninety minutes later, sixteen men and women lay dead and another thirty wounded. Prior to the incident, Whitman had complained of periodic murderous rages. When doctors performed an autopsy, they found a tumor in the temporal lobe of his brain.

Did the tumor cause Whitman's deadly behavior? We have no way of knowing. But Lewis wanted to show the jury that as a result of a small benign temporal-lobe cyst that showed up on Shawcross's MRI, a form of epilepsy she characterized as "partial complex-seizure state," post–traumatic stress from Vietnam, and what he claimed was severe childhood physical and sexual abuse at the hands of his mother, Arthur Shawcross was not responsible for his episodes of extreme violence. In fact, she testified, he was in some kind of fugue state when he killed each woman; his memory of each episode would have been impaired or nonexistent.

One of the problems with this line of reasoning is that weeks and months after the murders, Shawcross was able to relate the details to Boriello and Blythe in minute detail. In some cases, he actually brought them to body dump sites the police had been unable to find. He was probably able to do this because he had fantasized about each one so many times that they were fresh in his mind.

He took steps to destroy some of the evidence so the police wouldn't find him. After his arrest, he also wrote a rather analytic letter to his girlfriend (he had a wife, too), saying that he hoped for the insanity defense because doing time in a mental hospital would be a lot easier than doing time in prison.

On that score, Shawcross clearly knew whereof he spoke. His troubles with the law began in 1969 when he was convicted of burglary and arson in Watertown, north of Syracuse. Less than a year later, he was arrested again and admitted strangling a young boy and girl. The girl had also been sexually molested. For those two crimes, Shawcross was sentenced to twenty-five years in prison. He was paroled after fifteen. That, if you recall from a previous chapter, was why age was the one aspect of the profile that Gregg McCrary had called wrong. Shawcross's fifteen years in stir had merely been a holding pattern.

Now let's take this step-by-step. First of all, if you ask me or just about any of the many thousands of cops, prosecutors, and federal agents I've worked with over the course of my career, you'll get a resounding consensus that twenty-five years for ending the lives of two children is pretty obscene in and of itself. But second, to let this guy out early, it seems to me you have to presume one of two opposite premises.

Premise number one: despite this guy's bad background, despite his dysfunctional family, the alleged abuse, the lack of good education, his violent past, and everything else, prison life was such a wonderful, spiritually uplifting, eye-opening, and rehabilitative experience that Shawcross saw the light, realized the error of his ways, and because of all the good influence in prison resolved to turn over a new leaf and be an upright, law-abiding citizen from that moment hence.

Okay, if you don't accept that one, how about premise number two: prison life was so completely horrible, so unpleasant and traumatic every day, so thoroughly punishing in every way, that despite his bad background and continuing desire to rape and kill children, he never wanted to be back in prison and resolved to do anything he could to avoid going back.

I agree, that one's just as unlikely. But if you don't accept either of these two premises, how in the hell do you let someone like that out without considering the strong possibility that he's going to kill again?

Quite clearly, some types of killers are much more likely to repeat their crimes than others. But for the violent, sexually based serial killers, I find myself agreeing with Dr. Park Dietz that "it's hard to imagine any circumstance under which they should be released to the public again." Ed Kemper, who's a lot brighter and has a lot more in the way of personal insight than most of the other killers I've talked to, acknowledges candidly that he shouldn't be let out.

There are just too many horror stories out there. Richard Marquette, whom I interviewed and who had a string of disorderly conduct, attempted rape, and assault and battery charges against him in Oregon by his early twenties, progressed to rape, murder, and mutilation after an unsuccessful sexual experience with a woman he'd picked up in a Portland bar. He fled the area, was placed on the FBI's Most Wanted list, and was arrested in California. He was convicted of first-degree murder and sentenced to life in prison. Paroled after twelve years, he killed and dissected two more women before being captured again. What in God's name led a parole board to think this guy was no longer dangerous?

I can't speak for the FBI, the Justice Department, or anyone else. But I can say that for myself, I would much rather have on my conscience keeping a killer in jail who might or might not kill again if sprung, than the death of an innocent man, woman, or child as a result of the release of that killer.

It's an American attribute to think that things are always getting better, that they can always be improved upon, that we can accomplish anything we set out to do. But the more I see, the more pessimistic I become about the concept of rehabilitation for certain types of offenders. What they went through as children is often horrible. That doesn't necessarily mean the damage can be undone at a later date. And contrary to what judges, defense attorneys, and mental health professionals might want to believe, good behavior in prison isn't necessarily predictive of acceptable behavior in the outside world.

In virtually every respect, Shawcross had been a model prisoner. He was quiet, kept to himself, did what he was told, and didn't bother anyone. But what my colleagues and I have found and have tried desperately to get across to others in the business of correction and forensic psychology is that *dangerousness is situational*. If you can keep someone in a well-ordered environment where he doesn't have choices to make, he may be fine. But put him back in the environment in which he did badly before, his behavior can quickly change.

Take the case of Jack Henry Abbott, the convicted murderer who wrote *In the Belly of the Beast*, a moving and penetrating memoir of life in prison. Realizing his exceptional talent as a writer and believing that anyone so sensitive and insightful must be rehabilitated, such literary lights as Norman Mailer campaigned to have Abbott paroled. He became the toast of New York. But within a few months of his release, he got into an argument with a waiter in Greenwich Village and killed him.

As Al Brantley, a former Behavioral Science instructor who is now a member of the Investigative Support Unit, put it in one of his National Academy lectures, "The best predictor of future behavior, or future violent acting out, is a past history of violence."

No one would accuse Arthur Shawcross of being anywhere near as bright or talented as Jack Henry Abbott. But he was also able to convince a parole board he could be released. After his parole, Shawcross first settled in Binghamton, where an angry community mounted a campaign against him and he left after two months. He was relocated to the larger and more anonymous metropolitan area of Rochester, where he took a job as a salad preparer with a food-distribution company. A year after his arrival, he began killing again—a different targeted victim this time, yet no less vulnerable.

During her examinations of Shawcross, Dorothy Lewis put him under hypnosis several times and "regressed" him to earlier phases of his life where he acted out such episodes of abuse as his mother's insertion of a broom handle far up his rectum. During these recorded sessions, he is seen to take on other personalities, including that of his mother, in a scene eerily reminiscent of *Psycho*. (Shawcross's mother, however, denied ever abusing her son and denounced him as a liar.)

In her work at Bellevue, Lewis has documented some compelling cases of multiple personality in children who had been abused. They are so young that it would be difficult to conceive of them being able to fake this. But as Lewis has demonstrated, the rare cases of multiple personality disorder begin early in childhood, often during the preverbal phase. In adults, it seems the only time you really hear about multiple personality disorder is after someone is on trial for murder. Somehow, it never comes up until then. Kenneth Bianchi, one of two cousins who together committed the Hillside Strangler murders in Los Angeles in the 1970s, claimed after his arrest to be a multiple. John Wayne Gacy tried the same approach.

(I've often joked that if you have an offender with multiple personalities, I'll let the innocent personalities go as long as I can lock up the guilty one.)

For the Shawcross trial, lead prosecutor Charles Siragusa, who did a masterful job, called on Park Dietz to present the other side. Dietz examined Shawcross just as extensively as Lewis had, and Shawcross came up with a lot of specific details about the murders. While Dietz didn't make any absolute judgment about the veracity of the stories of abuse, he thought they sounded at least plausible. Nevertheless, he did not think Shawcross was delusional, found no evidence he had suffered from blackouts or loss of memory, found no correlation between his behavior and any organic neurological findings, and concluded that whatever mental or emotional problems he might have, Arthur Shawcross understood the difference between right and wrong and was able to make the choice as to whether he killed or not. And on at least ten occasions here, and probably more, he had chosen to do so.

When Len Boriello asked him why he had killed these women, he replied simply, "Taking care of business."

True psychotics—those who have lost touch with reality—don't commit serious crimes very often. And when they do, they are usually so disorganized and make so little attempt to avoid detection that they are generally caught fairly quickly. Richard Trenton Chase, who killed women because he thought he needed their blood to stay alive, was a psychotic. If he couldn't get human blood, he'd settle for what was at hand. When Chase was placed in a mental institution, he continued to catch rabbits, bleed them, and inject their blood into his arm. He would catch small birds, bite off their heads, and drink their blood. This one was for real. But for a killer to avoid detection and get away with ten murders, he has to be pretty good at it. Don't make the mistake of confusing a psychopath with a psychotic.

During the trial, Shawcross always maintained a stoic and immobile, almost catatonic, demeanor toward the jury. It was as if he were in a trancelike state, unable to comprehend what was going on around him. Yet the police officers and marshals who guarded and escorted him reported that as soon as he was outside the jury's sight and hearing, he would loosen up, become talkative, sometimes joke around. He knew a lot was at stake in selling the insanity plea.

One of the cleverest, most resourceful—and, I have to say, most charming—criminals I've ever studied and interviewed was Gary Trapnell. He'd been in and out of prison most of his adult life and at one point actually convinced a young woman to secure a helicopter to land in the middle of the prison yard and rescue him. During one of his notable crimes—an airplane hijacking in the early 1970s—Trapnell is in the plane on the ground trying to negotiate terms for his getaway. In the midst of this, he raises his fist in the air for cameras to catch and demands, "Free Angela Davis!"

" 'Free Angela Davis'? What's this 'free Angela Davis'?" This comes as something of a shock to most of the law enforcement people working on the case. There's nothing in Trapnell's background to suggest that he's in any way emotionally committed to the young black California professor's radical causes. There's nothing to suggest he's political in any way, and here, as one of his demands, he wants Angela Davis freed from prison. The guy must be loony. That's the only logical explanation.

Later, after his surrender and conviction, when I interviewed him in the federal penitentiary in Marion, Illinois, I asked him about this demand.

He said something to the effect of, "When I saw I wasn't going to work my way out of this one, I knew I'd be doing some hard time. And I figured if the big black brothers thought I was a political prisoner, I'd be less likely to get my ass raped in the shower."

Not only was Trapnell fully rational at the time, he was planning ahead, virtually the opposite of being crazy. In fact, he wrote his own memoirs, entitled *The Fox Is Crazy, Too*. This nugget of information also gave us tremendous insight into negotiations. If some totally off-the-wall demand suddenly comes up, it could mean that in his mind, the offender has already moved on to the next stage and the negotiator can react accordingly.

Trapnell told me something else I found very, very interesting. He said that if I gave him a copy of the current edition of *DSM*, the *Diagnostic and Statistical Manual of Mental Disorders*, and pointed to any condition described in it, by the next day he could convince any psychiatrist that he was genuinely suffering from the affliction. Again, Trapnell's got a lot more on the ball than Shawcross. But just as it doesn't take all that much imagination to know you've got a better shot at parole if you tell the shrink you're feeling much better and no longer have any interest in molesting little boys, it stands to reason that your fugue-state explanation will play better if the jury can actually see you in something of a trance.

For a long time, the law enforcement community tried to

rely on *DSM* for guidance and definition about what constituted a serious mental disorder and what did not. But most of us found the reference book to be of little value in what we did. This was one of the motivations for developing the *Crime Classification Manual*, which was published in 1992. The basic structure of the book grew out of my doctoral dissertation. Ressler, Ann Burgess, and her husband, Allen, a professor of management in Boston, collaborated with me as coauthors. Other members of the Investigative Support and Behavioral Science Units, including Greg Cooper, Roy Hazelwood, Ken Lanning, Gregg McCrary, Jud Ray, Pete Smerick, and Jim Wright, worked with us as contributors.

With *CCM* we set about to organize and classify serious crimes by their behavioral characteristics and explain them in a way that a strictly psychological approach such as *DSM* has never been able to do. For example, you won't find the type of murder scenario of which O. J. Simpson was accused in *DSM*. You will find it in *CCM*. What we were trying to do was separate the wheat from the chaff as far as behavioral evidence was concerned and help investigators and the legal community focus in on which considerations may be relevant and which are not.

Not surprisingly, defendants and their attorneys will bring up anything they possibly can to avoid assuming responsibility for their actions. Among the laundry list of factors Shawcross's team suggested had contributed to his insanity was the post–traumatic stress disorder from Vietnam. Research indicated that Shawcross had seen no combat. But this wasn't a new one. It had been used many times before. Duane Samples, who disemboweled two women in Silverton, Oregon, on the night of December 9, 1975, claimed PTSD as his defense. Only one of the women died, but I've seen the crime-scene photos. Both of them look like autopsies. Robert Ressler discovered that Samples hadn't seen action, either, despite his claims. The day before the attack, however, Samples had written a letter describing his long-standing fantasy of disemboweling a beautiful naked woman.

In 1981, Ressler went out to Oregon to help prosecutors explain why the governor should not follow through with his intention to parole Samples. The argument worked, though he was finally paroled ten years later.

Is Samples insane? Was he temporarily insane when he cut up the two women? The natural tendency would be to say that anyone who could do such a horrible, perverse thing must truly be "sick." And I wouldn't disagree with that. But did he know what he was doing was wrong? And did he choose to do it anyway? Those are the important questions as far as I'm concerned.

Arthur Shawcross's trial in Rochester City Court lasted more than five weeks, during which prosecutor Siragusa displayed a deeper and more complete understanding of forensic psychiatry than I have seen from virtually any doctor. During the trial, every minute of which was televised, he became a local hero. When the jury was finally handed the case after closing arguments, they took less than a day to reach a verdict of guilty of murder in the second degree on all charges. This judge made sure Shawcross would not have the opportunity to repeat his actions. He sentenced him to two hundred fifty years to life in the state penitentiary.

And this brings up another aspect of the insanity defense, one that a good many people don't realize: juries don't like it and don't often go for it.

They don't go for it for two reasons, I believe. One is that it strains credibility that multiple killers are so compelled to commit their crimes that they have no choice. Keep in mind that no serial killer in my experience ever felt so compelled to kill that he did so in the presence of a uniformed police officer.

The second reason juries don't go for the insanity defense is an even more basic one. After all the legal and psychiatric and academic arguments are stripped away, when it finally gets down to the deliberation of a defendant's fate, jurors realize instinctively that these guys are *dangerous*. Whatever the decent men and women of Milwaukee might intellectually have felt about Jeffrey Dahmer's sanity or lack thereof, I don't believe they were willing to entrust his future (and their community's) to a mental institution about whose security and judgment in keeping him they couldn't be sure. If they put him in prison, his dangerousness would more likely be held in check.

I don't mean to imply that most psychiatrists or mental health professionals are hot to spring dangerous offenders from incarceration and put them back in situations where they can do more harm. What I am suggesting is that in most instances, from my experience, these people don't see enough of what we do to be able to make informed judgments. Even if they have forensic experience, it's often limited to a particular area, which is what they will then rely on.

One of my first cases as a profiler involved the murder of an elderly woman, Anna Berliner, in her home in Oregon. The local police had consulted a clinical psychologist about the type of UNSUB they were looking for. Among her injuries were four deep pencil stab wounds in the chest. The psychologist had conducted interviews with about fifty men charged with or convicted of homicide. Most of these examinations had been done in prison. Based on his experience, he predicted that the offender would be someone with a fair amount of prison time, probably a drug dealer, because only in prison is a sharpened pencil widely considered a deadly weapon. People on the outside, he reasoned, wouldn't think to use an ordinary pencil to attack someone.

When the police contacted me, I gave them an opposite opinion. I thought the age and vulnerability of the victim, the overkill, the fact that it was a daytime crime and that nothing of great value was missing, suggested an inexperienced juvenile offender. I didn't believe that he carefully analyzed the pencil's use as a weapon. It was there and he used it. The killer turned out to be an inexperienced sixteen-year-old who had gone to her house trying to get a contribution to a walkathon in which he was not actually participating.

The key feature of this crime scene was that all behavioral evidence suggested to me an offender who was unsure of himself. An ex-con attacking an elderly woman in her home would be very sure of himself. Merely picking up on a single piece of evidence (such as the African American hair in the Francine Elveson case) doesn't give the entire picture. In fact, in the Anna Berliner murder, it could have led in just the opposite direction from the truth.

The most difficult question any of us in this business are asked has to do with whether a particular individual is, or will be, dangerous. For psychiatrists, it's often posed in terms of "a threat to himself or others."

Around 1986, the FBI was contacted about a roll of film sent in from Colorado to a photo lab for developing. The pictures depicted a man in his late twenties or early thirties, dressed in camouflage gear, posed on the tailgate of his 4X4 with his rifle and a Barbie doll that he had subjected to various tortures and mutilations. No law had been broken in doing this, and I said that the guy would not have a criminal record. But I also warned that at his age, this fantasy he was acting out with the doll would not be satisfying much longer. It would evolve. Just from the photographs, I didn't know how important it would be in his life, but for him to have gone to the care and trouble he did, it must have had some important significance. I said that this guy should be watched and interviewed, because this was a case of dangerousness waiting to happen. I'm not sure if most psychiatrists would have had the same perspective.

As strange as this incident may sound, I can think of several "Barbie doll cases" brought to me over the years, all involving adult men. One subject out in the midwest would stick pins in every inch of the doll and leave it on the grounds of the local psychiatric hospital. Occasionally you get this kind of thing with satanic cults, voodoo, or people who think they're into witchcraft, but there was none of that here. Nor did he attach a name to the doll, indicating an orientation to a particular person. This was a general sadistic tendency, characteristic of someone who has a real problem with women.

What else can we say about this individual? We can say that he has probably experimented with torturing small animals and may do it regularly. He will have difficulty dealing with people his own age, either men or women. When he was growing up, he would have been a bully or sadistic with younger, smaller children. And he either has or will soon reach the stage in which acting out his fantasies on a doll won't be enough. You can argue about whether or not he's "sick," but sick or not, I can tell you I'd have a real concern about his dangerousness.

So when is this dangerous behavior likely to occur? This guy is an inadequate loser. In his mind, everyone's out to get him and no one recognizes his talents. If the stressors in his life become unbearable, that's when he'll go one step further with his fantasy. And with a doll mutilator, one step further doesn't equal going after someone in his age group, it means going after someone younger, weaker, or lamer. He's a coward. He's not going to go after a peer.

That doesn't mean he's going to go for children necessarily. Barbie is portrayed as a mature, developed woman, not a prepubescent girl. No matter how warped this guy is, what he desires is contact with a mature woman. If he's mutilating or abusing a baby doll, we've got another set of problems.

And yet the guy who's sticking pins in the doll and leaving it at the hospital is going to be fairly dysfunctional, he won't have a driver's license, he'll stand out in a crowd as being weird. The guy in camouflage is going to be much more dangerous. He's got a job because he has money for his rifle, his truck, a camera. He can get around and function "normally" in society. The minute he snaps, someone's in real trouble. Do I trust most psychiatrists or health-care professionals to make this distinction? No. They just don't have the background or the orientation for it. They haven't verified their findings.

One of the key features of our serial-killer study was the idea of verifying what people told us by studying tangible evidence. Otherwise, you're relying on self-reporting, which is incomplete at best and scientifically meaningless at worst.

The evaluation of dangerousness has many uses and applications. On Friday, April 16, 1982, U.S. Secret Service agents met with me about a series of letters written by the same individual beginning in February 1979, threatening the life of the president (the first one targeted Jimmy Carter, all the others Ronald Reagan) and other political figures.

The first letter had been sent to the Secret Service in New York, from "Lonely and Depressed." It was two pages long, handwritten on notebook paper, and threatened to "shoot and kill President Carter or someone else who has power."

Between July 1981 and February 1982, eight more letters followed. Three were sent to the Secret Service in New York, one to the FBI in New York, one to the FBI in Washington, one to the *Philadelphia Daily News*, and two directly to the White House. They were handwritten by the same hand as "Lonely and Depressed," but these were all signed "C.A.T." They were mailed from New York, Philadelphia, and Washington. The letters expressed C.A.T.'s intent to kill President Reagan, who was variously referred to as "the evil of God" and "the Devil." Other politicians who supported President Reagan were also threatened. The writer also made references to John Hinckley, promising to carry out his failed mission.

There were more letters, with the mailing list expanded

to Congressman Jack Kemp and Sen. Alfonse D'Amato. Of particular concern to the Secret Service was the inclusion of photographs of Senator D'Amato and Congressman Raymond McGrath of New York City. Taken at very close range, they demonstrated C.A.T.'s ability to get close enough to carry out his threats.

Finally, on June 14, 1982, the fourteenth letter was sent to the editor of the *New York Post*. It declared that everyone would know who he was after he did away with the president, whom he referred to as "the Devil." He claimed that no one listened to him and everyone laughed at him, none of which surprised me.

But within the text of this communication he also gave the newspaper "permission" to talk to him after he had completed his historic mission. This was the opening we were looking for. C.A.T. was willing, probably eager, to engage in a dialogue with a newspaper editor. We would supply one.

From the language and usage in the letters, as well as where they were sent and to whom, I was pretty sure this guy was from New York City. I profiled a single white male in his mid-twenties to early thirties, a native New Yorker living on the outskirts of the city, probably alone. He would be of average intelligence with a high school diploma and maybe some further courses in political science and literature and was probably the youngest or only son in his family. I suspect that in the past, he was heavily into drugs and/or alcohol, but now would be only an occasional user. He would see himself as a failure, having never fulfilled the dreams his parents or others had set for him, and had a lifelong list of incomplete tasks and goals. In his early to mid-twenties I expected him to have been psychologically taxed by an uncontrollable stress, perhaps related to military service, divorce, illness, or loss of a family member.

There was a lot of speculation about what "C.A.T." stood for or symbolized. I told the Secret Service not to spend too much time worrying about that, since it might not mean anything at all. There is often a tendency to read too much into every detail when, in fact, the UNSUB might just like the sound of it or the way it looked written out.

The issue for the Secret Service, as it always is, was whether or not this guy was actually dangerous since a lot of people who make threats and spout in letters would never follow through. But I told them that personalities like this one are always searching for something. They turn to political groups and cults, but don't find it. Other people think they're weird and don't take them seriously, so the problem worsens as time goes by. They focus on a mission to give their lives some meaning. This is the first time he's felt any control, and he likes the feeling, which will lead him to take frequent and greater chances. People who take chances are dangerous.

I thought he would be familiar with weapons and prefer close-range assault, even though that would mean he couldn't get away. Because his mission might be suicidal, he'd be keeping a diary for posterity, so the world would know his story. Unlike a personality like the Tylenol poisoner, C.A.T. doesn't want to be anonymous. When the fear of life becomes greater than the fear of death, he will perpetrate his act of violence. He will seem very calm just prior to his act. He will camouflage himself and blend into his surroundings. He will chat with police or Secret Service agents nearby, and he will seem ordinary and nonthreatening.

In certain ways, he was the same type as John Hinckley, whose case and trial were much in the news. He also seemed fixated on Hinckley, about whom we knew a fair amount. I thought he might want to hear the trial verdict or sentence and suggested to the Secret Service that at that time, they go to Ford's Theatre in Washington, where Abraham Lincoln had been shot and where Hinckley visited before he shot President Reagan. I also told them to watch the nearby hotel where Hinckley had stayed. If anyone requested Hinckley's room, that could very well be him.

The hotel did report a request for that specific room. Secret Service agents swooped in and raided an elderly couple who had spent their wedding night in that room and had been back many times since.

In August, the Secret Service got two more letters signed "C.A.T." addressed to the "Office of the President, Washington, D.C." These were both postmarked from Bakersfield, California. Since a lot of assassins travel around the country stalking their prey, there was real concern that the guy might be on the move. In these letters he said, "Being of sound mind & Sound Body [I] am takeing it upon myself to organize as many United States Citizens as I can, to bear arms, and exterminate from my country, the enemies from within."

In a long, paranoid rambling, he talked about the "torture & Hell" he had been through and acknowledged the possibility that he could be killed "in my attemps to bring to Justice the scumb at the top."

I went through these letters carefully and concluded we were dealing with a copycat. For one thing, these were written in script rather than the block capitals of the earlier letters. They referred to President Reagan as "Ron" rather than "the Devil" or "the Old Man." I thought it likely the writer was a woman, and as unpleasant as the sentiments and threats expressed were, I did not think this individual would be dangerous.

The real C.A.T. was a different story. I thought a "tactical stall" would be the best approach, engaging him in a dialogue until we could locate him. We cast a Secret Service agent as the newspaper editor and briefed him on how to seem and what to say. I emphasized that he should try to get C.A.T. to open up to him so that his "full story" could be told. Once the level of trust was built up, the "editor" should suggest that they meet, but make it late at night, someplace out of the way, because the editor was even more concerned than C.A.T. about keeping it secret.

We placed a carefully constructed classified ad in the *New York Post*, which C.A.T. answered. He began having regular conversations with our man. I thought he'd be calling from some large public facility such as Grand Central or Pennsylvania Station, or possibly one of the libraries or museums.

Around this time, the FBI got another evaluation from Dr. Murray Miron, the noted psycholinguistics expert at Syracuse University. Murray and I had collaborated on research and articles on threat assessment, and I thought he was one of the best in the business. After the telephone dialogue began, Murray wrote an analysis for the FBI stating he no longer considered C.A.T. dangerous, but instead, a publicity-seeking fraud who was getting off on manipulating all of these important people. Murray certainly thought he ought to be caught, but didn't see him as the threat I did.

Gradually, we were able to keep him on the phone long enough to establish a trap and trace. On October 21, 1982, a combined Secret Service–FBI team picked him up in a phone booth in Penn Station while he was talking to the "editor." His name was Alphonse Amodio Jr., a twenty-seven-year-old, white, native New Yorker with a high school education.

FBI and Secret Service agents went to his cramped, roach-infested apartment in Floral Park. The family seemed quite dysfunctional, and when Mrs. Amodio was interviewed, her description of her son matched the profile. "He hates it [the world] and feels it hates him," she told the agents. She described his violent mood swings. He had been clipping newspaper stories for years and had filled two filing cabinets with folders labeled with the names of various politicians. As a child, he had had such a bad stutter that it had held him back from starting school. He had joined the Army but went AWOL after basic training. Other than several diary references to himself as an "alley cat," the agents could find no logic or explanation for the C.A.T. moniker.

Amodio was placed in the psychiatric lockup at Bellevue. Before his trial, U.S. District Court judge David Edelstein requested an evaluation from a psychiatric social worker, who found the defendant severely emotionally ill and therefore a serious danger to the president and other government officials.

Amodio did confess to being C.A.T. Agents questioning him could find no political component to his thinking. He just did it for the power and attention.

He is no longer institutionalized. Is this type of person still dangerous? I don't think he would be an immediate threat, but if the stressors built up again and there was no way for him to cope, I would begin getting nervous again.

What do I look for? One of the key things is tone. If I see a series of letters to a politician, a movie star, an athlete, or any celebrity in which the tone becomes increasingly rigid and urgent ("You're not answering my letters!"), I take them seriously. It becomes mentally and physically exhausting to maintain that obsessive-compulsive rigidity. In time, the individual will begin to break down. Again, you can call behavior a form of mental illness, but what I have to concern myself with is how *dangerous* it may be.

Though we have interviewed women such as attempted assassins and Manson family sympathizers Lynette "Squeaky" Fromme and Sara Jane Moore, our published prison study only involved men. While you find the occasional woman assassin type, you will note that every case of serial murder or lust killing I've mentioned involves a male offender. Our research has shown that virtually all serial killers come from dysfunctional backgrounds of sexual or physical abuse, drugs or alcoholism, or any of the related problems. Women come from these same backgrounds, and if anything, girls are even more subject to abuse and molestation than boys. So why do so few of them grow up to commit the same kinds of crimes as the men? A female serial killer suspect such as Aileen Wuornos, accused of killing men on interstates in Florida, is so rare as to be instantly noteworthy.

For this subject we're on shakier ground, because there simply haven't been the studies to answer this question definitively. As some have speculated, it may be related directly to testosterone levels and otherwise hormonally and chemically based. The only thing we can say with an experiential authority is that women seem to internalize their stressors. Rather than lashing out at others, they tend to punish themselves through such things as alcoholism, drugs, prostitution, and suicide. Some may repeat the psychological or physical abuse within their own families, as the mother of Ed Kemper appears to have done. From a mental health viewpoint, this is very damaging. But the fact remains, women do not kill in the same way or in anywhere remotely near the numbers men do.

So what can be done about dangerousness? How can we intervene in cases of mental instability or character defect before it's too late? Unfortunately, there's no quick or simple answer. In many instances, law enforcement has become the front line of order and discipline, rather than the family. This is a dangerous situation for society to be in, because by the time we enter, it's too late to do any good. The best we can do is to keep more bad from happening.

If you're asking the schools to be the answer, you're also asking a lot. If you take a kid from a bad background and expect the overburdened teachers to turn him around in seven hours a day, it might or might not happen. What about the other seventeen hours in a day?

People often ask us if, through our research and experience, we can now predict which children are likely to become dangerous in later life. Roy Hazelwood's answer is, "Sure. But so can any good elementary school teacher." And if we can get them treatment early enough and intensively enough, it might make a difference. A significant role-model adult during the formative years can make a world of difference.

Bill Tafoya, the special agent who served as our "futur-ist" at Quantico, advocated a minimum of a ten-year com-mitment of money and resources on the magnitude of what we sent into the Persian Gulf. He calls for a wide-scale re-instatement of Project Head Start, one of the most effective long-term, anticrime programs in history. He doesn't think more police are the answer, but he would bring in "an army of social workers" to provide assistance for battered women, homeless families with children, to find good foster homes. And he would back it all up with tax incentive programs.

I'm not sure this is the total answer, but it would certainly be an important start. Because the sad fact is, the shrinks can battle all they want, and my people and I can use psychol-ogy and behavioral science to help catch the criminals, but by the time we get to use our stuff, the severe damage has already been done.

Sometimes the Dragon Wins

When the body of a sixteen-year-old girl was found in the Green River outside Seattle in July of 1982, no one thought too much about it. The river, linking Mount Rainier with Puget Sound, was a popular illegal dump site, and the victim was a young prostitute. The significance of the find didn't become apparent to police until later that summer—another woman was found dead in the river on August 12, with three more discovered three days later. The ages and races of the victims differed, but all were suffocated. Some were weighted down in an apparent effort to keep them hidden. All were undressed, and in two cases, small rocks were found inside the victim's vagina.

Now, the serial nature of the crimes was unavoidable and brought back haunting reminders of Seattle's last serial murders, the kidnapping and killing of at least eight women in the area in 1974 by a subject known only as "Ted." Those cases had remained unsolved for four years until a handsome, articulate young man named Theodore Robert Bundy was arrested for a brutal series of sorority-house murders in Florida. By that time, he had worked his way across the country, killing at least twenty-three young women and earning himself a permanent place in the chamber of horrors of our collective psyche.

Maj. Richard Kraske of the King County Criminal Investigations Division had been in charge of that investigation, and wanting to apply what he had learned, he now turned to the FBI for assistance in developing a psychological profile of the "Green River Killer." Although the investigators on the newly formed, multijurisdictional task force were divided over whether all the cases were really linked, there was one clear common factor: all the dead women were prostitutes who worked the Sea-Tac Strip, the Pacific Coast Highway near Seattle-Tacoma International Airport. And now, more young women were missing.

In September, Allen Whitaker, the Seattle SAC, was at Quantico for an in-service and presented us with a detailed package on the five original cases. As I often did when I wanted to be able to concentrate away from constant staff and phone interruptions, I sequestered myself on the top floor of the library, where I could be alone, stare out the window (always a pleasant novelty for those of us who work underground), and get myself into the minds of the offender and the victims. I spent about a day looking through the materials—crime-scene reports and photos, autopsy protocols, victim descriptions. Despite the variances in age and race and MO, the similarities were strong enough to indicate all the murders were committed by the same subject.

I developed a detailed profile of a physically powerful, inadequate, underemployed white male, comfortable with the river, who felt no remorse for what he was doing. Quite the contrary, he was a man on a mission who'd had humiliating experiences with women and was now out to punish as many as he could of what he considered to be the lowest of them. But at the same time, I warned the police that because of the nature of the crimes and the victims, many people would fit this profile. Unlike an Ed Kemper, say, this was no mental giant. These were unsophisticated, high-risk crimes. The emphasis had to be on proactive techniques that would lure the UNSUB into some type of contact with the police. Whitaker took the profile back with him when he left Quantico.

Later that month the badly decomposed body of another young woman was found in an area of condemned houses near the airport. She was nude, with a pair of men's black socks tied around her neck. The medical examiner estimated she'd been killed around the same time as the river victims. Perhaps the killer had changed his MO after hearing about surveillance of the river.

As detailed in *The Search for the Green River Killer*, a carefully researched account by Carlton Smith and Tomas Guillen, the strongest suspect was a forty-four-year-old taxi driver who matched the profile in virtually every way. He'd injected himself into the investigation early, calling police with tips on how to find the killer and advising them to look for other taxi drivers. He spent a lot of time with prostitutes and street people along the Strip, was nocturnal, drove around compulsively, drank and smoked as the profile suggested the UNSUB would, and professed concern for the prostitutes' safety. He had five failed marriages, grew up near the river, lived with his widower father, drove an older, conservative car that wasn't well maintained, and followed the press on the case closely.

Police scheduled him for an interview in September and called me for a strategy. I was traveling at a feverish pace then, hopping around the country on an almost weekly basis trying to keep up with my cases. When the police called, I happened to be out of town. They spoke to Roger Depue, the unit chief, who said I would be back in a few days and strongly suggested they wait to conduct the interview until they'd had a chance to talk to me. Thus far, the subject had been cooperative and wasn't planning to leave the area.

But the police went ahead with the interview, which lasted an entire day and turned into a confrontation. From a perspective of twenty-twenty hindsight, perhaps it could have been done differently. Polygraph results were ambiguous, and even though the police put him under bumper-lock surveillance and continued gathering circumstantial evidence, they could never make a case against him.

Not personally having been involved in that part of the investigation, I can't say whether or not this individual was a promising suspect. But this lack of coordination and focus greatly hampered the investigation in the early stages, when a subject is usually most catchable. He's concerned, he doesn't know what to expect, the "ass-pucker factor" is at its highest. As time goes by and the UNSUB realizes he's getting away with it, he becomes more comfortable. He settles down, refines his MO.

At the beginning of this case, local police didn't even have a computer. And as the investigation grew, at the rate they were processing leads, it would have taken fifty years to evaluate properly what they had. Were a Green River type of investigation launched today, I hope and trust the early organization would be more efficient and the strategy more defined. Still, the task would be formidable. These prostitutes lived a nomadic existence. Oftentimes, when a boyfriend or pimp would report one missing, she had disappeared on purpose or simply relocated to another area up or down the coast. Many of them used aliases, making identification of bodies and tracking of cases a nightmare. Medical and dental records were therefore hard to locate and authenticate. And relations and cooperation between police and the prostitute community are always tenuous at best.

In May 1983, a young prostitute was found fully clothed in a carefully staged scene: a fish was placed across her throat, another on her left breast, and a wine bottle between her legs. She had been strangled with a thin cord or rope. The police chalked her death up to the Green River Killer. But while I thought the last victim found on land had been related, this one struck me as more of a personal-cause homicide. This one wasn't random. There was too much anger here. The killer knew this victim well.

Nearing the end of 1983, the body count had risen to twelve, with seven more reported missing. One of the dead women had been eight months pregnant. The task force asked me to come out and give them on-scene advice. As I've mentioned, I was trying to handle various stages of the

Wayne Williams case in Atlanta, the .22-Caliber Killer in Buffalo, the Trailside Killer in San Francisco, the Robert Hansen case in Anchorage, an anti-Semitic serial arsonist in Hartford, and more than a hundred other active cases. The only way I could keep up with them all was to force myself to dream about them at night. I knew I was running myself ragged. I just didn't know how ragged, how fast. And when the Green River Task Force said they needed me, I knew I had to squeeze that one in, too.

I was confident my profile would fit the killer, but I also knew it would fit a lot of people, and more than one of these could be involved by now. The longer this went on, the greater the chance for more killers to become involved, either as copycats or simply because of the territory and the victims. The Sea-Tac Strip was easy pickings for a killer. If you have a will to kill, that's the kind of place you go. The prostitutes were readily available, and since many of them plied the entire West Coast corridor from Vancouver all the way down to San Diego, when a girl disappeared, often she would not be missed.

I thought proactive techniques were more important than ever. These could include convening town meetings on the murders at rural schools, then passing around sign-up sheets and taking note of license plates of those attending, using the media to put forth one investigator as "supercop" to lure the killer to contact him, stories personalizing the pregnant woman to try to encourage some remorse and revisits from the killer, surveillance of unpublicized dump sites, use of decoy police officers, and any number of other possibilities.

I brought Blaine McIlwain and Ron Walker, two of the newer profilers, on the December trip to Seattle, figuring this would be a good case to get them some on-site experience. It was a good thing I did, as if God or some cosmic order had planned it. They saved my life.

When they broke through the locked, bolted, and chained door to my hotel room and found me unconscious and convulsing on the floor, I was near death from the fever that was raging through my brain.

By the time I finally recovered and returned to work in May of 1984, the Green River Killer was still at large, as he is at this writing more than a decade later. I continued consulting with the task force, which grew into one of the largest organized manhunts in American history. The longer the investigation went on, as the number of bodies continued to grow, I became increasingly convinced that several killers were at work, all sharing some similar traits, but each acting on his own. Police in Spokane and Portland brought me clusters of murdered and missing prostitutes, but I found no clear connection to the murders around Seattle. San Diego police thought another cluster in their city might be related. All in all, the Green River Task Force was investigating more than fifty deaths. More than twelve hundred solid suspects had been reduced to about eighty. They ranged from boyfriends and pimps of the dead women to a john in Portland from whom a prostitute had escaped after threats of torture, to a Seattle-based trapper. At times, even members of the police force were considered possible suspects. But none of this was enough for closure. At this point, I'm convinced there were at least three killers, possibly more.

The last major proactive thrust came in December 1988, with a two-hour live television program broadcast nationally. Entitled *Manhunt . . . Live* and hosted by *Dallas* star Patrick Duffy, the show offered background on the search for the killer or killers and provided a bank of toll-free numbers for viewers to give tips and leads. I flew out to Seattle to appear on the show and to train police officers on how to screen calls and quickly ask pertinent questions.

In the week following the broadcast, the telephone company estimated that more than one hundred thousand people had tried to call, but fewer than ten thousand had gotten through. And after three weeks, there just weren't the financial resources or the volunteers to continue manning the crime-stoppers hot lines. In the end, it was symbolic of so many other aspects of Green River—many dedicated people expending tremendous effort, but ultimately, too little, too late.

For years, Gregg McCrary had a cartoon tacked to the bulletin board in his office. It shows a fire-breathing dragon standing fiercely over a prostrate knight. The caption reads simply, "Sometimes the dragon wins."

This is a reality none of us can ever escape. We don't catch them all, and since the ones we do catch have already killed or raped or tortured or bombed or burned or maimed, none of them is ever caught soon enough. It's true today, just as it was more than a hundred years ago when Jack the Ripper became the first serial killer to haunt the public imagination.

Ironically, though the *Manhunt* broadcast didn't solve the Green River murders, that same year I appeared on another national television show in which I did determine through profiling the possible identity of that most infamous serial killer of all. It was timed to coincide with the hundredth anniversary of Jack the Ripper's Whitechapel murders, which meant my profile was only a century too late to do any good.

The brutal prostitute murders took place in the gaslit streets and alleys of Victorian London's rough and teeming East End between August 31 and November 9, 1888. Over that time, the viciousness of the killings and the postmortem mutilation escalated. In the early morning of September 30, he killed two women within an hour or two, an unheard of event at the time. The police received several taunting letters, which were published in the newspapers, and the horrors became a huge media event. The Ripper was never caught, despite the fervent efforts of Scotland Yard, and his identity has remained a subject of intense speculation ever since. Like the "true" identity of William Shakespeare, the choice of suspects often reveals more about the people doing the speculating than it does about the mystery itself.

Among the favorite and most fascinating possibilities over the years has been Prince Albert Victor, Duke of
Clarence, eldest grandson of Queen Victoria and, after his
father, Edward, the Prince of Wales (who became Edward
VII upon Victoria's death in 1901), the next in line to the
throne. The Duke of Clarence is supposed to have died
in the great influenza epidemic of 1892, but many Ripper
theorists have him actually dying of syphilis or possibly
poisoning at the hands of a royal physician to remove the
taint of scandal from the monarchy. It's certainly an intrigu-
ing possibility.

Other strong candidates have included Montague John
Druit, a teacher in a boy's school who matched eyewitness
descriptions; Dr. William Gull, chief royal physician; Aaron
Kosminski, a poor Polish immigrant who'd been in and out
of mental asylums in the area; and Dr. Roslyn D'Onstan, a
journalist known to dabble in black magic.

Much has been made of the fact that the Ripper murders
stopped abruptly, leading to speculation that he might have
taken his own life, that the Duke of Clarence was sent on a
royal trip, that one of the other suspects might have died.
Looking back from our current knowledge, it seems to me
just as likely that he was picked up for some other lesser
offense as many are, and this was what stopped the killing.
Another issue was the "ripping" itself. One of the reasons
for the focus on someone with medical training was the
degree of disembowelment of the later victims.

The aim of *The Secret Identity of Jack the Ripper*, broadcast nationally in October 1988, was to present all available
evidence in the case and then have experts from various
disciplines present their analyses about who Jack really
was, solving this century-old riddle "once and for all." Roy
Hazelwood and I were invited to be on the program, and the
FBI thought this would be a good opportunity to showcase
the kind of work we do without compromising any ongoing
investigations or trials. The live, two-hour presentation was

hosted by British actor, writer, and director Peter Ustinov, who really got into the mystery as the drama unfolded.

Now any exercise of this kind has the same rules and strictures as a current investigation—that is, our product can only be as good as the evidence and data we have to work with. A hundred years ago, forensic investigation was primitive by modern standards. But I thought that, based on what I knew about the Ripper murders, if such a case were presented to us today, it would be very solvable, so I thought we ought to take a flyer on it. When you do the kind of work we do, there is actually some sport and relaxation when the only thing on the line if you screw up is making a fool of yourself on national television rather than having another innocent victim dead.

Before the program aired, I developed a profile as I would for a modern case, with the same-style heading:

UNSUB; AKA JACK THE RIPPER
SERIES OF HOMICIDES
LONDON, ENGLAND
1888
NCAVC—HOMICIDE (CRIMINAL INVESTIGATIVE
ANALYSIS)

The last line, NCAVC, refers to the National Center for the Analysis of Violent Crime, the overall program established at Quantico in 1985 to include the Behavioral Science and Investigative Support Units, VICAP—the Violent Criminal Apprehension Program computer database—and other rapid-response teams and units.

As in a real consultation, once I had come up with the profile, we were given the possible suspects. As appealing as the Duke of Clarence was from a dramatic standpoint, after analyzing all the evidence available, Roy and I independently came up with Aaron Kosminski as our likeliest candidate.

As in the Yorkshire Ripper case ninety years later, we were convinced the taunting letters to the police were written by an impostor, someone other than the "real" Jack. The type of individual who committed these crimes would not have the personality to set up a public challenge to the police. The mutilation suggested a mentally disturbed, sexually inadequate person with a lot of generalized rage against women. The blitz style of attack in each case also told us he was personally and socially inadequate. This was not someone who could hold his own verbally. The physical circumstances of the crimes told us that this was someone who could blend in with his surroundings and not cause suspicion or fear on the part of the prostitutes. He would be a quiet loner, not a macho butcher, who would prowl the streets nightly and return to the scenes of his crimes. Undoubtedly, the police would have interviewed him in their investigation. Of all the possibilities we were presented, Kosminski fit the profile far better than any of the others. As for the supposed medical knowledge needed for the postmortem mutilation and dissection, this was really nothing but elementary butchery. And we have long since learned that serial killers need nothing but will to commit whatever atrocities they want on a body. Ed Gein, Ed Kemper, Jeffrey Dahmer, Richard Marquette—to name but a few—were in no way held back by their lack of medical training.

Having presented this analysis, I now have to backpedal on my original declaration with the qualification that from this vantage point a hundred years later, I can't be sure that Aaron Kosminski was the Ripper. He was simply one of the ones given to us. But what I can state with a high degree of confidence is that Jack the Ripper was someone *like* Kosminski. Were this criminal investigative analysis taking place today, our input would help police and Scotland Yard narrow their focus and come up with the UNSUB's identity. That's why I say that by modern standards, this case would be very solvable.

• • •

In some cases our methods point to a type of suspect, but we can't get enough evidence for an arrest and indictment. Such a case was the "BTK Strangler" in Wichita, Kansas, in the mid-1970s.

It began on January 15, 1974, with the murder of the Otero family. Thirty-eight-year-old Joseph Otero and his wife, Julie, were tied and strangled with venetian-blind cords. Their nine-year-old son, Joseph II, was found tied in his own bedroom, a plastic bag over his head. Eleven-year-old Josephine was hanging by her neck from a pipe in the basement ceiling, clad only in a sweatshirt and socks. All the evidence suggested that this was not an impulsive act. The telephone lines had been cut and the cord had been brought to the scene.

Ten months later, a local newspaper editor got an anonymous call directing him to a book in the public library. Inside was a note from the UNSUB, claiming credit for the Otero killings, promising more and explaining that "the code words for me will be: Bind them, Torture them, Kill them."

Several more killings of young women followed in the ensuing three years, after which a letter to a local television station revealed much about the psyche of this UNSUB, who had carefully given himself his own nickname: "How many do I have to kill before I get my name in the paper or some national attention?"

In one of his published communications, he compared his work to that of Jack the Ripper, the Son of Sam, and the Hillside Strangler—all obscure losers who had become media celebrities through their crimes. He attributed his deeds to a "demon" and "factor X," leading to extensive psychological speculation in the newspapers about his personality.

But he also included graphic drawings of naked women in various poses of binding, rape, and torture. These hideous drawings were not published, but they gave me a good picture of the type of person we were looking for. From that, it was only a matter of narrowing down the suspects.

Like those of his hero Jack the Ripper, BTK's murders stopped abruptly. In this case, though, I believe the police had interviewed him, he knew they were closing in on him, and he was intelligent and sophisticated enough to stop before sufficient evidence could be gathered. I hope we've at least neutralized him, but sometimes the dragon wins.

Sometimes the dragon wins in our own lives as well. When a murderer kills one person, he takes a lot of victims along with that individual. I'm not the only one in my unit to lose work over stress-related problems; far from it. And the instances of family problems and marital strife are too numerous not to be worried about.

In 1993, my marriage with Pam broke up after twenty-two years. We would probably give differing perspectives on what happened between us, but certain things are undeniable. I was away much too often when our daughters, Erika and Lauren, were growing up. When I was in town, I was still so consumed by what I was doing that Pam often felt like a single parent. She had to run the house, pay the bills, get the kids to school, meet with the teachers, make sure the homework got done, all the while keeping up with her own teaching career. By the time our son, Jed, was born in January of 1987, we had other profilers working with me and I wasn't spending as much time on the road. But I have to admit, I have three bright, loving, charming, wonderful children, and I don't think I really got to know them well until shortly before I retired from the Bureau. I spent so much time over the years learning about the victimology of dead children that I shortchanged and didn't learn enough about my own brilliantly alive ones.

Many times Pam would come to me with some typical minor problem involving one of the kids, say a cut or scrape from falling off a bike. With all the stress and pressure I felt, we both remember how often I would lash out, describing the mutilated bodies of kids the same age that I had seen, and didn't she realize that a fall off a bike was normal and nothing to get charged up about?

You try never to fully desensitize yourself from the horrible stuff, but you find yourself building up immunity against anything that's less than horrible. One time I was eating dinner with the kids while Pam was opening a package in the kitchen. The knife slipped and she cut herself badly. She screamed and we all came rushing in. But as soon as I saw that the injury wasn't threatening to life or limb, I remember how interesting I found the blood-spatter pattern to be and began mentally correlating it to spatter patterns I'd seen at murder scenes. I was joking around, trying to diffuse the tension. I started pointing out to her and the children how we saw a different pattern every time she moved her hand, and that was one of the ways we could tell what happened between an attacker and a victim. But I don't think the rest of them took it as casually as I did.

You try to develop defense mechanisms to deal with what you see on the job, but you can easily end up coming off as a cool, aloof son of a bitch. If your family's intact and your marriage is solid, you can put up with a lot of what you face at work. But if there are any weaknesses at home, various stressors can magnify everything, just as they do for the people we hunt.

Pam and I ended up with different friends. I couldn't talk about what I did in her circle, so I needed my own kind around me. And when we socialized outside Bureau or law enforcement circles, I often found myself bored by the mundane concerns discussed. As cold as it sounds, when you spend your days getting inside the heads of killers, where the neighbor puts his trash can or what color he paints his fence just isn't all that stimulating.

I am glad to say, though, after a period in which we both went through the emotional wringer, that Pam and I are now good friends. The kids live with me (Erika is off at college), but Pam and I are together much of the time, and we both now take an equal role as parents. I'm grateful Lauren and Jed are still young enough for me to enjoy some of their growing-up years.

From a lonely position in the early 1980s in which I was the entire full-time FBI profiling staff—assisted as their time permitted by Roy Hazelwood, Bill Hagmaier, and a few others—the unit grew to more than ten. That's still not enough to handle the volume of cases we're presented, but it's probably just about as large as we could be and still maintain the personal contact with each other and the local departments that has become the hallmark of our own modus operandi. Many of the police chiefs and detectives who call on the unit first met us in National Academy classes. Sheriff Jim Metts contacted me to help find Shari Smith's and Debra Helmick's murderer, and Capt. Lynde Johnston called on Gregg McCrary to help determine who was slaughtering prostitutes in Rochester because they were both National Academy graduates.

By the mid-1980s, Behavioral Science had been divided up into the Behavioral Science Instruction and Research Unit, and the group I worked for as criminal-personality profiling program manager, the Behavioral Science Investigative Support Unit. The other two key divisions besides mine in Investigative Support were VICAP, which Jim Wright had taken over from Bob Ressler, and Engineering Services. Roger Depue was chief of Instruction and Research and Alan "Smokey" Burgess was chief of Investigative Support. (He is not related to Ann Burgess, but her husband, Allen Burgess, was our coauthor on the *Crime Classification Manual*. Got it?)

As taxing and challenging as my job was in many ways, I had managed to establish a prominent and satisfying career for myself. Fortunately, I'd been able to avoid the step virtually everyone else who wants to get ahead in the organization has to take—administration. That changed in the spring of 1990. We were having a unit meeting when Smokey Burgess announced he was retiring as unit chief. Later, the new deputy assistant director, Dave Kohl, who'd been my squad supervisor in Milwaukee and a fellow member of the SWAT team, called me into his office and asked me my intentions.

I told him I was so burned out and fed up with everything that I was thinking of applying for a desk job uptown in violent crime and finishing out my career that way.

"You don't want to do that," Kohl told me. "You'll lose yourself up there. You can make a much greater contribution as unit chief."

"I don't know if I want to be unit chief," I told him. I was already performing a lot of the unit-chief functions and acting as institutional memory because I'd been there so long. But at this stage of my career, I didn't want to get bogged down in administration. Burgess was an excellent administrator, adept at running interference so that those of us who worked for him could do our jobs effectively.

"I want you to be unit chief," Kohl announced. He's a dynamic, hard-charging, aggressive type.

I said I wanted to continue doing cases, trial strategy, court testimony, and public speaking. That's what I thought I was good at. Kohl assured me I'd be able to and nominated me for the job.

My first act as unit chief, as I've said many times, was to "get rid of the BS" by getting rid of "Behavioral Science" in our name and calling it, simply, the Investigative Support Unit. I wanted to give our local police clients and the rest of the FBI a clear message about where we were—and were not—coming from.

With the help and unending support of Roberta Beadle, who was in charge of personnel, I got VICAP staffing from four up to sixteen. The rest of the unit grew, too, and soon we were up to a total complement of about forty people. To relieve some of the administrative burden created by our new size, I instituted a regional management program in which individual agents would be responsible for a specific region of the country.

I thought these people all deserved to be GS-14s, but headquarters was only willing to give us four or five 14 slots. So I got them to agree that as each one got through a two-year specialized training program, they would each be "anointed" as experts and recognized as supervisory special agents entitled to that rating and pay. The program involved auditing all National Academy Behavioral Science Unit–taught courses, taking two Armed Forces Institute of Pathology courses, working on psychiatry and law at the University of Virginia (Park Dietz was there at the time), attending John Reed's interrogation school, studying death investigation with the Baltimore Medical Examiner's Office, riding with NYPD homicide units, and writing profiles under one of the regional managers.

We also did much more international work than ever before. In the last year before he retired, for instance, Gregg McCrary worked major serial murders in both Canada and Austria.

Functionally, the unit ran well. Administratively, I ran something of a loose ship, which is merely a function of my personality. When I would see someone burning out, I'd go around the rules and regulations, sign them out, or tell them to take some time off. Ultimately, they would be much more efficient than if I had them working by the rule book. When you've got top people and you can't reward them monetarily, you have to help them out in other ways.

I also always got along well with the support staff, and when I retired, they seemed the most sorry to see me go. This probably goes back to my time in the Air Force. So many of the leaders in the Bureau were military officers (and many, like my last SAC, Robin Montgomery, were decorated war heroes) that they approached things from an officer's perspective. There's nothing wrong with this, and large organizations would function less smoothly if most of the administrators were like me. But I was an enlisted man and so always identified emotionally with the support people. I was therefore a lot more likely to get the help I needed than some of the other chiefs.

A lot of people think of the FBI the same way they used to think of IBM: a huge bureaucratic organization of bright and accomplished, though interchangeable, humorless men and women in white shirts and dark suits. But I've been fortunate enough to be part of a small group of truly unique individuals, each of whom is a standout in his or her own right. As time went by and behavioral science's role in law enforcement grew, we all naturally developed our own special interests and fields of expertise.

From the early days of our study, Bob Ressler pursued research while I devoted myself to the operational side. Roy Hazelwood is the expert on rape and lust murder. Ken Lanning is the leading authority on crimes against children. Jim Reese started off in profiling but found his great contribution to be made in the field of stress and stress management for police officers and federal agents. He has a Ph.D. in the field, has written extensively, and is sought after for his counseling ability throughout the law enforcement community. Once he came into the unit, Jim Wright not only took on the training of new profilers but also became the leading authority on stalking, one of the fastest growing of the serious interpersonal crimes. And each of us has developed many, many personal relationships with field offices, police departments, sheriff's offices, and state agencies around the country so that when someone calls for help, he or she knows and trusts whom they're talking to.

It's sometimes daunting for the new people coming into the unit, trying to blend in with all these "stars," especially after the film *The Silence of the Lambs* came out and such intense national interest was focused on what we do. But we try to assure them that the reason they were selected is because we feel they have what it takes to be full and equal members of the team. They all come from strong investigative backgrounds, and once they're with us, we put them through a full two years of on-the-job training. Add to that their intelligence, intuition, diligence, integrity, and self-confidence, together with an equal capacity to listen to and evaluate other people's points of view. From my perspective, one of the things that has made the FBI Academy the premier institution of its kind in the world is that it is made up of individuals, each pursuing his or her own interests and talents for a common purpose. And each of those individuals, in turn, encourages the same qualities in others. I hope and trust that the collegial and mutually supportive system we set up in the unit will survive as we first-generation people retire.

At my retirement dinner at Quantico in June 1995, a lot of people had nice things to say about me, which I found both humbling and extremely moving. Frankly, I was prepared for a real roast and figured all my people would use this last official chance to dump everything on me they'd been saving up. I ran into Jud Ray in the men's room afterward, and he was already expressing regret at having held off. Once they'd blown their opportunity, though, and it was my turn to speak, I felt no obligation to restrain myself and let loose with all the zingers I'd armed myself with in anticipation of what they'd say. I had no particular wisdom or serious advice to impart that night; I just hope I've managed to strike a chord by the example I've tried to set.

Since my retirement, I've gone back to Quantico to teach and consult, and my colleagues know I'm always available to them. I continue to lecture and speak as I always have, giving the perspective of my twenty-five years of experience delving into the mind of murder. I've retired from the FBI, but I don't think I'll ever truly be able to stop what it is I've trained to do. Unfortunately, ours is very much a growth industry, and we'll never run out of customers.

People often ask me what can be done about our horrendous violent-crime statistics. While there are definitely practical things that can and should be done, I believe that the only chance of solving our crime problem is if enough people want to. More police and more courts and more prisons and better investigative techniques are fine, but the only way crime is going to go down is if all of us simply stop accepting and tolerating it in our families, our friends, and our associates. This is the lesson from other countries with far lower numbers than ours. Only this type of grassroots solution, in my opinion, will be effective. Crime is a moral problem. It can only be resolved on a moral level.

In all my years of research and dealing with violent offenders, I've never yet come across one who came from what I would consider a good background and functional, supportive family unit. I believe that the vast majority of violent offenders are responsible for their conduct, made their choices, and should face the consequences of what they do. It's ridiculous to say that someone doesn't appreciate the seriousness of what he's done because he's only fourteen or fifteen. At eight, my son, Jed, has already known for years what's right and what's wrong.

But twenty-five years of observation has also told me that criminals are more "made" than "born," which means that somewhere along the line, someone who provided a profound negative influence could have provided a profound positive one instead. So what I truly believe is that along with more money and police and prisons, what we most need more of is love. This is not being simplistic; it's at the very heart of the issue.

Not too long ago, I was invited to speak before the New York chapter of the Mystery Writers of America. The talk was well attended and the reception was warm and cordial. These men and women who made their living writing stories about murder and mayhem were acutely interested in hearing from someone who had worked thousands of actual cases. In fact, ever since Thomas Harris and *The Silence of the Lambs,* writers and newspeople and filmmakers have been coming to us for the "real story."

But what I quickly realized as I related the details of some of my more interesting and graphic cases was that many people in the audience were turning off and tuning out. They were getting seriously grossed out by hearing about the things that my people and I saw every day. I saw that they had no interest in hearing the details, at the same moment that it must have dawned on them that they didn't want to write about it like it really was. Fair enough. We each have our own clienteles.

The dragon doesn't always win, and we're doing whatever we can to see to it that he wins less and less. But the evil he represents, the thing I've confronted throughout my career, isn't going to go away, and somebody has to tell the real story. That's what I've tried to do here, just as I've lived it.

Index